Twilight War

Twilight War
The Folly of U.S. Space Dominance

MIKE MOORE

The **INDEPENDENT INSTITUTE**

Oakland, California

The Independent Institute
100 Swan Way, Oakland, CA 94621-1428
Telephone: 510-632-1366 · Fax: 510-568-6040
Email: info@independent.org
Website: www.independent.org

Cover Design: Roland de Beque
Cover Photo: © Stockbyte Photo/VEER

Library of Congress Cataloging-in-Publication Data

Moore, Mike
  Twilight war : the folly of U.S. space dominance / Mike Moore.
      p. cm.
  Includes bibliographical references and index.
  ISBN-13: 978-1-59813-018-8 (alk. paper)
  ISBN-10: 1-59813-018-8 (alk. paper)
  1. Space control (Military science) 2. Space weapons--Government policy--
United States. 3. United States--Military policy. 4. Space warfare. I. Title.
  UG1523.M585 2008
  358'.80973--dc22

                                        2007041954

Printed in the United States of America

12 11 10 09 08   1 2 3 4 5

*To David and Katie, Michael and Sue,
and Melanie and Jack*

Acknowledgments

A number of men and women, experts and lay readers, have read *Twilight War* in one version or another and they have offered cogent advice, copious criticism, and considerable encouragement. They are John Blades, Jo Alice Buxton, Joseph Cirincione, Dwayne A. Day, Everett C. Dolman, Amb. Jonathan Dean, Susan Eisenhower, Steve Fetter, Nancy C. Gallagher, Lt. Gen. Robert Gard, Jr., Amb. Thomas Graham Jr., Jack Harris, Robert Higgs, Theresa Hitchens, John Isaacs, Marlene Lee, Diane and Vivek Likhite, Gerald E. Marsh, John J. Mearsheimer, John C. Polanyi, Alexander Tabarrok, David J. Theroux, and Frank von Hippel. I thank them all.

I owe special thanks to Linda Rothstein, my editor and friend, and to my wife Sandy for her patience, support, and cogent criticism—which in sum was, "Write it so I can understand it!" Good advice; I hope I met her standard.

I also thank the John D. and Catherine T. MacArthur Foundation for a generous research and writing grant, which made *Twilight War* possible, the Independent Institute, for its enthusiasm in overseeing and publishing it, and the Secure World Foundation for underwriting a book tour.

Finally, the author claims sole responsibility for all factual errors in *Twilight War* as well as any outrageous idiosyncrasies that you, the reader, may encounter.

Contents

Preface

America's policy toward military space is headed in the wrong direction. That's what *Twilight War* is all about. But an important subtext in *Twilight War* is the long tradition of American exceptionalism, which tends to derail any attempt to devise a more sensible policy.

When applied to foreign affairs, exceptionalism can be a dangerous thing, and I speak of it now and then in *Twilight War*. For now, I offer just one expression of it, a passage that captures the ageless exceptionalist ethos with unerring accuracy. "[W]e Americans are the particular, chosen people—the Israel of our time; we bear the ark of the liberties of the world," wrote Herman Melville in *White-Jacket*, his largely autobiographical description of life aboard an American Man-o'-War, published in 1850.

> God has predestined, mankind expects, great things from our race; and great things we feel in our souls. The rest of the nations must soon be in our rear. We are the pioneers of the world; the advance guard, sent on through the wilderness of untried things, to break a new path in the New World that is ours....
>
> Long enough have we been skeptics with regard to ourselves, and doubted whether, indeed, the political Messiah had come. But he has come in *us*, if we would but give utterance to his promptings. And let us always remember that with ourselves, almost for the first time in the history of Earth, national selfishness is unbounded philanthropy; for we cannot do a good to America, but we give alms to the world.[1]

Provocative words, especially when applied to space and to foreign policy. Nonetheless, you will hear echoes of Melville throughout *Twilight War*, with and without the God language. "National-security space" is the new "wilderness of untried things," say America's space warriors, and they hope to try out some very new things...things that may make the nation we love less secure, not more secure.

Introduction
The Biography of an Idea

More than a decade ago I read, to my surprise, that America had reached a defining moment in "operationalizing" space. That was the message of Gen. Joseph W. Ashy as he prepared to retire in 1996 from his triple-threat post as commander of North American Aerospace Defense Command, U.S. Space Command, and Air Force Space Command. He was quoted in the August 5, 1996 issue of *Aviation Week & Space Technology* as saying that the United States was going to "engage terrestrial targets some-day—ships, airplanes, land targets—from space. We will engage targets in space, from space.... It's politically sensitive, but it's going to happen. Some people don't want to hear this, and it sure isn't in vogue...but—absolutely—we're going to fight *from* space and we're going to fight *into* space."

I came across General Ashy's words while serving as editor of the *Bulletin of the Atomic Scientists,* the home of the Doomsday Clock, the so-many-minutes-to-midnight metaphor for global peril. His views startled me. Working at the *Bulletin,* I had talked to academics at many of the world's leading universities as well as men and women in the Defense Department, at national security and arms control think tanks, and at the national research laboratories. Some of the experts I dealt with carried high security clearances; all were knowledgeable. But nothing I had heard from them suggested that the United States faced much of a national security threat when it came to space. Certainly America did not seem to face the kind of threat that would justify the claim that "we're going to fight *from* space and we're going to fight *into* space."

Did General Ashy know something the rest of us didn't? Men and women like Ashy have access to "intelligence" that can be astounding. But are the things they "know" necessarily true? In national security matters—as seen in the run-up to the war in Iraq—the answers to strategic questions may be the result more of personal and collective worldviews than of hard intelligence.

Was the Korean War the product of Moscow's long-range plan to take over the world? That view was widely held at the time, but few if any credible historians or political scientists would endorse it today. Did North Vietnamese naval forces intentionally launch a second unprovoked attack on U.S. ships in international waters in the Gulf of Tonkin? It seemed so in August 1964; we now know it didn't happen.

General Ashy was an archetypal "space warrior"—one of the men and women who believe that conflict in space is inevitable. There is a certain circular truth to that belief: If the United States acts as if conflict in space is inevitable, it will be. It will be a self-fulfilling prophecy.

The American people have a narrowing window of opportunity in which to ensure that space remains a domain free of conflict. Seizing that opportunity will not be easy; it will require new ways of thinking. Americans like to be realistic and tough-minded. But in this case, being realistic and tough-minded means having the will and the guts to work with other nations to ensure that space remains a conflict-free sanctuary. Unilateral military actions in space will not guarantee American security; they will guarantee conflict and, possibly, a new cold war. True multilateral cooperation is a better bet.

CHINA'S CHALLENGE

On January 11, 2007, China destroyed a Chinese weather satellite orbiting about five hundred miles above the Earth. The satellite, launched in 1999, was an aging but still functioning bird. Nonetheless, the People's Liberation Army fired a medium-range ballistic missile carrying a kinetic-kill vehicle that smashed into the satellite, creating a cloud of debris including thousands of fragments large enough to damage or even destroy another satellite unlucky enough to encounter one of them. The debris cloud will circle the globe for decades.

The Chinese satellite was the victim of a weapons test, the first such test since September 13, 1985, when an American Prototype Miniature Homing Vehicle launched by a high-flying F-15 fighter slammed into an old U.S.

scientific satellite called Solwind. Like the hapless Chinese weather satellite, Solwind was still sending data back to Earth.

That China pulverized one of its own satellites in a test of an antisatellite weapon—commonly called an "ASAT"—was probably not illegal according to international law. Nonetheless, the test was a diplomatic faux pas, eliciting protests and expressions of concern from a host of nations. And especially from the United States, which owns more than half of the eight-hundred-plus scientific, commercial, and military-oriented satellites operated by spacefaring nations. Commercial satellites are essential to the functioning of the U.S. post-industrial economy, and military-oriented satellites are pivotally important to the American way of high-tech war.

The test was widely interpreted by America's space warriors as an ominous event, an unmistakable declaration that China was playing military hardball with the United States. China had demonstrated a space weapon, and that was reason enough for the United States to get tough regarding space issues.

The space-warrior prescription for reckoning with China's space challenge—or for dealing with any other wayward spacefaring nation—is for the U.S. military to preemptively develop and deploy the means to dominate space. Which is to say, America must field its own antisatellite "space-control" weapons.

SENDING A SIGNAL...

What is a space weapon? It could be space-based hardware that can disrupt, disable, or even destroy another satellite in space. It can be space-based hardware that can attack *earthly* targets from space. No nation today possesses such weapons. But my definition of a space weapon also includes hardware based on the ground, in the air, or at sea that can disrupt, disable, or destroy satellites in space. In short, an ASAT. The United States, Russia—and now China—have such weapons.

What do we mean by "space"? For the purposes of this book, space is a sharply limited concept. We are concerned with *orbital* space, sometimes called "circumterrestrial space." Outer space is infinite, but circumterrestrial space is a finite thing that lies well within the orbit of the Moon and thus within the binding force of Earth's gravity. Think of it this way: If Earth were an orange, orbital space would be the rind that surrounds the juicy bits.

Put *Star Wars* and *Star Trek* out of mind. They boldly go where only film-makers go, thanks to lively imaginations and the convenient suspension of the laws of physics. This book deals with reality, not fantasy. It is not about lasers and phasers and Death Stars. It is the biography of an idea—unilateral dominance of orbital space.

This idea has deep roots. Since the dawn of the Space Age more than fifty years ago, American space warriors have vigorously if unsuccessfully advocated a policy of U.S. military dominance of orbital space—not because they seek control of the world, as some people suggest, but because they believe that unilateral space dominance would help the United States protect its own space assets while it maintained law and order in space as a benign, though self-appointed, policeman. A space cop, as it were.

The United States would be a friendly and agreeable space cop, but a cop nonetheless. A major plus, insofar as space warriors are concerned, is that American dominance of space would assure that the United States would also retain military dominance on the ground, at sea, and in the air. That dominance relies heavily on America's space "assets."

While the Soviet Union lived, the dream of American military dominance of space was empty rhetoric. The United States and the Soviet Union possessed impressive and roughly equal capabilities in space, making it dangerous for either to attempt to achieve anything approaching dominance. After the collapse of the Soviet Union, things changed. In the early 1990s, America's space warriors began to assert that the time had come for America to take control.

This newly belligerent rhetoric toward space has not gone unnoticed. Many nations have said—in generally polite diplomatic language—that the United States is heading down the wrong road with its many conceptual plans for military space hardware, which may include positioning offensive weapons in space. By custom and by international treaty—the Outer Space Treaty of 1967—space is the "province of all mankind" and must remain devoted to "peaceful purposes."

Virtually all of the world's nations, save the United States and Israel, have repeatedly gone on record as favoring the negotiation of a new space treaty called, somewhat awkwardly, Prevention of an Arms Race in Outer Space (PAROS). That treaty would, presumably, plug loopholes in the four-decades old Outer Space Treaty, thus more comprehensively securing space as a weapons-free sanctuary.

For more than a quarter of a century, the United States has exercised its veto power at the Conference on Disarmament in Geneva to prevent formal negotiations. American diplomats finesse the issue with smiley-face assertions that there is no arms race in space, so why get lathered up about a problem that does not yet exist? And that is technically correct. What kind of race has only one entrant?

According to space warriors, America's military space dominance would be exercised *only* if the United States faced a direct military challenge. Unfortunately, in January 2007, China upped the ante with its ASAT test.

One eminent space warrior, Jeff Kueter, president of the George C. Marshall Institute, said that with its ASAT test, China had crossed the Rubicon; it had "signaled to the world its capability to threaten essential satellites." China's test *did* send a signal, but the message was more likely that it was time for the United States to begin serious, good faith negotiations that might lead to a new space treaty. China, as you'll learn in these pages, has taken the point position in advocating a new space treaty.

Why did China send the message in the form of a debris-rich ASAT test? Ticking off nations whose satellites might now be in jeopardy from Chinese space debris seems like a near-perfect example of the old shoot-yourself-in-the-foot syndrome, a malady that afflicts nations as well as individuals.

The answer may be that under the administration of George W. Bush, space warriors have made great headway in selling the space-dominance idea. For several years, China has tried to convey its dismay over America's military-space plans through diplomatic channels. That didn't work. China's smash-up test in space produced a lot of blowback; but at least it focused attention on the issue.

DO AS I SAY...

Although most of the world's nations say they favor negotiations for a PAROS treaty, the administrations of Ronald Reagan, George H. W. Bush, Bill Clinton, and George W. Bush have blocked negotiations. Indeed, the latter administration has been openly contemptuous toward the idea. The Bush administration's no-treaty stance was reflected in a revision of America's National Space Policy, issued in October 2006.

The United States, the 2006 policy said, remains "committed to the exploration and use of outer space by all nations for peaceful purposes, and for the benefit of humanity." Solid, comforting, boilerplate. A little later, though, it takes on a more truculent tone than the Clinton policy issued a decade earlier:

> The United States considers space capabilities—including the ground and space segments and supporting links—vital to its national interests. Consistent with this policy, the United States will: preserve its rights, capabilities, and freedom of action in space; dissuade or deter others from either impeding those rights or developing capabilities intended to do so; take those actions necessary to protect its space capabilities; respond to interference; and deny, if necessary, adversaries the use of space capabilities hostile to U.S. national interests.

A casual reading of the paragraph is not alarming. Why wouldn't the United States—or any other state—have the right to defend its assets in space? That's simple self-defense. But what does "dissuade or deter others from either impeding those rights or *developing capabilities intended to do so*" actually mean? The United States is developing the very antisatellite capabilities it says others must *not* develop. America's new space policy also says, with conspicuous clarity: "The United States will oppose the development of new legal regimes or other restrictions that seek to prohibit or limit U.S. access to or use of space. Proposed arms control agreements or restrictions must not impair the rights of the United States to conduct research, development, testing, and operations or other activities in space for U.S. national interests."

WHO DECIDES?

The public's concept of America's future in space includes returning to the Moon and establishing a permanent presence there, as well as thinking seriously about one day sending astronauts to Mars. Meanwhile, in the name of national security, the United States is pursuing a research and development program aimed at achieving the military capability to control orbital space and—possibly—to place weapons in space, once a sitting president gives the go ahead and Congress agrees.

Are we talking eyes-glaze-over rocket science here? Questions fit only for "experts"? No. We're talking about the meaning of America, and you and I are all expert enough to tackle that one. America's founders shared a very big idea—that the people, not a monarch, were sovereign. They also believed that for such a republic to work, citizens must be well informed and deeply involved in important public-policy questions. That's Civics 101.

If the United States chooses to go the space-control and space-weapons route—and *that choice has not yet been definitively made*—that decision will become a central feature of American foreign policy, a policy that since 2001 has had a decidedly unilateralist and triumphalist cast. A policy of space dominance would set the tone for decades to come. It would be a lulu of a mistake for which America's children and grandchildren would pay the price.

We the people can no longer afford to let the question of unilateral space dominance remain in a hazy leave-it-to-the-experts twilight. There's a policy war going on regarding space that, in the end, comes down to a conflict over fundamental American values. That policy struggle has largely gone unnoticed. We need to examine these issues in the clarifying light of day; we must become more involved in shaping this vital facet of our nation's future. *Twilight War* gives you the background needed to come to grips with that issue.

The first two chapters introduce the notion of unilateral space dominance, a term you probably have not run into outside of the world of science fiction. Keep in mind throughout *Twilight War* that space dominance is not yet settled national policy. But our nation is heading in that direction.

Chapters three, four, and five elaborate on what's actually happening in regard to national-security space. An example: The missile defense system the United States is currently deploying is not likely to work well if missiles are ever launched against the United States. But it would be a dandy system if used in an offensive mode against the satellites of other nations. Space warriors call that "space control."

Chapter six—"Put to the Sword"—takes you back to the early years of the twentieth century when the notion of precision warfare, in the form of precision strategic bombing, began to develop. Precision bombing was supposed to be a new and humane way of fighting wars, but it didn't work as it was supposed to. Hundreds of thousands of German and Japanese civilians died in that early type of "precision" war. Today, the United States can do precision war better, thus sparing civilian lives. A variety of space satellites make such precision possible. These space assets must be protected, but unilateral space dominance is not the way to go about it.

Chapters seven through eleven provide the historical background you need to understand why President Eisenhower established a space-for-peaceful-purposes policy—as well as why men and women I call "space warriors" have tried for five decades to overturn it. Eisenhower's peaceful-purposes legacy is under intense assault today; the spirit of Wernher von Braun, who imagined a kind of orbiting battlestar sixty years ago, is still with us.

Chapter twelve argues that the best way to preserve the use of space for all is for the United States to take the lead in negotiating a hard-nosed and fully verifiable space treaty that would prevent any nation, including the United States, from developing space-related weapons. All spacefaring nations say they favor such a treaty, but the United States has systematically blocked serious work on one.

Why is that? The United States ardently and eloquently champions the rule of law on every continent. Why doesn't America at least engage in serious treaty talks? The final chapters attempt to answer that question, in part, by linking the dream of unilateral space dominance to the grand old tradition of American exceptionalism—the notion that the United States, and only the United States, is free to do what it wants on the world's stage, perhaps because Providence has favored it above all other nations.

Don't overlook the appendices. The first will give you some sense of how old the dream of space travel is—and how even early visionaries saw weapons possibilities in space. Appendix B will help you understand why satellites stay up instead of falling back to Earth. Appendix C links the notion of space control to the much older concept of control of the air. Appendix D demonstrates that old ideas never die. For more than six decades space warriors have dreamed of having a spacebomber—and even as you read this, the dream lives. The final appendix— "Useful Websites"—is a must. Mining these sites will put you on the road to Expertville.

Finally, a note about the term "space warrior," which I use throughout these pages: Space warrior is not a one-size-fits-all descriptive, nor is it meant as a pejorative. Space warriors often use the term about themselves and their colleagues. We live in an unstable and unpredictable world and America needs warriors who have demonstrated a passionate love for their country and a devotion to defending it. The space warriors I have met have been—without exception—direct and honorable regarding their beliefs. *Twilight War* questions their views, not their motives.

1

Triumphalism in Space

The history of humankind has been largely a tale of organized armed conflict. From the moment a warrior first huffed up a hill so he could lay eyes on the enemy, reconnaissance from the highest point has been basic to the successful conduct of war.

Warriors had to settle for hills and ridges for millennia until French brothers Joseph-Michel and Jacques-Etienne Montgolfier began a series of experiments that led to the first balloon ascension with a human aboard on October 15, 1783. Physicist Jean François Pilatre de Rozier rose some eighty feet in a basket attached to a tethered bag of hot air.

Progress was rapid. The public was enchanted by balloons, whether hot air or hydrogen. Ascensions became such picnic-friendly events in Paris that tickets were sometimes sold to limit crowds. But ballooning was not confined to France. In January 1793, French aeronaut Jean-Pierre Blanchard lifted off in a hydrogen-filled balloon in Philadelphia, the first such flight in the United States. President George Washington had previously given him a "passport" with which to identify himself upon landing. Forty-six minutes later, Blanchard touched down fifteen miles away and presented the passport to a befuddled farmer who could not read.[1]

Ungainly and colorful, balloons were joyful manifestations of the human spirit and imagination. And just as surely, the balloon would be useful in war, another ageless though darker manifestation of the human spirit. In 1783, just two days after de Rozier first went aloft, Andre Giraud de Villette ascended with de Rozier. Villette offered this prediction in a Paris newspaper:

> I observed St. Cloud, Isty, Ivry, Charenton, and Choisy with ease, and perhaps Corbeil, which a light mist prevented me from distin-

guishing clearly; from this moment I was convinced that this apparatus, costing but little, could be made very useful to an Army for discovering the positions of its enemy, his movements, his advances, and his dispositions, and that this information could be conveyed to the troops operating the machine. There, gentlemen, is an undeniable utility that time will perfect for us.[2]

In April 1794, France, besieged by Austrian and Prussian forces, established the world's first military air service, which would be used for observation. In June, a tethered hydrogen-filled balloon, *L'Entreprenant*, played a role in a battle between French and Austrian forces. Two aeronauts were aloft for about ten hours during an engagement near Fleurus, and they communicated with officers on the ground by lowering bags containing their observations.

The astonished Austrians surrendered. Were balloon observations decisive? The commanding French general, a man who kept his feet on the ground, did not think so. But one of the aeronauts said: "I shan't say that the balloon won the battle of Fleurus. What I can say is that, being trained to use my glasses in spite of the oscillation and swaying due to the wind, I was able to distinguish infantry, cavalry, and artillery, their movement and, in general, their numbers."[3]

And so began the modern military quest to gain the highest ground possible during conflict and to enjoy the "undeniable utility" it confers upon those who can hold it against all comers. For most of the twentieth century, air was the high ground; nations expended tens of thousands of lives and considerable treasure to control it during conflict. In the twenty-first century, orbital space is widely said to be the ultimate high ground. The question today: Will there be another cold war as nations seek to dominate it?

The first Cold War was a joint enterprise. Neither the United States nor the Soviet Union fully controlled their fate. Each reacted to the moves and perceived intentions of the other. The tensions were real and the Cold War may have been inevitable. But that is not the case today regarding space. The space-dominance paradigm is as American as the Stars and Stripes. If a cold war in space develops, perhaps with China, the United States will have incited it. It is as simple as that. Conversely, if the United States refrains from adopting a policy of space dominance, a new cold war, this time in space, is less likely.

REAP THE BENEFITS

Sputnik, launched on October 4, 1957, weighed just 184.3 pounds, but its thin A-flat beeps were politically deafening. Sputnik II followed in November; it weighed half a ton and carried Laika, a soon-to-be-martyred dog. The ability to accelerate payloads like that to seventeen thousand miles per hour, the minimum necessary to achieve a temporarily sustainable low-Earth orbit, implied that the Soviets had powerful rockets that could be used to lob hydrogen bombs at the United States. All sorts of sensible people were spooked.

The director of the Smithsonian Astrophysical Observatory said, "I would not be surprised if the Russians reached the Moon within a week." When asked what we might find there, Edward Teller, the "father" of the H-bomb, answered, "Russians." The *New York Times* declared that the United States was "in a race for survival." Labor leader Walter Reuther called Sputnik a "bloodless Pearl Harbor." G. Mennen Williams, governor of Michigan, resorted to edgy humor:

> *Oh Little Sputnik, flying high*
> *With made-in-Moscow beep,*
> *You tell the world it's a Commie sky,*
> *And Uncle Sam's asleep.*[4]

Stuart Symington, a Missouri senator and Democratic presidential hopeful, said in a Veterans Day address on November 11, 1957 in Jefferson City, Missouri, "The race for the conquest of space is today's major engagement in the technological war. We must win it because the nation that dominates the air spaces [sic] will be in a position to dominate the world."[5]

Senate Majority Leader Lyndon B. Johnson, whose chance of becoming president was considerably greater than Symington's, was chairman of the Senate Preparedness Committee. In that capacity, he organized hearings designed mostly to demonstrate that an incompetent administration had let the nation fall abysmally behind the Soviet Union in space. The hearings began in late November 1957 and continued into January 1958. Seventy-eight witnesses testified, producing 2,313 pages of testimony. On January 7, 1958, Johnson told Democratic senators in well-publicized remarks: "Control of space means control of the world, far more certainly, far more totally than any control that has ever or could ever be achieved by weapons, or troops of occupation.… Whoever gains that ultimate position gains control, total control, over the Earth, for purposes of tyranny or for the service of freedom."[6]

Democratic presidential hopefuls had de facto allies in the active-duty military. Air Force Chief of Staff Thomas Dresser White launched a very public campaign urging the Eisenhower administration to seize control of space. An intellectual who studied Italian, Spanish, Portuguese, Greek, Russian, and Chinese as well as military history and strategy as he rose through the ranks, White was the archetypal space warrior. On November 29, 1957, the general launched his crusade at the National Press Club in Washington, a forum that ensured maximum headline attention.

"The compelling reason for the preeminence of airpower is clear and unchallenged, because those who have the capability to control the air are in a position to exert control over the land and seas beneath." But now, White said, the Soviet Union had one-upped the United States. For the first time since 1814, the U.S. homeland was in mortal danger; no longer would the Atlantic and Pacific moats protect it. America's answer to the Soviet challenge would require the military use of space. "I feel in the future whoever has the capability to control space will likewise possess the capability to exert control of the surface of the Earth."

The following February, White elaborated his space vision in a speech at the national conference of the Air Force Association, a nongovernmental organization that sings the praises of the Air Force.

> The United States must win and maintain the capability to control space in order to assure the progress and preeminence of the free nations.… You will note that I stated the United States must win and maintain the *capability* to control space. I did not say that we should control space. There is an important distinction here. We want all nations to join with us in such measures as are necessary to ensure that outer space shall never be used for any but peaceful purposes.
>
> But until effective measures to this end are assured, our possession of such a capability will guarantee the free nations liberty—it does not connote denial of the benefits of space to others. In the past when control of the seas was exercised by peaceful nations, people everywhere profited. Likewise, as long as the United States maintains the capability to control space, the entire world will reap the benefits that accrue.[7]

Control of space, White said in his windup, "should be the goal of all Americans." One did not need to be a rocket scientist (presumably most rocket scientists throughout the world quickly became aware of White's words) to parse the general's argument: The United States should become the Wyatt Earp of space.

PEACEFUL PURPOSES

President Eisenhower was more complicated, thoughtful, and analytical than the syntax-challenged, golf-playing, nap-taking, do-nothing president Democrats often portrayed him as being. Although he and Secretary of State John Foster Dulles are remembered today for having employed the rhetoric of "massive retaliation," that phrase was, in the weirdly counterintuitive logic of the Cold War, part of their strategy for preserving the peace. The rhetoric was designed to dissuade the Kremlin from taking reckless actions that might lead to war.[8]

Nuclear war, Eisenhower believed, would be so terrible that neither side would let it happen. But after Sputnik, many of Eisenhower's top military officers—with General White in the lead—as well as some of the nation's most prominent politicians and opinion shapers urged him to move the nuclear arms race into space. Eisenhower believed that would be unwise. In the face of take-control-of-space-now demands, the president reaffirmed his policy of "space for peaceful purposes," which he had tentatively established two years earlier.[9]

Eisenhower's peaceful-purposes policy eventually became the basis of one of the most honored international agreements in history, the Treaty on Principles Governing the Activities of States in the Exploration and Use of Outer Space, including the Moon and Other Celestial Bodies. The document is commonly (and thankfully) known as the "Outer Space Treaty."

Before leaving office, the Eisenhower administration began working with the Soviet Union and the United Nations on military space issues, negotiations that were carried forward by the Kennedy and Johnson administrations. The Outer Space Treaty "entered into force," as diplomats put it, on October 10, 1967, just a few days past the tenth anniversary of the first Sputnik. Ambassador Anatoly Dobrynin of the Soviet Union said the treaty ensured the "peaceful activities of states in outer space for the benefit of all mankind." In contrast, President Johnson was decidedly Kennedyesque:

"Whatever our disagreements here on Earth, however long it may take to resolve our conflicts whose roots are buried centuries-deep in history, let us try to agree on this. Let us determine that the great space armadas of the future will go forth on voyages of peace—and go forth in a spirit not of national rivalry but of peaceful cooperation and understanding."[10]

The treaty is stuffed with grand language about the "common interest of all mankind," the "use of outer space for peaceful purposes," the virtues of "international cooperation," and the need to develop "mutual understanding" to strengthen "friendly relations between States and peoples." Unlike similar feel-good language that often makes its way into arms control documents like verses in a Hallmark card, the words in the Outer Space Treaty may have been sincere. Moving the Cold War into space was a profoundly scary business in the mid-1960s.[11]

"Most of the participants [in drafting the treaty] had only hazy ideas of what would come to pass in the space field, and how it would affect their own destinies," wrote two space law experts in 1998. "Even the United States and the Soviet Union seemed far more willing than usual to be persuaded by one another on most issues. Paradoxically, this comparative lack of specifically self-serving goals may be one reason why the Outer Space Treaty is viewed with such respect—approaching reverence at times—by so many.... The treaty can be said to represent a more general view of the interests of humanity instead of being merely a compromise among interested parties, shaped primarily by the balance of power."[12]

The core of the treaty is the notion that outer space, including the Moon and other "celestial bodies," is the "province of all mankind" and that space should be used exclusively for peaceful purposes. The words "peace" and "peaceful" appear seven times in the treaty; the phrase "peaceful purposes" pops up four times.[13]

According to the treaty, the Moon and other celestial bodies could not be appropriated by any state. A nation might plant its flag on the Moon, as the United States did in July 1969, but it could not claim ownership. No military installations of any kind would be permitted there; no testing of weapons; no military maneuvers. Military personnel would be welcome as explorers, but only if they were engaged in nonmilitary scientific research or other "peaceful purposes."

Orbital space—the region between the Earth and the orbit of the Moon—was a different matter. Only nuclear or other weapons of mass destruction were barred from orbital space. The United States and the Soviet Union already had a variety of military-oriented hardware circling the Earth—mainly spy, communication, and missile-launch-warning satellites—and the Cold War adversaries were not about to deal those assets away.

Spy satellites were too useful to both sides to be banned—and they were not in themselves weapons. Given the fact that the retaliatory nuclear forces of the United States and the Soviet Union were on a hair trigger, satellite imagery, even if blurry or full of static, served the interests of peace. In matters nuclear, ambiguity breeds mistrust, fear, miscalculation, and possibly accidental or preemptive war. Spy satellites helped clear away the fog, giving each side bits and pieces of the puzzle regarding the other side's military capabilities, if not the other side's political intentions. Small comfort, to be sure, but it was some comfort.

The U.S. and Soviet teams who worked on the treaty simply accepted the limited militarization of space, mainly for intelligence gathering and communications. That was a given. Spy, communications, and warning satellites were OK but orbital weapons—"shooters" in today's argot—were not. The treaty's negotiators focused solely on nuclear weapons and other weapons of mass destruction during their deliberations. Space weapons so accurate that they could take out buildings or bunkers or airplanes in flight were the stuff of science fiction, not of humankind's real-life future. In the mid-1960s, when the major work on the treaty was done, there was no reason to worry about non-nuclear weapons in space. What would be the point? No conventional weapon fired from space would have enough accuracy or explosive power to be militarily significant.

A space-based conventional weapon—if developed and deployed—might be aimed at a bunker, but it was as likely to blow apart a barn thirty, if not three hundred, miles from the target. Further, conventional weapons in space would not be cost effective, even if they could be made reasonably accurate. Lifting anything into orbit was (and remains) hugely expensive. Only weapons with *mass* effects would be worth the cost, and now they were barred.

Although the drafters of the Outer Space Treaty believed they were peering far into the future, they could not foresee the incredible shrinking world of microprocessors, a computing-power race that the United States has always led by many laps. As U.S. processors got smaller, they also became more powerful. In turn, that made the miniaturization of space hardware possible. Powerful but minuscule processors opened the door for today's array of made-in-America precision weapons, many of which are dependent on an ever more sophisticated array of U.S. space satellites, especially surveillance and geo-positioning satellites.

After the collapse of the Soviet Union—and in an age of true precision weaponry—visionaries in the armed forces, in hardline think tanks, and in Congress could at last imagine weapons in space that would be both useful *and* non-nuclear. There are, as they endlessly point out, no legal impediments to deploying such weapons.

THE NEXT MANIFEST DESTINY?

In recent years, no one did more to promote space-dominance than former senator Bob Smith of New Hampshire. Senator who? No one would accuse Smith, a right-wing Republican who represented New Hampshire in the U.S. Senate in the 1990s, of having been a Capitol Hill heavyweight. A big man—six-feet-six—he was short on political heft, charisma, and voter appeal, and he eventually lost his seat to John E. Sununu in 2002.

Senator Smith would be little more than a footnote in political history if not for "The Challenge of Space Power," a speech he delivered November 18, 1998 at an aerospace conference in Cambridge, Massachusetts. "America has always been a nation of discoverers and explorers," said Smith, then chairman of the Senate Subcommittee on Strategic Forces. "It suits our national character to pursue the permanent frontier of space. Like Columbus, we must dare to move away from the 'old world'—old vision, old strategy, and old institutions—if we are to truly enter the 'new world' of space."

In Smith's vision, the new world of space would be an American sea, generously open to all nations as long as the United States approved. "Control of space is more than a new mission area—it is our moral legacy, our next Manifest Destiny, our chance to create security for centuries to come."

Elected to the House in 1984, Smith first served on the Space Subcommittee of the Science and Technology Committee, a yeasty experience for a young conservative, particularly during the Reagan years. Smith admired Reagan, loathed the Soviet Union, and mistrusted China, which he considered a likely future adversary. If America were to flourish in the twenty-first century, Smith believed, it must build upon Ronald Reagan's Star Wars program. The United States must strive to dominate space lest an enemy come to control it—and thus the planet below.

Although Smith was not influential on Capitol Hill in the traditional let's-make-a-deal sense, no senator is devoid of power. If a senator chooses to stake a claim on previously unspoken-for territory, he or she can eventually own it. Smith made military space, national security space, his domain.

Smith argued that space was already heavily militarized with a variety of satellites increasingly vital to Pentagon planners and combat commanders. He was right about that. But, he said, space had never been "weaponized." He was right about that, too—and a little angry. The United States had dropped the ball; beginning with the Eisenhower administration, the United States had intentionally chosen not to weaponize space. That must change. The space-for-peaceful-purposes policy, established by President Eisenhower, was the dragon Smith hoped to slay.

"My approach to space," Smith said, "has come to rest on three assertions. First, America's future security and prosperity depend on our constant supremacy in space. Second, while we are ahead of any potential rival in exploiting space, we are not unchallenged and our future dominance is by no means assured. Third, to achieve true dominance we must combine expansive thinking with a sustained and substantial commitment of resources and vest them in a dedicated, politically powerful, independent advocate for space power." In the twenty-first century, the United States must shift "substantial" military resources to space. "Space offers us the prospect of seeing and communicating throughout the world; of defending ourselves, our deployed forces, and our allies; and, if necessary, of inflicting violence—all with great precision and nearly instantaneously and often more cheaply. With credible offensive and defensive space control, we will deter and dissuade our adversaries, reassure our allies, and guard our nation's growing reliance on global commerce. Without it, we will become vulnerable beyond our worst fears."[14]

Although the Defense Department had repeatedly spoken over the years of the importance of "space control," Smith said, nothing much had happened. "Even the Air Force's Space Warfare Center and Space Battlelab are focused primarily on figuring out how to use space systems to put information into the cockpit in order to drop *bombs* from *aircraft* more accurately. This is not space warfare. It is using space to support air warfare."[15]

WE ARE ON NOTICE...

Senator Smith's speech drew little press attention. News people at the time were distracted by the possibility that a president of the United States might be impeached for lying under oath about his sexual indiscretions. Meanwhile, journalists who actually paid attention to Smith and knew of his continuing passion for space power were inclined to snicker and call him "space man." The senator was not dismayed. He knew how to move his concerns to the next level. He would draft Donald Rumsfeld, then a high-powered business executive in Chicago, to take the point position.

Smith conceived the idea of assembling a congressionally mandated and funded panel of space-minded men, with Rumsfeld as its chair. The assemblage was called the Commission to Assess United States National Security Space Management and Organization—universally known as the Space Commission.[16]

Rumsfeld was an astute choice. A long-time Washington insider, he wore power as easily as many of us wear jeans and sweatshirts. He was brilliant, charming, tough, and politically savvy, and he had impeccable right-wing credentials extending back to the Nixon and Ford years, when he played hardball against a host of heavyweights, including Henry Kissinger, and often won.[17] Despite having reached an age when other financially secure men are inclined to play golf in the morning and take naps in the afternoon, Rumsfeld was in permanent hyperdrive.

More important was the fact that Rumsfeld had a passionate interest in military space issues. Rumsfeld had last served in the federal government as President Gerald Ford's second secretary of defense. After leaving the Pentagon, he turned his energies to private enterprise but remained on call for high-level volunteer assignments for the government.[18] Most significantly, he had chaired the Commission on the Ballistic Missile Threat to the United States, which issued its final report in July 1998.[19]

That commission argued that U.S. intelligence estimates were too sanguine about the immediacy of the presumed missile threat. North Korea and Iran could produce crude and inaccurate missiles that would "be able to inflict major destruction on the U.S." within five years of a decision to do so, said the commission; Iraq would take about ten years. North Korea fired a primitive three-stage missile shortly after the report appeared, persuading a lot of people that Rumsfeld and his crew were extraordinarily prescient.

The commission, however, did not recommend that the United States build a national missile-defense system, the sort of thing that Ronald Reagan had in mind in the 1980s with his Star Wars vision. Such a recommendation—either for or against—would have gone beyond the commission's charter. The commission had been asked to *evaluate* the threat, Rumsfeld explained, not to suggest remedies. In contrast, Rumsfeld II—the Space Commission—had a more expansive charter. Its task was to analyze threats and recommend steps the United States should take to meet them.

The Space Commission issued its report on January 11, 2001.[20] The United States was at risk, the report said. America had failed to take bold action to protect its commercial assets in space, which had become vital to the functioning of an increasingly interconnected global economy. Further, the United States had been unconscionably derelict in its duty to properly defend the country's military and intelligence assets in space, which were essential to the new U.S. way of precision war. The report contained this stunning (if not quite original) metaphor, rumored to have been drafted by Rumsfeld:

> History is replete with instances in which warning signs were ignored and change resisted until an external, "improbable" event forced resistant bureaucracies to take action. The question is whether the U.S. will be wise enough to act responsibly and soon enough to reduce U.S. space vulnerability. Or whether, as in the past, a disabling attack against the country and its people—a "space Pearl Harbor"—will be the only event able to galvanize the nation and cause the U.S. government to act.
>
> We are on notice, but we have not noticed.[21]

Most Americans did not notice Rumsfeld's wake-up call, mostly because the news media overlooked it. That was understandable. Distinguished panels, commissions, and task forces are common in Washington. They meet, hear witnesses, and issue staff-written reports that are, with rare exception, filed in drawers labeled "Obscurity," where they molder away unless rescued years later by historians who pronounce them far-sighted, shortsighted, or alarmist. The report of the Space Commission seemed to follow the pattern. The Associated Press distributed a nuts-and-bolts piece about it and the *New York Times*, the *Washington Post* and a few other newspapers carried short staff-written articles. TV news essentially ignored it.

Why didn't a report with such headline-friendly rhetoric attract attention? Bad timing. On December 28, 2000, president-elect George W. Bush nominated Rumsfeld as secretary of defense. In a peculiar coincidence, Rumsfeld's confirmation hearing before the Senate Armed Services Committee was held January 11, 2001, the same day the Space Commission report was released. Rumsfeld's testimony during the hearing focused on how he would transform the military to meet the challenges of the new century. That was *the* Rumsfeld story of the day; the findings and recommendations of Rumsfeld's Space Commission were buried, sidebar material at best.

The Space Commission's report deserved more vigorous treatment than Rumsfeld's comments at the confirmation hearing. Any nominee for defense secretary at the beginning of the twenty-first century, Republican or Democrat, would have focused on the need to transform the armed forces to fit the needs of a new century. That's How to Give Testimony 101. But the Space Commission's report was revolutionary. Its recommendations, if implemented, would overturn four decades of established practice in the national security space field. Among many things, it spoke of possibly deploying weapons in space, a thing that had never been done by any nation. In a nod to those who might not be enamored of that, the commissioners said they "appreciate the sensitivity that surrounds the notion of weapons in space for offensive or defensive purposes. They also believe, however, that to ignore the issue would be a disservice to the nation. The Commissioners believe that the U.S. Government should vigorously pursue the capabilities called for in the National Space Policy to ensure that the President will have the option to deploy weapons in space to deter threats to and, if necessary, defend against attacks on U.S. interests."[22]

High on the commission's priority list was the need to develop and test antisatellite (ASAT) weapons, largely because the commissioners believed that unfriendly nations might someday deploy observation and command-and-control satellites that would imperil U.S. forces on land, sea, and air in a time of conflict. "The senior political and military leadership needs to test these [ASAT] capabilities in exercises on a regular basis, both to keep the armed forces proficient in their use and to bolster their deterrent value." By "test," the commissioners meant not only computer simulations and war games, but also "live-fire events." The latter would require "testing ranges in space."

The United States would also need "assured access to space." Although space-launch facilities at Vandenberg Air Force Base in California and Cape Canaveral Air Force Base and the Kennedy Space Flight Center in Florida were sufficient "to meet the projected needs of all users under normal conditions," the United States should develop the capacity for "surges." That is, if some U.S. satellites were ever disabled or destroyed by an unfriendly power at a critical moment, the United States would need to quickly insert replacements into orbit.

The nation must build a more sophisticated "space situational awareness" network not only to keep track of satellites, space debris, and asteroids, but "to reduce the possibility of surprise by hostile actors." Radars and cameras used to track objects in space are now based on Earth, the commissioners noted. In the future, the "evolution of technology and the character of this problem argue for placing elements of the surveillance network in space."

"Earth surveillance from space" was another big-ticket item on the commission's agenda. "The U.S. needs to develop technologies for sensors, communication, power generation, and space platforms that will enable it to observe the Earth and objects in motion on a near real-time basis, twenty-four-hours a day." That is, the United States should work toward developing technology that could keep track of almost anything of military importance anywhere in the world at all times. Such a capability "could revolutionize military operations." Space-based radar, for instance, aimed toward Earth "could provide military commanders, on a near-continuous and global basis, with timely, precise information on the location of adversary forces and their movement over time." That ability "coupled to precision strike weapons delivered rapidly over long distances" would greatly enhance the U.S. ability to deter "hostile action."[23]

As for the endlessly controversial matter of national missile defense, the commissioners turned cagey, presumably because it was still American policy in January 2001 to preserve, with modifications, the 1972 Anti-Ballistic Missile Treaty. The report simply said: "Some believe the ballistic missile defense mission is best performed when both sensors and interceptors are deployed in space." (Once in office, George W. Bush dumped the ABM Treaty, as he had repeatedly pledged to do during his presidential campaign.)

But the Space Commission's money shot, the rationale for a future program of space dominance, was not about anything as specific as antisatellite weapons or space-based radars or missile interceptors based in space.

Rather, it was a generalized vision of what *might* be, if the United States would only get on with it.

> Many think of space only as a place for passive collection of images or signals or a switchboard that can quickly pass information back and forth over long distances. *It is also possible to project power through and from space in response to events anywhere in the world.* Unlike weapons from aircraft, land forces, or ships, space missions initiated from Earth or space could be carried out with little transit, information, or weather delay. Having this capability would give the U.S. a much stronger deterrent and, in a conflict, an extraordinary military advantage.[24] (Italics added.)

By word count alone, the commission's report did not seem to focus on the weaponization of space. Only 109 words were devoted explicitly to power projection "from and through space." Only forty-four words directly addressed the possibility of a space-based missile-defense system. "Negating satellite threats"—that is, the development of antisatellite weapons—got just three paragraphs.

In contrast, a substantial portion of the report was devoted to examining the debilitating effects of the bureaucratic maze—how dozens of departments, agencies, bureaus, military commands, intelligence centers, councils, research laboratories, and House and Senate committees and subcommittees had their thumbs in the national security space pie. As anyone who has ever worked within a large bureaucracy knows, diffuse authority is often a recipe for incoherence, incompetence, and inaction. The commissioners insisted that Congress and the Defense Department rationalize outdated, nonproductive, and counterproductive structural relationships.

In his "Challenge of Space Power" speech in 1998, Senator Smith had called for a separate Space Force, to be coequal with the Army, Navy, and Air Force. It was too soon for that, said the Space Commission. Nonetheless, Smith was a happy man. The overall message of the Space Commission was clear. Just as Smith had advocated, Rumsfeld and his fellow commissioners said it was time for the United States to get tough regarding space.

The old Eisenhower-era space-for-peaceful-purposes dragon was not yet slain but it was being stalked. At a Rumsfeld press conference on May 8, 2001, in which the secretary of defense outlined some early space initiatives, Smith turned to Rumsfeld and said: "You are a true visionary. I am really delighted that you are secretary of defense."[25]

DOMINATING THE SPACE MEDIUM

Rumsfeld resigned as George W. Bush's secretary of defense in November 2006, after it became apparent in mid-term elections that a majority of Americans had come to reject the Rumsfeld-Cheney-Bush war of choice in Iraq. Given that, it is difficult to recall that Rumsfeld was a superstar in the early days of the Bush administration, a man whose impact on the public mind was great and influence on foreign policy huge. The cover of the December 31, 2001 issue of the conservative *National Review* featured a caricature of a grinning, rakish Rumsfeld. The coverline said: "The Stud: Don Rumsfeld, America's New Pin-Up." The cover of the January 27, 2003 issue of *Time* depicted a grimly determined Rumsfeld. The coverline: "Donald Rumsfeld's Blueprint for War."

Yet Rumsfeld and his colleagues on the Space Commission were not the alpha and the omega of the space-weapons debate. The observations made by the commissioners were far from original. Rumsfeld and his fellow commissioners poured old wine into new bottles and pasted new labels on them.

In 1997, for instance, U.S. Space Command, a combined Army, Navy, and Air Force umbrella organization established in 1985 and headquartered in Colorado Springs, issued the sixteen-page *Vision for 2020*. Printed on glossy, heavyweight paper and heavily stocked with full-color illustrations, *Vision* was rather like a prospectus for a gated retirement community in Florida, the sort of thing typically peppered with punchy paragraphs and salted with bromides that describe the planned community's unparalleled amenities.

Instead of depicting a proposed championship golf course and tennis courts or pools and clubhouses, *Vision* hustled dreams of unlimited space power. On the first page, in oversize type against the black background of space, it reads: "U.S. Space Command—dominating the space dimension of military operations to protect U.S. interests and investment. Integrating Space Forces into warfighting capabilities across the full spectrum of conflict." The type, a rousing yellow, seems to fall away from the reader, like the text at the beginning of George Lucas's first *Star Wars* movie. ("A long time ago in a galaxy far, far away…") Turning the page:

> Historically, military forces have evolved to protect national interests and investments—both military and economic. During the rise of sea commerce, nations built navies to protect and enhance their

commercial interests. During the westward expansion of the continental United States, military outposts and the cavalry emerged to protect our wagon trains, settlements, and railroads.

As air power developed, its primary purpose was to support and enhance land and sea operations. However, over time, air power evolved into a separate and equal medium of warfare.

The emergence of space power follows both of these models. Over the past several decades, space power has primarily supported land, sea, and air operations—strategically and operationally. During the early portion of the twenty-first century, space power will also evolve into a *separate and equal medium of warfare.* Likewise, space forces will emerge to protect military and commercial national interests and investment in the space medium due to their increasing importance.[26]

A little later, we are told that U.S. control of space is essential—control being defined as the "ability to assure access to space, freedom of operations within the space medium, and an ability to deny others the use of space, if required." Control of space will allow the United States to "evolve into the guardian of space commerce—similar to the historical example of navies protecting sea commerce."

Next comes "global engagement," an ominous thing that "combines global surveillance [of Earth] with the potential *for a space-based global precision strike capability* (italics added)." "The two principal themes of the USS-PACECOM Vision," says a bit of centerfold text, "are dominating the space medium and integrating space power throughout military operations."

The visual clincher is on the inside back cover, where a painting depicts a device that has topped the wish list of space warriors for more than two decades: a space-based laser. The vantage point is near-Earth space, a couple of hundred miles up. Below is a pie-wedge portion of the Earth depicted in the sere shades of a rock-baked desert—the easternmost tip of the Mediterranean Sea and below that, the Red Sea, partly obscured by clouds. Above the Mediterranean is a bit of the Black Sea; to its right, the Caspian; below that, the Persian Gulf. A few yards ahead, hanging in the blackness of space, is an orbiting laser. It glows orange as it zaps a missile rising from a point on the Iraq-Iran border.

The following year, 1998, Space Command followed up *Vision 2020* with its *Long Range Plan.* The plan's introduction said that the United States "does not expect to face a global military peer competitor within the next two decades." Given that, the nation had "entered a period of 'strategic pause,'" which would give the United States "an opportunity similar to the period between World War I and World War II" to explore "innovative warfighting concepts and capabilities."

The "growth of space power," Space Command added, "closely resembles air power's evolution during the first half of this century. Air power evolved from supporting warfighters (e.g., communications and reconnaissance), to air combat, and finally to strategically projecting force on the battlefield. Similarly, space power started out mainly as support (e.g., communications and surveillance) and may move toward space combat operations. Eventually, as it continues to mature, it may allow us to project force from space to Earth."

That last phrase—"it may allow us to project force from space to Earth"—is intriguing. Chapter Six of the plan, titled "Global Engagement," explains what it means: The United States could hold "a finite number of targets at risk anywhere, anytime with nearly instantaneous attack from space-based assets."[27]

Indeed, space-based weapons would give the United States attack options that "offer reduced risk, increased speed, and short cycle times to counter some high-value targets that may threaten U.S. and allied forces and interests." The meaning of "high value targets" is not always precise, but in Pentagon-speak it generally covers "leadership" (think of the many air-launched bunker-buster weapons expended in the futile attempts to kill Saddam Hussein and his top lieutenants in March and April 2003), command-and-control centers, key industries and services related to the war effort, and—of course—weapons of mass destruction.

Unlike nuclear weapons, said the *Long Range Plan*, space-based precision weapons could "neutralize threats without widespread destruction." Among the "evolving concepts" for these weapons, the plan said, were "common aero vehicles" that could be inserted into orbit and later reenter the atmosphere and head for their targets at hypersonic speeds, as well as the old standby, lasers, which would do their work at the speed of light.

As for the "threat," the plan's authors peered into their crystal ball and everywhere saw darkness. Losing the use of space in a future conflict, they said, would be "intolerable." Space-based systems and products "will increase our enemies' potency and level the military playing field."

The explosive commercial development of space capabilities will make space products accessible to any organization with resources. The blending of military and civilian systems complicates our ability to distinguish when an enemy is gaining advantage from space systems....

Technological advances also provide unparalleled capability and access to potential adversaries. For example, higher bandwidths, better imagery resolution (less than one meter), and the sheer number of payloads in space will act as combat multipliers. An adversary's ability to command and control forces will gain much from dynamic, global, communication networks.... Anyone with Internet access will get highly accurate imagery almost instantly. Satellites for navigation are proliferating and adversaries will use them to enable precise military operations.[28]

Space Command would ensure that this dark vision of how an enemy might someday "level the military playing field" would never come to pass. Space Command would develop the capability to control space in a time of conflict, mostly with ground-based and space-based antisatellite weapons. That would require systematic effort and heavy investment; it would be neither easy nor cheap. But it would be necessary. By 2020, the United States would have a "robust and wholly integrated suite of capabilities in space and on the ground"—it would achieve "dominance of space."

In fairness to Space Command, the authors of the *Long Range Plan* inserted a disclaimer at the beginning of the "Global Engagement" chapter: *"At present, the notion of weapons in space is not consistent with U.S. national policy. Planning for this possibility is the purpose of this plan should our civilian leadership later decide that the application of force from space is in our national interest."* (Emphasis in the original.)

The United States has not yet publicly chosen to pursue a full-blown Pax Americana policy in which a comprehensive space-dominance capability would be a central feature. Despite a relentless beating of the drums by space warriors since the late 1950s, presidents, with the exception of Ronald Reagan and George W. Bush, have demonstrated considerable restraint regarding national security space.[29] That de facto policy of restraint is under assault today, particularly under cover of the national missile defense program.

In late 2002, U.S. Space Command was folded into Strategic Command, the nation's global-strike unit and the lineal descendant of the Cold War-era Strategic Air Command. U.S. Space Command's sister organization, Air Force Space Command, took the point position regarding the development of space-dominance theory and doctrine. Air Force Space Command issued its *Strategic Master Plan FY06 and Beyond* in October 2003. In it, Air Force Space Command amplified earlier project-force-from-space language: "Non-nuclear *prompt global strike* from and through space can transform the warfighter's role in the future. Most notably, a non-nuclear strike capability, possibly in the form of a Common Aero Vehicle (CAV) launched by a ballistic missile, air launch system, or a SOV [Space Operations Vehicle], could provide the President and the Secretary of Defense with a range of space power options. These options are for deterrence and flexible response when time is absolutely critical, risks associated with other options are too high, or when no other courses of action are available."[30] (Italics added.)

A GRAND SCENE AND DESIGN

Today's space warriors, like their godfather, one-time Air Force Chief of Staff Thomas Dresser White, believe the capability to control space should be the goal of the United States, if not of all Americans. That vision is uniquely in tune with twenty-first century American triumphalism, the dominant *leitmotif* in American foreign policy since the collapse of the Soviet Union. Triumphalists believe that America's values, perhaps divinely inspired, ought to be the world's values. Triumphalists are not shy about proclaiming the United States as *the* global hegemon.

Are space warriors right when they say the United States must unilaterally develop and deploy the capability to control space to defend America and its vital interests? Everett C. Dolman, a professor at Air University's School of Advanced Air and Space Studies, a clout-heavy institution, is among the most thoughtful and articulate of space-warrior theorists. He insists that U.S. control of space would place "as guardian of space the most benign state that has ever attempted hegemony over the greater part of the world." It would be a bold and decisive step, and "at least from the hegemon's point of view, morally just."[31]

Or are liberal internationalists (like me) on track in suggesting that America and its vital interests would be better served if the United States took the lead in developing a new, tougher, and more comprehensive space treaty that would decisively prevent any nation from developing a capability to militarily dominate space?

Unilateral space dominance would be viewed by many nations as an exercise in imperial arrogance. If we go down that road, it might well trigger a new and costly cold war, most likely with China. In contrast, the treaty route can potentially deter *any* nation, including the United States, from testing and deploying the dangerous hardware necessary for space dominance.

2

Full Spectrum Dominance

Colonel John R. Boyd, a retired Air Force fighter pilot and Pentagon consultant, died of cancer on March 9, 1997 at seventy years age. Shortly after Boyd's death, Charles Krulak, commandant of the Marine Corps, described him as "a towering intellect who made unsurpassed contributions to the American art of war" and "one of the central architects in the reform of military thought." Thousands of officers in all the services, said Krulak, "knew John Boyd by his work on what was to be known as the Boyd Cycle or the OODA loop."[1]

High praise. Who *was* this obscure Air Force officer who never made it to the top ranks of the Air Force but who is now said to have made "unsurpassed contributions to the American art of war"? What possessed James Fallows, then editor of *U.S. News & World Report* and a savvy observer of military affairs, to assert that Boyd's "ideas about weapons, leadership, and the very purpose of national security" changed the modern military? What compelled Charles Grassley, a Republican senator from Iowa, to call Boyd "the leader of the military reform movement," a man who "always set the example of excellence—both morally and professionally"?

And…what *is* an OODA loop?

Boyd was a self-educated super-achiever, a voracious reader of history and philosophy, and an original military thinker. He didn't crave fame or money; he lived simply. His passion was to do whatever he could to give the United States an edge in any future conflict. By the mid-1970s, Boyd had come up with critical design innovations that made the F-15, the F-16, and the F/A-18 the best fighter planes in the world. Meanwhile, he wrote the book—literally—on fighter-plane tactics: *New Conception for Air-to-Air Combat*. Then he began reinventing the American way of war.

Boyd reflected on the long-ago air battles of the Korean War. He had flown the F-86 *Sabre* during the latter months of the war; the other side flew Soviet-made MiG-15s. In many ways, the MiG-15 was a superior machine; it could out-turn and out-climb the F-86, which would seem to make it a pretty lethal tool. And yet, American pilots enjoyed a "kill ratio" of about ten to one. Why? For decades the Air Force insisted the reason was "better training."

Boyd had no quarrel with the idea that American pilots had a training edge over their North Korean, Chinese, and Soviet counterparts. (Soviet pilots were heavily engaged in the war, a fact that neither Josef Stalin nor President Harry Truman publicized for fear that it would make a bad situation worse.) But how, Boyd asked, could American pilots have a *ten to one* advantage over their adversaries? Could superior training alone account for that? He eventually concluded that something more profound was also at work.

Although the MiG-15 was arguably the better airplane, the F-86 had a couple of advantages. The American craft had a more generous bubble canopy than the MiG. That meant U.S. pilots could see the airspace around them more easily than could MiG-15 pilots. In an aerial dogfight, that was vital. In today's Air Force terminology, dedicated as it is to making even simple ideas sound arcane, American pilots had greater "situational awareness."

More important, the F-86 had a fully powered hydraulic flight-control system; in contrast, the MiG-15 had a mechanical system with a hydraulic boost. An F-86 pilot could move the control stick with one finger; the MiG-15 pilot had to work up a muscle sweat to rapidly change direction. That enabled the F-86 pilot to flip from maneuver to maneuver more easily and more quickly.

Boyd's insight eventually led to his OODA loop theory: A pilot in a dogfight who could Observe, Orient, Decide, and Act more quickly than the enemy, thus disrupting the enemy's decision cycle, was more likely to win the battle. Boyd took that idea and turned it into meta-theory that applied to all combat—whether in the air, at sea, or on the ground.

FAST-BREAK WARFARE

Confusing the enemy is old stuff. War is not all guns and guts. It is also a mind game. A successful commander tries to get inside the head of his enemy and work on his mind. As China's Sun-tzu put it nearly 2,500 years ago:

Warfare is the art of deceit. Therefore, when able, seem to be unable; when ready, seem unready; when nearby, seem far away; and when far away, seem near. If the enemy seeks some advantage, entice him with it. If he is in disorder, attack him and take him. If he is formidable, prepare against him. If he is strong, evade him. If he is incensed, provoke him. If he is humble, encourage his arrogance. If he is rested, wear him down. If he is internally harmonious, sow divisiveness in his ranks. Attack where he is not prepared; go by way of places where it would never occur to him you would go.[2]

Boyd admired Sun-tzu and adapted many of his insights to late twentieth-century warfare. Boyd believed that victory awaited the side that could disrupt the enemy's decision cycle so rapidly and intensely and unpredictably as to drive the enemy crazy, making him incapable of coping with the onslaught. The enemy should be enmeshed "in an amorphous, menacing, and unpredictable world of uncertainty, doubt, mistrust, confusion, disorder, fear, panic, chaos" so daunting that there would be no way out. The result would be mental paralysis and defeat.[3]

Speed was important, but it was not the main thing. Boyd biographer Robert Coram writes that the "key thing to understand…is not the mechanical cycle itself, but rather the need to execute the cycle in such fashion as to get *inside* the mind and decision cycle of the adversary. This means the adversary is dealing with outdated or irrelevant information and thus becomes confused and disoriented and can't function."[4] Although many of his ideas are widely accepted today in America's armed forces, Boyd is seldom credited. He was too extreme, too uncompromising, too obsessive, too coarse, too unkempt, too mercurial, too abrasive—qualities that did not endear him to the power structure. Coram recounts an incident in which Boyd, then a lieutenant colonel who liked to tell the high brass precisely why they were wrong, accosted a general in a Pentagon corridor and began an intense conversation about one of Boyd's favorite projects.

Boyd was smoking a cigar and waving his arms and jabbing his finger. The general grew bored and turned and began edging away just as Boyd reached out to emphasize a point. The cigar burned a hole in the general's tie. For a moment those passing by froze as they stared at the tableau of an astonished general looking down at the hole in his tie. The hole smoldered on the edges and grew larger and larger and smoke rose around the general's face. He slapped out the burning tie, then spun and walked away. Boyd did not know the reason for the general's abrupt departure until someone said, "Damn, John, you just set the general's tie on fire."[5]

Boyd was not the only military strategist and tactician who was thinking about how best to exploit America's advantage in a new information-rich, high-tech, fast-moving way of war. Boyd had plenty of company. By the Gulf War in 1991, it was clear to nearly everyone that the American way of war had moved away from the force-on-force attrition style of warfare to a fast-break way of fighting in which U.S. forces were always a step or two or three ahead of the enemy.

In basketball, an expert fast-break team will almost always beat a slower and more methodical team—*if* it can sustain its tempo while its players remain fully in touch with one another, no matter how fast the pace. In the military sphere, there is only one world-class fast-break team; and no other team on the planet is capable of slowing it down, at least in a conventional war. (Urban or guerrilla war, in which much of America's high-tech advantage is lost, is an altogether different matter.)

Boyd's theory of fast-break OODA-loop war—whether adopted and refined by others or arrived at independently—dominates today's strategic and tactical thinking in the Army, Air Force, Navy, and Marines. A great variety of space assets—satellites—play the pivotal role in a new "netcentric" way of ground, air, and sea warfare. Without them, America's Boyd-style way of war would not be possible.[6]

About two months before the March 2003 Anglo-American invasion of Iraq, the Pentagon began leaking to the press that Iraq would face an unprecedented "shock and awe" campaign if Saddam Hussein did not see the light. A few days later, think-tank expert Harlan K. Ullman, the man most closely identified with the development of the post-Boyd shock-and-awe concept, said in an interview with the *Christian Science Monitor* that the war would likely begin with "simultaneous attacks of hundreds of warheads, maybe thousands, so that very suddenly the Iraqi senior leadership, or much of it, will be eviscerated." The aim would be to "make the situation look virtually hopeless for Saddam Hussein and the leadership."[7]

The origins of the phrase can be found in *Shock & Awe: Achieving Rapid Dominance*, a slim study-group volume published in October 1996 by the

Directorate of Advanced Concepts, Technologies, and Information Strategies at National Defense University.[8] Ullman, a major player at the Center for Strategic & International Studies in Washington, was the principal author. The main objective of rapid dominance, the study said, was to impose an

> ...overwhelming level of Shock and Awe against an adversary on an immediate or sufficiently timely basis to paralyze its will to carry on.
>
> In crude terms, Rapid Dominance would seize control of the environment and paralyze or so overload an adversary's perceptions and understanding of events that the enemy would be incapable of resistance at tactical and strategic levels. An adversary would be rendered totally impotent and vulnerable to our actions....
>
> Theoretically, the magnitude of Shock and Awe Rapid Dominance seeks to impose (in extreme cases) the non-nuclear equivalent of the impact that the atomic weapons dropped on Hiroshima and Nagasaki had on the Japanese. The Japanese were prepared for suicidal resistance until both nuclear bombs were used. The impact of those weapons was sufficient to transform both the mindset of the average Japanese citizen and the outlook of the leadership through this condition of Shock and Awe. The Japanese simply could not comprehend the destructive power carried by a single airplane. This incomprehension produced a state of awe.[9]

The study—in many ways, an elaboration of Boyd's concepts—was well received at high levels in the American military in the late 1990s. It also found favor with a quartet of unusually influential civilians: Harold Brown, Frank C. Carlucci, James R. Schlesinger, and Donald Rumsfeld, all former secretaries of defense. In October 1999, the men, hardliners all, sent a letter to Secretary of Defense William S. Cohen, who had acquired a reputation, perhaps unfairly, for being a bit of a softy. "We are writing to you," they said, "in support and endorsement of the concept of rapid dominance."[10]

Rumsfeld remained enamored of the rapid dominance concept. In *Plan of Attack*, reporter Bob Woodward wrote of the moment when Rumsfeld, by then secretary of defense, introduced President George W. Bush to the shock-and-awe concept during preparations for the invasion of Iraq: "The president chuckled a little bit. 'Shock and awe,' he noted, was a catchy notion. Was it a gimmick? he wondered."[11]

It was no gimmick. Despite the inflammatory Hiroshima-and-Nagasaki rhetoric, *Shock & Awe* focused on precision attacks against military and militarily important targets rather than civilian-oriented targets. The pace, the precision, and the overwhelming number of attacks were to create panic and confusion, not massive, indiscriminate destruction. America's space assets make shock and awe possible.

THE TIN EAR SYNDROME

Shock and awe as well as the rhetoric of the space-warrior community is embedded in a wider context summed up in the Defense Department's phrase "full spectrum dominance," a fast-break style of warfare first widely advertised by the Joint Chiefs of Staff in *Joint Vision 2010*, issued in 1996. "The label *full spectrum dominance*," says a follow-up document, *Joint Vision 2020*, published in June 2000, "implies that U.S. forces are able to conduct prompt, sustained, and synchronized operations with combinations of forces tailored to specific situations and with access to and freedom to operate in all domains—land, sea, air, *space*, and information. Additionally, given the global nature of our interests and obligations, the United States must maintain its overseas presence and the ability to rapidly project power worldwide in order to achieve full spectrum dominance."[12] (Italics added.)

The *National Security Strategy of the United States of America*, issued by the Bush White House in September 2002 (and reaffirmed and refined in 2006) endorsed full spectrum dominance. It declared that the United States must remain so militarily powerful that no nation would ever again challenge it.[13]

There may not be much wrong with that—if U.S. military dominance could always be moderated by presidential caution, realism, a commitment to a high degree of multilateralism, and a reasonable degree of humility in the conduct of foreign policy. The world does not need another Cold War–style arms race in which global civilization might be destroyed in a matter of hours if matters get seriously out of hand. The knowledge in world capitals that the United States has—and will retain—a capacity for full spectrum dominance in any conventional conflict may indeed short-circuit any such arms race, just as the *National Security Strategy* suggests. But the words themselves, "full spectrum dominance," are a near-perfect example of the tin ear syndrome that infects bureaucracies everywhere. What were they thinking when they came up with such a menacing phrase?

The uniformed military interprets full spectrum dominance in relatively narrow battlefield terms: If U.S. military forces are called upon to fight, they must be so well prepared with doctrine, training, and hardware that they can prevail quickly and efficiently. That's reasonable. Short, decisive wars are generally better than long wars. There's less time to spill blood and treasure. But a lot of people around the world, particularly those who already mistrust America for a variety of reasons, are inclined to interpret full spectrum dominance differently. Their reasoning is straightforward. The United States is the richest and most powerful nation in the history of the world and, in its foreign policy, possibly the most arrogant.

That the United States suffers from arrogance is not jaw-dropping news. Every rich and powerful state in recorded history has suffered from arrogance. *Thrived* on it. Think ancient Mesopotamia, Egypt, Persia, Periclean Athens, Imperial Rome. Or consider Britain, on whose empire the "sun never set"; or Nazi Germany, which in living memory sought to conquer all of Europe; or France, which believed that its beloved army and its impregnable Maginot Line were sufficient to tame Hitler's ambitions; or the Soviet Union, which was persuaded that it represented the endpoint of human history. If America is arrogant, as it assuredly is, it is breaking no new ground.

And yet, many of today's critics combine the adjectives "rich," "powerful," and "arrogant" with the uniquely American phrase "full spectrum dominance" and conclude that the United States is an imperial power determined to run the world.

CONTROLLING THE "GREAT COMMONS"

If the Defense Department had a slogan, it would be, "You ain't seen nothin' yet." One of the key operational concepts of the technology-driven revolution in military affairs is the development of "network-centric warfare" in which all military units, from individual soldiers ("land warriors," the Defense Department sometimes calls them) to field commanders to Pentagon chieftains would have instant access to all militarily significant information, allowing officers and enlisted troops at every level to adapt to changing battlefield conditions with fast-break speed.

We saw a bit of that during the first shock-and-awe weeks of Gulf War II in March 2003, in which Iraq's conventional forces were hopelessly outmaneuvered and paralyzed. Space assets played a principal role. Nonetheless, say the folks at the Pentagon, U.S. forces are still in the early stages of refining the techniques of space-dependent, information-rich war, in which a precision attack by a small unit can replace massed attacks by larger units.

The Holy Grail is something planners call the "global information grid," or GIG. At the center of the grid would be a constellation of "transformational" communications satellites—which do not yet exist—that would tie into a host of ultra high-tech subsystems, most of which also do not exist. In theory, land, sea, and air forces would be linked together by a "global space internet" that would enable small combat units and even individual soldiers to download all the information they need to win whatever skirmish or battle they might be involved in.

On a moonless night, for instance, a two-man ground patrol would be able to "see" everything around them—not with night-vision goggles, but with "heads-up" digital images displayed on shields attached to their helmets. The images would be generated by unmanned aerial vehicles loitering overhead as well as by new-generation observation satellites, including space-based radar that could penetrate darkness and clouds and smoke.

If the "warfighters" should "see" a couple of enemy tanks on their displays, they could destroy them without firing a shot or exposing themselves to enemy fire. They would simply call in artillery shells from guns stationed miles away. Only two rounds would be needed, one for each tank, because each round would be "smart"—that is, it would be guided directly to its target by Global Positioning System satellites.[14]

Fantasy? Who knows? Many of the keenest proponents of military transformation—and that includes a lot of space warriors—tend to be True Believers in the digital battlefield. For them, the global information grid is just around the corner. But in the real world of contending priorities and cost overruns, the development of space-dependent "future soldier" systems, including the grid, is proving far more difficult and more costly than expected. Will transformational communications satellites and the global information grid ever become realities? Possibly, barring a long-term downturn in the U.S. economy. American ingenuity in all things military is extraordinary.

The Bush administration assigned a high priority to military transformation with a heavy emphasis on new space hardware, and even a Democratic administration would likely retain that high priority, albeit with different emphases. Neither party wants to be soft on defense, and enhanced space capabilities are at the heart of the transformation effort. In Senate testimony in March 2004, Arthur K. Cebrowski, then director of the Defense Department's Force Transformation Office, spoke glowingly of America's space superiority, and then continued:

> From all indications our space forces are providing us with an asymmetric advantage that no adversary currently enjoys. Although that is clearly true, evidence suggests that our space supremacy is not guaranteed. An adversary might turn our asymmetric advantage into an asymmetric vulnerability if we cannot maintain space supremacy...
>
> Alfred Thayer Mahan, a prominent naval historian and strategist, described the oceans as a Great Common. Today, space and cyberspace must be added to the list of commons that must be controlled. One of the recognized barriers to becoming a hegemonic power is the ability to operate and control the commons. Therefore, we can expect nations with hegemonic aspirations to try to erode our ability to operate effectively in the commons and to achieve the ability to control the commons for their own use.[15]

In other words, the United States must become a hegemonic power in space because other nations, which have their own "hegemonic aspirations," will try to prevent it from doing so. Call it "magical circularity."

Even if the United States remains far ahead of everyone else in its military-space capabilities, Cebrowski argued, it must not succumb to complacency. As the "sole superpower," it must *compete with itself to avoid stagnation.* That last bit is worth pondering. Is it sound advice for a nation to "compete with itself" in building military capabilities? It might seem rational to some; to others, it suggests a straight-arrow highway to national bankruptcy.

Cebrowski's allusion to Alfred Thayer Mahan in his testimony was intriguing. Mahan was more than just a "prominent naval historian and strategist." In the 1890s, he was widely recognized as the Western world's premier naval strategist and one of the nation's most influential imperialists—a mentor to Theodore Roosevelt. In his most important work, *The Influence of Sea Power Upon History 1660–1783*, Mahan wrote: "It is not the taking of individual ships or convoys, be they few or many, that strikes down the money power of a nation; it is the possession of that overbearing power on the sea which drives the enemy's flag from it, or allows it to appear only as a fugitive; and which, by controlling the great common, closes the highways by which commerce moves to and from the enemy's shores."[16]

At the turn of the twentieth century, Mahan saw command of the seas as the key to achieving global power. A century later, space warriors universally assert that control of space is the door to global military dominance during a time of conflict. Mahan, a man of the nineteenth century, is studied by today's space warriors.

AN "UNDISCOVER'D COUNTRY"

Despite all this heavy-duty space-warrior rhetoric, there is not yet a consensus regarding space in national security circles. The pros and cons of space control and weapons in space are debated regularly within the higher ranks of the Air Force, in the Pentagon, and at national security–oriented think tanks. Arguments over control of space range from leave-well-enough-alone conservatism to unapologetic let's-take-over-space-*now* radicalism. *Twilight War* focuses on the let's-do-it-now end of the spectrum because the notion of space control has gained substantial momentum since the end of the Cold War.

Space warriors say that land, sea, and air have long seen conflict. By analogy, they predict that conflict in space is inevitable. Given that, the United States must prepare for it now by developing the means to take control of space when that day comes. It must be the firstest with the mostest. If it isn't, Americans may someday face—in the words of Donald Rumsfeld's Space Commission—a "space Pearl Harbor."

That is a deceptive analogy. Allusions to Pearl Harbor—an event regularly cited by space warriors—trigger potent images for Americans, visions of a sleepy Sunday morning turned into a nightmare of roaring aircraft and staccato gunfire, of exploding bombs and torpedoes, of roiling smoke and foundering ships, of mass death in a fire-flooded bay. It also brings to mind a nation that was woefully unprepared for global war despite desperate attempts by the Roosevelt administration to get the country into some sort of fighting trim. But the Pearl Harbor analogy is little more than a dramatic device.

The December 7, 1941 attack was a swaggering wager by an arrogant and highly militarized government. Japan assumed that the United States, once its Pacific fleet was crippled, would work out a negotiated settlement that would fall far short of all-out war with a powerful seafaring nation five thousand miles distant. The United States had no close Asian ties, Tokyo noted. Why *should* America fight? Why should American men die to shield Asians from Japanese control when for two years Americans had refused to fight for their British cousins, their blood and cultural kin?

Japanese leaders were desperately ignorant of American history and the American character and they lost their bet, thus bringing destruction upon their homeland. Would any national leader make that kind of irrational bet today? Or tomorrow? The United States was militarily weak in 1941, although its potential power was enormous. Today, the United States is universally acknowledged as the world's hyperpower. It has no "peer competitor," a fact the Defense Department acknowledges. The United States has the means and the will to fight effectively with new generations of conventional weapons as well as a vast assortment of nuclear weapons, should it come to that.

What twenty-first-century leader would risk his nation's survival on a spin of the old, creaky, surprise-attack wheel of fortune? Any nation wishing to launch a Pearl Harbor–style attack on U.S. space assets would first have to conduct tests—many tests—in space. U.S. observation satellites and ground stations would detect these tests. Would anyone really believe that the United States would fail to respond decisively to such a provocation?

The United States does not lack for enemies. But tigers do not attack healthy bull elephants. It is difficult to imagine that any nation would *directly* challenge the United States in space. Could a nation secretly mount a program capable of taking out a few U.S. satellites? Possibly. Could a nation secretly develop the capability to eliminate enough U.S. satellites to radically tip the balance of power in a surprise attack? Not likely. The question proposes a suicidal scenario as unreal as anything the old bolt-from-the-blue crowd dreamed up during the Cold War.

"Purposeful interference with U.S. space systems," says a Department of Defense Directive issued in 1999, "will be viewed as an infringement on our sovereign rights. The U.S. may take all appropriate self-defense measures, including, if directed by the National Command Authorities, the use of force, to respond to such an infringement on our rights."[17]

The meaning of "appropriate self-defense measures" is ambiguous. But again, what national leader would bet his life and the life of his state against a nation with an annual defense budget of $500 billion a year, thousands of nuclear weapons, and conventional weapons of such precision they can reliably strike targets as small as a house from twenty thousand feet?

America's space warriors see things differently. To them, the superiority of the U.S. military during these post–Cold War years offers an opportunity of another kind. The United States must use these years of "strategic pause" to preemptively develop a comprehensive and demonstrated capability to control space—and to get on with the deployment of weapons in space.

Official rhetoric regarding space control and weapons in space is often stilted, guarded, and bureaucratic, but the meaning is plain. Consider this observation offered in October 2002 by Lance Lord, who then headed Air Force Space Command:

> Our [Air Force Space Command] strategy will enable us to trans-
> form space power to provide our Nation with diverse options to glob-
> ally apply force in, from, and through space with modern ICBMs,
> offensive counter space, and new conventional prompt global strike
> capabilities.... As Guardians of the High Frontier, Air Force Space
> Command has the vision and the people to ensure the United States
> achieves Space Superiority today and in the future.[18]

The words of General Lord and even those of the Space Commission report pale when compared to the dreams of some of the most ardent space warriors, men such as Everett C. Dolman, mentioned in the previous chapter. Dolman argues in *Astropolitik: Classical Geopolitics in the Space Age* that the United States should "endeavor at once to seize military control of low-Earth orbit." Only America, he says, can be trusted to regulate space for the benefit of all:

> If any one state should dominate space, it ought to be one with
> a constitutive political principle that government should be respon-
> sible and responsive to its people, tolerant and accepting of their
> views, and willing to extend legal and political equality to all. In
> other words, the United States should seize control of outer space
> and become the shepherd (or perhaps watchdog) for all who would
> venture there, for if any one state must do so, it is the most likely to
> establish a *benign* hegemony.[19] (Italics added.)

Dolman is no right-wing zealot. His arguments are sophisticated and coherent. He is receptive to contrary ideas, not contemptuous of them. He believes that American control of space, once the people of the world became accustomed to it, would bring enormous benefits to humankind.

Professor Dolman has a following but he does not run the show. He is an academic theorist, not a policymaker. Over the past forty-plus years, national security space issues have been handled with a good deal of common sense and wisdom. The sky is not yet falling. The United States has long used space for military purposes, including the deployment of satellites that permit U.S. land, sea, and air forces to fight more efficiently. Space is not a pristine sanctuary but neither is it weaponized. The largely internecine debate over whether the United States should attempt to achieve military dominance of space continues.

Nonetheless, since the end of the Cold War, the United States has been lurching, albeit uncertainly, in the direction of space control and perhaps the weaponization of space—full spectrum dominance applied to space. If the trend continues, America would enter an "undiscover'd country" more profoundly treacherous than anything Hamlet ever dreamt of.

VELVET GLOVE, STEEL FIST

America's space warriors argue that a unilateral decision to deploy a comprehensive space-control system and to place weapons in space involves nothing more sinister than building a navy to control the seas or an air service to command the air. But that analogy is off the mark. U.S. air and sea power, while overwhelming, cannot be deployed everywhere all of the time, even during war. In contrast, space weapons, *if* they are developed and deployed, would be an always thing. Swords of Damocles orbiting overhead seven days a week, twenty-four hours a day, in times of peace and war.

Even "responsive launch weapons"—"pop-ups," as space warriors ingenuously call them, designed to be deployed in orbit only in times of high tension or actual conflict—would be seen by others as an ever-present threat. On a city street, a man with a gun is usually regarded as potentially dangerous, whether the weapon is in his hand or tucked into his jacket pocket. Similarly, any nation that has tested and deployed a capability to insert weapons into space, even temporarily or only "when needed," would be scary to nations lacking that capability.

Not so, say space warriors. U.S. space-power plans should not alarm anyone because U.S. intentions are "non-aggressive." The assumption that other nations would be comfortable with that formulation is bizarre. What major state would be willing to subject its national fortunes to changing U.S. whims and geopolitical aims?

In assessing the threat posed by existing or potential rivals, national leaders throughout the world are more interested in capabilities, demonstrated or presumed, than in intentions. Capabilities are thought to be roughly measurable. In contrast, divining the intentions of another nation's leaders is a speculative art that often can be futile. Intentions can change as quickly as governments; capabilities have a modest degree of permanence.

In the world in which we live, saints seldom wind up as presidents or prime ministers and certainly not as dictators. "The sad fact is that international politics has always been a ruthless and dangerous business," says political-science realist John J. Mearsheimer, "and it is likely to remain that way. Although the intensity of their competition waxes and wanes, great powers fear each other and always compete with each other for power."[20] That, says Mearsheimer, is the "tragedy of great power politics."

Like most nations, the United States has always attempted to assess the intentions of other nations while focusing keenly on their actual capabilities. In the last century, Franklin D. Roosevelt tracked Japanese military expansion in the western Pacific in the 1930s as well as the rearmament of Germany. Both nations were building industrial and military capabilities that could eventually imperil the United States.

In response to that presumed threat, Roosevelt acted as forcefully as he could in a domestic climate of non-involvement to prepare the country for war. The research program that would lead to the creation of the atomic bomb was well under way, with FDR's blessing, *before* Pearl Harbor. (At a key meeting on Saturday, December 6, 1941 at the Cosmos Club in Washington, Arthur Holly Compton of the University of Chicago argued that plutonium would be a "worthy competitor" to highly enriched uranium to form the bomb's explosive core.)[21]

After the war, the Truman administration devised the Marshall Plan, in part because the administration feared the Soviet Union had, or might soon have, the military capability to take over a war-ravaged and demoralized Western Europe. An economically vigorous and future-oriented Western Europe would resist Soviet expansion.

Although President Eisenhower tried endlessly to divine the intentions of Soviet leaders, he put U-2 spy planes into the air and ordered that spy satellites be developed to gather hard evidence of actual Soviet bomber and missile capabilities.

A few years later, the United States almost went to war during the Cuban missile crisis, not because President Kennedy believed the Soviet Union would wantonly attack the United States with nuclear-tipped missiles based in Cuba, but because the Soviet Union was developing a capability in Cuba that could limit U.S. freedom of action in the brutal Cold War chess game.

Later still, the Carter-Reagan arms buildup in the 1980s was inspired by the fear among U.S. hardliners that the balance of power was shifting and the Soviet Union might develop superior missile capabilities that could tempt it to launch a "disarming first strike." Ronald Reagan resurrected the Russian proverb, "Trust, but verify" in his later pursuit of arms control. Soviet expressions of good intentions were welcome, Reagan said, but the United States needed technical means to assess actual Soviet capabilities.

Since the end of the Cold War, many American strategists have pointed to China as the next major threat, partly because China is developing more sophisticated long-range ballistic missiles. Fear of its future capabilities is an important driver in the current U.S. missile defense program. Ironically, China is modernizing its nuclear forces in part because it has believed since September 1967 that a "limited" U.S. missile defense system would be designed to negate China's minuscule and antiquated deterrent force— not an altogether unreasonable belief. In 1967, Defense Secretary Robert S. McNamara described a proposed limited missile-defense system as Chinese rather than Soviet oriented.[22]

For the last four decades of the twentieth century and into the twenty-first century, high-level space warriors have regularly asserted that the United States must preemptively develop the capability to control space because if it fails to do so, America will be doomed to a vulnerable second-class status.

All major powers value their own sovereignty and the freedom to act in defense of their vital national interests. They do not like to be at the mercy of another state, particularly a nation that, like the United States, has repeatedly demonstrated technological wizardry and amazing capabilities in warfighting. To U.S. space warriors, a demonstrated capability to dominate space seems sensible and necessary. But to other nations, such a capability may suggest a velvet-glove hegemony that could one day turn to steel-fisted imperialism.

Any nation with a comprehensive and demonstrated space-dominance capability would be able, by definition, to deny access to space to another nation *at any time*, not just during a time of conflict.

INVESTIGATOR, PROSECUTOR, JUDGE, JURY, AND EXECUTIONER

In August 2002, I spoke at an international arms control meeting in Italy. During the question-and-answer session, a British scholar suggested that he did not like some portions of my presentation; he thought I had defended the modern U.S. military rather too vigorously, especially in regard to my comments suggesting that America's new way of precision war—as demonstrated in the skies over Yugoslavia and, later, in Afghanistan—had certain positive values, such as sparing the lives of civilians. He accused U.S. forces of not fighting "fair." Americans, he said, fought with high-tech weapons, inflicting enormous casualties on the other side's forces while sustaining few casualties on their side. It just wasn't right.

I responded by saying that if a nation is called upon to fight, the idea is to get the thing over with quickly within the bounds of international law and the generally accepted rules of war, not to send one's own young men into a meat grinder in the interest of someone's sense of fairness. That was the meaning—and the virtue—of full spectrum dominance. The Brit didn't buy that.

And yet, my British colleague had a point. In later conversations, he made it clear he believed that a circular process was under way. America's high-tech military capabilities were not, in themselves, a bad thing. But the widening gap between the United States and all other nations in military capabilities was contributing to a growing arrogance among civilian policymakers regarding the conduct of foreign policy. In turn, increased arrogance at the highest policymaking levels reinforced the determination of decision-makers to use military force more often, more unilaterally, and more imperially. Even as we spoke, my British colleague asked, was not the United States planning to invade Iraq?

Shortly after that meeting, the new *National Security Strategy of the United States* was issued in September 2002 by the administration of George W. Bush. It was an extraordinary expression of American triumphalism. In his cover letter, President Bush asserted,

[T]he great struggles of the twentieth century between liberty and totalitarianism ended with a decisive victory for the forces of freedom—and a single sustainable model for national success: freedom, democracy, and free enterprise.

Today the United States enjoys a position of unparalleled military strength and great economic and political influence. In keeping with our heritage and principles, we do not use our strength to press for unilateral advantage. We seek instead to create a balance of power that favors human freedom: conditions in which all nations and all societies can choose for themselves the rewards of and challenges of economic liberty. In a world that is safe, people will be able to make their own lives better. We will defend the peace by fighting terrorists and tyrants. We will preserve the peace by building good relations among the great powers. We will extend the peace by encouraging free and open societies on every continent.[23]

Inspiring words, certainly—particularly for someone like me who cherishes individual liberty. But how, exactly, were we to go about creating "a balance of power that favors human freedom" without appointing ourselves the world's policeman? After all, the *National Security Strategy* endorsed global U.S. military dominance more or less to the end of time. Among other things, it outlined a doctrine of preemption. The United States would henceforth consider taking anticipatory military action against a presumably hostile state or terrorist organization "even if uncertainty remains as to the time and the place of the enemy's [potential] attack."

Or as President Bush's cover letter put it, "As a matter of common sense and self-defense, America will act against such emerging threats *before* they are fully formed. We cannot defend America and our friends by hoping for the best.... In the new world we have entered, the only path to peace and security is the path of action." (Italics added.) That strike-first language was breathtaking. In common with other great powers throughout history, the United States had always stood ready to engage in preemptive—even preventive—war if sufficiently provoked. Most famously, John F. Kennedy was prepared to bomb Soviet missile sites in Cuba before they became fully operational, if diplomatic efforts failed. That would have been an example of preventive, not preemptive war. Soviet missiles were being installed in Cuba to constrain U.S. behavior vis-à-vis the Soviets, not to attack the United States.

Nonetheless, until Bush's *National Security Strategy* was issued, the "inherent right" of either preemptive or preventive war had never before been spelled out in an official U.S. policy statement, much less in playground-bully language: "Watch it, or I'll hit you first!"

One could argue that this *National Security Strategy* was a breath of fresh air. If the United States was always ready, willing, and able to engage in preemptive or preventive war, why not say so? To ignore the issue in an official strategy document would be both timid and hypocritical. Candor is often the best policy, even in the cynical world of foreign policy.

And yet, at a time when many of the world's national leaders were already alarmed about America's military power and growing arrogance and what it might mean for the future, was it productive to tell everyone everywhere that the United States—alone among nations—reserved the right to preemptively attack any nation it merely perceived as a threat? Imagine Washington's reaction if Moscow or Beijing or even London had issued a document focused on its "right" to conduct preemptive strikes?

Defense Secretary Rumsfeld's early word games with the meaning of "preemption" did not inspire confidence. Shortly after the new strategy was unveiled, a reporter asked him why he had used "preemption" and "prevention" almost interchangeably during testimony on Capitol Hill. Rumsfeld acknowledged that there were differences between the two words and that he had been "a bit sloppy in using them somewhat interchangeably."

In international law and diplomacy, life and death issues are not defined so breezily. That is especially true if you head the defense ministry of the world's most powerful state.[24] At the time the *National Security Strategy* was published, the Defense Department's own *Dictionary of Military Terms* defined "preemptive" as an action "initiated on the basis of *incontrovertible evidence* that an enemy attack is imminent." In contrast, "preventive war" was "initiated in the *belief* that military conflict, while not imminent, is inevitable, and that to delay would involve greater risk."[25] (Italics added.)

The difference between incontrovertible evidence and belief is not trivial. In international law and practice there is a huge difference between preemptive and preventive war. The former is often justified, morally and legally. The latter is unworthy of a country that regards itself as a law-abiding nation, the prime mover behind the creation of the United Nations.

Preventive war based on mere belief is highly subjective, as we saw in the run-up to the American invasion of Iraq in 2003. Nation A believes, rightly or wrongly, that Nation B has hostile intentions; therefore it had better strike first. In doing so, Nation A acts as investigator, prosecutor, judge, jury, and executioner. And there are many potential Nation Bs out there.

Further, might such an assertive doctrine of preemption prove counter-productive? After the first Gulf War in 1991, Gen. Krishnaswamy Sundarji, former chief of staff of the Indian army, concluded that India needed a nuclear deterrent "to dissuade big powers from lightly pursuing policies of compellence vis-à-vis India. The Gulf War emphasized once again that nu-clear weapons are the ultimate coin of power....[T]he United States could go in because it had nuclear weapons and Iraq didn't."[26] India became a nuclear state in 1998.

Sundarji understood more clearly than most what the United States was up to after the end of the Cold War: it was developing an increased ca-pacity to coerce and compel non-nuclear states, if necessary, with its new generations of high-tech weapons. A February 2001 study for the Defense Threat Reduction Agency defined the coercion/compellence dynamic "as the threat of force or limited use of such force in pursuit of national security objectives. Thus, coercion includes both compellence (attempts to get other states to take actions desired by the asserting state) and deterrence (attempts to get other states to refrain from taking action opposed by the asserting state)."[27]

The intriguing issue is not that the United States is interested in coer-cion. It would be dangerous for the American people if the United States were not interested in getting its own way as often as reasonably possible, within the framework of international law. But the 2002 *National Security Strategy* publicly pushed the boundaries of the coercion/compellence en-velope by conflating the terms *preemptive* and *preventive*, no small matter in the early years of the twenty-first century, when the United States is the world's sole remaining superpower.

A BRIDGE TOO FAR?

More than a decade after the end of the Cold War, the world remains un-predictably dangerous. The United States must have well-trained and well-equipped military forces to help ensure its security. But at what point does overwhelming military superiority, combined with an official policy of preemption and prompt global strike, inspire fear and loathing? Political-science realists talk endlessly of the "security dilemma," a zero-sum business in which a state that becomes so extraordinarily powerful that its superior power, in itself, diminishes other states' sense of their own security, thus prompting a hostile response.

The desire to enjoy freedom of action in world affairs is not a uniquely American aspiration. Governments, whether democratic, authoritarian, totalitarian, monarchical, or theocratic, attempt to maximize their own freedom of action. In a conventional war, no state would stand a chance against the United States. As an American who loves his country, I am not unhappy with that. The United States is not Hitler's Germany nor Stalin's Russia. As great powers go, America is—just as triumphalists say—a relatively benign state. But is there a bridge too far? If so, would a unilateral policy of space dominance be it?

3

Nightmare Scenarios

Going to lay down
My sword and shield
Down by the riverside
Ain't going to study war no more.

It's a lovely sentiment, but one seldom practiced anywhere in the world. According to figures compiled by the Stockholm International Peace Research Institute, a reliable purveyor of military-related facts and figures since 1966, global military expenditures topped a trillion dollars in 2005. The United States spent roughly 48 percent of the total, with Britain (5 percent), France (5 percent), Japan (4 percent), and China (4 percent) rounding out the top five.[1]

Narrowly viewed, the systematic study of war has paid off for the United States. America's military forces can now fight conventional wars more efficiently and more "humanely" than ever before—and U.S. space assets are the key. In Pentagon-speak, they are a "force multiplier" or "enhancer." America's precision weapons almost always hit their targets, a rarity in the history of warfare. If the targets are military in nature, the ability to hit them precisely means fewer civilian casualties.

Consider NATO's intervention in the remaining Republic of Yugoslavia in 1999. A minor conflict by today's standards, it was nonetheless a preview of things to come. On March 24 of that year, NATO—a de facto extension of U.S. foreign policy—went to war with Slobodan Milosevic.

Milosevic was a terrorist in presidential garb, a man who ordered systematic ethnic cleansing throughout much of the 1990s as he sought to build a Greater Serbia on the bones of Tito's rapidly disintegrating state.[2] In the summer of 1998, in an attempt to drive Kosovar Albanians from their homes, Milosevic's army and police burned their houses and destroyed the crops of tens of thousands of ethnic Albanians who had long lived in the province of Kosovo. The United Nations estimated that some two hundred and thirty thousand Kosovar Albanians were "displaced" that summer. U.N. Security Council Resolution 1199, adopted on September 23, 1998, demanded that immediate steps be taken "to avert the impending humanitarian catastrophe." It was a toothless resolution. Russia and China were ready to veto any effective action by the United Nations.

NATO acted without U.N. endorsement. The justifications of NATO's "humanitarian intervention" are endlessly controversial. Was the intervention a just war? Or was it an abuse of a nation's sovereignty? In any event, the decision to go to war, even with a limited bombing campaign, was not easily made.

The leaders of NATO eventually approved air strikes as a way of forcing Milosevic back to the bargaining table. In opting for air attack, NATO had to weigh its goals against the certainty that at least some civilians, and perhaps many, would be killed by NATO bombs and missiles. In the end, the decision was made only because NATO's leaders were certain that the U.S. Air Force, which would organize the operation and fly the greatest number of missions, was capable of minimizing civilian casualties.

The calculus was straightforward. The citizens of NATO nations would likely tolerate the inevitable killing of Serbians in the course of a "humanitarian" war if they believed it would save a greater number of Kosovar Albanians. (Serbs were not well liked in much of NATO Europe, and Milosevic was then characterized as a minor-league Hitler.) But was there a tipping point? If too many Serbian civilians were killed, public sympathy in Europe would likely turn toward the Serbs and the operation would fall apart.

If U.S. precision weapons—terrain-hugging cruise missiles and laser-, television-, and radar-guided missiles—had not been available, there would have been no air campaign. It would have been clear from the get-go that NATO bombs would kill too many Serbs; the Kosovar Albanians would have been left to whatever fate awaited them.

NATO believed the campaign would be short—possibly as brief as three or four days. Milosevic would get the message and the bombing would stop. But Milosevic did not respond as hoped. The bombing dragged on for seventy-seven days before he fully capitulated. NATO gradually escalated the rate of attacks on military, industrial, transportation, and even a few "psychological" targets. Roughly twenty-three thousand bombs and missiles were used. Of that number, six hundred and fifty-one were JDAMs (Joint Direct Attack Munitions, or jay-dams), a weapon that came along just as the conflict began. Jay-dams were quasi-space weapons.[3]

In the late 1990s, the United States began turning tens of thousands of "dumb" bombs into "smart" bombs—"jay-dams"—with the addition of guidance kits manufactured by Boeing. The average cost of a kit was then about twenty thousand dollars. Once a kit was attached to a bomb—an operation that took about ten minutes under good conditions—the dumb bomb became something akin to an engine-less guided missile. A guided *gravity*-powered bomb, one could say.

Jay-dam kits added three movable fins as well as winglets—"strakes"—to the bombs, giving them both lift and a limited degree of maneuverability. But the kit's central elements were an inertial guidance system and a computer tuned to signals from a constellation of Global Positioning System (GPS) satellites orbiting some eleven thousand, nine hundred nautical miles above the surface of the Earth. Once the proper target coordinates were fed into the jay-dam's memory before release, the bomb would almost invariably glide to its target, generally hitting its "aimpoint" with an accuracy measured in a few yards.[4]

Critics of the war in the United States, Europe, and throughout much of the world, condemned NATO for going to war in the first place—and especially for ordering its aircraft to fly above fifteen thousand feet in the early weeks of the war. One reason for the high ceiling was to make it difficult for Milosevic's men to hit NATO aircraft with surface-to-air missiles. That, the critics said, demonstrated an outrageous moral lapse on NATO's part. It seemed to show that NATO was more interested in saving the lives of its air crews than in sparing the lives of Serbians living in and around the selected targets. And how could bombs accurately hit those targets, no matter how carefully chosen, from such heights?

A reasonable question. Precision is fundamental to the "lawful" prosecution of air war. If a bomb hits its target dead-on—and *if* the target has been properly chosen for its military value according to the widely accepted laws of war—the possibility of "collateral damage" is reduced. "Collateral damage" is a sanitized term for the incidental killing or maiming of ordinary men, women, and children unlucky enough to be near the target.

NATO's air campaign quickly demonstrated that the accuracy of jay-dams, even when delivered from high altitudes, was staggering. The jay-dam guidance computer receives signals from GPS satellites as it heads in, allowing it to refine its course as it glides. Counterintuitively, the ability to fine-tune their trajectories made jay-dams more accurate when released from higher altitudes than from lower altitudes.

After the bombing ceased, Human Rights Watch, a nongovernmental organization not known to champion the use of military force, conducted an exhaustive on-the-ground survey with particular emphasis on document-ing reports of civilian deaths from the bombing campaign.

"As few as 489 and as many as 528 Yugoslavs [civilians] were killed," the organization's report said. Human Rights Watch did not defend NATO. Although the designers of the air campaign went to great lengths to mini-mize civilian casualties, the report noted, the alliance could have done an even better job of protecting civilians.[5] But to military officers, government officials, and think-tank warriors everywhere, the number of civilian deaths was startlingly low. How could some twenty-three thousand bombs and missiles—only about thirty-five percent of which were true precision weap-ons—have produced, by historical standards at least, so few deaths?

Welcome to the "Revolution in Military Affairs."[6] The RMA describes a way of fighting in which—as seen in the "major combat phases" of the inva-sion of Afghanistan in 2002 and the invasion of Iraq in March 2003—the United States has a huge "asymmetric" edge in conventional combat.

...OR SOMEONE ELSE WILL

The military services are said to be loaded with officers forever fighting the last war. That is not quite true, at least in the United States. U.S. forces may have an abundance of men and women mired in parochial "stove-piped" thinking, especially when it comes to slicing up the Defense Department's budgetary pie. But it also has an ample number of officers who possess imagination, vision, and keen intelligence, and that includes Richard B. Myers, an Air Force general who served as chairman of the Joint Chiefs of Staff from the fall of 2001 to the summer of 2005.

Among Myers's way stations to the top was a concurrent stint as com-mander of U.S. Space Command, Air Force Space Command, and North American Aerospace Defense Command. While still in his three-hat post, Myers wrote an article for the January 1, 2000 issue of *Aviation Week & Space*

Technology in which he reflected on the historic importance of space assets to NATO's seventy-seven-day air campaign against Yugoslavia in 1999.

"Operations in Kosovo," he said, "gave us just a glimpse of what the future holds, and it's a future largely predicated on space." Although the United States demonstrated during the NATO campaign that it was the "world's space superpower," the people of the United States should not be deceived. "Space superiority is fleeting." The United States "enjoyed space dominance" against Serbia because "we controlled the high ground, not because of superior technologies or strategies, but because our adversaries simply didn't use space....

> We gained space superiority by default; the world took notice. Just as Milosevic modified his air defenses to try to deny our air superiority, others will modify their forces to try to deny our space superiority.
>
> Fortune may not be so kind in the twenty-first century. The worldwide proliferation of space-based capabilities will accelerate. Practically anyone with a credit card and an Internet account can buy global satcom [satellite communications] and one-meter [reconnaissance satellite] imagery. Precision navigation is free to everyone with a GPS receiver. Inevitably, these capabilities will be used for purposes hostile to the U.S. and its allies.
>
> The American military is built to dominate all phases and mediums of combat. We don't assume air, land, or sea superiority, but instead plan for, execute and seize the initiative.

"What we are witnessing today in space," Myers added, "is a modern-day version of the 1849 gold rush. Everyone is in a mad scramble, events occur at breakneck speed.... Space is a military and economic center of gravity. We can't afford to take it for granted. Only through a robust space control and modernization vision can we thwart military or terrorist attacks, and manage the space 'gold rush.'"[7]

Myers's article has been a Rorschach test for those who have encountered it. To some, it sounds like made-in-America common sense; to others, it is definitive proof of America's imperial design to dominate the globe from space. It is neither. But it is a clear expression of the space warrior's greatest nightmare: that enemies will somehow develop the means to negate America's many high-tech military advantages in space if America does not march smartly into the world of space control.

A couple of years later, Peter B. Teets, then undersecretary of the Air Force, director of the National Reconnaissance Office (the outfit that operates America's intelligence-gathering satellites), and the Defense Department's executive agent for space, amplified that idea while speaking at the Air Force Association's 2002 National Symposium. His topic was the control of space.

Today, Teets said, the U.S. military must use space for the "collection of all kinds of intelligence, precision navigation and...for weapons delivery, communication and transmission of information to users worldwide...."

> How long before an adversary, realizing the tremendous benefit that we gain from our space capabilities across the spectrum of warfighting, will seize an opportunity to deprive us of the use of them? How long will we continue to assume zero percent losses to our space systems during hostilities? The need to continue our thinking about space control is not just doctrinal rhetoric, but military reality.

The mission of space control, Teets added, "has not been at the forefront of military thinking because our people haven't yet been put at risk by an adversary using space capabilities." That would change:

> If we do not pursue control of space, then someone else will. If we do not exploit space to the fullest advantage across every conceivable mode of war fighting, then someone else will—and we allow this at our own peril. If we do not develop a new culture of space professionals—a new form of warfighter—then someone else may do so first....
>
> Our success at wielding airpower has come with a realization that we need to do it before—and better than—anybody else. Let us do the same for space.[8]

The undeniable need to protect U.S. assets in space—military, intelligence, and commercial—is the most powerfully persuasive argument space warriors have for a policy of space dominance. It is not a trivial argument. The United States has more than four hundred commercial, scientific, and military-related satellites in orbital space, ranging from a few hundred to thousands of miles high. That's slightly more than all the other spacefaring nations combined. (Communications satellites, from which live TV pictures come into your living room from all over the world, are true high flyers: they orbit at about 22,300 miles above the equator.)

VULNERABILITIES

"The ability to restrict or deny freedom of access to and operations in space is no longer limited to global military powers," said the Space Commission. "Knowledge of space systems and the means to counter them is increasingly available on the international market. Nations hostile to the U.S. possess or can acquire the means to disrupt or destroy U.S. space systems by attacking the satellites in space, their communications nodes on the ground and in space, or ground nodes that command the satellites."[9]

All space warriors repeat that thought; it is their core rationale. Future enemies of the United States will attempt to compromise America's new way of fast-break precision war by attacking U.S. space systems. The Space Commission offered a variety of methods bad actors might use to compromise U.S. space systems.[10] The first involves attacking ground stations—facilities that exercise command and control over satellites and receive data from satellites. In theory, ground stations could be attacked by bombs, missiles, and even World War II–style sabotage. This being the twenty-first century, computer hackers might be an even bigger threat—"computer network intrusion" it's called.

Until September 11, 2001, direct attacks on U.S. ground stations seemed unlikely; after 9/11, one cannot be so sure. And yet, achieving unilateral control of space or inserting weapons into space would not help the United States defend itself against such attacks. Old-fashioned hardnosed, well-armed, keep-'em-away security would be the best bet, including the "hardening" of facilities by expanding and toughening physical and electronic barriers.

As for computer intrusion, the situation is less straightforward. The Defense Department has long been aware of the damage hackers can do; DoD systems have been a favorite target of hackers. Perhaps the department ought to be thankful for that. By defending their systems from sophisticated amateurs, they learn how to better ward off true evildoers.[11]

How well is the protection effort working? Alan Paller, director of research at the SANS Institute, a nonprofit organization that monitors computer security, has misgivings. He warned in 2005 that American military forces are becoming too dependent on information technology. "The risk of losing the engagement because the systems were hacked grows explosively."[12] The possible impact of network intrusion in a future conflict is, to use a favorite Rumsfeldian phrase, is one of the greatest "unknown unknowns." Regardless, the threat of network intrusion cannot be met by either space-control systems or weapons in space.

The Space Commission report also lists "denial and deception" as a major concern. That's a no-brainer for a possible adversary. It simply means that the orbits of America's spy satellites are pretty well known; amateur satellite trackers routinely report their locations. Knowing when an American reconnaissance satellite will be overhead gives bad guys an edge in hiding what they are up to.

But only a very slight edge. Traditional camouflage does not work well these days, given the sophisticated "multispectral" sensors American spy satellites contain. "Multispectral" simply means that two or more images are taken simultaneously, each in a different part of the electromagnetic spectrum. Such techniques see through simple camouflage, though the skilful use of smoke or other "obscurants" can be effective at times.

Deceit is another matter. In earlier days, tricking the other side involved the art of allowing the enemy to see or hear things that were not quite true. Historians still study the many ruses used by the Allies in their successful effort to persuade Hitler that the D-Day landings in Normandy were a feint, and the real invasion would be at Pas de Calais. Decoys were a major part of that effort, including the huge invasion "army" Gen. George S. Patton had presumably assembled near Dover, complete with inflatable tanks, plywood artillery, empty trucks shuttling back and forth, and false radio messages.

In the Space Age, deceit is more likely to involve electronics than inflatable tanks. Unauthorized electronic entry into a computer system—"spoofing"— can plant false and thus misleading data into a command-and-control system, eroding the confidence of the users of the system. Space control and space weapons are not the answer to spoofing; the answer is to employ extraordinary multi-level precautions to ensure that only authentic messages get through.

Jamming is another space-warrior worry. Radio frequencies that link ground stations to satellites or satellites to ground stations ("uplinks" and "downlinks") could be jammed during a conflict. Although jamming is an old technology that was widely used by the belligerents in World War II, it is not a trivial concern. Space warriors spend considerable time and energy in devising ways to defeat jamming on the battlefield (while learning how to jam adversaries). One anti-jamming technique captures, amplifies, and relays the faint signals from Global Positioning System satellites by using un-manned air-breathing aerial vehicles as pseudo-satellites (or "pseudolites"). The enhanced signals are not easily jammed.

One team of analysts suggests that pseudolites flying at sixty thousand feet can provide "ten thousand times the received signal strength on Earth as a GPS satellite with equivalent transmission energy."[13] Another way to take care of jammers, employed in the March 2003 invasion of Iraq, is simply to use the radio frequency of the jammer to guide American missiles to it.[14]

On a global scale, jamming could be serious problem during a major conflict. America's military communications satellites are, by design, rela-tively jam-proof; in contrast, commercial communications satellites are not. During a major conflict, the U.S. military relies heavily on commercial satellites to provide much of the high-data-rate bandwidth it needs. "It is likely," says a reliable report on space weapons issues, "that a large fraction of the communications bandwidth the U.S. military relies upon will remain susceptible to jamming until at least 2015."[15]

Even that estimate may be optimistic. Building anything resembling a jam-resistant global information grid is proving more difficult and expensive than anticipated. The Transformational Satellite Communications System, or TSAT, slated to come on line by 2014 or later, will be the key component of the grid. In the words of a Government Accountability Office (GAO) report issued in 2006, the constellation of five extraordinarily capable satel-lites will "provide survivable, jam-resistant, global, secure, and general pur-pose radio frequency and laser cross-links with air and other space systems." Unhappily, the Department of Defense "is not meeting original cost, sched-ule, and performance goals established for the TSAT program."[16]

The GAO report, however, did not suggest that the program was yet another Defense Department boondoggle, of which there have been many over the decades. It simply said that some of the technologies required for the TSAT program were not yet "mature" and that the Defense Department had been too optimistic regarding both schedule and cost.[17] Whatever the fate of the TSAT program may be, the United States does not need to pur-sue control of space or to place weapons in space to defeat jamming.

Another major concern of the Space Commission was the possibility that other nations could use a variety of antisatellite weapons to directly degrade, disable, or destroy American satellites. "Direct-ascent" interceptors—the sort of thing the Chinese used in their January 2007 test—could kill American satellites in low-Earth orbit by hitting them at high speeds, transforming expensive U.S. satellites into space junk. Direct-ascent interceptors would not have to be terribly sophisticated.

In theory, a more advanced interceptor, far beyond the reach of most nations, could be inserted into a "parking" orbit. It would later maneuver into an orbit designed to bring it close to the target satellite, upon which it would then work its mischief, perhaps with a burst of electromagnetic radiation designed to fry the electronic innards of the target satellite. An even more sophisticated killer could be inserted into a "storage orbit" where it might remain for months or years before maneuvering for an attack. Such an interceptor might be one of several housed in a mother ship.

A variant of the storage-orbit satellite killer would be a "space mine," a nasty little device that would regularly intersect the target's orbit. Eventually the mine would be detonated during one of the close encounters. Yet another variant is the so-called co-orbital satellite, a stealthy killer that could maneuver into the orbit of the target satellite and travel with it until it receives a signal from the ground to attack, a bit like a lioness creeping up on an unsuspecting gazelle and then—*wham*! One less gazelle.

Yet another class of nightmarish devices trotted out by space warriors is a variation of the direct-ascent interceptor mentioned a few paragraphs back. But instead of hitting the target satellite, or exploding near it, the satellite killer would release a cloud of metal shot, sand, or debris into the target's path. At orbital speeds, collisions with intentional space garbage could gravely damage or destroy a satellite. Once again, space control or weapons in space would not offer protection from such an attack. Shields, or "Whipple Bumpers," that would orbit protectively in front of the satellite would offer some protection.[18]

Ground-based lasers also could cause problems for a spy satellite—either by temporarily "dazzling" its sensors (a condition from which it would presumably recover), or by permanently "blinding" them. The United States conducted a laser test against a worn-out American satellite in 1997, and China may have tested a low-power ground-based laser by "illuminating" at least one American satellite.[19] Control of space or weapons in space are helpless in the face of such attacks, but a defensive "shutter" system on a satellite is feasible. "Detection of the low-power aiming phase of the ground-based lasers would give time for closing a shutter to eliminate the exquisite vulnerability of the satellite's focal plane."[20]

There are other ways, some highly speculative, to damage or kill a U.S. satellite even before getting into far more technically difficult (if not science fiction) weapons like space-based lasers and microwave, particle-beam, and electromagnetic-pulse weapons. The problem, though—which is a lucky thing for the United States—is that developing ASAT weapons that could knock out a *significant* portion of U.S. satellites (the "space Pearl Harbor" scenario) is not easy. In fact, it would be so staggeringly difficult as to beggar the imagination.

A nation intent on launching a massive ASAT attack against the world's most advanced spacefaring nation could get only so far with laboratory work and covert Earth-based testing. At some point, testing would have to move into space, and at that point it would become visible to the United States.

As noted earlier, even the United States, according to the Space Commission, would have difficulty developing an advanced and reliable ASAT system. Although the United States needs such a system, the commission said, ASAT capabilities must be tested on a "regular basis, both to keep the armed forces proficient in their use and to bolster their deterrent effect on potential adversaries."

> Besides computer-based simulations and other wargaming techniques, these exercises should include "live-fire" events. These "live-fire" events will require the development of testing ranges in space and procedures for their use that protect the on-orbit assets of the U.S. and other space-faring nations. While exercises may give adversaries information they can use to challenge U.S. space capabilities, that risk must be balanced against the fact that capabilities that are untested, unknown or unproven cannot be expected to deter.[21]

There are a couple of things going on in this paragraph. One has to do with deterrence. If America wants to intimidate potential adversaries, it must demonstrate in space what it can do; it must show the world that it can "negate" the satellite systems of bad actors. Beyond that is a fundamental fact: Reliably degrading, disabling, or destroying satellites is not easy. Even the United States, the most technologically advanced state in the world, would need "live-fire events" against targets in space to perfect it.

THE TRUE NIGHTMARE

There is, however, one scenario offered by space warriors that is truly nightmarish. It assumes that a rogue state like North Korea or even a major state like China might someday feel so threatened by U.S. military prowess in space that it would choose an attack option called HAND—High Altitude Nuclear Detonation. "Perhaps the most devastating [antisatellite] threat," the Space Commission said, "could come from a low-yield nuclear device, on the order of fifty kilotons, detonated a few hundred kilometers above the atmosphere."[22] (A kiloton is equivalent to a thousand metric tons of TNT in explosive power.)

The assumption that nuclear weapons detonated in space might wreak havoc with U.S. space assets has been conventional wisdom since 1962, when "Starfish Prime," a U.S. nuclear test in space, disabled six satellites.[23] Since then, weapons experts have generally believed that nukes with even relatively small yields on the order of the Hiroshima and Nagasaki bombs could possibly degrade or disable satellites in low-Earth orbit—even those that have been "hardened" to some degree against radiation. According to the Defense Threat Reduction Agency, "A 10–15 kiloton nuclear weapon [roughly the yield of the Hiroshima bomb] detonated at 120–150 kilometers altitude would pump up the radiation levels in low Earth orbit space by three to four orders of magnitude. Satellites designed to survive for years at natural low-Earth-orbit radiation levels could degrade in this radiation environment in a matter of weeks."[24]

For some satellites, the end would come much sooner. The electronic hearts of satellites within line of sight of the detonation could be destroyed by direct exposure to "prompt radiation," especially X-rays. The good news, according to the Defense Threat Reduction Agency, is that the "geometry" of low-Earth orbit space is such that only five to ten percent of a given satellite constellation would be in a line-of-sight position at the time of detonation. Satellites not within line of sight would take much longer to fizzle out—perhaps weeks, perhaps months—as their innards "accumulate ionizing radiation damage in key electronic components from gamma rays, X-rays, neutrons, debris gamma interactions, and beta-decay electrons trapped in the Earth's magnetic field."[25]

How would the United States react to such an attack? How *could* it react? Nuclear detonations in space, if at night, would produce spectacular light shows—something like Northern Lights on steroids—but there would be no direct loss of life. "Direct loss of life," however, should be used cautiously. Depending on the altitude of the blast and other variables, the electromagnetic pulse from the detonation(s) would likely have some affect on terrestrial electrical and electronic systems. Worst-case scenarios were described in a 2004 report by a congressionally mandated task force: "Depending on the specific characteristics of the attacks, unprecedented cascading failures of our major infrastructures could result.... The primary avenues for catastrophic damage to the Nation are through our electric power infrastructure and thence into our telecommunications, energy, and other infrastructures."[26]

If the United States chose to retaliate, what would it hit? The offending nation, such as North Korea, might not have many, if any, assets in space, so retaliation in kind would be pointless. Would the United States strike back by hitting ground targets in the offending state? Perhaps. Or perhaps not. While nuclear detonations in space would not directly kill anyone, U.S. retaliatory strikes against ground targets, no matter how precise, would kill at least a few people, perhaps many. In diplo-speak, U.S. retaliation against ground facilities might well "shock the conscience of mankind."[27]

No rogue state currently has the ability to launch enough nuclear weapons into low-Earth orbit to sharply compromise U.S. military space capabilities. (Global Positioning System satellites, for instance, are in orbits too high to be reached by states such as North Korea.) But space warriors are looking a decade or two down the road. What will be the threat in 2018, in 2028? Who can say what sorts of nuclear and ballistic-missile capabilities unfriendly states might develop over the years?

Detonating a number of nuclear weapons in space could, in theory, wipe out a lot of America's low-Earth-orbit infrastructure—commercial, scientific, and military—over a period of weeks or months, as repeated exposure to jacked up radiation levels chewed away at the satellites' electronic guts. Although a "rogue state" might be able to someday detonate a bomb or bombs in low-Earth orbit, only powerful states such as Russia and China would have the capability to detonate weapons in higher orbits. Many of America's most important military-oriented satellites—especially Global Positioning and communications—are in higher orbits and thus out of range of a rogue-state attack. And because military satellites in higher orbits are exposed to more natural radiation than satellites in low orbits, they have more radiation hardening.

Detonating a nuclear weapon in space—and certainly detonating several—would be an extreme act. It would not go down well with the world's other spacefaring states, whose space assets might be degraded or disabled. Would a rogue state like North Korea consider committing an act guaranteed to bring it international opprobrium while inviting economic, political, and perhaps military retaliation?

The answer is a firm "maybe." If the leaders of a rogue state came to believe that the United States was intent on getting rid of them through military means—America's ever-popular call for "regime change"—they might figure they had nothing to lose by frying a bunch of satellites in low-Earth orbit. Having missiles advanced enough to loft nuclear weapons into the lower reaches of space might give North Korea enough leverage to make the United States think twice about preemptive military action. In U.S. military lingo, the United States could be "dissuaded" from doing that which it might otherwise do.[28]

Space warriors worry about nuclear detonations in space, as should we all. But neither U.S. control of space nor weapons in space can fix that vulnerability. The first fix, of course, is to work ever more closely with other like-minded states to enforce the international nuclear nonproliferation regime, which has worked pretty well over the decades. It is easy to forget that it was inspectors from the much-maligned International Atomic Energy Agency, or IAEA, a U.N.-affiliated outfit, who uncovered the fact that North Korea was violating the terms of the Nuclear Nonproliferation Treaty, to which it was a signatory.[29] And it was IAEA and U.N. inspectors in the early 1990s who revealed the extent of Saddam Hussein's covert bomb program after Gulf War I, despite Saddam's unrelenting efforts to hide it.[30]

Another fix to the vulnerability problem requires the further development of U.S. "surge" capabilities. ("Surge" is space-warrior talk for being able to launch replacement satellites into orbit quickly, should the need arise.) Developing a surge capacity has been a sensible space-warrior priority for many years; nonetheless, the United States has made little headway in actually doing it. Space expert Jim Oberg got it right when he wrote in 1999 that

> [the] most obvious limitation on space operations is cost. In recent decades, little progress has been made in reducing the transportation cost per pound of placing payloads into orbit....

Associated with the cost factor is the narrowness of the bottlenecks through which space operations pass. Not only launch facilities but also equally crucial ground control facilities exist in limited number, often with no redundancy. This creates both vulnerabilities to loss of function and severe upper limits on surge capacity for expansion or replacement of in-space assets.[31]

LESSONS OF THE PAST

With the exception of nuclear detonations in space, the ASAT "threat" may not amount to much. Hitting a satellite in low-Earth orbit, even with a "direct ascent" missile, is a tricky business that currently lies well beyond the capabilities of North Korea-type rogue states. Orbital or co-orbital ASATs require an even higher degree of sophistication; ditto for ground-based lasers. Although spreading a cloud of pellets in the path of a satellite is theoretically simpler, it is not nearly as easy as some space warriors suggest.

Meanwhile, America's space warriors, to their credit, are actively working on a host of defenses. Among them are shutters to protect the sensors of satellites from laser beams, increased maneuverability to get out of the way of incoming kill vehicles, additional radiation hardening against nuclear explosions, and "distributed" networks in which the work of a large and expensive satellite can be done by several smaller and cheaper and widely dispersed satellites. A lucky shot might damage or destroy one of the smaller satellites, but the others would pick up the load.[32]

Second-rank powers would encounter extraordinary difficulties in attempting to develop an antisatellite system comprehensive enough to seriously compromise America's military space capabilities. And their ASAT systems would still have to be thoroughly tested in space, where they would be easily detected. Finally, America's space warriors have a host of techniques available to "passively" protect key U.S. satellites.[33]

Is there a need for the United States to develop and deploy "offensive" counterspace capabilities? Space warriors say "yes." They see the future as uncomfortably threatening. Eventually, they say, another powerful state will challenge the United States for global preeminence, and the United States must be ready to meet that threat. Vegetius's maxim, "He who aspires to peace should prepare for war" is the guiding principle of space warriors.

There's some truth to that. It is not a bad idea to prepare for the worst *realistically* assessed threat. But in the military sphere, the meaning of "realistic" may have more to do with ideology than with real-world facts.

4

Joined at the Hip

Soon after the first Sputniks were launched, many Americans, civilian and military, began to believe that if the Soviet Union could place scientific satellites in orbit, it would soon be able to spy on the United States from space. More ominously, the Soviet Union might someday soon be able to insert nuclear bombs into orbit—bombs that could rain fire and radiation on American cities without warning.

The United States, said an Army briefing in November 1957, has an "urgent national requirement for a satellite defense system.... Sooner or later, in the interest of survival, the United States will have to be able to defend itself against satellite intrusion, otherwise it will be helpless before any aggressor equipped with armed reconnaissance satellites."[1]

The Eisenhower administration took pains, privately and publicly, to point out that an orbital bombardment system made no sense, either for the United States or for the Soviet Union. Orbital weapons would be vastly more expensive than conventional weapons. Further, they would be far less accurate, overwhelmingly provocative, and prone to catastrophic failure. If a weapon were ever called down on an American or Soviet city by accident, nuclear war would be the likely outcome. On March 26, 1958, the administration issued a detailed explication of Eisenhower's space policy.

"It is useful to distinguish among four factors which give importance, urgency, and inevitability to the advancement of space technology," the statement said. The first of these is the compelling urge of man to explore and to discover, the thrust of curiosity that leads men to try *to go where no one has gone before*."[2] (Italics added.) The latter phrase was boldly adapted by a TV enterprise called *Star Trek*.

The second reason for a space program was "the defense objective." "If space is to be used for military purposes, we must be prepared to use space to defend ourselves." That is, the president would abandon his peaceful-purposes policy if he obtained solid information that the Soviets were up to no good in space.

The third rationale for the space program was national prestige: "To be strong and bold in space technology will enhance the prestige of the United States among the peoples of the world and create added confidence in our scientific, technological, industrial, and military strength."

The fourth driver of the space program was that "space technology affords new opportunities for scientific observation and experiment which will add to our knowledge and understanding of the Earth, the solar system, and the universe."

The bulk of the statement was devoted to explaining basic scientific principles of space flight as well as the scientific objectives of the space program. The subheadings tell the story—"Why Satellites Stay Up"; "The Thrust Into Space"; "The Moon as a Goal"; "A Message from Mars"; "Will the Results Justify the Costs?"; "The View From a Satellite"; "A Close-Up of the Moon"; "On to Mars"; and "The Satellite Radio Network."

Then came the heading, "Military Applications of Space Technology." The section was short and blunt. It said the most important and foreseeable military uses for satellites were for reconnaissance, communication, and meteorology. In contrast, space weapons, such as orbital bombs, would be pointless.

> Much has been written about space as a future theater of war, raising such suggestions as satellite bombers, military bases on the Moon, and so on. For the most part, even the more sober proposals do not hold up well on close examination or appear to be achievable at an early date....
>
> Take one example, the satellite as a bomb carrier. A satellite cannot simply "drop" a bomb. An object released from a satellite doesn't fall. So there is no special advantage in being over the target. Indeed, the only way to "drop" a bomb directly down from a satellite is to carry out aboard the satellite a rocket launching of the magnitude required for an intercontinental missile. A better scheme is to give the weapon to be launched from a satellite a small push, after which

it will spiral in gradually. But that means launching it from a moving platform halfway around the world, with every disadvantage compared to a missile base on the ground. In short, the Earth would appear to be, after all, the best weapons carrier.[3]

The administration's explanation was intended to reassure the public that the president was pursuing a reasonable and budget-wise space program devoted to the peaceful search for scientific knowledge, which would then be shared with all humankind. Administration statements, and there were many, were also designed to suggest that Sputnik did not represent a military threat.

The public was not reassured, however, because highly placed military men continued to urge that the administration adopt a more aggressive stance toward Soviet advances in space. One of the most influential was Lt. Gen. James B. Gavin, chief of research and development for the U.S. Army, an intellectual and soon to be a member of Sen. John F. Kennedy's brain trust.

Gavin's public discontent was no small matter for the president. As commander of the 82nd Airborne in World War II, Gavin had returned to the United States as a hero, the "Jumping General," a leader who always had been among the first to leap into fight. Gavin was immensely popular. Upon retiring from the Army in 1958, he wrote *War and Peace in the Space Age*, published later that year. Gavin's book elegantly captured the mood of many high-ranking military men regarding the presumed folly of the president's space-for-peaceful-purposes policy.

If the United States did not achieve control of space first, Gavin said, the Soviet Union would. The purpose of U.S. land, sea, air—and now, space—dominance, he said, was to preserve global peace though deterrence and to prevail if conflict came. That required a proactive policy. To ensure peace, the United States must be prepared to police the world. "The [city] policeman on the beat must by virtue of his reputation and appearance maintain law and order. He must have power available to him that can be applied quickly.... In the world community similar power, although of a much greater degree, must be available."[4]

Policing the world included space. In the "very near future it will be possible to place a satellite in orbit that will be able to conduct detailed photography. Its accuracy should be such that it will be possible to distinguish separate aircraft on an airfield."[5] That accuracy, said Gavin, would enable the United States to determine the precise coordinates of Soviet targets; these coordinates would be needed if war came.

But turnabout was not fair play. The United States must be prepared to destroy Soviet spy satellites. "It is inconceivable to me that we would indefinitely tolerate Soviet reconnaissance of the United States without protest, for clearly such reconnaissance has an association with an ICBM [ballistic missile] program." There were "delicate legal problems" involved in smashing Soviet satellites, Gavin admitted. Nonetheless, it was "urgently necessary" that the United States "acquire at least a capability of denying Soviet overflight—that we develop a satellite interceptor."[6]

Gavin stirred the antisatellite pot with vigor, influencing editorial writers, pundits, and—through them—the public. Nonetheless, Eisenhower remained adamant in his opposition to antisatellite systems, believing that they were unnecessary, provocative, and counterproductive—and were inconsistent with his space-for-peaceful-purposes policy. If the United States destroyed Soviet spy satellites, went the argument, the Soviets would destroy U.S. satellites. In the end, America would be the clear loser; it needed to peer inside the tightly closed Soviet Union far more than the Soviet Union needed to look into the already open United States.

EARLY ASATS

On April 12, 1961, Cosmonaut Yuri A. Gagarin circled the Earth in an hour and forty-eight minutes and landed safely. He was the first human to orbit Earth. Four months later, Cosmonaut Gherman Titov completed seventeen and a half orbits in twenty-five hours and eighteen minutes, and returned safely. Once again, the American public, as well as its top military men, were alarmed. A nation with such advanced space technologies could surely place nuclear weapons in orbit.

Nor did Nikita Khrushchev's truculence calm anyone's nerves. During an August 1961 Kremlin reception for Titov, Khrushchev famously said: "If you want to threaten us from a position of strength, we will show you strength. You do not have fifty- and one-hundred-megaton bombs. We have bombs stronger than one hundred megatons. [A megaton is equal in explosive power to a million metric tons of TNT.] We placed Gagarin and Titov in space, and we can replace them with bombs which can be diverted to any place on Earth."[7] Khrushchev's remark came at the height of the Berlin crisis, a Cold War turning point when nuclear war seemed possible, perhaps imminent.

In an orbital bombardment system, the sort of thing Khrushchev hinted at, nuclear weapons would be housed in satellites that could be called down on targets essentially without warning, even when compared to ICBMs, in which the best-case warning would have been fifteen or twenty minutes. However, an orbital system was so technically difficult and so dangerously provocative that the Soviet Union was probably never keen on it, despite the bluster. Indeed, the Soviet Union agreed to a ban on nuclear weapons in space when it signed the Outer Space Treaty of 1967.

The other heavy-duty Soviet threat in the 1960s was the so-called *Fractional* Orbit Bombardment System, or FOBS, which the Soviet Union seemed to favor, at least to the extent of conducting a dozen or so non-nuclear tests. With FOBS, a bomb carrier could be launched and the bomb released toward its target *before* a full orbit had been achieved. In that respect, FOBS would be akin to an intercontinental ballistic missile; but instead of an attack coming from the north, where radar picket lines would have given some kind of warning, the attack might come from the south, where warning systems were hopelessly inadequate. That was frightening to Air Force officers charged with defending the American mainland.[8]

In 1962, President John F. Kennedy and Defense Secretary Robert S. McNamara ordered that the Army's primitive (and probably useless) Nike Zeus antiballistic missile system be adapted as an ASAT weapon. They believed it would be possible to direct a Nike Zeus missile toward an offending satellite and detonate a nuclear warhead near it. The program was canceled when even its supporters realized that its range was so limited that it had little chance of intercepting an orbiting satellite.[9]

But the administration approved a competing Air Force ASAT effort, Program 437. The Air Force system centered on two liquid-fueled Thor intermediate-range ballistic missiles based on Johnston Island, about eight hundred miles southwest of Honolulu. Thor wasn't much to brag about. It had such a slow reaction time—six to twelve hours—that it was unlikely to be effective. And it wouldn't take much to overwhelm a two-interceptor system. Launching three or more FOBS would do the job.

Because the missiles were deployed on open pads near the sea, they were subject to the corrosive forces of storms, sea spray, heat, and humidity. (Johnston was a flyspeck—three thousand by six hundred feet—and everything on it was near the sea.) Like Zeus, the Thor system would zap target satellites with intense radiation and an electromagnetic pulse from a nuclear detonation. Unfortunately, the EMP would also damage the electronic components of friendly satellites. Beyond that, the system had another and potentially more serious problem: "The use of an atomic weapon to kill an enemy satellite might inadvertently signal the start of a nuclear war. The U.S. might launch such an attack suspecting that the Soviets were launching a surprise strategic attack from space. The U.S.S.R. in turn might react by launching an all-out nuclear offensive thinking the United States was preparing for a nuclear first strike."[10]

Given that spectacular downside, the existence of Program 437 was more of a we-are-all-skating-on-thin-ice political message than a workable antisatellite weapon. It told the Soviets that if they launched a space weapon, the United States would try to destroy it, and that might well lead to a nuclear-fire-and-brimstone holocaust that no one really wanted. The Thor system, never credible, was allowed to fade into obscurity in the late 1960s and early 1970s.

While the United States focused on killing Soviet satellites with nukes, the Soviet Union developed its own antisatellite weapon, a co-orbital killer that could theoretically maneuver within striking distance of a U.S. satellite and explode. The explosive would be conventional, not nuclear; shrapnel would presumably kill the American bird. Or the Soviet satellite might simply shoot it with shotgun-like pellets.

The Soviet system was tested on an off-and-on basis from 1963 to 1972, the year when the U.S.-Soviet Antiballistic Missile Treaty was signed.[11] That treaty eased East-West tensions for a bit, but the Soviets resumed their ASAT tests in 1976, perhaps in reaction to America's Space Shuttle program, which was moving along nicely after receiving President Richard M. Nixon's blessing in January 1972. ("It will revolutionize transportation into near space by routinizing it," the president said of the Shuttle. "It will take the astronomical costs out of astronautics.")[12]

The Shuttle program—which was designed to launch twenty-four missions a year—worried Soviet leaders. Moscow believed that if shuttle launches became as routine as the president promised, the American orbiter could scoop up Soviet satellites in low-Earth orbit as easily as it deployed American satellites.[13]

The U.S. national security community was divided over how best to respond to the renewed Soviet drive to perfect its co-orbital ASAT. Hardliners said the United States must launch a truly workable ASAT program of its own to counter the Soviet threat. (Few believed that the Johnston Island system was worth resurrecting.) In contrast, men and women who favored arms control pacts advocated a treaty that would ban ASATs. In his fiscal year 1978 report to Congress, Donald Rumsfeld, President Gerald Ford's secretary of defense, said: "Space has thus far been a relative sanctuary, but it will not remain so indefinitely. The Soviets could use their antisatellite capability during a crisis or conflict to deny us the use of a vital element in our total military system."

Therefore, he added, the Ford administration would "increase significantly the U.S. space defense effort over a broad range of space-related activities which include space surveillance, satellite systems survivability, and the related space operations control function."[14] The last bit meant that the United States would develop an ASAT system featuring a missile that would be launched from a high-flying fighter plane. The missile would be tipped with a separate kinetic-kill vehicle that would break free from the missile booster and home in on the target satellite. The KV, as it was commonly called, would hit the target with enough force to pulverize it, or at least to disable it. (The kinetic-kill idea had been percolating in Air Force circles since the early 1970s.)

Two decades after President Eisenhower had declared that space should be a sanctuary free of weapons and conflict, the Soviet Union and the United States seemed to be turning that policy on its head. The Ford administration, however, did not return to office, and Jimmy Carter, whose view of Soviet intentions was marginally more sanguine, took over the White House.

Carter favored the Eisenhower give-diplomacy-a-chance view of antisatellite weaponry. He would conduct arms control negotiations while developing a backup plan—research and development of the kinetic-kill ASAT system. In a report to Congress, Secretary of Defense Harold Brown said this of the administration's two-track policy:

> As the president has clearly stated, it would be preferable for both sides to join in on an effective, and adequately verifiable ban on antisatellite systems; we certainly have no desire to engage in a space

weapons race. However, the Soviets with their present capability are leaving us with little choice. Because of our growing dependence on space systems we can hardly permit them to have a dominant position in the ASAT realm. We hope that negotiations on ASAT limitations lead to a strong symmetric control. But in the meantime we must proceed with ASAT programs.[15]

Hardliners were generally pleased that ASATs were being developed. Meanwhile, arms controllers were reassured by the fact that the administration was pursuing a diplomatic solution. The unexpected Soviet entry into Afghanistan—a de facto invasion—changed everything. Newly sharpened East-West tensions buried ASAT negotiations.[16]

With the election of Ronald Reagan, Carter's two-track policy was abandoned. The United States would no longer attempt to negotiate an ASAT treaty. A new presidential direction had been established: U.S. space security would not be ensured by treaty, but by developing and building ASATs.[17]

Early in Reagan's tenure, the fighter-plane-launched ASAT idea came to be called the Miniature Homing Vehicle. The MHV needed no explosives to do its job; an F-15 fighter climbing at a steep angle at a high altitude would simply fire a rocket carrying the homing vehicle. As its name implied, the MHV would pick up the satellite with its sensors and lock in a collision course. In one test of the system, a thirty-five-pound homing vehicle launched from an F-15 destroyed Solwind, an aging one-ton American satellite on September 13, 1985. The kinetic energy released at impact was equal to about five tons of TNT.[18] (The Chinese test in January 2007 was similar, although a mobile medium-range ballistic missile instead of an airplane boosted the kinetic-kill vehicle into space.)

The Defense Department hoped to build more than a hundred of these Kamikaze homing vehicles, but the program ran into technical problems and costs skyrocketed. Congress, alarmed by an apparent escalation of the Cold War into space, banned further tests in 1988, and the Air Force subsequently canceled the program.[19] By then the Reagan administration had a far grander space-related vision, the Strategic Defense Initiative, a.k.a. "Star Wars."

Star Wars once again proved the validity of an ancient truth: labels can be deceptive. On the surface, ballistic-missile *defense* systems and *offensive* antisatellite systems seem unrelated. They are not. Any system presumably capable of striking an incoming intercontinental ballistic missile in space can far more easily hit satellites, at least those in low-Earth orbit.

To fully understand the ardor today's space warriors have for full spectrum dominance in space—which encompasses antisatellite systems—we need to take a brief look at Reagan and the hair-trigger national security policies he inherited.

SUICIDE PACT

As the war in Europe ground down in 1945, few Americans did more in the futile attempt to preserve the U.S.-Soviet alliance than Gen. Dwight D. Eisenhower. He liked the Russians, especially Marshal Georgi Zhukov, his Soviet counterpart, and he did everything possible to preserve good relations with Moscow, even though many of his superiors in Washington had already defined the Soviet Union as the next threat. But as president, Eisenhower dedicated himself to saving the world from the "slavery" of communism.

No internal conflict was as great as Eisenhower's decision to rely chiefly on nuclear weapons to preserve the peace. Immediately after atomic bombs were used against Japan, Eisenhower understood that the post war world had taken a bad turn. "Before the atom bomb was used," Eisenhower told journalist Edgar Snow in August 1945, "I would have said yes, I was sure we could keep the peace with Russia. Now I don't know."

> I had hoped the bomb wouldn't figure in this war. Until now I would have said that we three, Britain with her mighty fleet, America with the strongest Air Force, and Russia with the strongest land force on the continent, we three could have guaranteed the peace of the world for a long, long time to come. But now, I don't know. People are frightened and disturbed all over. Everyone feels insecure again.[20]

In 1953, Eisenhower, by then president, asked J. Robert Oppenheimer, who had been the scientific director of World War II's Manhattan Project, to write an article suggesting that the United States and the Soviet Union ought to work together to find a way out of the nuclear impasse. "The atomic clock ticks faster and faster," Oppenheimer wrote. "We may be likened to two scorpions in a bottle, each capable of killing the other, but only at the risk of his own life."[21]

In July 1954, a year after the Korean armistice had been signed, South Korean president Syngman Rhee met with Eisenhower. Rhee was not happy that the Korean War had ended in armed stalemate, with Korea divided at roughly the 38th parallel, which had been the boundary before the war. He wanted reunification—and he wanted the United States to take the lead in accomplishing that objective through military means.

"We have to know where our great ally, the United States, the champion of democracy, stands in relation to the attempts of communist Russia and the communists of China to take over our country and to keep it divided," Rhee said. How can the United States sit by "and let the communists conquer and conquer and conquer?"

A few minutes later, Rhee came to his closer. "You are the hope of the world." Will the United States "tell the free nations that if they stand up for their freedom against communism, the United States will help them? There will be no more talk, no more appeasement. We will all stand and work together. That is what the world is crying for today." When it was Eisenhower's turn, the president said:

> What you are in effect suggesting is that there can be no peace in the world until the head of the communist octopus is destroyed. That means Russia is destroyed.... The free nations of the world have never gone to war deliberately—they cannot....
>
> When you say that we should deliberately plunge into war, let me tell you that if war comes, it will be horrible. Atomic war will destroy civilization. It will destroy our cities. There will be millions of people dead. War today is unthinkable with the weapons which we have at our command. If the Kremlin and Washington ever lock up in war, the results are too horrible to contemplate.[22]

Despite his aversion to nuclear weapons and his conviction that nuclear war would be immoral as well as suicidal, Eisenhower presided over a massive buildup of nuclear weapons, bombers, and missiles. By the time Eisenhower turned the White House over to John F. Kennedy, the United States and the Soviet Union were locked in a nuclear arms race that was spiraling out of control. Doomsday scenarios abounded, in popular culture and even in serious analyses.[23]

Although never stated officially (at least in an unclassified forum) U.S. missiles were on a launch-on-warning hair-trigger; the United States was prepared to go to war on virtually a moment's notice.[24] Hair trigger status was barely bearable in the bomber age, when the officers in charge of early-warning radar systems would have had a few hours to determine whether Soviet bombers were headed for America's airfields and cities. But as Soviet intercontinental ballistic missiles began to come online in the early 1960s, warning time was cut to minutes. By the time a warning got to him, the president might have five minutes or so to decide whether to get U.S. missiles off the ground.

If the warning of a Soviet attack were false—caused perhaps by a technical malfunction in the early-warning system or a human error—the launch of America's retaliatory missiles would initiate an accidental nuclear war. In contrast, if the warning was correct but the president failed to launch U.S. missiles, much of America's retaliatory missile force would be destroyed on the ground. In the deceptively homey argot of the Pentagon, this dilemma was known as "use 'em or lose 'em." Soviet leaders were caught in the same dilemma. At every moment of every day, particularly in the 1970s and 1980s, the globe was never more than a half hour away from near-total destruction.

The most influential American proponent of the Moscow-may-strike-first idea was the late Albert Wohlstetter, an analyst at the RAND Corporation; later, he became a powerfully influential academic at the University of Chicago. Wohlstetter's spirit lives on; he is the intellectual godfather of a generation of neoconservatives, including Richard Perle and Paul Wolfowitz, two of the chief architects of the war against Saddam Hussein in 2003.[25]

By the late 1950s, both President Eisenhower and many of America's defense analysts understood the all-or-nothing dilemma. At one point in November 1957, after receiving an unusually pessimistic report about America's supposed vulnerabilities to a surprise Soviet attack, Eisenhower simply commented, "You can't have this kind of war. There just aren't enough bulldozers to scrape the bodies off the streets."[26]

By 1957, nuclear strategists were working up a "counterforce" strategy. They assumed that in a surprise Soviet attack, America's missile fields and bomber bases would be the first targets; the Soviets would try to catch America's missiles and bombers on the ground. The United States, counterforce theory said, should do roughly the same: America's retaliatory attacks should go after Soviet missiles and bombers in the hope of catching a fair number of them still on the ground. Further, America's retaliatory strikes should be "restrained," which would "signal" to Soviet leaders that the United States was not trying to wipe out their cities.

Once the Soviet leadership understood that the U.S. response was limited, the war could somehow be called off with perhaps only a few million deaths on either side rather than tens of millions. President Kennedy's defense secretary, Robert S. McNamara, a man who believed that virtually everything could be quantified and controlled, ran with the counterforce idea and outlined an elaborate doctrine of "assured destruction," which quickly morphed into *mutual* assured destruction—MAD.

An uncontrolled arms race would probably end in disaster for everyone, according to the proponents of MAD. It didn't make sense for the United States and the Soviet Union to continually try to get an edge on the other in numbers of weapons and missiles. Sooner or later, by intention or more likely by accident or miscalculation, the weapons would be used during a time of high East-West tension.[27]

MAD theory said that the United States and the Soviet Union ought to achieve a rough nuclear balance instead of continually attempting to one-up the other in weaponry. The key to achieving such a balance would be to deploy large numbers of "survivable" weapons, nukes that could "ride out" a first strike by the other side in super-hardened silos or in missile submarines hiding in the ocean depths.

With a sufficient number of survivable weapons, each nation would be able to "absorb" a nuclear strike and still be able to launch a devastating retaliatory strike—a so-called "second strike." Those missiles would be able to inflict "unacceptable damage" on the aggressor. The threat of that second strike would deter the leaders of the bad-guy nation from launching the first strike.

It is uncertain how many high-level people on either side of the Iron Curtain really believed that a nuclear exchange could be so rationally controlled. A spasm of nuclear destruction seemed more likely to follow even the limited use of nuclear weapons. In 1983, for instance, I was party to an off-the-record conversation with an American general very near the top of the nuclear-weapons chain of command. It was then U.S. policy—which meant it was NATO's policy—to use tactical nuclear weapons to help repel a Soviet invasion of Western Europe, even if the Soviets used only conventional weapons.

In theory, NATO's nukes would be used with restraint against the invading force, not against targets in the Soviet Union. That would tell Moscow to call off the invasion or risk escalation to full-scale nuclear war against the Soviet homeland. The general was intensely skeptical that things would work that way in the heat of battle. It was more likely, he said, that once NATO's forces used nuclear weapons, even in a defensive mode, "It would all be over." The conflict would escalate into a global holocaust.

Mutual assured destruction richly deserved its acronym. It was, in effect, a bilateral suicide pact—in the popular phrase, a "balance of terror." MAD embraced a set of arcane assumptions and strategies that added up to: "If you kill me, I'll kill you."[28]

The balance of terror did not stop the arms race; rather, it channeled it into new directions—especially the deployment of superlatively accurate missiles with multiple warheads, each of which could hit a different target. Under MAD's umbrella, the United States and the Soviet Union simply went nuclear nuts. By 1987, the two nations had between them more than sixty-six thousand nuclear weapons of all shapes, sizes, and yields, and in varying states of readiness.[29] Many of the weapons (nuclear mines, for instance) were "small" enough that they were thought to be useful against bridges or dams. Thousands of weapons were large enough to consume vast areas of cities in radioactive firestorms.[30]

The "stability" of MAD depended, in large measure, on the assurance that neither side had a way to defend against a nuclear strike. That was the push behind the U.S.-Soviet Anti-Ballistic Missile Treaty of 1972. The core purpose of the treaty was to prevent either side from deploying a system that might prevent the other side's missiles from hitting their targets.[31]

The dark logic of the treaty was clear. If one side seemed to be developing a potentially effective missile defense system, the other side would simply build more missiles and warheads to overwhelm it. That would lead to a dangerously unstable offense-defense race. In contrast, if neither side had a comprehensive missile-defense system, the men, women, and children of each nation would be held hostage to the other side's nuclear weapons. That was said to be desirable; holding entire populations hostage was assumed to be a powerful incentive for avoiding actions that might lead to nuclear war.[32]

IMPOTENT AND OBSOLETE

Despite his undeniable public charm, President Reagan was a divisive figure. The majority of Americans, including most Republicans and many Democrats, have come to regard him as a virtual demigod who ended the Cold War more or less single-handedly. A minority of Americans, mostly on the left, viewed him as a dangerously misguided man who came close to bringing on a secular Armageddon.

Generally forgotten is that Reagan, the ultimate hardliner, was determined to rid the world of nuclear weapons, a goal most often associated with anti-nuclear activists rather than with men who have occupied the Oval Office. Reagan repeatedly said that nuclear abolition was his ultimate aim. Nonetheless, he did not trust Soviet leaders or the system they controlled. He made that plain in a speech delivered June 8, 1982 at Britain's House of Commons. The Soviet Union was an "evil" totalitarian state that belonged on the "ash heap of history."[33]

Kenneth Adelman, one of President Reagan's top national security advisers and a quintessential hardliner, was shocked by Reagan's antinuclear beliefs. "The more I sat at NSC (National Security Council) meetings with him," he told author Paul Lettow, "the more I was surprised that for an anti-Communist hawk, how antinuclear he was. He would make comments that seemed to me to come from the far left rather than from the far right. He *hated* nuclear weapons."[34] A comprehensive, space-based missile-defense system, Reagan believed, would be an indispensable first step toward the goal of nuclear abolition.

To the surprise of many close advisers who had not been consulted, Reagan told the world on March 23, 1983 that he would attempt to do away with the balance of terror. "The defense policy of the United States," he said, "is based on a simple premise: The United States does not start fights. We will never be an aggressor. We maintain our strength in order to deter and defend against aggression—to preserve freedom and peace."

Soviet leaders, he said, seemed to have a different idea: "For twenty years the Soviet Union has been accumulating enormous military might. They didn't stop when their forces exceeded all requirements of a legitimate defensive capability. And they haven't stopped now. During the past decade and a half, the Soviets have built up a massive arsenal of new strategic nuclear weapons—weapons that can strike directly at the United States."[35]

Reagan asserted that he would devote himself to revitalizing America's military forces, which were not up to snuff. That would help meet the Soviet threat. But he would also try to change the nation's deterrence policy, which relied heavily on nuclear retaliation. "The human spirit," he said, "must be capable of rising above dealing with other nations and human beings by threatening their existence." He would therefore "call upon the scientific community in our country, those who gave us nuclear weapons, to turn their great talents now to the cause of mankind and world peace, to give us the means of rendering these nuclear weapons *impotent and obsolete.*" (Italics added.) He would ask scientists to come up with a comprehensive antiballistic missile system.

Although a startling speech, it was not overly surprising to Reagan's closest confidantes who had known of the president's antipathy toward nuclear weapons, reaching as far back as 1945 when atom bombs were used against Japanese cities. Reagan later characterized the balance of terror as a kind of Old West standoff—"two westerners standing in a saloon aiming their guns to each other's head—permanently."[36]

In January 1967, Reagan, the newly installed governor of California, visited bomb scientist Edward Teller at Lawrence Livermore National Laboratory, about eighty miles southwest of Sacramento, the state capital. (Livermore is one of the nation's three principal nuclear weapons labs; the other two are Los Alamos and Sandia, both in New Mexico.) Teller, who briefed Reagan on ballistic-missile defense systems, later recalled: "My impression was that his questions showed very little knowledge of the subject but real interest in the subject. And furthermore, they were perfect questions, they were good questions...coming from a man who had not looked into that situation before."[37]

President Reagan was as scientifically naïve as he was politically optimistic.[38] The kind of missile defenses he envisioned—which relied heavily on space-based hardware—was beyond the reach of U.S. scientists in the 1980s. Arguably, the far simpler and more limited system now being deployed still lies beyond the capabilities of today's scientists—the antimissile defense system ordered up by George W. Bush is a pale imitation of Reagan's "Star Wars" vision. No one would suggest that "Son of Star Wars" or "Star Wars Lite" could handle the massive attack the Soviet Union was capable of launching in the 1980s.[39]

The technical improbability of Reagan's Star Wars system was just one knock against it. Men and women in the arms control field also opposed it because of its possible psychological impact on Soviet leaders. From Moscow's point of view, a comprehensive space shield in addition to America's increasingly accurate ICBMs could add up to an American ability to launch a preemptive first strike.

From the Soviet perspective, Star Wars was a "space-strike system"—a "Sword of Damocles designed to curtail their ability to retaliate after an initial American attack."[40] Whatever America's actual intentions might be, such a capability was seen in Moscow as powerfully coercive. If the Strategic Defense Initiative really worked, the Motherland could end up under America's nuclear thumb.

The Soviet Union, already highly stressed by a huge military budget, could not afford to build its own version of Stars Wars. But it didn't need to. Soviet leaders, as well as Western arms control experts understood that a bigger and better Soviet missile offense could always overwhelm a defense system—and at a much lower cost. Even proponents of Star Wars conceded, at times, that no matter how good the missile shield was, there would always be "leakage." During a massive Soviet attack, some Soviet warheads would always get through.[41]

Richard L. Garwin, one of the century's most respected American scientists in the national security field, put it this way in 1985: "SDI is seen by the Soviets as a threat to their survival—seen as leaving the U.S. with a powerful nuclear attack capability, while disarming the Soviet Union.... [It] will drive the Soviets to an urgent expansion of their nuclear force, from the present 9,000 warheads to 50,000 or more."[42]

THREAT CLOUDS AND KILL VEHICLES

Although vastly scaled down, today's homeland defense system described by the Missile Defense Agency embraces three subsystems, as did the Star Wars concept. The first subsystem would attempt to shoot down missiles as they rise from the enemy's launch pad and head into space atop a booster rocket; this is known as "boost-phase" defense. The second subsystem would try to intercept and destroy warheads as they arc through the vacuum of space, "midcourse" defense. Like the "free safety" in American football, the third subsystem, "terminal" defense, would kill warheads that made it through the first two.

Of the three, the midcourse system is the most advanced component—and it is the most relevant to the space-control mission. It is difficult to find scientists thoroughly familiar with the physics of the midcourse system now being deployed who believe it will work as advertised. The idea of hitting a bullet with a bullet, a simile universally used by missile-defense partisans, is daunting almost beyond comprehension.

Presumably no one in the United States would know exactly when evil-doers might fire missiles toward the United States, although they would presumably have a pretty good idea where the missiles might come from. North Korea is usually cited as the most likely candidate, an assumption that requires a considerable suspension of disbelief.

North Korea is a backward society in technology as well as in politics. Its long-range missile program embraces 1950s systems that have been refined with upgrades and add-ons.[43] Yet the fundamental question remains: Even if North Korea could fire a missile toward U.S. territory, why would it? To do so would be tantamount to national suicide, and whatever one may think of North Korea's wretchedly solipsistic leadership, it does not seem overtly suicidal. Ditto for Iran, another nation that is said to be a future missile threat to the United States. The real focus of space warrior concern is, once again, China.

A functioning midcourse system would take a few minutes to detect the launch of enemy missiles (with a combination of technically ingenious ground-, sea-, land- and space-based sensors), assess their trajectories with an astonishing degree of accuracy, and then dispatch interceptors composed of fast-accelerating booster rockets topped with maneuverable kinetic-kill vehicles. Once in space, the kill vehicles (which by then would have separated from their boosters) would use onboard sensors to spot the enemy warheads (now detached from their boosters) and adjust course with such exquisite precision as to smack into the warheads.

There are staggering problems with this scenario. Space is a very big place and the warheads are very, very small. Score one for the offense. But the defense has one advantage in picking out the warheads: the warheads, which have ridden into space atop fire-spewing rockets, are warm. America's interceptors are equipped with infrared sensors, which means that the warheads will be visible in the infrared spectrum. Score one for the defense.

Well, maybe not. Anyone who might seek to throw missiles at the United States understands the vexing heat-makes-the-warheads-visible problem, and they have a variety of options available to foil the defense. These are generally called "penetration aids" or, to use a more prudish term, "countermeasures." One of the simplest countermeasures is to deploy "threat clouds"—warheads would travel through space in the company of multiple decoys. Because there is no air resistance in space, the decoys can be pretty simple; aluminized balloons, inflated in space, would do nicely. Given the fact that kill vehicles have just seconds to "discriminate" real warheads from decoys and lock in, one has to score another point for the offense.

And yet… the warheads are still warm, which means that the kill vehicles might still have a chance of telling warm warheads from cold decoys. Score another point for the defense. Again, maybe not. The warheads could be hidden *inside* one of the balloons and even cooled. Or the decoys could be warmed. In either case, the kinetic-kill vehicles would be looking at many objects without a reliable means of detecting which are the actual warheads.

Sounds fantastic, doesn't it? But tricking interceptors is old stuff. The United States and the Soviet Union developed multiple techniques for doing just that during the Cold War. *Countermeasures*, a classic analysis of the deception problem issued in April 2000, remains relevant today.[44]

And then there is the matter of velocity. The combined "closing speed" of the threat clouds and the kill vehicles, each of which would be on a different trajectory, would be in the fifteen- to twenty-thousand miles-per-hour range or more. Further, neither the warheads nor the kill vehicle would be large, which means the collision course would have to be almost unimaginably precise. Think of aiming one office-size refrigerator at another, with each traveling many times faster than a speeding bullet at cross-angles to one another.

For more than a decade, proponents have insisted that the midcourse missile defense scheme sketched here could be made to work. Tens of billions of dollars have been spent on it. In recent years, however, the Missile Defense Agency seems to have tacitly admitted that the midcourse system is—well—flawed. The agency is in the early stages of experimenting with "MKVs"—multiple-kill vehicles, each of which would be small—perhaps the size of a bag of sugar in one common analogy. With MKVs, the interceptors could presumably go after the entire threat cloud, popping all of the balloons at once, so to speak. Don't hold your breath.[45]

THE FACES OF JANUS

The antiballistic missile system being deployed today is a lose-lose proposition. It is unlikely to work as hoped in any of its three incarnations (boost, midcourse, or terminal phase), and it is prohibitively expensive. Perhaps the most striking cost analysis of missile defense was released in January 2003 by the Center for Arms Control and Non-Proliferation. The center is regarded in the arms control world as a reliable outfit, and the five economists who prepared the report have solid academic credentials. (One, Kenneth J. Arrow, shared the 1972 Nobel Prize in Economics.)

The report estimates that the cumulative cost of a "layered" missile defense system could be between $800 billion and $1.2 trillion. Admittedly, the economists employed worst-case cost assumptions: that the sort of system envisioned by the Bush administration, which would include expensive space-based interceptors, would be deployed by 2015, a break-neck timeline.

Such rapid deployment is not likely to happen. Historically, congressional Democrats have not been as enthusiastic about dumping bales of money into the bottomless missile-defense well as have Republicans. And in the mid-term elections in 2006, Democrats regained control of both houses of Congress after more than a decade of wandering in the wilderness. Nonetheless, anyone who hopes to follow the unfolding missile-defense debate should consider reading the report. It provides much helpful background.[46]

In a sense, whether the system would actually work or that it might be horribly expensive is, to some space warriors, somewhat irrelevant. Antiballistic missile systems are Janus-faced. Seen from one angle, they are purely defensive. Seen from another, they are offensive. Antiballistic missile systems and antisatellite systems are joined at the hip.

People knowledgeable about national security space issues, including the space warriors I have met, concede that the United States already has a reliable ASAT system in the guise of the "midcourse" phase of the anti-ballistic missile system. It is a classic "open secret." "Ballistic missile defense overlaps somewhat with space weaponry," says *Reinventing Multilateralism*, a study produced by the Program in Arms Control, Disarmament, and International Security at the University of Illinois.

This overlap occurs not because BMD (ballistic missile defense) interceptors and the missiles they target fly through outer space but because BMD interceptors have some residual antisatellite (ASAT) capability.

Ballistic missile defense necessarily implies a low-altitude ASAT capability, but not geosynchronous or high-altitude ASAT capability. This ASAT capability by itself would not justify the deployment of ballistic missile defense, but it is a collateral mission.

In addition, the technologies for ballistic missile defense (e.g., kinetic-kill vehicles) can be directly transferred to produce dedicated ASAT weapons. However, the modest ASAT capability provided by BMD systems should not sound the death knell for larger multilateral efforts to control weapons in space, especially ASAT weapons.[47]

Or to put it another way, America's midcourse anti-ballistic missile system, which is regularly portrayed by its proponents as strictly defensive in nature, can be used offensively as a space-control weapon. It might not be able hit enemy warheads headed for the United States, but even in its present not-ready-for-prime-time form, its missile interceptors could do a dandy job of smashing satellites in "low-Earth orbit."[48] As it happens, much of the infrastructure needed to intercept missiles overlaps with the infrastructure required for an antisatellite system. As they say in national security circles, the hardware is "dual purpose."

Surprise weighs heavily against the success of anti-ballistic missile systems; no defender would know exactly when missiles might be launched from the attacking nation or precisely what paths they would take. In contrast, satellites follow predictable paths. The attacker would know precisely where the satellites would be at any given time. Further, satellites are bigger than missile warheads; the larger the target, the easier the task. Satellites are also considerably more fragile than warheads and easily damaged or destroyed; they are built to operate in the no-resistance vacuum of space; in contrast, warheads must be tough enough to withstand the fiery reentry into the atmosphere.

Finally, anyone who chooses to damage or destroy a satellite can choose the time of attack, when everything is most favorable to success. If a nation ever launched missile warheads against the United States, it would surely do so when the warheads would travel in the Earth's shadow. That makes them difficult to pick out from the India-ink blackness of space. But if a nation attacks a satellite, it would likely do so when the target was a sparkling diamond in full sunlight.

Even if they are whizzing along at seventeen thousand five hundred miles per hour, satellites in low-Earth orbit can be killed by America's existing anti-missile interceptors. America's space warriors, however, have been reluctant for a couple of decades to rely on an ASAT system that creates debris that—as the world saw in the Chinese test—would endanger American satellites as well as the satellites of other nations. Air Force General Ralph Eberhart, who oversaw the development of U.S. Space Command's Long Range Plan, put it this way in 2000 while talking to a group of defense reporters: "First and foremost, I'm concerned about the debris in space and not knowing what's going to happen once you blow it [a satellite] up.... I have to admit that I would also be concerned about the threshold that you cross if you do that…what it might mean in terms of weapons in space and other space activities."[49]

The general added that destroying another country's communications or spy satellites by using a weapon launched into space would be "a last-ditch option." He would use negotiations to resolve the conflict. If that didn't work, he "would much rather interfere with the [satellite's] uplinks and downlinks—I would much rather…bomb a ground station."

Space warriors—at least those in the military—are dead set against creating debris that would damage U.S. satellites in low-Earth orbit. They are much more interested in developing more sophisticated systems that could temporarily disable, damage, or destroy satellites in any orbit, without creating debris. And they are working on such systems with vigor.

5

Prompt Global Strike

Strategic Air Command, organized in 1946, was at first fitted out with World War II–style conventional bombs and bombers. But from the 1950s on, it was a nuclear force with new generations of bombs and bombers. SAC's core mission was deterrence; that meant having the men and the equipment and the determination to hit the Soviet Union with nuclear weapons if the Cold War turned hot. Even SAC's bellicose let-the-bombs-fall commander, Gen. Curtis LeMay, said that SAC was all about deterrence.

"Our national policy," LeMay said in 1956, "is one of deterrence.... We must deter aggression. We deter it by making it clear that we have strength and that its application will cost the enemy more than he could possibly gain by attacking us."[1]

In those days, SAC presumably would strike after deterrence had failed and Soviet bombers or missiles were on their way. Why "presumably"? Because LeMay had a well-earned reputation, even within SAC, for hoping that SAC's frequent spy flights in Soviet airspace would provoke a war while the United States still had many more nuclear weapons than the Soviets.[2] Nonetheless, he denied that he advocated preventive war. In his 1965 autobiography, he said:

> There was, definitely, a time when we could have destroyed all of Russia (I mean by that, all of Russia's capability to wage war) without losing a man to their defenses.... This period extended from before the time when the Russians achieved The Bomb, until after they had The Bomb but didn't yet own a stockpile of weapons....
>
> It would have been possible, I believe, for America to say to the Soviets, "Here's a blueprint for your immediate future. We'll give you

a deadline of five or six months"—something like that—"to pull out of the satellite countries, and effect a complete change of conduct. You will behave your damn selves from this moment forth."

We could have done this. But whether we *should* have presented such a blueprint was not for me to decide. That was a question of national policy.[3]

In 1992, Strategic Air Command was folded into a new organization called Strategic Command or StratCom, which also embraced the Navy's submarine-based nuclear strike force. StratCom's mission statement includes the wording "global strike operations," a phrase that has evolved to embody the possibility of *preemptive* strikes with conventional, and possibly nuclear, warheads, anywhere in the world at any time.[4] General LeMay, who died in 1990, would have approved.

After the collapse of the Soviet Union, America's strategic planners were at a loss. The decades-long existential threat to the United States was gone, or at least greatly diminished. Joint Chiefs Chairman Colin Powell famously said in 1991 during an interview, "Think about it. I'm running out of demons. I'm running out of villains. I'm down to Castro and Kim Il Sung."[5]

Planners had long recognized that veiled U.S. threats to preemptively strike certain targets with nuclear weapons lacked credibility—it would be like hitting a beetle with a sledgehammer. Nuclear weapons had been extensively tested but never used after August 1945. Their use was widely regarded as taboo, and the leaders of rogue states knew it.[6] Nukes still had credibility as weapons of retaliation, but not as weapons of preemption.

Beginning in the early 1990s, the question of the day was how to persuade rogue states that it was dangerous to assume that the United States would *never* preemptively strike their military facilities. One idea was to develop low-yield nuclear weapons, devices that would somehow be perceived by rogue state leaders as small enough to be used.[7] The idea that smaller nukes would be gentler didn't play well with Congress, which believed it was unwise to design new nuclear weapons. Congress nixed the idea.

Another means for going after rogues was designed to make it impossible for them to safely hide their weapons, or themselves, beneath the surface of the Earth. The B61-11 program turned an older nuclear bomb into a "bunker buster"—a weapon that might be able to penetrate a few yards below the surface to blow up underground military facilities. The program was heavily criticized because, even though the bomb detonated below the surface, it would still throw up huge amounts of radioactive fallout that would endanger innocent civilians. Although it remains in the stockpile, it is not generally viewed as a credible preemptive weapon.

After a decade of high-level discussion and debate in the 1990s among the members of the nuclear priesthood, a secret *Nuclear Posture Review* was submitted to Congress on December 31, 2001.[8] It was a watershed document, parts of which were quickly leaked. Unlike earlier statements on nuclear policy, it added the use of conventional explosives to the bunker-buster mix.

The major emphasis in the *Nuclear Posture Review* was on developing effective means to "defeat hard and deeply buried targets." According to the document, there were some ten thousand underground facilities of military importance worldwide and about fourteen hundred of them "were known or suspected strategic (WMD, ballistic missile basing, leadership or top echelon command and control) sites." A majority of them, the document said, were deeply buried and thus "difficult to defeat because of the depth of the facility and the uncertainty of the exact location."

> In general, current conventional weapons can only "deny" or "disrupt" the functioning of HDBTs [hard and deeply buried targets] and require highly accurate intelligence and precise weapon delivery—a degree of accuracy and precision frequently missing under actual combat conditions. Similarly, current conventional weapons are not effective for the long term physical destruction of deep, underground facilities....
>
> The United States currently has a very limited ground penetration capability with its only Earth-penetrating nuclear weapon, the B61 Mod 11 gravity bomb. This single-yield, non-precision weapon cannot survive penetration into many types of terrain in which hardened underground facilities are located. Given these limitations, the targeting of a number of hardened, underground facilities is limited to an attack against surface features, which does not provide a high probability of defeat of these important targets.
>
> With a more effective [nuclear] Earth penetrator, many buried targets could be attacked using a weapon with a much lower yield than would be required with a surface burst weapon. This lower yield

would achieve the same damage while producing less fallout (by a factor of ten to twenty) than would the much larger yield surface burst. For defeat of very deep or larger underground facilities, penetrating weapons with large yields would be needed to collapse the facility.[9]

The *Nuclear Posture Review* is one of the prime national security documents from which other plans and operations flow. Many national security analysts who saw leaked excerpts believed the 2001 revision was a recipe for preemptive nuclear attack. That seemed to be the clear message of the section on how to "defeat" hard and deeply buried targets. Later in 2002, the possibility (if not the probability) of preemptive attacks, conventional and possibly nuclear, became explicit national policy. The *National Strategy to Combat Weapons of Mass Destruction*, issued in December 2002, says: "Because deterrence may not succeed, and because of the potentially devastating consequences of WMD [weapons of mass destruction] use against our forces and civilian population, U.S. military forces and appropriate civilian agencies must have the capability to defend against WMD-armed adversaries, including in appropriate cases through preemptive measures."[10]

After that, the buzz in national security circles over the possibility that the United States was planning preemptive nuclear attacks against certain facilities in rogue states became so intense that Linton F. Brooks, the administrator of the National Nuclear Security Administration, attempted to defuse the talk during a May 12, 2004 speech at the Heritage Foundation.

> I have had a committee chairman tell me we were planning on developing low-yield [nuclear] weapons to use preemptively against terrorists in places like Afghanistan. I assume you all understand this is nonsense. While no one wants to constrain a president's options in advance, I've never met anyone in the administration who would even consider nuclear preemption in connection with countering rogue state WMD threats. But we've allowed this misconception by not being clear about our policy.[11]

Brooks's speech did little to ease fears. Meanwhile, the Defense Department officially assigned the born-again global-strike mission to StratCom. In military and civilian national security circles, the mission generally takes the adjective, "prompt," as in "prompt global strike." The goal of prompt global strike is to acquire the ability to put explosives on targets anywhere in the world within an hour or two after a decision to do so.[12]

The prompt global strike mission was assigned to StratCom during the tenure of Adm. James O. Ellis. At Ellis's retirement dinner in July 2003, General Myers, then chairman of the Joint Chiefs of Staff, told an appreciative Omaha audience that "the president charged you [Ellis] to 'be ready to strike at any moment's notice in any dark corner of the world' [and] that is exactly what you've done."[13]

In 2005, StratCom announced that its "Joint Functional Component Command for Space and Global Strike" had become operational. According to a StratCom press release, written in the Defense Department's traditional klutzy style, "the command's performance during Global Lightning demonstrated its preparedness to execute its mission of providing integrated space and global strike capabilities to deter and dissuade aggressors and when directed, defeat adversaries through decisive joint global effects in support of USSTRATCOM missions."[14]

According to William M. Arkin, a civilian analyst with extraordinarily good sources within the military and intelligence communities, the November 2005 "Global Lightning" exercise involved the planning and execution of a mock attack on North Korea. It was not, however, a preemptive attack; it was a retaliatory strike against North Korea—identified in the StratCom scenario as the "Purple" force—that had hit the United States "with a number of intermediate-range ballistic missiles" with nuclear warheads. (Arkin wrote about Global Lightning in his *Washington Post* blog more than a week before the exercise began.)[15]

According to Arkin, Global Lightning was conducted within the framework of the new and secret Contingency Plan 8022, invariably referred to as Conplan 8022. That plan, says Arkin, lies at the heart of the new global-strike mission: "In the secret world of military planning, global strike has become the term of art to describe a specific preemptive attack. When military officials refer to global strike, they stress its conventional elements. Surprisingly, however, global strike also includes a nuclear option, which runs counter to traditional U.S. notions about the defensive role of nuclear weapons."[16]

Arkin is right about the nuclear option; it has not been ruled out. But the thrust of the prompt global strike mission is to develop the capability to preemptively hit "time-sensitive" targets quickly with high-tech, precision, conventional weapons. General James E. Cartwright, commander of Strategic Command, put it this way in congressional testimony on March 29, 2006.

USSTRATCOM [has] championed the need for a prompt, precise conventional global strike capability to bridge the gap between prompt nuclear weapons and less timely, but precise, conventional weapons. Key initiatives include:

- Deploy[ing] an initial precision-guided conventional Trident sea-launched ballistic missile capability within two years. The speed and range advantage of a conventional Trident missile increases decision time and provides an alternative to nuclear weapon use against fleeting, high value targets. The conventional Trident missile would be particularly useful in deterring or defeating those who seek to coerce or threaten the U.S. with WMD.

- Develop[ing] a new land-based, penetrating long-range strike capability to be fielded by 2018.

- Study[ing] alternative options for delivering prompt, precise conventional warheads using advanced technologies such as hypersonic vehicles from land, air, or the sea.[17]

The Bush administration did not invent the notion of "prompt global strike." The conceptual work on prompt global strike flourished during the Clinton administration, and it was fairly well formed by July 1998, when the Air Force Space Command Directorate of Requirements issued a "draft mission statement."[18] The Bush administration simply carried the concept further and eventually "operationalized" it, in Pentagon-speak.

"Operationalized" or not, the first phase of conventional global strike—adapting twenty-four long-range and supremely accurate Trident II D-5 submarine-launched missiles—has not yet gotten anywhere with Congress, which has refused to fully fund the program. This lack of congressional enthusiasm can be traced mostly to the ambiguity issue. Trident missiles armed with conventional warheads (up to four per missile) would be stored in submarine silos next to Trident missiles armed with nuclear warheads. At any given moment, several submarines would be on patrol, ready to launch missiles on short notice if ordered to do so.[19]

If a Trident II D-5 missile with conventional warheads was launched, how would other nations—Russia and China, perhaps?—know that the missile was non-nuclear and its target a rogue state? Defense planners argue the missile's trajectory would not resemble, say, a Moscow or Beijing trajectory. Nonetheless, launching a missile from a submarine stuffed to the gills with nuclear warheads strikes many members of Congress as more than a little risky.

A SPECTRUM OF TARGETS

Despite the ambiguity issue, the drive toward preemptive prompt global strike is real. Defense planners still hope to get the conventional Trident D-5 online in a few years. But how does space fit into the picture, other than facilitating possible strikes with surveillance, reconnaissance, communications, and global-positioning satellites? The answer is that the Trident program is projected as a "near-term" solution to the prompt-global-strike "requirement." The longer-term scheme involves the Air Force; Air Force Space Command hopes to be in the prompt-global-strike business by 2025 or thereabouts.

As described in Chapter One, the Air Force Space Command's October 2003 *Strategic Master Plan FY06 and Beyond* said:

> Non-nuclear *prompt global strike* from and through space can transform the warfighter's role in the future.
>
> Most notably, a non-nuclear strike capability, possibly in the form of a Common Aero Vehicle (CAV) launched by a ballistic missile, air launch system, or a SOV [Space Operations Vehicle], could provide the President and the Secretary of Defense with a range of space power options. These options are for deterrence and flexible response when time is absolutely critical, risks associated with other options are too high, or when no other courses of action are available.[20] (Italics added.)

In its closing section, "The Way Ahead," the master plan describes conventional strike:

> Our vision calls for *prompt global strike space systems* with the capability to directly apply force from or through space against terrestrial targets. International treaties and laws do not prohibit the use or presence of conventional weapons in space. Policymakers are working to create conditions for a new Strategic Triad that includes non-nuclear global strike weapons. *Non-nuclear prompt global strike*

space capabilities are being studied. Our nation's leadership will decide whether or not to pursue the development of conventional, space based systems for global strike to fully exploit the advantages of space.[21] (Italics added.)

The Common Aero Vehicle (or CAV), a nifty conceptual space weapon, began to be mentioned regularly in space-warrior literature in the late 1990s.[22] A CAV would be a small, unmanned, unpowered, steerable, hypersonic machine that could be launched into space and then return to the atmosphere at high speeds. It would then glide through the atmosphere while maneuvering left and right toward a target.

It is called "common" because it would be able to carry a variety of payloads, from tiny unmanned reconnaissance vehicles to precision weapons, and because it could be launched into space using a variety of means, ranging from an expendable rocket to a so-called Space Operations Vehicle. It could even be launched, piggyback style, from a large airplane like a modified Boeing 747. The CAV would be an all-purpose sort of thing that might contain bombs, kinetic-energy rods, or even reconnaissance gear. The "aero" in Common Aero Vehicle does not come from "aerospace" as one might suppose. The CAV's "aerothermodynamic" shell would protect the hardware inside from the ferocious frictional heat generated by reentering the denser atmosphere at hypersonic speeds.

Conceptual work and research on maneuverable reentry vehicles began in the 1960s with a tongue-twisting Air Force program called Aerothermodynamic/Elastic Structural Systems Environmental Tests. Concepts with less challenging names followed, among them the Precision Recovery Including Maneuvering Entry program; the Small Evader Vehicle program; the Small High Accuracy Reentry Vehicle program; the Advanced Maneuvering Reentry Vehicle program; and the High Performance Reentry Maneuvering Reentry Vehicle program.[23]

Underlying these early studies was the assumption that someday the United States might be required to hit distant targets fast with something other than nuclear-tipped intercontinental ballistic missiles. In the early 1990s, concepts for Transatmospheric Vehicles, or TAVs, were the rage.[24] One "notional" TAV was labeled the "Black Horse." Never built, it was depicted in Spacecast 2020, a futuristic study conducted by the Air Force's Air University, as having varied and wondrous functions, not the least of which would have been the ability to launch stealthy attacks against earthly targets.

Strategic surprise results from the ability to strike enemy targets at any depth with little or no warning. Because kinetic energy multiplies the effect of weapons delivered from a suborbital trajectory, the weapons themselves can be small (e.g., brilliant micromunitions); therefore, a single vehicle could simultaneously strike a large number of targets. *Operational* surprise results from the rapidity of the completed attack, which may be timed to catch an adversary in the process of deployment or employment of inadequately prepared forces. *Tactical* surprise results from a variety of suborbital profiles that these vehicles can use to exploit gaps in any enemy's defense.[25] (Italics added.)

In *Air Force 2025*, another Air University exercise conducted in the mid-1990s, Transatmospheric Vehicles were still prominent, but now enthusiasm for lasers was on the rise.

The Global Area Strike System consists of a continental U.S.-based laser system which bounces high energy beams off a constellation of space-based mirrors. Inherently precise, megawatt-class, light speed weapons can potentially act within seconds or minutes to impact on events in space, the atmosphere, or the Earth's surface.

A transatmospheric vehicle [launched when needed] serves as a weapons platform for kinetic energy projectiles, directed energy weapons, and manned strike and provides flexibility in the response. It can thus deliver a variety of forces to anywhere on Earth within hours.

The combined system has near instantaneous response capability, a full range of lethality, and global reach and adequate flexibility. Although it can strike from space, no actual weapons are based in space. Its greatest asset is that it provides power projection without forward basing.[26]

In June 2003, the Defense Advanced Research Projects Agency (DARPA) and the Air Force described the newest version of the old dream machine in their Sunday-best bureaucratic prose. They were soliciting ideas from the aerospace industry regarding an unmanned high-flying "Hypersonic Cruise

Vehicle" that might someday be built as part of Project FALCON (*Force Application and Launch from CONUS*—"CONUS" is government-speak for the continental United States.) The request for proposals said the "Government's vision of an ultimate prompt global reach capability (circa 2025 and beyond) is engendered in a reusable Hypersonic Cruise Vehicle (HCV)."

> This autonomous aircraft would be capable of taking off from a conventional military runway and striking targets nine thousand nautical miles distant in less than two hours. It could carry a twelve-thousand-pound payload consisting of Common Aero Vehicles (CAVs), cruise missiles, small-diameter bombs, or other munitions. This HCV will provide the country dominant capability to wage a sustained campaign from CONUS on an array of time-critical targets that are both large in number and diverse in nature.[27]

Hypersonic Cruise Vehicles may be designed, developed, and deployed in time and under budget. But don't count on it. The whole FALCON business may turn out to be something like the endless quest to achieve useful quantities of electricity from nuclear fusion—a goal forever receding forty years into the future.

Even if built, a Hypersonic Cruise Vehicle would not qualify as a true "space" weapon. It would fly high and fast, touching the lower edge of space, but it would not itself achieve orbit. Rather, it would be a component in a "system of systems," a buzz phrase endlessly repeated by high-ranking military officers and think tankers, including space warriors. Hypersonic Cruise Vehicles would be ferries and their cargo could be weapons—hypersonic cruise missiles, the newest generations of "smart" bombs or other munitions. It could also carry our old friend, the Common Aero Vehicle.

Common Aero Vehicles, which do not yet exist anywhere except in the fertile imagination of space warriors, are among the coolest machines in the phantasmal space arsenal. Lance Lord, who then headed Air Force Space Command, said in 2005 that CAVs would have

> an incredible capability to provide the warfighter with a global reach capability against high payoff targets.
>
> The Common Aero Vehicle matched to a responsive launch platform would provide a truly transformational capability to anywhere in the world regardless of the level of access. The Common Aero Ve-

hicle capability could…deliver a conventional payload precisely on target within minutes of a valid command and control release order. This is the type of Prompt Global Strike I have identified as a top priority for our space and missile force.[28]

Congress has never been as enamored of the Common Aero Vehicle concept as has Air Force Space Command. Democrats and even some Republicans have expressed strong reservations now and then regarding the actual deployment of weapons in space, and that includes CAVs. In agreeing on a funding package for the FALCON/Common Aero Vehicle program in 2004, House/Senate conferees said they were "concerned that safeguards are not in place to guarantee that nations possessing nuclear weapons capabilities would not misinterpret the intent or use of the FALCON/CAV programs."

Therefore, the funds provided herein are for the development of hypersonic technologies for *non-weapons related research*, such as micro-satellite or other satellite launch requirements and other purposes as listed under the conferees recommendations. *The conferees direct that none of the funds provided in this Act may be used to develop, integrate, or test a CAV variant that includes any nuclear or conventional weapon.* The conferees further direct that none of the funds provided in this Act may be used to develop, integrate, or test a CAV for launch on any Intercontinental Ballistic Missile or Submarine Launched Ballistic Missile. The Committees on Appropriations *will consider expanding the scope of this program in subsequent years if safeguards negotiated among our international partners have been put in place.*[29] (Italics added.)

Two different concerns are expressed here. The first is general wariness about inserting weapons into orbital space. That concern is based on a not unreasonable fear that weapons in space would trigger a new arms race. The second concern is that Russia or China might mistake the launch of Common Aerial Vehicles as a nuclear attack. Space warriors have a host of ideas for allaying this second fear, such as basing launch facilities for CAVs in locations far removed from American intercontinental ballistic missile fields. For now, there is a moratorium on developing a Common Aero Vehicle as a space weapon.

But the main issue may be cost; even space warriors concede that basing Common Aero Vehicles in space would be frightfully expensive and therefore more than a little foolish. The preferred mode would be to use them as "pop-ups"—CAVs would be deployed only when needed. They would be fired into the lower reaches of space only to be called down immediately to their targets, much like intercontinental ballistic missiles.

The difference, though, is that ICBM warheads cannot be guided once they reenter the atmosphere. In theory, Common Aero Vehicles would be highly maneuverable in the atmosphere, something like the classic space-bomber concept that certain Air Force visionaries have dreamed of since the close of World War II. Munitions carried by CAVs would be able to strike their aimpoints within a few yards or even feet, according to space-warrior theory.

Air Force Space Command has spoken less freely of Common Aero Vehicles since congressional testimony by SpaceCom's Lance Lord triggered news stories in the spring of 2005. The *Washington Post* headlined Walter Pincus's article, "Pentagon Has Far-Reaching Defense Spacecraft in Works: Bush Administration Looking to Space to Fight Threats." The *New York Times* called its later story by Tim Weiner, "Air Force Seeks Bush's Approval for Space Weapons Programs." As one might imagine, space warriors generally regarded these stories as inflammatory.[30]

NO KEYS TO THE VAULT

Cost is now the central issue in the space-warrior world. Many of their schemes are so fantastic as to be doomed to fall of their own weight. Every military system in space is outrageously expensive, a fact of life space warriors increasingly acknowledge. If a given military mission can be accomplished by a terrestrial system, goes the rule of thumb, go with it.

The Government Accountability Office (known before 2004 as the General Accounting Office) has repeatedly found that cost overruns on military-oriented space hardware—mainly observation, communications, radar, and geo-positioning systems—to be both routine and substantial. In July 2005, a top analyst at the GAO testified before Congress: "There is a vast difference between the Department of Defense's budgeting plans and the reality of its space systems. Over the next ten years, space systems, each year, on average, will cost DoD in excess of $1.5 billion more than it originally planned.... This means there is $1.5 billion less that DoD has to spend on other priorities annually and tens of billions less available for DoD's overall weapons portfolio over time."[31]

At a time when routine defense-related appropriations (including funds provided to the Energy Department for nuclear weapons work) are closing in on $500 billion a year, $1.5 billion may seem paltry. In the context of the overall federal budget, which is now in the $3 trillion range, military-space costs have not been budget breakers.[32]

The total cost for space systems development and procurement has yet to reach the $10 billion-a-year mark. Beyond that, much of the space-control effort is tucked away in the National Missile Defense budget, which for Fiscal Year 2007 was a little over $10 billion.[33] And, of course, there is always the top secret "black" budget, which you and I—as well as most members of Congress—are not privy to.[34]

With remarkable irony, Donald Rumsfeld, who for many years was the prince of space warriors, contributed to the temporary derailing of some of the long-range plans space warriors had for developing and deploying space dominance hardware at a relatively early date. The war-of-choice invasion of Iraq, which Rumsfeld did herculean work to promote and make happen, slammed the Pentagon with huge unbudgeted costs—at this writing, somewhere in the neighborhood of $500 billion-plus. Given that unexpected hit, a host of expensive high-tech programs cherished by the Army, Navy, Marines, and Air Force have been scaled down, delayed, or killed.

Robert S. Dudney, editor of *Air Force Magazine*, commented in the August 2006 issue that the "armed forces are entering what officers believe will be the bleakest period of fiscal belt-tightening in a decade.... The Air Force, as a result, should prepare itself for budget combat. Apparently, it is doing so. One operations officer at Air Force headquarters, Maj. Gen. Roger W. Burg, recently declared, 'The Air Staff is focused on one thing, and it's spelled c-u-t-s.'"[35] The cuts would be in traditional "air-breathing" aircraft programs as well as space programs.

In commenting on the president's proposed Fiscal 2008 budget, the *Wall Street Journal*, which usually takes a congenial line toward space-warrior projects, headlined a story, "Pentagon Lowers Space Horizons: Satellite Effort Is Likely to Face Budget Pressures." The story, by Andy Pasztor, spoke of how the Defense Department budget proposal would "generally rein in spending on space programs—previously one of the fastest-growing defense segments—partly by slashing funding and slowing development of the military's most advanced satellite communications system, according to industry and government officials."

> The move highlights how funding for various space programs is being curtailed partly to help pay the bills for the conflicts in Iraq and Afghanistan.
>
> The tighter lid on space budgets is expected to affect a range of programs, from space-borne radar initiatives to ground-based technology to track foreign satellites and orbiting debris. At the same time, Pentagon planners face escalating pressure to find interim solutions to boost space-based communications and surveillance capabilities, ranging from expanded leasing of commercial capacity in orbit to stepped-up procurement of existing military-satellite hardware.[36]

Spending levels on space-dominance programs, such as those noted by the *Journal*, were already modest in the grand scheme of things, even if one includes the closely related spending on the variegated missile defense programs. But if the United States should opt to pursue and deploy an all-out space-dominance policy, including space-based weapons, it would enter new and unexplored cost territory. None of us, space warriors included, could predict the long-range economic implications of that.[37]

In addition, the struggle to keep the economy healthy while attempting to meet domestic needs and entitlements will mean the Defense Department no longer will have the keys to the vault, as was generally the case during the Cold War. The Defense Department inevitably will remain the most powerful player in the federal budget battle. Sooner rather than later, though, it will have to figure out how to maintain full-spectrum dominance without breaking the bank. Expensive and exotic new space Common Aero Vehicle-type hardware may not be the Defense Department's first choice. Right now, the first choice appears to be ASATs.

FIRST, A REALITY CHECK

Space historian Dwayne A. Day began an opinion piece for the May 23, 2005 issue of *The Space Review*, an online publication, by quoting Gen. Thomas S. Power, the one-time head of the old Strategic Air Command

and one of the most demented guys ever to wear four stars on an American uniform.[38] According to Day, Power wrote the following in a secret 1962 telex explaining why the Air Force needed a manned nuclear-powered space bomber:

> [The] basic strategic space requirement is for a manned strike force that is highly survivable, capable of sustained operation, independent of Earth support during periods of hostilities, subject to assured positive command and control at all levels of operations before, during, and after initial strike, and capable of delivering weapons with precision and discrimination in the face of any conceivable defense in the period under question.

The space bomber General Power envisioned was not approved by his Air Force superiors or by the Secretary of Defense. That, however, was not Day's point. Rather, his essay zeroed in on the "overheated warrior rhetoric" (such as that offered by Power) that has always existed in the U.S. Air Force when it came to space programs.[39]

> Unfortunately, a lot of people…fall for the rhetoric with regularity. The press reports these speeches and the occasional wild study as if they represent real Pentagon plans. Conservatives believe that if an Air Force general states the need for an antisatellite weapon or an expensive piece of hardware it must be vital. Moreover, so-called "peace and justice" groups claim that the sky is falling and that we are about to enter the era of space militarization. The gulf between rhetoric and reality is filled with a lot of clueless people.

In fact, Day added, "One could assemble a pretty neat comic book containing all of these over-ambitious, unaffordable, or just plain unnecessary military space weapons systems" that Air Force generals have insisted over the decades are vital to preserving democracy.

> But the hidden story behind all of these plans is that over a period of time support for space programs, particularly space weapons, faded from the upper echelons of the Air Force.
>
> A former civilian Air Force chief scientist once remarked that one of his jobs consisted of serving as a reality check for goofy proposals from Air Force Space Command, like using lasers to blow up tanks.…

The problem is that most of the programs in rhetorical military space do not abide by the laws of physics, few of them abide by the laws of bureaucratic and international affairs, and none of them abide by the laws of fiscal reality.

Day is squarely on target. There is a profound disconnect between what the most ardent space warriors want and that which might be possible in the real world. But there is a twist. Although no one can predict whether the wishes of today's space warriors will ever be endorsed by an American president and funded by Congress, however fantastic their ideas may be, they still have consequences.

What leader of a reasonably powerful state, such as China, could safely dismiss America's "overheated warrior rhetoric?" When America's space warriors speak of developing and deploying a space-control capability as well as space-related weapons, can they be ignored?[40]

During the Cold War, America's defense planners were inclined to take Soviet rhetoric and boasts as gospel, as if the Soviet Union was overflowing with military supermen and technological geniuses. In 1981, the Reagan Pentagon began issuing a series of glossy booklets filled with ominous text, graphs, fanciful illustrations, and retouched photos, all to demonstrate how extraordinarily powerful the Soviet Union was and why it was a continuing threat to the very existence of the United States.

The ninth edition of *Soviet Military Power* was issued in September 1990. The foreword, which carried the name of Defense Secretary Dick Cheney, noted that many changes were then occurring in the Soviet Union. And yet, "prudence demands that we focus on the most dangerous challenge to our national security. The military might of the Soviet Union is enormous and remains targeted on the United States and our allies. *All evidence indicates that this fact will not change.*" (Italics added.)

Two months after those words were written, the Berlin Wall was hacked to pieces and the Soviet Union began to crumble. At the end of 1991, the Soviet flag was lowered for the last time. This is not said to hammer Cheney—but the point is that the nine-volume *Soviet Military Power* series is just one more testament to the fact that defense planners everywhere seem genetically predisposed to devising (if not embroidering) worst-case scenarios.

A man who understood the power of worst-case scenarios better than most was George Lee Butler, a quintessential nuclear-weapons insider. Butler wore four stars when he retired in 1994 after thirty-three years in the Air Force. He had taught nuclear strategy at the Air Force Academy in his younger years; worked on nuclear policy at the Pentagon; and commanded a nuclear-armed B-52 wing, logging three thousand flying hours.

Later he was director of plans and policy for the Joint Chiefs of Staff and, later still, director of the Joint Strategic Target Planning Group, the organization that prepared America's nuclear-war options. Butler capped his military career as commander-in-chief of Strategic Air Command and as the first commander-in-chief of StratCom, SAC's successor.

A couple of years after retiring, the general became a nuclear abolitionist. He could think more objectively about the madness of it all after the Cold War had ended. "The moment I entered the nuclear arena," he said in a 1998 speech at the National Press Club, "I knew I had been thrust into a world beset with tidal forces, towering egos, maddening contradictions, alien constructs, and insane risks."

> Its arcane vocabulary and apocalyptic calculus defied comprehension. Its stage was global and its antagonists locked in a deadly spiral of deepening rivalry. In every respect, it was a modern day holy war, a cosmic struggle between the forces of light and darkness. The stakes were national survival, and the weapons of choice were eminently suited to this scale of malevolence. The opposing forces each created vast enterprises, each giving rise to a culture of messianic believers infused with a sense of historic mission and schooled in unshakable articles of faith.[41]

An arms race in space would not be as bad as the Cold War rivalry described by General Butler, but it could still be a very nasty thing.

As for the ability to deliver a prompt global strike—that is a real U.S. doctrine that could be carried out, if necessary, by long-range missiles, hypersonic cruise missiles, and stealth bombers such as the B-2. But prompt global strike from *space*? The United States is not likely to have that capability in the near future. But when planners in China and elsewhere read documents such as the *Nuclear Posture Review* and Air Force Space Command's series of master plans, how can they be sure?

The United States and the Soviet Union ratcheted up the Cold War year after year because defense planners in each nation thought the other side was either ahead or threatening to pull ahead. Following that pattern, other nations, particularly China, are likely to assume the worst about America's military plans for space. If the United States talks about unilateral space dominance, the leaders of at least a few nations will believe that it actually may be achievable, and they will try to stop it by developing their own antisatellite weapons.

DEFENSIVE AND OFFENSIVE COUNTERSPACE

I have not written much about lasers based in space, or space-based microwave weapons, or electromagnetic-pulse weapons, and so on—the bread-and-butter of peace activists who believe that space warriors are out of control and space warfare is just over the horizon. These exotic weapons concepts seem to me, as well as to many space warriors, to be little more than fantasies in the current cost-constricted environment. These days, the only potential space-to-Earth weapon that space warriors seem to take seriously is the Common Aero Vehicle, and even it would be developed as a "pop-up," not as a weapon that would be based in space. But that does not mean space warriors are not working tirelessly on space-dominance weapons.

The ability to control space in a time of conflict lies at the heart of space dominance, and the space-warrior community is well along in developing antisatellite weapons. China's ASAT test in January 2007 was a disaster, a device that left in its wake a literal ton of debris. Many more "tests" like that and low-orbit space will be useless to all nations.

U.S. space warriors moved beyond the debris issue more than two decades ago when the Air Force's miniature kinetic-kill vehicle demolished the Solwind satellite. Although that test created a large amount of debris, Solwind was in a lower orbit than the Chinese satellite, which meant the debris was subject to some degree of atmospheric drag and had settled out by 2002. The debris created by the Chinese test will circle the Earth for a much longer period.

Meanwhile, America's defensive and offensive "counterspace" program, unmatched by any other nation, is perking along nicely. *Counterspace Operations*, an Air Force doctrinal document issued in August 2004, is must reading for anyone who wants to explore space dominance and how the United States plans to achieve it.[42]

Chapter Four of *Counterspace* lists the many satellite defensive measures the United States is working on, including "camouflage, concealment, and deception, hardening of systems, and the use of dispersal." Camouflage, concealment, and deception means hiding satellite ground stations and telemetry uplinks and downlinks.

System hardening would help protect the electronic innards of satellites from electromagnetic-pulse radiation. Physical hardening of ground-based facilities is also called for. "Robust networks" —the Defense Department loves the adjective, "robust"— "hardened by equipment redundancy and the ability to reroute, ensure operation during and after information-operations attack."

Dispersal means that satellites can be deployed "into various orbital altitudes and planes." Terrestrial nodes could be spread out by "deploying mobile ground stations to new locations." Though the use of mobile technology is expanding, *Counterspace* later says, "many of today's ground-based systems are not mobile, making physical security measures essential."

Run-and-hide in space would be an option, too. America's "satellites may be capable of maneuvering in orbit to deny the adversary the opportunity to track and target them. They may be repositioned to avoid directed-energy attacks, electromagnetic jamming, or kinetic attacks from antisatellite weapons." The ability to maneuver, however, is "limited by on-board fuel constraints, orbital mechanics, and advanced warning of an impending attack."

America's space-based and terrestrial nodes, *Counterspace* says, could use "different modes of operation" to flummox adversaries. "Examples include changing radio-frequency amplitude and employing frequency-hopping techniques to complicate jamming."

And then, there is *offensive* counterspace. For a decade, space warriors have referred to the various kinds of possible attacks on the adversary's space assets as the "Five Ds": deception, disruption, denial, degradation, and destruction.

Offensive techniques could include illuminating the spy satellites of a nosy nation with a ground-based laser to "deny, disrupt, degrade, or destroy" the satellite's optical sensors. The prevailing belief among space warriors is that "dazzling" an optical sensor may be the best way to go in certain cases because it is a "reversible effect" that does not permanently damage the sensor.

Reversible effects are thought to be useful if the adversary nation is simply sparring rather than fighting. Dazzling is less likely to lead to escalation than would the permanent blinding of the other guy's satellite. Further, the owner of the satellite may not even know it has been dazzled; if optical sensors fail, it could be because of other reasons. And it is much easier to dazzle a sensor than to destroy it. Permanently damaging a sensor with a tightly focused laser requires locking in on the fast-moving satellite for a longer time, and in the end it may not be technologically possible given atmospheric turbulence.

Another way to get rid of a satellite, says *Counterspace*, is simply to smash it with a kinetic-kill weapon. As noted a moment ago, that course is not favored by America's space warriors because it causes debris—debris that could threaten the satellites of the United States and its friends and allies.

Radio-frequency and laser-communications nodes—ground stations, uplinks and downlinks, and satellite-to-satellite nodes—can be attacked. "Most space systems" *Counterspace* dryly notes, "are ineffective without communication links."

Launch facilities are excellent targets; they represent a "primary choke-point for interdicting an adversary's efforts to augment or reconstitute space forces."

Earth-based military command, control, communication, computer, intelligence, surveillance, and reconnaissance systems are also potential targets. "Destruction of such systems," *Counterspace* says with some understatement, "would substantially reduce the enemy's capability to detect, react, and bring forces to bear against friendly forces."

"An adversary may gain significant space capabilities by using third-party space systems," says *Counterspace*. "Using diplomatic or economic means to deny an adversary access to these third-party (commercial or foreign) space capabilities will generally require the assistance of other U.S. governmental agencies." Translation: Parties not involved in a conflict might not be altogether willing to cooperate with the U.S. military. That's why the good Lord gave America the State Department.

ON THE ATTACK

This discussion has been largely theoretical—a highly truncated summary of current doctrine. The fundamental question is this: Is the United States working on hardware that could actually attack the satellites of other nations? The answer is yes.

In October 1997, the Army fired its ground-based Mid-Infrared Advanced Chemical Laser (MIRACL) at a nearly defunct Air Force satellite.[43]

The results of the test are not fully known to people who lack the proper security credentials. But it was undeniably a preliminary test of a possible antisatellite weapon.[44] The Pentagon continues to refine ground-based antisatellite lasers, principally with work on "adaptive" optics. While it is possible to "illuminate" a satellite in orbit, one needs a more tightly focused laser beam to do any real damage. Given the turbulence of the atmosphere, which scatters laser beams, correcting for that will not be easy. Will adaptive optics actually enable laser beams to reach satellites in highly concentrated form? Maybe, maybe not. The jury is out on that one, and maybe deadlocked.[45]

If fully developed—a very large "if"—ground-based lasers could attack satellites in low-Earth orbit, but satellites in higher orbits would be well beyond range. Not to worry. Space warriors seem to have other plans for these high-flying satellites. First, consider this from a background paper prepared for the Space Commission:

> Advances in miniaturization and the proliferation of space technologies enable many countries to enter space with small, lightweight, inexpensive and highly capable systems that can perform a variety of missions. Included in this list of missions is *counterspace operations*, such as long-duration-orbital inspection and intercept.…
>
> Microsatellites can perform satellite inspection, imaging and other functions and *could be adapted as weapons*. Placed on an interception course and programmed to hone-in [sic] on a satellite, a microsatellite could fly alongside a target until commanded to disrupt, and then disable or destroy the target. Detection of and defense against such an attack would be difficult.[46] (Italics added).

As Tom Wilson, the paper's author, suggested, microsatellite work is also being done elsewhere. The University of Surrey in England, the pioneer in microsatellite research, is a global leader in selling low-cost scientific satellites to other nations, including China.[47] But the most technologically advanced microsatellites almost surely bear the made-in-USA label.

American research into microsatellite technologies, most of which is classified, has intriguing program designations: XSS, or Experimental Satellite System; DART, or Demonstrator to Test Future Autonomous Rendezvous Technologies in Orbit; MiTEx, or the Micro-satellite Technology Experiment; ANGELS, or Autonomous Nanosatellite Guardian for Evaluating Local Space; and the Orbital Express Space Operations Architecture program.[48]

These are disparate but related experimental programs that are variously overseen by DARPA, the Air Force Research Laboratory, Air Force Space Command, NASA, and a variety of aerospace contractors. The common goal is to develop small satellites that can autonomously find and rendezvous with satellites already in orbit—that is, get up close and personal with orbiting satellites with little or no direction from ground controllers.

The DART mission in April 2005 was so successful in locating its target that it accidentally ran into it. DART was supposed to come within a hundred meters of its target and then stay with it for a while. Instead, the spacecraft knocked its target—a "retired" communication satellite launched by DARPA in 1999—into a slightly higher orbit.[49]

Bumping into the target instead of simply coming close would seem vaguely comical if not for the weapons implications. All of the organizations involved in testing these devices say that their principal purpose is to develop technologies to robotically find, refuel, service, and even repair satellites in orbit. That sounds like a good thing. The ability to refuel and service and even repair satellites could potentially prolong the lives of these machines, some of which are hugely expensive. (America's most advanced surveillance satellites are said to be in the billion-dollar-plus range.)

Another purpose of the experiments is to develop the technology needed to get close enough to other nations' satellites to inspect them. That would come in handy if the United States ever had reason to believe that Country X had put a weapon into orbit. The United States has people who are pretty good at figuring out the function of a satellite in orbit if they get a good close look at it. Further, American microsats are so small as to be stealthy; the United States could presumably inspect a satellite without Country X knowing it.

Now consider for a moment what an ideal space-based antisatellite weapon would be like. First, it would be small enough to be stealthy. Second, it would have the ability to get very close to the target satellite, even close enough to touch it. Finally, it would have the onboard means to negatively affect the operation of the target satellite—jamming its radio-frequency telemetry, perhaps, or coating its optical sensors with paint, or "tugging" it into a useless orbit with a mylar net, or frying its electronic innards with a non-nuclear electromagnetic burst, or simply by ramming it hard enough to damage or destroy it, but not hard enough to pulverize it.

A microsatellite might even fire off a small explosive charge while in orbit next to the target. Satellites are delicate creatures, easily damaged, and it would not take much of a charge to disable a satellite, while creating only minimal debris. As the Space Commission's Tom Wilson aptly said, micro-sats *can* be adapted as weapons.[50]

Is the United States developing a highly sophisticated antisatellite system capable, in theory, of reaching satellites in *any* orbit? That's a matter of conjecture. There is no smoking gun, at least in the non-classified world. But in view of America's stated doctrine of full spectrum dominance in all things military, in view of its plans to develop a prompt global-strike capability, in view of its elaborate and sophisticated counterspace doctrine, and in view of its stated intent to develop and deploy a space-control capability, it would not be surprising, would it?

6

Put to the Sword

On the eve of the American-led invasion of Iraq in 2003, Marc Ash, editor of Truthout, a liberal-left web site, wrote an impassioned editorial. George W. Bush and Tony Blair were planning, he said, "the greatest act of human slaughter since Pol Pot and the Khmer Rouge orchestrated the Cambodian genocide in the mid-1970s." Pol Pot and the Khmer Rouge, Ash added, had killed "some 1.5 to 2 million largely defenseless and quite peaceful Cambodians."

> Civilian Iraq is utterly defenseless and totally unprepared for the carnage that is about to be visited upon them. It is murder plain and simple, murder on an unimaginable scale.
>
> There is no "war" looming, no "conflict" with Iraq, and no "stand-off." What exists is a vast military force poised to inflict death and destruction on a major population center. Those who live there will attempt to defend themselves, but they will fail, and the dead will cover the ground like a fallen forest.
>
> Should this act of insanity proceed, it will stand as one of the greatest crimes against humanity ever recorded.[1]

Ash was wrong. George W. Bush and Tony Blair were not planning mass murder. Neither were U.S. military forces. To even suggest that the many Iraqi deaths of the last four years would be a direct result of the acts of the allied forces would be a grotesque misunderstanding of events. Ash's assessment is a near-perfect example of how some peace activists (among others) have failed to take note of the radical changes in American military capabilities over the last several decades.

The twenty-first-century edition of America's armed forces can fight conventional wars just as effectively and lethally as ever, yet spare civilians to a degree never before thought possible. Space hardware, information technology, focused brainpower, and systematic "lessons learned" programs are keys to a new American way of war. There has been a "revolution in military affairs," just as military analysts have been saying for years, and the United States leads that revolution by a huge margin.

The Bush administration's road to war against Saddam Hussein was colored by the assumption that America's space-dependent precision weapons would produce few Iraqi civilian casualties relative to the size of the task—conquering a large and well-armed nation headed by a ruthless dictator. Further, the Bush administration was concerned with a range of humanitarian issues related to the invasion.[2]

If the Bush administration had known from the get-go that the invasion would produce tens of thousands of Iraqi civilian deaths, it would likely have been far more reluctant to go to war. The blowback would have been staggering. Anger in the Arab and Islamic worlds, in the European nations, in Russia and China, and nearly everywhere else would have been overwhelming. The administration's calculus leading up to the invasion was that space-enabled precision warfare would ensure a quick, easy, and relatively clean outcome. In early March 2003, according to Bob Woodward's *Plan of Attack*, Secretary of Defense Rumsfeld called seven of his key people together. He asked them to assess how long the war would last. The estimates ranged from a week to a month.[3]

The aftermath of the invasion would be wholly positive, the administration believed. Admiring world leaders would applaud; the United States would have removed a madman from the global stage at minimal human cost. Iraqis would dance in the streets, giddy with their newfound freedom and eager for democracy. Authoritarian Arab regimes would take note of America's righteous might and unswerving determination and begin instituting democratic reforms in their respective states. Persian Iran would be intimidated and North Korea's Kim Il Jung would be cowed.

Most Americans now understand that such ideologically driven assumptions were dead wrong. (The role of "exceptionalist" ideology in foreign policy as well as in space policy is explored in Chapter Fourteen.) More pointedly, many astute observers of American foreign policy knew the administration's assumptions were wrong-headed long before the actual invasion. James Webb, secretary of the Navy in the Reagan administration and now a Democratic senator from Virginia, wrote this in a September 4, 2002 op-ed in the *Washington Post*:

> The issue before us is not simply whether the United States should end the regime of Saddam Hussein, but whether we as a nation are prepared to physically occupy territory in the Middle East for the next 30 to 50 years. Those who are pushing for a unilateral war in Iraq know full well that there is no exit strategy if we invade and stay. This reality was the genesis of a rift that goes back to the Gulf War itself, when neoconservatives were vocal in their calls for "a MacArthurian regency in Baghdad." Their expectation is that the United States would not only change Iraq's regime but also remain as a long-term occupation force in an attempt to reconstruct Iraqi society itself.

After the American-led invasion of Iraq began in March 2003, Defense Department spokesmen emphasized in daily briefings that coalition forces were taking precautions to minimize civilian casualties. A comprehensive Human Rights Watch investigation confirmed those assertions, especially in regard to air strikes. "Coalition forces took significant steps to protect civilians during the air war, including increased use of precision-guided munitions when attacking targets situated in populated areas and generally careful target selection."

Bombs were dropped whenever possible, the Human Rights Watch report said, "when civilians were less likely to be on the streets, using penetrator munitions and delayed fuzes to ensure that most blast and fragmentation damage was kept within the impact area, and using attack angles that took into account the location of civilian facilities such as schools and hospitals." In contrast, the report condemned hasty, jury-rigged bombing strikes designed to kill senior Iraqi leaders. There were fifty acknowledged air strikes against "leadership" targets, including Saddam Hussein. All failed. "While they did not kill a single targeted individual, the strikes killed and injured dozens of civilians."[4]

Although 29,199 bombs were dropped during the invasion, the majority of noncombatant civilian deaths during the "major combat phase" were attributed to ground combat in urban areas, according to Human Rights Watch. And many of those deaths were caused, at least in part, by Iraqi tactics employed to minimize America's high-tech advantage.

The investigation showed that Iraqi forces committed a number of violations of international humanitarian law, which may have led to significant civilian casualties. These violations included the use of human shields, abuse of the Red Cross and Red Crescent emblems, use of antipersonnel landmines, location of military objects in [legally] protected places (such as mosques, hospitals, and cultural property), and a failure to take adequate precautions to protect civilians from the dangers of military operations. The Iraqi military's practice of wearing civilian clothes tended to erode the distinction between combatants and civilians, putting the latter at risk, although it did not relieve Coalition forces of their obligation to distinguish at all times between combatants and civilians and to target only combatants.[5]

During combat in March and April 2003, American and British forces fought a high-tech conventional war according to the highest standards of the military art, employing precision weaponry wherever possible. With few exceptions, Anglo-American forces operated in a manner calculated to spare the lives of noncombatant civilians. The other side, however, did not always fight according to Anglo-American rules, particularly after the major combat phase ended and low-intensity guerrilla war began. Precision weaponry is much less valuable when the other side is engaged in guerrilla operations, especially in urban areas.

For a moment, recall George W. Bush's televised "Mission Accomplished" speech delivered on May 1, 2003 from the flight deck of the aircraft carrier *Abraham Lincoln* loitering off the coast of San Diego. "In the battle of Iraq, the United States and our allies have prevailed.... Now our coalition is engaged in securing and reconstructing that country.[6] By May 2007, four years after the president's triumphal speech, at least seventy thousand Iraqi citizens had died, deaths caused by the American response to guerrilla tactics as well as by the seemingly endless acts of violence employed by insurrectionists and fanatical Islamists.[7] The U.S. population is roughly eleven times that of Iraq's. Seventy thousand Iraqi deaths would be the equivalent of more than seven hundred thousand deaths inside the United States.

Iraq disintegrated into brutal civil war, and the discomfiting fact remains: Suicide bombers and hide-in-the-shadows fighters were a predictable byproduct of the American-led invasion. Ironically, though, the invasion would not have occurred if not for the availability of space-enabled precision weapons that seemed to guarantee a speedy, conclusive, and nearly bloodless outcome.

The fact that U.S. forces are capable of conducting precision, civilian-sparing *conventional* warfare when called upon to fight seems like a moral plus—if, to echo Shakespeare, the cause be just and the "quarrel honorable."[8] For some eighty years, many of America's leading airmen have been wedded to the idea that precision airpower could make warfare more humane. Today, an analogous idea animates space warriors.

THE HAMMER IS IN OUR HANDS

In *Thus Spake Zarathustra*, published in the mid-1880s, Friedrich Nietzche asked: "And if man were to learn to fly—woe, *to what heights* would his rapaciousness fly."[9] The twentieth century provided the answer.

By the fall of 1914, Europe was at war, and British, French, and German airmen began dropping bombs on enemy troops. "We took to bombing with enthusiasm," a British officer later recalled, "although we may now wonder what good we thought we were doing." These early efforts were hopelessly inaccurate but also dangerous for the airmen. In February 1915, the Royal Flying Corps recommended releasing bombs from five hundred feet in order to get bombs within fifty yards of a target. At that height, rifle fire could bring an airplane down.[10]

Whether effective or not, the bombs were generally directed toward clear-cut military targets. But that soon changed. The long-dreaded Zeppelin raids against Britain began on January 19, 1915. One of the three airships turned back because of engine trouble; the remaining two dropped bombs on towns on the southeastern coast of England, killing twenty-four people. Although facilities directly related to the war effort were targeted, they were seldom damaged because they were seldom found. Or, if found, the bombs simply missed. That established a bombing pattern that would persist throughout the Great War—and which would be repeated on a far greater scale in World War II, Korea, and Vietnam.

Zeppelins, being large and slow targets for anti-aircraft guns, visited the British Isles under cover of darkness. On the night of January 31, 1916, for instance, Zeppelin L21 (585 feet long, 61 feet in diameter) was searching for the militarily important port of Liverpool. Instead, it dropped its bombs by mistake on several towns in the West Midlands, many miles from Liverpool. The captain of the Zeppelin was hopelessly lost. Early in the twentieth century, before lights in rural areas became commonplace, swaths of unlighted countryside could be mistaken at high altitudes for bodies of water; lighted rural towns on the edge of dark voids could be interpreted as seaports.

On that night in Wednesbury, Mrs. Joseph Smith, of 14 King Street, heard explosions shortly after 9 p.m. She left her house and ran into the street to see what was happening. Upon returning home, she found that her house had been destroyed and her husband, her thirteen-year-old daughter, and her eleven-year-old son, had been killed. Her youngest girl, Ina, seven years old, was missing. Her body was found the next day on the roof of a nearby factory. In all, thirty-five civilians were killed that night.[11]

"You must not suppose that we set out to kill women and children," said a Zeppelin commander captured by the British. "We have higher military aims. You would not find one officer in the German army or navy who would go to war to kill women and children. Such things happen accidentally in war."[12]

Over the long run, the Zeppelin raids caused little physical damage and few casualties. In 51 raids, 196 tons of bombs killed 557 people and injured 1,358.[13] As militarily futile as the raids were, a precedent had been set. Although the German high command intended to bomb war-related targets, they were not averse to killing a few civilians. Civilian deaths, they believed, would cause panic and demoralize the population, which would then press the government to sue for peace. *Schrecklichkeit*—acts of "frightfulness"— would paralyze the enemy's will to resist.[14]

On May 25, 1917, the Germans turned to the Gotha bomber, a biplane with a forty-foot fuselage and a seventy-eight-foot wingspan. Its two Mercedes engines could propel the machine to a speed of eighty miles an hour. The Gotha had a range of five hundred miles and it could drop bombs from a height of fourteen thousand feet. In December 1917, a handful of *Riesenflugzeug* or "Giant" bombers joined the Gothas in raids on England. The Giant was a biplane with a wingspan just three feet shorter than the World War II B-29, and it carried a crew of five to seven, depending on the mission. It bristled with defensive machine guns.

As with the Zeppelin raids, the Gothas and the Giants had little military effect, but they killed civilians. That did not altogether displease the

German High Command. The British, after all, had established a naval blockade that was bringing hardship, malnutrition, disease, and death to hundreds of thousands of German civilians. "The German people, under pressure of English starvation and the war, has become a hard race with an iron fist," said a warning from the German government. "The hammer is in our hands, and it will fall mercilessly and shatter the place where England is forging weapons against us."[15]

In twenty-seven Gotha and Giant raids, 835 people were killed and 1,972 injured.[16] That was hardly enough to destroy British home front morale, although the raids caused anxiety, occasional panic, and considerable anger. But the raids impressed Winston Churchill, then a key minister in the Lloyd George government. In the next great war, Churchill said, Britain would wield the hammer.

> We are sure that if, after a prolonged spell of peace, war on a great scale suddenly broke out again, the Power which had made the most intensive study of aerial warfare would start with an enormous initial advantage, and the Power that neglected this form of active defence might well find itself fatally situated.
>
> Proceeding on this assumption, we contend that the British policy is to develop the independent conception of the air as an art, an arm, and a service; and that this method alone will secure the qualitative ascendancy and superiority which the safety of the country requires.[17]

A FEELING OF IMMINENT DEATH

Many thousands of aircraft were ultimately involved in the Great War; nevertheless, airpower did not play a decisive role. The second decade of the twentieth century was the age of ground- and sea-based industrial war. Machine guns, barbed wire, shrapnel-filled artillery shells, poison gas, and submarines were the engines of mass destruction, not aircraft.

No one knows how many men in uniform died in the Great War of 1914–1918, partly because it is impossible to get a grip on carnage on such a vast scale and partly because it is not easy to separate combat deaths from those caused by diseases directly related to combat conditions. The 1980 edition of *Encyclopaedia Britannica* estimates that of the sixty-five million men mobilized, about eight and a half million died as a result of combat. Another twenty-one million men were wounded. Similarly, no one knows how many civilians died of hunger and disease, mainly because of the British naval blockade of Germany, but estimates start at about a million and range upward.

Ernest Hemingway captured the madness of the war in his novel of love, death, and disillusion, *A Farewell to Arms*, published in 1929. At one point, Henry, an American ambulance driver on the Italian front, recalls how he put a log on a campfire one night. The log was full of ants. As the log began to burn, "the ants swarmed out and went first toward the center where the fire was; then turned back and ran toward the end. When there were enough on the end they fell off into the fire."

Henry watched for a time, thinking that it was the end of the world for the ants but "a splendid chance to be a messiah and lift the log off the fire and throw it out where the ants could get off onto the ground." Instead, he threw a cup of water on the log so he could use it for whisky. "I think the cup of water on the burning log only steamed the ants."[18]

Like Hemingway, many airmen involved in the war came to believe that mass slaughter in war, any war, was morally unacceptable. Unlike Hemingway, they could do something concrete about it; they could ensure that future wars would be fought more humanely. Never again, they thought, would nations throw millions of young men against wire, machine guns, shrapnel, and gas. The next war would be won in the air. Large, high-flying, long-range bombers would destroy the enemy's industrial capacity to fight, thus shortening wars and saving lives.

After the Armistice, the air services of the victorious nations were dismantled with startling speed and air-minded men everywhere were adrift on a sea of peace. Nonetheless, theoretical planning for the next great war proceeded among the most visionary of the air-minded men. It was an Italian, Giulio Douhet, who developed the first systematic theory of victory through airpower.

According to Douhet's seminal work, *Command of the Air*, published in 1921 and later amplified, the Great War had demonstrated that future great-power conflicts were likely to be total war. Defensive weapons had trumped offensive weapons. Artillery and machine guns made it easier to defend fortifications than to attack them.

In the next war, said Douhet, military aircraft would be decisive. Bombers would range far behind fortified defensive lines and strike at the enemy's vital centers, its industrialized cities. Noncombatant civilians in those cities would become targets—and properly so, according to Douhet. Modern wars were not fought solely by men in uniform. Food and weapons and munitions produced by civilians sustained war. Therefore, "the entire population and the resources of a nation" would be "sucked into the maw of war.... No longer can areas exist in which life can be lived in safety and tranquility, nor can the battlefield any longer be limited to actual combatants. On the contrary, the battlefield will be limited only by the boundaries of the nations at war, and all of their citizens will become combatants. There will be no distinction any longer between soldiers and civilians."[19]

The Great War had been so enormously destructive because it lasted so long, said Douhet. "The fighting was sporadic and drawn out over a long period of time, so [the belligerents] could replace their successive material and moral losses and go on throwing all their resources into the struggle until they were exhausted. Never, at any time during the war, was a deathblow struck—a blow which leaves a deep, gaping wound and the feeling of imminent death."[20]

Douhet consigned land and naval forces to the dustbin. Airpower would be *the* offensive weapon of the future. An independent air force would get the job done in days or weeks or months, possibly before an army could be mobilized or ships deployed. Long-range bombers would instill the feeling of imminent death. If an enemy attacked, retaliation should be swift, relentless, brutal. The enemy's cities must be bombarded with explosive, incendiary, and poison-gas bombs. Civilians must be killed and the survivors demoralized. Sooner rather than later, the survivors would force their governments to capitulate.

"What could happen to a single city in a single day could also happen to ten, twenty, fifty cities," he wrote. "What civil or military authority could keep order, public services functioning, and production going under such a threat? And even if a semblance of order was maintained and some work done, would not the sight of a single enemy plane be enough to stampede the population into panic?"[21]

Douhet believed he was serving humanity in advocating the incineration and gassing of civilians. While major conflicts were inevitable, his peace-through-death plan would at least make them brief: "Mercifully, the decision will be quick in this kind of war, since the decisive blows will be directed at civilians, that element of the countries at war least able to sustain them. These future wars may yet prove to be more humane than war in the past in spite of all, because they may in the long run shed less blood."[22]

A DISTINCT BENEFIT TO CIVILIZATION

Billy Mitchell, a flamboyant hero of the Great War, was the son of a U.S. senator and the grandson of a minor-league robber baron. He was wealthy, handsome, articulate, and charming, and he was well acquainted with Douhet and his theories. Mitchell had frequent conversations with the air-power partisan during a visit to Italy in 1922, and he possessed a synopsis of Douhet's *Command of the Air*.[23]

In Mitchell's day, the Air Service was part of the Army, and insofar as the Army's General Staff was concerned, its principal mission was to support ground troops in battle. Nonsense, said Mitchell, repeatedly and publicly. In future wars, air power must play the pivotal role. Land armies were in a "stage of arrested development" and surface navies were in a "period of de-cline," both throwbacks to a simpler age. Wars would now be decided in the air. "It is probable that future wars again will be conducted by a special class, the Air Force, as it was by the armored knights of the Middle Ages."[24]

Like Douhet, Mitchell's central belief was that bombing the enemy's vi-tal centers would "make the contest much sharper, more decisive, and more quickly finished." Unlike Douhet, Mitchell believed that air forces should not directly attack civilians; rather, airmen should go after the "means of making war." Bombers should "attack centers of production of all kinds, means of transportation, agricultural areas, ports and shipping." The intel-ligent application of airpower would result in "diminished loss of life and treasure and will thus be a distinct benefit to civilization."[25]

Sparing civilians was not, however, an absolute with Mitchell. Sooner or later, he believed, the United States would have to fight Japan. It was fortunate, he said, that Japan's densely populated cities were exceptionally vulnerable to air attack. "These towns are built largely of wood and paper to resist the devastations of earthquakes and form the greatest aerial targets the world has ever seen.... Incendiary projectiles would burn the cities to the ground in short order. An attack by gas, surging down through the valleys, would completely block them out."[26]

If Mitchell had played the game more astutely, he might have found a receptive audience. But "Mitchell tried to convert his opponents by killing them first," said Mitchell's friend and colleague, Hugh Trenchard, the man chiefly responsible for organizing Britain's Royal Air Force.[27] In 1925, Mitchell was demoted because of his unrelenting attacks on the Army and Navy and banished to an outpost in San Antonio. Shortly thereafter, he issued a six-thousand-word public indictment of the War and Navy departments, accusing them of "incompetency, criminal negligence, and almost treasonable administration of the National Defense."[28]

Mitchell got the showdown he sought: a court-martial. After being convicted in the fall of 1925 for "conduct prejudicial to good order and discipline," Mitchell resigned from the Army and campaigned on behalf of airpower for another ten years, offering lurid visions of the destruction that would befall the United States if the country's leaders failed to heed his warnings. In the May 1, 1926 issue of *Collier's*, for instance, he described an air attack on New York City in dire terms: Survivors would "claw and clutch and scramble, clambering on top of those who have fallen. Before long there is a yelling, fighting mass of humanity."[29]

Even at his death in 1936, Mitchell took a jab at the Army and Navy. He left instructions to be buried in Milwaukee, his hometown, rather than in Arlington National Cemetery.

ACTS OF FAITH

Mitchell's ideas flourished at the Army Air Corps Tactical School, commonly called ACTS, founded in 1920 by the War Department. Some seventy years later, the Air Force's School of Advanced Airpower Studies, an ACTS descendant, became one of the key incubators of military space theory. *Beyond the Paths of Heavens: the Emergence of Space Power Thought*, an anthology assembled at the school and published in 1999, is a good starting point for exploring the pros and cons of space control and the weaponization of space.[30]

By the early 1930s, a Mitchell-inspired team of bomber enthusiasts—called the "Bomber Mafia" by airpower historians—dominated ACTS, making it a hothouse for incubating theories of independent airpower and strategic bombardment. ACTS graduates became the senior leadership of the Army Air Forces during World War II. Eleven of thirteen three-star generals in the Army Air Forces had attended ACTS, as had all three four-star generals.[31]

Strategic bombing theories took shape at ACTS. High-altitude, daylight, precision bombardment would be the winning trifecta in the next great war. The Bomber Mafia was composed of men who simply assumed that U.S. bombers would get bigger, faster, and better; that bombsights would become ever more accurate; that enemy fighter planes would not present much of a threat to well-armed bomber formations; and that enemy ground defenses would not be effective against high-flying intruders.

Haywood "Possum" Hansell, who later became a key player in designing the strategic bombing campaign against Germany, summarized the prevailing ACTS philosophy in a 1938 lecture. Strategic bombing against industrial and transportation targets would win wars "by paralyzing the industrial machinery which must be relied upon to sustain the means to fight." An added benefit: Bombing would make life miserable and unsafe for enemy civilians, thus breaking their morale, their "will to resist." Civilians would come to "prefer the acceptance of peace terms to endurance of further hardship" and force their government to end the war.

The Bomber Mafia, however, rejected intentional Douhet-style terror bombing. "We may find the Air Force charged with breaking the will to resist of the enemy nation," Hansell said. "Let us make it emphatically clear that that does *not* mean the indiscriminate bombing of women and children."[32]

By 1935, Boeing had produced a prototype B-17, the four-engine "Flying Fortress"; 12,726 were ultimately built.[33] Contracts for the equally formidable B-24 "Liberator" were let in March 1939; 18,190 were constructed. The B-29 "Superfortress" program got under way in May 1941, nearly seven months before Pearl Harbor; some 4,000 were manufactured.[34] (The B-29 program rivaled the atom bomb project in scientific and technological complexity and scale, and it was a good deal more costly.)

These huge planes were said to be civilian-sparing precision weapons. In a favorite ACTS metaphor, crews would be able to put bombs into pickle barrels from great heights. Surgically precise strikes against military and militarily important targets far behind the front lines would be possible, which meant that residential neighborhoods would be largely spared. The Bomber Mafia was tragically mistaken in that belief.[35]

DE-HOUSING CIVILIANS

Britain and the United States were the only nations to enter World War II with systematic theories of *strategic* daylight precision bombing of militarily important targets far behind the lines. The idea of "daylight" should be emphasized. With the technology then available, bombardiers had to see their targets plainly with optical bombsights to have a chance of hitting them. Precision night-time bombing was an oxymoron.

In contrast, Germany, Japan, Italy, France, and Russia entered the war with a near-total emphasis on the *tactical* use of air power to support ground and naval forces. Germany's air attacks on Britain, which began in June 1940, were supposed to pave the way for a cross-channel invasion, Operation Sealion, which was eventually aborted. They were strategic in nature, but ill-conceived, badly planned, and poorly executed. A German scholar later characterized the campaign as "a confused arrangement looking much more like the aimless destructive outbursts of a child with conflicting impulses than the results of clear, decisive planning.[36] Further, the Luftwaffe's twin-engine bombers lacked the bomb-carrying capacity of the four-engine heavy bombers soon to be fielded by the British and the Americans.

Although the United States and Britain began the war with similar precision bombing doctrines, they rejected Douhetism. Douhet believed that killing and terrorizing civilians in war was morally acceptable because it would end the conflict quickly. He was not much concerned with pinpoint accuracy; precision was unnecessary when the object was terror. In contrast, accuracy was the chief concern within the U.S. Army Air Corps and, to a lesser extent, within the Royal Air Force.

That is not to say that the British or the Americans went wobbly at the thought of killing civilians. Strategic bombing would always put civilians at risk—and it should put them at risk, according to Anglo-American theory. Civilians must feel the pain; otherwise, they would not pressure their government to come to terms.

Hugh Trenchard, commander of the Royal Air Force and a principal architect of Britain's bombing doctrine in the interwar years, wrote in 1928 that terror bombing would be illegitimate. However, it would be all right to terrorize workers in industrial plants by making them fearful that they might be killed. Fear would keep them from showing up for work, a desirable outcome that would help cripple the enemy's industry. But, said Trenchard, "I emphatically do not advocate indiscriminate bombardment, and I think that air action will be far less indiscriminate and far less brutal and will obtain its end with far fewer casualties than either naval blockade, a naval bombardment, or sieges."[37]

Similar sentiments were expressed by America's Bomber Mafia. High-ranking officers in the U.S. Army Air Forces, men who were committed to winning wars by daylight precision bombing of military, industrial, and transportation targets, believed that at some point, civilians might become legitimate targets. Months before Pearl Harbor, Air War Plan-1 was developed, outlining the type of German targets that must be attacked once the nation went to war—electric power plants, rail switching yards, canals, petroleum and synthetic-oil plants, aircraft factories, and aluminum and magnesium plants. Under the heading of "Morale," it envisioned some amount of terror bombing: "Timeliness of attack is most important in the conduct of air operations directly against civilian morale. If the morale of the people is already low because of sustained suffering and deprivation and because the people are losing faith in the ability of the armed forces to win a favorable decision, then heavy and sustained bombing of cities may crush that morale entirely."[38]

Meanwhile, the Royal Air Force's theoretical airpower doctrine, which emphasized the selective bombing of industrial targets, proved difficult under real-world conditions. Selective bombing required solid intelligence, accurate bombsights, reasonably clear skies, and daylight. Daylight bombing, however, turned out to be horrendously costly to men and machines. The British lost so many planes and airmen to enemy fire during daylight raids that they quickly switched almost exclusively to night bombing.

In June and July 1941, the British conducted the "Butt report"—a photo analysis of the performance of 4,065 RAF bombers over the course of a hundred night raids. Although returning crews usually reported that they had hit their targets, the photos told a different story. Not one bomb in three had struck within five miles of the aimpoint. In the heavily defended

Ruhr Valley, the ratio was less than one in ten. A few crews even bombed cities in France and Switzerland thinking they were over German cities.[39]

By turning to night bombing, Bomber Command was mounting de facto "area" raids on cities, although it persisted in saying that it was still engaged in selective bombing. Air Chief Marshal Sir Charles Portal issued Directive No. 22 on February 14, 1942, which put an end to that self-delusion, at least among bomber crews. Bomber Command would now focus "on the morale of the enemy civil population and in particular of the industrial workers."[40]

A little more than a month later, on March 30, 1942, Prime Minister Winston Churchill's science adviser, Lord Cherwell, recommended that Bomber Command destroy working-class homes in fifty-eight German cities. Having "one's house demolished is most damaging to morale," Cherwell said. "People seem to mind it more than having their friends or even relatives killed." An intense "de-housing" program would "make about one-third of the whole German population homeless" by 1943. "There seems little doubt that this would break the spirit of the people."[41]

THE ROAD TO DRESDEN

Air Marshall Arthur Harris, an extraordinarily blunt man who took over as commander-in-chief of Bomber Command on February 23, 1942, knew he did not yet have the planes, men, and bombs to carry out a comprehensive morale-busting plan. But he would work on it. Meanwhile, as he put it in his memoir, *Bomber Offensive*, the "idea was to keep on at small targets for their strategic importance but, to put it crudely, not to mind when we missed them, or at any rate to regard a miss as useful provided that it disturbed morale."[42]

Harris experimented with different combinations of munitions in an effort to most efficiently de-house civilians. Torching their cities, Harris decided, would be best. His experiments in arson were elaborate and systematic; they focused on developing navigation aids to get his bombers to the targeted city at the right time, even though the planes started from different airfields and followed different routes. He also explored better ways to "mark" aimpoints so that his massed bomber formations could drop their bombs in the proper patterns. Determining the right mix and sequence of explosive bombs and incendiaries—the former to knock down buildings and to rupture water mains and the latter to set the rubble afire—was perhaps the most essential element. If Harris got it right, Bomber Command would be able to frighten or kill firemen with a second round of explosive bombs.

"If a rain of incendiaries is mixed with high explosive bombs, there is an irresistible temptation for the fireman to keep his head down," Harris noted.[43] If enough firemen were killed or prevented from fighting the fires, small fires would combine into a larger blaze. An early experiment was Lubeck, a historic port city on the Baltic, about twenty miles northeast of Hamburg. It was hit in March 1942.

> It was a city of moderate size, of some importance as a port, and with some submarine building yards of moderate size not far from it. It was not a vital target, but it seemed to me better to destroy an industrial town of moderate importance than to fail to destroy a large industrial city. However, the main object of the attack was to learn to what extent a first wave of aircraft could guide a second wave to the aiming point by starting a conflagration.... At least half the town was destroyed, mainly by fire."[44]

By July 24, 1943, Harris was ready for big game: Hamburg, Germany's second largest city. In Project Gomorrah, 731 bombers managed to start the war's first self-sustaining firestorm or "fire typhoon," as Harris called it. Some forty thousand civilians are thought to have died, according to U.S. estimates. Other estimates are higher.

Those who succumbed were not necessarily caught in the open or killed by falling debris; thousands of men, women, and children were in air raid shelters where they were asphyxiated as fire consumed the oxygen. In some shelters, temperatures were so high that only ashes remained, and the number of deaths could only be roughly estimated.[45]

By the end of the war in Europe, Bomber Command had attacked seventy German cities. According to the post-war reckoning of Bomber Command's Operational Research Section, twenty-three of these cities had more than sixty percent of their built-up areas destroyed while forty-six had lost about half of their built-up areas— apparently, one city sustained only light damage.[46] The last major Bomber Command raid of the war was on Dresden, Germany's seventh largest city.

Dresden, the capital of Saxony, was a lovely medieval city in eastern Germany with a pre-war population of about six hundred and fifty thousand. It was arguably of no great importance to the German war effort compared to the industrial cities of western and northern Germany, and it had suffered just two small American daylight attacks during the war. Despite those attacks, Dresden's residents believed their city to be relatively safe. American bombs had been directed at militarily important targets and they had struck with reasonable accuracy. Although dozens of German cities had by now been gutted by British fire raids, surely that would not happen to Dresden.

The city was too old—some buildings dated back a thousand years—too beautiful, and too historically significant to be wantonly destroyed. Dresden was the cultural capital of Germany, the "Florence of the Elbe." Many residents believed the Allies planned to make it the capital of the new Germany. Another common belief was that Dresden had been "paired" with Oxford. As long as Germany spared that ancient city, Dresden would survive.

More than a half century later, the reasons for the destruction of Dresden are still the subject of debate. I will not venture into that quagmire other than to note that the British, at the direction of Churchill, were eager to help the Red Army, which was advancing rapidly from the east. German refugees were fleeing westward from the Russians and German soldiers were heading east. Rail lines were already overtaxed; bombing Dresden's rail yards would create even more confusion and perhaps paralysis, thus helping the Soviets.

The attack plan Harris and his staff developed was ingenious, involving decoy strikes against other cities and a synthetic oil plant, all designed to draw German night fighters away from the real target, giving Harris's main bomber forces free passage. Nine light bombers, Mosquitoes, would hit Dresden first, marking the aimpoint—the cycle stadium—with enormous red flares. The flares would act as beacons for the heavy bombers, which would drop high explosives to create rubble and incendiaries to set it afire.

Some three hours later, a larger force would strike the city. The delay was critical; firefighters and rescue workers from nearby towns and cities would need time to get to Dresden to help the local brigades. The second wave would kill them or at least disrupt their efforts, thus ensuring a large conflagration and, with luck, a firestorm.

The plan worked. A British Air Ministry communiqué said that nearly six hundred and fifty thousand incendiaries were dropped on the city and the glow of the fire was visible nearly two hundred miles away. When daylight came, more than three hundred heavy U.S. bombers hit Dresden. The

Americans concentrated on the rail yards, but the smoke was so heavy that accurate bombing was impossible.

By the time of the raid, Soviet troops were just eighty miles from Dresden and the city was swollen with refugees from the east. Some historians believe that tens of thousands of men, women, and children may have been in the city awaiting rail transport to the west. There is simply no way to get an accurate accounting of how many of these refugees simply disappeared without a trace. Bodies or the remnants of bodies were quickly burned by German authorities in an attempt to stop the spread of disease. Death estimates range from about twenty-five thousand (the official British and U.S. estimates) to two-hundred and fifty thousand. The higher estimates had their roots in Nazi propaganda and were seldom taken seriously. The definitive account of the bombing is Frederick Taylor's *Dresden: Tuesday, February 13, 1945*. Taylor puts the death toll between twenty-five and forty thousand.[47]

The British people had so far failed to fret much about the torching of German cities, mostly because of a widespread belief, inspired by the German air attacks on Britain, that German civilians deserved to have some amount of death and destruction visited upon them—some sixty thousand British citizens had been killed in German air raids, including roughly forty thousand who died during the Blitz in 1941.

But Dresden was a watershed. Germany was beaten and Berlin would surely fall soon. Criticism of Bomber Command grew strident as reports of Dresden's destruction made their way into newspapers. Winston Churchill, an early and ardent champion of the bombing of cities, was disquieted. He drafted a memo to the Air Staff that said: "It seems to me that the moment has come when the question of bombing of German cities simply for the sake of increasing the terror, though under other pretexts, should be reviewed. Otherwise we shall come into control of an utterly ruined land.... I feel the need for more precise concentration upon military objectives, such as oil and communications behind the immediate battle-zone, rather than on mere acts of terror and wanton destruction."[48]

The air staff was so offended by the draft memo that they persuaded Churchill to tone it down, deleting references to "terror." After the war, Air Marshal Sir Arthur Harris, by then generally known in Britain as "Bomber Harris," defended himself in his memoirs:

I know that the destruction of so large and splendid a city at this late stage of the war was considered unnecessary even by a good many people who admit that our earlier attacks were as fully justified as any other operation of war. Here I will only say that the attack on Dresden was at the time considered a military necessity by much more important people than myself, and that if their judgment was right, the same arguments must apply... [to] the ethics of bombing as a whole.[49]

And what were those earlier arguments? "I never forget, as many do, that in all normal warfare of the past, and of the not distant past, it was the common practice to besiege cities and, if they refused to surrender when called upon with due formality to do so, every living thing in them was in the end put to the sword."[50]

WITH A STRONG WIND

In January 1943, Churchill and Roosevelt met at Casablanca where a number of basic war aims were worked out, including the formalizing of U.S. and British cooperation in a Combined Bomber Offensive against Hitler's Germany. The ultimate objective of the strategic air offensive was to "bring about the progressive destruction and dislocation of the German military, industrial, and economic system, and the undermining of the morale of the German people to a point where their capacity for armed resistance is fatally weakened."[51]

There was, however, considerable leeway in interpreting how the Casablanca Directive would be carried out. The Americans chose to pursue daylight precision attacks, insofar as possible, even in the face of very heavy losses of men and machines; in contrast, R.A.F. Bomber Command continued to bomb at night, with working-class residential areas as its principal targets.[52]

British crews understood what they were doing and often expressed dismay. "There were people down there being fried to death in melted asphalt in the roads," said one R.A.F. crewman after the raid on Hamburg. "They were being burnt up and we were shuffling incendiary bombs into this holocaust. I felt terribly sorry for the people in that fire I was helping to stoke up."[53]

Meanwhile, American crews took comfort in the fact that their targets were almost always militarily significant, even if many of their bombs went astray. As one top American commander, Ira Eaker, said late in the war, Americans would not go for "baby killing" plans. "We should never allow the history of this war to convict us of throwing the strategic bomber at the man in the street."[54]

In the fall and winter of 1944–1945, however, American crews flew ever more frequently in weather so bad that visual sightings, the key to precision bombing, were not possible. In overcast weather, the crews relied on radio beacons and primitive radar, H2X, to get them over the target. The fuzzy H2X images bore little relationship to today's crisp radar images. The Eighth Air Force Operations Analysis Section estimated that bombing under good visual conditions was about one hundred and fifty times more accurate than bombing through complete overcast.[55] Once the targets were "found" by radar, far more bombs missed their targets than hit them. Because the targets were almost invariably in built-up areas, civilians were killed by the hundreds and sometimes by the thousands.

The extent to which American strategic bombing forces slipped closer to de facto Douhetism in the skies over Germany is a matter of controversy among military historians. Some suggest that by the spring of 1945 the Americans were little better than R.A.F. Bomber Command at sparing civilians; other historians are mystified by such charges, asserting that in almost all cases the Americans hewed to their pre-war doctrine of precision attack.

German air officers were inclined to agree with the latter view. Erhard Milch, a field marshal in the Luftwaffe during the war and deputy to Luftwaffe chief Hermann Goering, analyzed the Combined Bomber Offensive after the war. Regarding the American end of it, he said, "It was only natural that a certain percentage of the bombs dropped during daylight operations did fall on civilian targets and population centers, but this was only a fraction when compared with that of the [R.A.F.] night bombing operations."[56]

But against Japan, the air war took a different turn. The United States abandoned precision bombing altogether and turned to area raids, in which civilians would die by the hundreds of thousands. Haywood Hansell, one of the leading figures in developing the pre-war doctrine of precision bombing, served with distinction in the European bombing campaign. In January 1945, he was in charge of the principal strategic bombing campaign against Japan, and his daylight precision tactics were not getting the results that General of the Army Henry "Hap" Arnold, who headed the Army Air Forces, wanted.

Hansell's team began flying missions from the Marianas in late 1944 with the new B-29 Superfortress. The weather over Japan in the winter was often heavily overcast, which seriously compromised the possibility of precision attacks. Further, high-altitude jet-stream winds, where the B-29s flew, were far faster than anything over Germany, making precision bombing runs an iffy thing at best. Finally, target sets were not easily defined. War industries were more widely dispersed in Japanese cities than in German cities, and a considerable number of items for war were produced in cottage industries.

Many men in the Washington-based air staff had long believed that the best way to destroy Japan's industrial war machine was simply to burn its cities. In 1939, a course at the Air Corps Tactical School, where precision bombing theory ruled, taught that "large sections of the great Japanese cities are built of flimsy and highly inflammable materials." The Tokyo earthquake of 1923 "bears witness to the fearful destruction that may be inflicted by incendiary bombs."[57] (The Tokyo-Yokohama earthquake was thought to have killed some one hundred and forty thousand people, mostly by fire. The quake hit around noon after gas burners had been lit to prepare the midday meal in homes and restaurants.)

About five months before the D-Day invasion of Europe, Hap Arnold submitted his "Outline of Presentation of Views of Commanding General, Army Air Forces, on the Role of the Air Forces in the Defeat of Japan" to President Roosevelt. Arnold wrote that "seventeen hundred tons of incendiaries will cause uncontrollable fires in twenty major cities," thus destroying numerous war industries.[58] Now, in the early weeks of 1945, Arnold was ready to sack Hansell; General Curtis LeMay would be his go-to guy. "LeMay realized that incendiary bombs would have an even more terrible effect upon Japan than they had on Germany," Arnold later wrote. "In Germany, buildings and whole towns that from a distance seemed to be unscathed were found, on closer approach, to be nothing but gutted, burned-out shells. In Japan there were so many old wooden buildings that a large load of incendiaries, with a strong wind, would normally destroy the major portion of a town with one attack."[59]

BOILED AND BAKED

LeMay's first massive fire raid was the night of March 9, 1945. Tokyo, the world's most densely populated major city, was the target. The death toll was 83,793, according to the post-war U.S. Strategic Bombing Survey. Later but plausible estimates put the actual number higher, perhaps around 130,000.[60]

The raid was cunningly planned. The planes would go in at night rather than during the day. Daylight was needed for precision bombing; darkness would do for area bombing. Some three hundred B-29s loaded with incendiaries—a mix of magnesium, because it burned hotter, and napalm, because it splattered—would fly at low altitudes, five to seven thousand feet instead of twenty-eight or thirty thousand feet. Because the planes would not have to climb as high, fuel requirements would be less. Bomb-bay fuel tanks were eliminated, allowing more bombs to be carried.

LeMay also stripped his planes of defensive ammunition except for the tail gun. That saved weight. Every pound of ammo not taken aboard meant another pound of magnesium or napalm could be carried. LeMay believed that disarming the planes would not jeopardize his crews; at that point in the war, Japanese night fighters were not much of a threat. He was correct.

The general recalled after the war that thermal updrafts caused by the Tokyo fires "bounced our airplanes into the sky like ping-pong balls. They got knocked up to twelve and fifteen thousand feet."[61] LeMay, however, failed to note that the stench of burning flesh, which permeated the aircraft at such low altitudes, made many crewmen gag and vomit. Japanese civilians were often reduced to limbless lumps of charcoal; in areas of more intense heat, they simply disappeared. In later raids, LeMay's crewmen often wore oxygen masks to mask the odor of burning flesh, even though oxygen was not needed. In later years, LeMay served as commander of Strategic Air Command and eventually chief of staff of the Air Force. In his autobiography, he echoed Air Marshall Harris. There was "nothing new about this massacre of civilian populations," LeMay wrote. "In ancient times, when an army laid siege to a city, everybody was in the fight. And when that city had fallen, and was sacked, just as often as not, every single soul was murdered."[62] A few pages on, he added: "We scorched and boiled and baked to death more people in Tokyo on [the] night of March 9–10 than went up in vapor at Hiroshima and Nagasaki combined."[63]

If you are among those inclined to believe that the twenty-first century American way of precision conventional war is inexcusably brutal, just think how much worse it was before.

PICKLE BARRELS

By the end of World War II, bombers armed with high-explosive and incendiary bombs had become as indiscriminately destructive as anything Giulio Douhet had imagined decades earlier. Just as the Italian airpower theorist had predicted more than two decades earlier, civilians had indeed been "sucked into the maw of war." The around-the-clock Anglo-American Combined Bomber Offensive against Germany claimed, even by conservative estimates prepared by the U.S. Strategic Bombing Survey, a "minimum of 305,000 civilian lives and injured another 780,000. About 485,000 residential buildings—a high percentage of them apartment houses—were totally destroyed and another 415,000 heavily damaged. An estimated 7.5 million German civilians were made homeless."

In Japan, the statistics were even more appalling, although the length of the bombing campaign was measured in months rather than in years. According to the Strategic Bombing Survey, some 330,000 civilians were thought to have been killed and more than 500,000 injured. About two and a half million buildings were destroyed by the raids and the Japanese themselves knocked down 615,000 buildings to create firebreaks.

Nonetheless, the survey's casualty figures are believed by many historians to be far too low, particularly because they also include the atom-bombed cities of Hiroshima and Nagasaki. Other estimates, based on varying degrees of hard data and reasonable extrapolation, go as high as nine hundred thousand.[64]

Robert S. McNamara, secretary of defense for Presidents Kennedy and Johnson, served on LeMay's staff in World War II and helped plan the incendiary campaign against Japan. In 2003 McNamara wrote in a newspaper op-ed that LeMay was "the ablest commander of any I met during my three years of service with the U.S. Army Air Corps in World War II." McNamara accepted the death figure of nine hundred thousand. According to McNamara, LeMay said at one point, "If we lose the war, we'll be tried as war criminals."[65] There is little moral clarity in war, especially total war.

Although the United States entered World War II with a highly developed doctrine of civilian-sparing daylight precision bombing, it didn't have the technology to pull it off. In 1940, one unusually keen champion of precision bombing extolled the virtues of a new Norden bombsight that would be coupled with a new automatic pilot for bomb runs, and said: "We do not regard a fifteen-foot square… as being a very difficult target to hit from an altitude of thirty thousand feet." Airpower historian Stephen L. McFarland wryly comments that that assertion was "the equivalent, in the idiom of the day, to dropping a bomb in a pickle barrel from six miles up."[66] (At the time, delivering a bomb within hundreds of yards of the aimpoint was thought to be good.)

Shortly after the end of Gulf War I in 1991, in which U.S.-led coalition forces evicted Iraqi troops from Kuwait, Gen. Buster C. Glosson, director of campaign plans and commander of the 14th Air Division during the war, offered this observation:

> Airpower advocates have long dreamed of a day when the weapon, platform, and willingness to use them properly would come together to make airpower a decisive force. Today, those dreams are reality. One need only to look back to our raids on Schweinfurt, Germany, in World War II to see how dramatically precision weapons have enhanced our capabilities over the last fifty years. Two raids of three hundred B-17 bombers could not achieve with three thousand bombs what two F-117s can do with only four…. To shut down an industry in World War II, we were forced to target entire complexes because of the inaccuracy of our weapons; today we would need to hit only a couple of key buildings."[67]

Although the Army Air Forces believed the B-17 Flying Fortress, the B-24 Liberator, and the B-29 Superfortress were precision weapons, they were not. In effect, they were weapons of mass destruction. In contrast, the United States finally possesses the technology to win conventional wars while minimizing civilian deaths—and much of that capability is rooted in space. The United States can now put bombs into those metaphorical pickle barrels. That degree of accuracy has moral implications. If a war must be fought, it ought to fought as cleanly as possible.

And yet, as always, the Law of Unintended Consequences comes into play. If Americans can now do war "*right*," then will they be inclined to do war more often? Do precision weapons lower the threshold for going to war? Do they inspire overconfidence—a kind of only-we-can-do-it-right hubris? If so, does that arrogance encourage national leaders to choose the war option too quickly, leaving other possibilities largely unexplored?

7

True Space Ships

Henry "Hap" Arnold, the man who oversaw Curtis LeMay's firebombing campaign against Japan, was born in 1886 in Gladwyne, Pennsylvania, on the "Main Line." His family had a long military history. Four ancestors on his mother's side and three on his father's had taken part in the American Revolution. His paternal grandfather had fought at Gettysburg and his father had been a cavalryman in Puerto Rico.

In 1903, the year of Wilbur and Orville Wright's first flight in North Carolina, Arnold entered West Point. In his 1949 autobiography, *Global Mission*, he claimed to have been unaware of the flight throughout his West Point years. He and his buddies, he said, were obsessed with becoming officers in the Horse Cavalry. The cavalry, Arnold wrote with exclamation-point extravagance, "was why we were all here! It was what we lived for—our whole future! It was the last romantic thing left on Earth." Yet it was Arnold, the would-be horse soldier, who would set the Air Force on a trajectory toward space.

After graduation from West Point, Arnold was assigned to the infantry; a commission in the Horse Cavalry was a high-prestige assignment and he had not earned it. He had been a middling student (sixty-sixth in a graduating class of 111) and a prankish, often-disciplined cadet. Only six classmates received more demerits in their final year.

After two years in the Philippines, Arnold's unit was shipped back to the States, to Governor's Island in New York Bay, a post so flat "it wasn't even fun to ride a horse on it." The flatness was a virtue. Governor's Island became New York's first landing field and Second Lieutenant Arnold was soon witnessing the exploits of aviators like Wilbur Wright and Glenn Curtiss, men willing to boldly go where no one had gone before, suspended on flimsy contraptions of wood, fabric, and wire.

Arnold recalled the day in 1909 when Wilbur Wright flew from Governor's Island (south of Manhattan's Battery Park) up the Hudson River to Grant's tomb (122nd Street and Riverside Drive) and back. An amazing feat. Less than a year later, Curtiss flew from upstate Albany to New York—143 miles in less than three hours, with a couple of stops along the way—and claimed a $10,000 prize offered by Joseph Pulitzer's *New York World*.[1]

In 1911, Arnold received a letter from the War Department asking if he would be willing to volunteer for pilot training with the Wright brothers at Simms Station near Dayton, Ohio, a post operated by the Aeronautical Division of the Signal Corps. Arnold went to his commanding officer for advice. "Young man, I know of no better way for a person to commit suicide!" That did it; Arnold was hooked.

The Army had organized the Aeronautical Division in 1907 "to study the flying machine and the possibility of adapting it to military purposes." It had one officer, two enlisted men, and too little money to accomplish anything. When President Theodore Roosevelt learned how little, he ordered the Army to allocate funds. In February 1908, the Army signed a contract with the Wright brothers to teach a few young men how to fly.

When Arnold arrived at Simms Station (now the sprawling, tech-heavy Wright-Patterson Air Force Base) in 1911, he found a cow pasture with a wooden shed, two airplanes, and a thorn tree at the far end. The Wright factory, where ground instruction took place, was in town. The airplanes were not complicated machines by later standards, but they were unforgiving. The pilot sat on a "hard seat located on the leading edge of the thin lower wing. The airman's feet rested on a slender bar before the wing." The craft was maneuvered largely through a system of levers, pulleys, moving belts, and clutches that "warped" the wings; the pilot operated the rudder by rotating handgrips. Flights were attempted in the early morning or evening hours when there was usually less wind than during the day.

Arnold's first takeoff with an instructor was on May 3, 1911. Ten days later, after twenty-eight flights with a total air time of three hours and forty-eight minutes, he had become a military aviator. Arnold's first contribution to military aviation occurred during a training flight at Simms. "I was coming back into the field when a bug hit me in the eye and left one of its transparent wings sticking to my eyeball. The pain was terrific; blinded by tears, I could scarcely see to make my landing.... The possibility of being rammed dead by a bug had not occurred to us before. After that we wore goggles."[2]

OUTRAGEOUS PLAN

In late March 1917, nearly six years after surviving his collision with a bug, Captain Arnold succeeded Billy Mitchell, by then his mentor, as executive officer of the Army Air Service. Mitchell had been dispatched to Europe where the Great War had been under way for three years, without the direct participation of the United States. Congress finally declared war on April 2, 1917. By August 5, Arnold was the youngest colonel in the Army, a temporary wartime rank. He was thirty years old and embarrassed. "Youngsters, in those days, just didn't get to be colonels. At first, I used to take back streets when I walked to the War Department from my house, imagining that people would be looking at me incredulously."[3]

Arnold pleaded to go overseas where he could join Mitchell and get into the fight. But the Army kept him in the States to organize the production of airplanes, a daunting task. When the United States entered the war, America's air arm had roughly one thousand, one hundred and fifty officers and airmen and about two hundred civilian mechanics. Of the one hundred and thirty pilots, only twenty-six were really qualified, Arnold believed. Of fifty five airplanes, fifty-one were "obsolete" and the remaining four "obsolescent."

The British, the French, the Belgians, the Italians, and certainly the Germans and Austrians were far ahead of the United States in hardware, in airmen, in air combat theory, and air combat experience. The difference in readiness, Arnold thought, was rooted in the fact that the Europeans were forever preparing to fight one another, a centuries-old pastime in the Old World. The United States, protected by the Atlantic and Pacific, seemed immune from invasion and thus unprepared for battle.

Shortly after the United States declared war, the French premier (secretly prodded by Billy Mitchell) asked the United States to send forty-five hundred fighting airplanes, five thousand pilots, and fifty thousand mechanics to the Western Front within a year or so. Previously, the Army had been devoting, on average, about a hundred thousand dollars a year to aviation. Arnold and his colleagues cooked up an outrageous plan: they asked for $639,242,452 to build 22,600 airplanes and 45,000 engines. The money also would be used to recruit and train tens of thousands of pilots, crew-

men, and mechanics. The Army's General Staff, annoyed by the imperti-
nence of the request, did not approve the plan, but the secretary of war
did. Congress passed the appropriations bill and the president signed it in
a matter of weeks.[4]

Building twenty-two thousand airplanes was hopelessly unrealistic. The
United States had no combat planes of its own, only trainers and observation craft. U.S. factories would have to build foreign designs, principally
the DeHavilland-4, a British two-seater. It was a good machine able to stay
aloft for three hours, fly at about a hundred and twenty miles per hour, and
climb to ten thousand feet in fourteen minutes. The DeHavilland could fly
reconnaissance missions, operate as a pursuit plane, and it could even drop
a few small bombs. There was a problem, though; the United States lacked
an aircraft industry.

In April 1917, America had twelve aircraft factories, ranging from small
to tiny. In the ten years the Army had been in the flying game, it had ordered just one hundred and fifty-four "military" planes, none designed for
combat. Arnold turned mostly to the auto industry, which *was* organized
for large-scale production. But in the end, the promised numbers were simply out of reach and the airplanes themselves too hard to build. Airplanes
were not autos. An automobile in those days might have a thousand parts;
a combat plane, many thousands.

By the time the Armistice was signed on November 11, 1918, the Army
Air Service had grown to about one hundred and seventy thousand men, including 2,768 pilots and observers. American industry had produced some
forty-five hundred DeHavilland-4s as well as several thousand trainers, mostly
the JN-4 or "Jenny," a name barnstormers immortalized during the 1920s.[5]

THE FLYING BUG

Arnold regarded the number of planes built as a personal failure. And it
was, if judged against the outrageous goal of more than twenty-two thousand. But in "failure," Arnold began to build close and lasting relationships
between military aviation and results-oriented scientists, engineers, and industrialists. Donald Douglas, Jack Northrop, Chance Vought, and Glenn
Martin were among the aviation pioneers Arnold worked with during the
Great War whose companies would later manufacture swarms of military
aircraft during World War II.

Arnold also turned to Henry Ford, who churned out cylinders for Liberty engines "so fast they stacked up at his Detroit factory like cords of wood." So good was the four hundred-horsepower Liberty engine that it was not only in great demand by the U.S. military but also by England, France, and Italy.[6]

At Ford's gritty River Rouge plant, Arnold worked with Bill Knudsen, who built Eagle boats to hunt German submarines. In 1940, President Franklin D. Roosevelt named Knudsen, by then president of General Motors, to take charge of mobilizing the economy to build armaments and airplanes. Arnold also worked with Charles Kettering of Delco, who later became director of research at General Motors. "It was [Kettering] who took the 'spark knock' out of gasoline," Arnold later wrote. "Whatever the problem, he made it seem simple."

One of the problems that Arnold and Kettering worked on in 1918—along with Orville Wright, Henry Ford, Elmer Sperry, inventor of the autopilot for ships and airplanes, and Robert Millikan, who was soon to receive a Nobel Prize for Physics—was a "Flying Bug," a pilotless, double-winged flying bomb.

"It was a complete little airplane built of papier-mâché and reinforced with wooden members, its smooth cardboard wing surfaces spreading less than twelve feet," Arnold recalled. "Its fuselage held three hundred pounds of explosives and it weighed, unloaded, three hundred pounds. It took off from a small four-wheeled carriage which rolled down a portable track, its own little two-cycle, forty-horsepower engine, built by Henry Ford, meeting the requirements for both pressure and vacuum necessary to operate the automatic controls."

The Bug was sent on its way by turning its launch tracks toward its distant objective and firing up the engine. Aiming it was not easy; the distance to the target as well as wind direction and speed had to be calculated as accurately as possible. Once launched, a Sperry gyroscope forced the Bug to fly straight and a barometer kept it at the right altitude. "The number of revolutions of the engine required to take the Bug to the target was then figured and a cam set. When the engine had turned exactly that proper number of revolutions, the cam fell into position, the two bolts holding on the wings were withdrawn, the wings folded up like a jack rabbit's ears, and the Bug plunged to Earth as a bomb."

The Flying Bug was the first cruise missile. Prototypes cost four hundred dollars. With mass production, Arnold believed, the unit price would drop. His hope was to launch thousands of Flying Bugs every day against German strong points, troop concentrations, munitions plants, and the like. But the war ended before he could push his plan to completion and the program died a few years later.

"The Bug," Arnold wrote, "was twenty-five years ahead of its time. For all practical purposes—as a nuisance weapon—it compared very favorably with the German V-1. It was cheap and easy to manufacture, and its portable launching track would have permitted its use anywhere. Considering the trends in air weapons today, and that the first German V-1 was not launched against Britain until the fifth year of World War II, it is interesting to think how this little Bug might have changed the whole face of history if it had been allowed to develop without interruption during the years between the wars."[7]

Arnold had an undying enthusiasm for unmanned aircraft. They could do a lot of damage to the enemy, he believed, while saving the lives of American crewmen by keeping them out of harm's way. Early in 1942, Arnold, who was by then the Army's top air officer, considered reviving the Bug, which had been greatly improved. For one thing, it was now radio controlled. "It would cost, per unit, between eight hundred dollars and a thousand dollars as compared to two-hundred thousand dollars for a medium, or four-hundred thousand dollars for a single heavy bomber," Arnold said. But the range of the improved Bug was not sufficient to reach the principal cities of Germany from bases in southern England. If not for that fact, Arnold might have used the Bug by "the thousands and tens of thousands."[8]

In the summer of 1944, Arnold suffered a setback in another unpiloted-aircraft scheme. Carl Spaatz, one of the Army Air Forces' top combat officers, came up with the idea of crashing "Weary Willies"—worn-out heavy bombers—into German targets. The life expectancy of a "heavy," no matter how skillfully patched up, averaged one hundred and sixty-one combat days. In an effort to retire the planes in a useful way, Arnold said, they "tried some interesting experiments" by loading worn-out B-17s and B-24s with TNT. Pilots took off but bailed out over England. At that point, the banged-up bombers were guided by a mother ship through radio control.[9]

The Weary Willie experiments, code-named "Aphrodite," fizzled—mostly because the pilotless B-17s and B-24s could not be controlled well enough to accurately hit military targets. Nonetheless, Arnold believed they could be sent "against large industrial target areas in Germany"—that is, used to hit cities in a random way. There was little enthusiasm for that plan beyond Arnold and it eventually died, in part because the British feared German retaliation.

The Navy was also involved in Aphrodite. The Navy's guidance system, featuring television images beamed to the mother plane, promised better accuracy than the Army's. Joseph P. Kennedy, Jr., a naval lieutenant and a wealthy young Irish-American from Boston, volunteered to fly the first Navy mission, an attack on a V-1 launch site. Kennedy's PB4Y, a Navy version of the B-24, was loaded with ten tons of TNT. The bomber exploded shortly after takeoff, before Kennedy could bail out. Faulty wiring was the likely cause.[10]

THE SEED COMES FIRST

Hap Arnold was neither modest nor patient. He was abrasive and "unable to tolerate delay," writes his biographer Dik Daso. "He was unable to sit in one place for very long, unless in a high-level meeting, and was always in the middle of one project or another. He rejected opposition and was intolerant. His disdain for 'can't do' attitudes was well known."[11] Nevertheless, Arnold was keenly aware that the United States had plenty of people smarter than he and he sought them out.

In 1931, Arnold found himself in Riverside, California, in command of March Field, which was about forty miles from the California Institute of Technology in Pasadena. Robert Millikan, a member of the World War I Flying Bug team, was president of Cal Tech; he and Arnold renewed their friendship.

Cal Tech was a global leader in aeronautics, but Millikan wanted it to become *the* unchallenged pacesetter. That would promote the aircraft industry in southern California and attract research funds from the likes of Douglas Aircraft, Boeing, and the Army.[12] Arnold was a good man to know. Meanwhile, the Army Air Corps, as it was then called, could benefit from its association with Cal Tech.

Millikan, the recipient of the 1923 Nobel Prize for Physics, was one of the nation's most respected scientists and he could put Arnold in touch with the best scientific minds in the country. One of those minds belonged to

Theodore von Karman, a Hungarian who, in 1930, had been lured from a professorship in Germany to Cal Tech by a princely salary. Von Karman was a genius. At the age of six, he could accurately multiply five- and six-digit numbers in his head.[13] Now, he was perhaps the world's leading aeronautical scientist. He headed the Guggenheim Aeronautical Laboratory at Cal Tech, an ancestor of NASA's Jet Propulsion Laboratory.[14]

"During the first half of the 1930s," writes Daso, "Arnold and Karman developed a similar vision for military aviation: The United States needed a cooperative aeronautics establishment which coupled civilian scientific and industrial expertise with the practical needs of the Army Air Corps. To Arnold, this collaboration meant better Air Corps hardware. To von Karman, it meant great possibilities for Cal Tech and the West Coast aviation industry."[15]

By the mid-1930s, Arnold wrote, the Army Air Corps had been hacked back from its World War I peak to the point that it was practically "nonexistent." There were just sixteen hundred and fifty officers and sixteen thousand enlisted men and only a few "first-class airplanes—a handful of P-26 fighters, and a small number of B-10 and B-12 bombers. The rest of our assorted equipment was obsolete." And yet, Arnold, who had become assistant chief of the corps in January 1936, was not entirely displeased. He had long pushed fellow officers in technical fields to go outside the Army and even NACA, the government's National Advisory Committee for Aeronautics, when they needed to solve really tough technical problems. That strategy was being followed.

The Air Corps' Materiel Division, which was responsible for developing new hardware, regularly consulted scientists including von Karman; Millikan; Karl Compton, president of the Massachusetts Institute of Technology, and his brother Arthur, a Nobel Prize-winning physicist at the University of Chicago; Vannevar Bush, then dean of Electrical Engineering at the Massachusetts Institute of Technology; Lyman Briggs, director of the National Bureau of Standards; and James B. Conant, president of Harvard. These were scientific heavyweights. Conant, Bush, and both Comptons were shortly to become principal decision-makers in the second largest scientific and industrial effort of World War II, the Manhattan Project. (The largest was the B-29 Superfortress.) Briggs was deeply involved in the bomb project, too, in its early stages.

In the 1930s, high-ranking Army officers were seldom aware of the close relationship between civilian scientists and the Air Corps. "Once, after George Marshall became chief of staff," Arnold recalled, "I asked him to come to lunch with a group of these men. He was amazed that I knew them. 'What on Earth are you doing with people like that!' he exclaimed. 'Using them,' I replied. 'Using their brains to help us develop gadgets and devices for our airplanes—gadgets and devices that are far too difficult for the Air Force engineers to develop themselves.'"[16] In September 1937, Arnold told an aviation planning conference:

> Remember that the seed comes first; if you are to reap a harvest of aeronautical development, you must plant the seed called experimental research. Install aeronautical branches in your universities; encourage your young men to take up aeronautical engineering. It is a new field but it is likely to prove a very productive one indeed. Spend all the funds you can possibly make available on experimentation and research. Next, do not visualize aviation merely as a collection of airplanes. It is broad and far reaching. It combines manufacture, schools, transportation, airdrome building and management, air munitions and armaments, metallurgy, mills and mines, finance and banking, and finally, public security—national defense.[17]

A year later, in September 1938, Arnold became chief of the Air Corps after his boss, Oscar Westover, was killed in a bad-weather landing at the Lockheed Aircraft plant in Burbank, California. The "cramped nature of our habitual thinking" was quickly brought home to him, Arnold later recalled. In an effort to gear up for the inevitable global war, the new chief called a roundtable meeting of his staff. How many planes were essential, he asked. "Let everyone use his imagination; nobody hold back!"

Each officer, in turn, produced an estimate. The estimates "added up to a total of fifteen hundred—fifteen hundred combat airplanes to meet American requirements all over the world! I was shocked." By the end of the war, nearly two-hundred and thirty-thousand fighters, bombers, trainers, transports, and reconnaissance aircraft had been produced for America's armed forces.[18]

During his career, Arnold was never quite content with NACA, which Congress had established in 1915 as a research and consulting arm for military and commercial aviation. NACA was composed of government officials and civilian scientists and developers, and it produced a host of technological advances and refinements for aircraft until replaced in 1958 by NASA, the National Aeronautics and Space Administration.

Despite a record of achievement, NACA was too bureaucratic, too unimaginative, too confining to suit Arnold. His displeasure grew steadily as it became ever more likely that the United States would soon be embroiled in another great war. In 1938, German airmen had taken Charles Lindbergh on a VIP tour of Luftwaffe facilities. They were eager to impress the world's most famous aviator with their aircraft, and they succeeded. Alarmed by the possibility that the Germans might have fighter planes that could reach speeds of four hundred miles per hour, Lindbergh pressed Arnold, the new head of the Air Corps, to develop a five-hundred-mile-an-hour fighter.

Arnold took the matter up with George W. Lewis, director of aeronautical research at NACA. "Why in the name of God," Arnold asked, didn't the United States have a four-hundred-mile-per-hour fighter? "Because you haven't ordered one," Lewis replied. Arnold learned that Lewis had been aware for some time that fast fighters could be built; he simply hadn't passed that information on to the Air Corps.

An outfit so lacking in initiative as NACA, Arnold believed, was not the best bet to come up with the ideas that would be necessary to defeat the Germans in the coming war. He increasingly turned to civilian experts to help push the Air Corps toward cutting-edge technology.[19]

"MECHANICAL" WARS

In the summer of 1944, Arnold commanded the world's largest Air Force. Nonetheless, he was haunted by the knowledge that the United States had entered the European conflict largely unprepared. The German military had focused in the 1930s on applying science and technology to winning the coming war. The Me-262 twin-engine jet fighter that went into production in the summer of 1944 had demonstrated that, as had the V-1 buzz bomb and the V-2 rocket.

The Germans also experimented with a host of lesser-known "wonder weapons." One was the Me-163 Komet, a stubby little plane built to intercept bombers. Like the Me-262, it appeared too late in the war to have much of an impact; unlike the Me-262, pilots had little enthusiasm for it.

Komets, powered by a combination of methyl alcohol and concentrated hydrogen peroxide, often blew up, sometimes while still on the runway. One Luftwaffe test pilot said it was probably the most dangerous aircraft ever built.[20]

After the successful D-Day landing, Arnold figured the war with Germany would soon end. It was time to start thinking about the next great war. Machines that flew faster than the speed of sound and even touched the edge of space would be the cavalry of the future. In World War II, the United States had been saved by its geographical isolation, by its industrial capacity, and by scientists who came up with advanced weapons ranging from radar and proximity fuses to B-29s and atom bombs. Even after Hitler invaded Poland in September 1939, the United States had still had the luxury of time. But Arnold was certain that whichever nation had the most creative and advanced technology on the first day of the next great war would prevail.

In August 1944, Arnold arranged a cloak-and-dagger meeting with Cal Tech's von Karman at New York's LaGuardia Airport, where Arnold was to change planes on a trip from Washington to Quebec. "When I arrived," von Karman recalled, "an aide drove me to the end of the runway, where an official U.S. Air Force car was parked. Then the aide disappeared. General Arnold was inside the car, and when he saw me approaching, he dismissed his chauffeur. Not another car was in sight."

Arnold asked von Karman to take a leave from Cal Tech and settle in at the Pentagon, where he and a group of top-drawer scientists chosen by von Karman would create a blueprint for post-war airpower research. By the end of the year, the Army Air Forces Scientific Advisory Group, with thirty-one scientists, had begun its work under von Karman's direction.[21] Von Karman quickly found that Arnold had bulldozed a path; every reel and spool of red tape had been pushed aside.

In his official charge to von Karman, dated November 7, 1944, Arnold said the group should remember that it is "a fundamental principle of American democracy that personnel casualties are distasteful. We will continue to fight mechanical rather than manpower wars." (Today, we might substitute the phrase "information-rich" for "mechanical.")

Von Karman's scientists should let their thoughts roam widely, Arnold said. They should assume that the air defenses of a potential enemy would become ever more sophisticated, making it difficult for America's long-range bombers to get through. "Is it now possible to determine if another totally different weapon will replace the airplane? Are manless remote-controlled radar or television assisted precision military rockets… a possibility? Is atomic propulsion a thought for consideration in future warfare?"

Two other questions had huge long-range implications: How much assistance "should we give or ask from our educational and commercial scientific organizations during peacetime?" And more provocatively, "Is the time approaching when all our scientists and their organizations must give a small portion of their time and resources to assist in avoiding future national peril and winning the next war?"[22]

The product of Arnold's LaGuardia initiative consisted of two reports: *Where We Stand*, an overview by von Karman that was given to Arnold in August 1945, and a much longer follow-up drafted by all the scientists: *Toward New Horizons*, dated December 15, 1945.

PREPARING FOR WAR IN TIMES OF PEACE

Where We Stand was largely a summary of a research trip to Germany in which von Karman and his colleagues interviewed German scientists and technicians to assess their accomplishments. The Germans never quite caught up with the Allies in radar, which put them in a desperate fix. But German research into other advanced technologies was first rate. *Where We Stand* insisted that the Army Air Forces must conduct intensive peacetime research into supersonic flight, pilotless aircraft, jet propulsion, radar, and atomic energy for propulsion.[23]

Where We Stand took a close look at German rocketry. Wernher von Braun and his rocket team had developed the V-2, and by the end of the war they were doing conceptual work on a multi-stage rocket that might have been capable of reaching the East Coast of the United States. Beginning in September 1944, 1,852 V-2s were sent against continental targets, mainly Antwerp, whose docks were important to sustaining the Allied invasion, and 1,403 against Britain, most of them toward London.[24] The latter attacks had little effect on the British war effort but they were psychologically devastating. Striking at more than three thousand miles an hour, V-2s outraced their own sound and hit without warning, day and night. The first indication of a V-2 attack was the explosion.

"A part, if not all, of the functions of the manned strategic bomber in destroying the key industries, the communication and transportation systems, and military installations at ranges of from a thousand to ten thousand miles will be taken over by pilotless aircraft of extreme velocity," *Where We Stand* said. One replacement might be an unmanned jet bomber flying at heights of up to sixty thousand feet at twice the speed of sound. Another replacement for manned strategic bombers would be long-range missiles, a "further development" of the V-2.

"By using two or more step [multi-stage] rockets for the acceleration, a very high speed is imparted to a missile, perhaps as high as seventeen thousand miles-per-hour or more, to give ranges of several thousand miles." A cartoonish illustration depicted a globe with a sleek "long range rocket" arcing through space from the United States to Japan. A tiny American flag was planted at the launch site; an equally small Japanese flag waved at the point of impact.[25] (*Where We Stand* was written before the Pacific war ended.)

The main body of the Scientific Advisory Group's study—in thirty-three sections strung over thirteen volumes—was the December 1945 report, *Toward New Horizons*. More than a half century later, *Horizons* is still admired in Air Force circles, but not because it is a useful blueprint. Even von Karman believed *Horizons* quickly became outdated. "What seemed like audacity in 1945," he said, "proved to be 'stick-in-the-mud' in 1957."[26]

Horizons is still spoken of with awe because it outlined a *process* for innovation. It helped institutionalize a way of thinking about the future. If the Army Air Forces were to remain the best in the world, it must continually give accomplished scientists free rein to imagine what might be. Simply projecting current trends into the future would not be good enough. As today's cliché goes, Air Force leaders had to think outside the box.

The topic headings of *Toward New Horizons* suggest its technical breadth: "Aerodynamics and Aircraft Design"; "Aircraft Power Plants"; "Aircraft Fuels and Propellants"; "Guided Missiles and Pilotless Aircraft"; "Explosives and Terminal Ballistics"; "Radar, Communications, and Weather"; "Aeromedics and Psychology." Nonetheless, von Karman's most urgent mission was outlined in his introduction, "Science, the Key to Air Supremacy." He insisted that the Army Air Forces must systematically encourage, nurture, and fund free-wheeling scientific research, including basic research with no clear application within the foreseeable future. (The awkward plural "Air Forces" terminology was abandoned in 1947, when the Air Force became an independent service.)

"Wars are fought with weapons based on fundamentals discovered during the preceding years of peace," von Karman wrote. "Discovery of fundamental results is dependent on an atmosphere of freedom from immediate specific goals and time tables." Government authorities, military or civilian, "should foster, but not dictate, basic research." Centralization of research should be avoided because it can too easily exclude "independent individuals and small groups of research men whose contributions are vital to the maintenance of an abundant scientific life within a nation." It was essential "that the Air Forces continue and expand their present direct relations, spiritual [sic] and contractual, with various universities, research laboratories, and individual scientists." Army Air Forces personnel should be assigned to civilian laboratories—not to supervise the labs or to be liaison officers "but merely to learn."

In times of peace as during the war, civilian consultants should be freely used. Close connections between universities and the government should be maintained. "Cooperative laboratories" should be established "in which the administrative and financial responsibility and management would remain with the government, and the scientific direction would be undertaken by faculty members. This method would solve the security problem and yet have the advantages of the geographical and spiritual connection with a place of scientific learning."[27]

Hap Arnold, who by now wore five stars as General of the Army (along with George C. Marshall, Douglas MacArthur, and Dwight D. Eisenhower), was pleased with the efforts of von Karman & Company. Arnold was intense, tough, and hard to work with. Von Karman was reflective, urbane, engaging, and easy to get along with. Both were wedded to the notion that visionary ideas today would produce decisive weapons tomorrow. Arnold's lasting legacy to the modern Air Force was his insistence that airmen cultivate vision with the help of men like von Karman.[28]

Arnold was a committed fast-tracker. He believed that von Karman's Scientific Advisory Group was terrific but it alone would not produce the roadmap to the future. Among Arnold's last official acts before retiring in March 1946 was the establishment of the office of Deputy Chief of Staff for Research and Development (headed by LeMay) and the creation of Project RAND (Research ANd Development). Although RAND was located at Douglas Aircraft, then the nation's largest defense contractor, it was staffed mostly with civilian scientists.

No other organization would be as pivotal in keeping the U.S. Air Force at the top of the game as RAND, which in 1948 became an independent think tank. The many reports it churned out in the late 1940s and early 1950s on the role that satellites might play in war and peace were chiefly responsible for the immense sophistication that has marked American military-oriented satellites for more than four decades.

By institutionalizing the role of civilian scientists in airpower research and development, Arnold created mutually reinforcing ties between military aviation, the aircraft (now aerospace) industry, defense-related think tanks, and the many worlds of fundamental and applied science. Without the systematic cross-pollination from the aerospace industry, laboratory scientists, and think-tank warriors, space-power theories (and fantasies) would not be as advanced as they are today.

Arnold's legacy lingers. Twenty-eight military and civilian laboratories and organizations advised U.S. Space Command as it put together its *Long Range Plan*, issued in 1998. Fifty aerospace contractors also contributed to the plan—among them, Aerojet, founded by von Karman, and RAND, which Arnold established with the help and cooperation of his old Flying Bug colleague, hunting companion, and in-law, Donald Douglas. (Arnold's son married Douglas's daughter.)[29]

"Any Air Force which does not keep its doctrines ahead of its equipment, and its vision far into the future, can only delude the nation into a false sense of security," Arnold said in his final report to the secretary of war in December 1945.[30]

In farewell remarks to the American people published in the February 1946 issue of *National Geographic*, Arnold said that the security of the United States now lay in continually preparing for war—and in always keeping the technological edge over possible adversaries. What country would attack the United States if it knew U.S. planes would immediately retaliate with atomic weapons? And if at some point Americans believed that bombers might not get the job done, long-range missiles of the "general type of the German V-2 rocket" should be developed and deployed.

But if an enemy somehow came up with a defense against such missiles, "We must be ready to launch [missiles] from unexpected directions"—perhaps "from true space ships, capable of operating outside the earth's atmosphere. The design of such a ship is all but practical today; research will unquestionably bring it into being within the foreseeable future."[31]

TAKE NOTHING FOR GRANTED

In November 1994, fifty years after Arnold first challenged von Karman to assemble a team of scientists to look into the future, Secretary of the Air Force Sheila Widnall and Air Force Chief of Staff Ronald Fogleman directed the Air Force Scientific Advisory Board, the successor to Arnold's Scientific Advisory Group, to produce a study as far-reaching as *Toward New Horizons.*

"We want you to rekindle that constant inquisitive attitude toward science," Widnall told the board during the fiftieth-anniversary celebration. "I challenge you, once again, to search the world for the most advanced aerospace ideas and project them into the future. Fifty years ago the Science Advisory Group stepped up to the challenge of writing *Toward New Horizons.* Today, let's begin the search for 'new world vistas.'"

Widnall and Fogleman received the two-thousand-plus pages of *New World Vistas* on December 15, 1995, fifty years after Arnold was given *Toward New Horizons.*[32] Like *Horizons, Vistas* was largely devoted to the future of the air-breathing Air Force, but it did not ignore space. The Air Force, it said, must evolve into a mix of piloted and unpiloted aircraft. Directed-energy weapons, such as lasers, should be developed. Information superiority must become the currency of battle. Ground-, air-, and space-based surveillance and command-and-control and information systems would inevitably become intertwined. Space itself might even become a battleground.

> The ability to deploy and use weapons from space is constrained by technology and policy issues. At this time national policy restraints are the most significant barrier to such implementation. It would be imprudent to ignore technological developments that could enable such a capability in the future.
>
> The function of a spaceborne weapon is essentially the same as a weapon on any other platform, to deliver a damaging or lethal amount of energy to a target of the warfighter's choosing. In future conflicts, the ability to destroy or incapacitate a target in the most timely manner and with the least collateral damage possible will be at a premium.[33]

Today's space warriors no longer speak of atomic weapons in space, as did Arnold. But the goal is the same: achieving overwhelming military dominance with the help of scientists and industrialists—the classic military/industrial/scientific complex.[34] That systematic collaboration of the military services with industry, civilian scientists, and think-tank analysts has produced a way of fast-break warfare that is overwhelmingly effective—and relies, in large measure, on Arnold's "true space ships."

8

Guardian of the Peace

"True space ships"? General of the Army "Hap" Arnold regu larly looked over the horizon, but even he could not fully see the sort of things that America's favorite ex-Nazi scientist, Wernher von Braun, envisioned. Von Braun, the charismatic German rocketeer who designed the V-2s that terrorized London and Antwerp late in World War II, was the first to systematically argue that the United States—and only the United States—should control space for the good of humankind. That overarching paradigm still energizes many of today's space warriors.

The cover of the March 22, 1952 issue of *Collier's*, then a widely read and influential weekly magazine, featured a painting of a sleek winged rocket silhouetted against the Earth, the surface of which glows in dawn's early light. The space plane thrusts into the blackness of space, its engines ablaze at the moment of separation from the second stage of its booster.

The lead article was by von Braun, the scientific spark behind the Apollo program that eventually got Americans to the Moon and back. But the Moon program lay a decade ahead. In March 1952, von Braun was developing missiles for the U.S. Army and, in *Collier's,* he was making the case that a slowly rotating "wheel-shaped satellite" two-hundred and fifty feet in diameter ought to be built by the United States. The space wheel would circle the Earth every two hours in a north-south orbit at an altitude of one thousand and seventy-five miles.[1]

"From this platform, a trip to the Moon itself will be just a step, as scientists reckon distance in space," said von Braun. If a nation had the vision to build such a space station, Mars finally would be within range. Although a Mars expedition would be an undertaking of "great magnitude," it was technologically possible, not science fiction. With the political will and the money, a "fleet of spaceships carrying fifty or one hundred people" would eventually "leave the Earth's orbit, not to return for more than two and a half years."

A space wheel, von Braun wrote, would advance science in many ways. Meteorologists would be able to observe cloud patterns over large areas of the Earth, enabling them to predict the weather more accurately and further into the future. Likewise, "navigators on the seas and in the air will utilize the space station as a 'fix,' for it will always be recognizable."[2]

"But wait!"—as a twenty-first century late-night TV pitchman might say—"There's *more!*" According to von Braun, a satellite would be an excellent observation and weapons platform. The first nation to build it would forever occupy the ultimate high ground of space, giving it an overwhelming military advantage over all other nations. The satellite would be in near-polar orbit, which meant that the men who manned it would be able to view nearly every point on Earth at least once in a twenty-four-hour period. Technicians "using specially designed, powerful telescopes attached to large optical screens, radarscopes, and cameras" would "keep under constant inspection every ocean, continent, country, and city.... It will be practically impossible for any nation to hide warlike preparations for any length of time."

It would cost about $4 billion to construct such a space station, von Braun estimated, and it would require building and reusing a small fleet of cargo rockets. In 1952, that was real money, nearly twice the cost of World War II's atomic bomb project. The space wheel would take some ten years to complete even if pursued at "top speed." But "if we don't do it, another nation—possibly less peace-minded—will."

Von Braun did not identify the "less peace-minded" nation. There was no need to. Six years earlier, Winston Churchill, no longer Britain's prime minister but still a near-mythic figure, had come to small-town Missouri, at President Truman's invitation, to describe how an "Iron Curtain" had fallen across Europe from "Stettin in the Baltic to Trieste in the Adriatic." In 1949, the Soviet Union had tested an atom bomb and China had succumbed to the Reds. In June 1950, communist North Korea had invaded non-communist South Korea, a war that quickly involved hundreds of thousands of Chinese "volunteers."

Meanwhile, according to Sen. Joseph McCarthy of Wisconsin and his like-minded colleagues, spies and fellow travelers infested organizations from local PTAs to the State Department. Herbert Philbrick's *I Led Three Lives* (loving husband and upstanding citizen, member of the Communist Party, and spy for the FBI) became a best seller and a TV series. Citizens of the United States thought they had reason to worry. Moscow, it was widely believed, was pulling the strings everywhere in its godless campaign to rule the world.

But, said von Braun, if a freedom-loving nation built the space station he described, that nation would become the "guardian of the peace." Technicians aboard the space wheel could keep an eye on what every other nation was up to as clearly as if they were in an airplane just four thousand feet above the ground. If a nation threatened war, "small winged rocket missiles with atomic warheads could be launched from the station in such a manner that they would strike their targets at supersonic speeds. By simultaneous radar tracking of both missile and target, these atomic-headed rockets could be accurately guided to any spot on the Earth."

According to von Braun's calculations, guardian-of-the-peace missiles could hit earthly targets from space with a high degree of accuracy; in contrast, missiles from Earth-bound evildoers could not destroy the well-defended space station. The first nation with a space wheel would have won the millennia-old game of war and peace. "The important point is that the station could defend itself in case of attack and that it could prevent rival stations from being established. Therefore, whether in the hands of a single peace-loving nation, or in the hands of the United Nations, the space station would be a deterrent which might cause a successful outlawing of war."[3]

Not everyone was as enamored of von Braun's space-station vision as Cornelius Ryan, his editor at *Collier's*. Von Braun "talks eloquently and writes well," wrote *Time* magazine's science editor John Norton Leonard in 1953. "He has won an enormous following, not only among the technically naïve, but among that even more credulous type, the semi-technical enthusiasts who have recently graduated from playing with hot-rod jalopies. All over the United States and in many other parts of the world are groups of enthusiasts who dream of hot-rodding off the tedious Earth. Von Braun is their hero because he tells them that it can be done in only ten years or so."[4]

Von Braun's rhetoric, wrote Leonard, gives men who actually work with rockets and missiles "cold chills." These men "spend their lives with detonating fuels, melting metals and psychotic artificial brains. They have seen many beautiful rockets explode into whizzing fragments or flop to inglorious ends a few hundred yards from their launching sites. They know that each forward step is difficult and dangerous, and they believe that von Braun proposes to take one thousand steps as if they were one."[5]

Leonard was right. Von Braun's notion that a huge space station could be built and staffed with the technology available in the 1950s was lofty but unrealistic. Nonetheless, the von Braun–Cornelius Ryan guardian-of-the-peace vision still animates a surprising number of space warriors. Today's von Brauns do not speak of putting nuclear weapons in space; twenty-first-century guardians of the peace would be armed with a variety of antisatellite weapons and other kinds of precision weapons based on land and possibly in space. In the words of Air Force Space Command, the United States would "own" space.

ONE OF THE MOST EXCITING VENTURES

Von Braun was born in 1912 into an upper class Silesian family whose ancestors included "knights, landowners, governors, jurists, diplomats, generals, even rectors of religious schools, but no engineers or scientists." Von Braun studied piano as a teenager with Paul Hindemith and later became proficient at the cello. When he was thirteen, his parents gave him an astronomical telescope, and astronomy and a passion for space flight replaced music.

Von Braun's father, Baron Magnus Freiherr von Braun, attempted to channel his son's "exorbitant" energies toward more "accepted standards of society." It didn't work. "I soon gave up," the baron later said, "and resigned myself to watching him grow, and to quietly paying the bills for broken windows, destroyed flower gardens, and other telltales that his early rocket experiments had left in the homes and yards of our neighbors."[6]

By the time he was twenty, von Braun was a star of the first magnitude in Germany's small constellation of civilian rocket enthusiasts. But he had also come to understand the facts of life in post–World War I Germany. No matter how diligently he and his fellow space-travel romantics tried to raise money for their experiments, the growth of rocket science would be agonizingly slow. Germany had been ravaged by the Great War and by the vengeful peace imposed upon it. The rocketeers needed an angel. In the summer of 1932, von Braun determined that the German Army would be his savior. He and a few colleagues joined forces with Army Ordnance.

Although trips to the Moon and voyages to Mars frolicked in von Braun's head, the leaders of Army Ordnance simply believed that in von Braun and his colleagues they had found a way to circumvent the Versailles Treaty of 1919, which forbade Germany from possessing long-range artillery. Rockets, which had been used in war for centuries, had not been mentioned in the treaty because of their apparent lack of offensive military utility. Powered by gunpowder, early rockets were used mainly to send up flares to illuminate the battlefield at night. Army Ordnance's leaders, however, believed that von Braun's liquid-fueled rockets might someday become a new strike-at-a-distance weapon. By 1932, German soldiers and airmen were already training secretly, some in the Soviet Union.

Von Braun and his colleagues were scientifically sophisticated but politically naïve. Or perhaps they were simply opportunists. Over the decades, many tens of thousands of words have been devoted to the topic. In any case, von Braun later wrote,

> There has been a lot of talk that [the civilian rocket experimenters] finally "sold out to the Nazis." In 1932, however, when the die was cast, the Nazis were not yet in power, and to all of us Hitler was just another mountebank on the political stage. Our feelings toward the Army resembled those of the early aviation pioneers, who, in most countries, tried to milk the military purse for their own ends and who felt little moral scruples as to the possible future use of their brainchild. The issue in those discussions was merely how the golden cow could be milked most successfully.[7]

Inmates of concentration camps were pressed into service as slave labor when V-2 production moved into gear in the summer and fall of 1943, principally at Mittelwerk, an underground plant near Nordhausen, about halfway between Berlin and Frankfurt. Workers, their bodies skeletal from malnutrition, starvation, and disease, died by the thousands. Mass executions and allied bombs also took a terrible toll. One scholar estimates that about ten thousand prisoners who helped build V-2s at Mittelwerk died or were killed.[8] Von Braun and his colleagues, based far to the north at Peenemünde on the Baltic Sea, did not run the production plants, but they made frequent problem-solving trips to Mittelwerk. After the war, von Braun said of one visit: "It is hellish. My spontaneous reaction was to talk to one of the SS guards, only to be told with unmistakable harshness that I should mind my own business, or find myself in the same striped fatigues! I would never have believed that human beings can sink that low, but I realized that any attempt of reasoning on humane grounds would be utterly futile. Such arguments as decency, fairness, morality, or ethics simply did not count here."[9]

As Germany collapsed in early 1945, the U.S. Army, the U.S. Navy, the British Army, and the Red Army sought to scoop up as many German scientists, technicians, and documents as possible, including von Braun's rocket team. The Americans had the most urgent need. The war against Japan was expected to continue into 1946 and German scientific and technical expertise might help defeat the Japanese.

The Americans were quick and clever. They not only took scientists and technicians and technical documents into custody in areas that the Soviets were scheduled to occupy, they poached on territory the British were slated to take over, a fact that greatly annoyed the Brits. At times, Americans even poached on one another. In one case, a Navy "exploitation team" boxed up captured documents and hardware and labeled the crates "U.S. Navy." Two days later, Army teams reached the same location, put the crates into bigger crates, and stenciled them "U.S. Army."[10]

The last months of the European war were chaotic for the scientists and technicians at Peenemünde. Von Braun and his band of brothers knew the Red Army, not the Americans, would capture Peenemünde. But they wanted to surrender to the Americans, not the Soviets. As one engineer later put it, "We despise the French; we are mortally afraid of the Soviets; we do not believe the British can afford us, so that leaves the Americans."[11] As the war wound down, the rocket team moved south so they could continue their work. (As late as January 1945, Hitler was still promising the German people a "wonder weapon" that would turn Germany's fortunes around.)

On May 2, 1945, six days before Germany surrendered, P.F.C. Frederick P. Schneikert, U.S. Army, was standing guard on a road in Bavaria near the Austrian-German border. A bicyclist, dressed in a long leather coat and a clean shirt and tie, came down the road. Schneikert ordered the bicyclist to halt. The man hopped off the bike, raised his hands, and came forward. He said he was Magnus von Braun, brother of Wernher von Braun, the inventor of the V-2. His mission was to find American soldiers to surrender to. The entire rocket team was hiding nearby, Magnus said. They wanted "to see Ike as soon as possible."[12]

The Peenemünders did not see the Supreme Allied Commander, who was otherwise occupied, but they were now safe and they had great expectations. If invited to the United States, they could—as civilians—haggle over terms, which some did. They wanted three-year contracts, but they had to settle for six-month deals, with the understanding that their services were likely to be renewed. They would not be permitted to bring their families, at least not right away. But they negotiated an agreement in which their families would be well looked after in Germany, where living conditions were harsh.

Von Braun's starting salary in America was seven hundred and fifty dollars a month, with perks. That was a handsome package in 1945, particularly for a man who had designed weapons that had randomly rained terror on England and Belgium just months earlier, and who had—albeit indirectly—employed slave labor to make his random-death machines. On the other hand, it would be a mistake to believe that von Braun had an overpowering interest in politics or money or machines of war. He wanted to continue building rockets. In May 1945, von Braun wrote a paper summarizing German rocket developments for his new American handlers. He said, in part:

> As a next step in rocket development, we should expect rockets with longer ranges, and also anti-aircraft rockets that can be guided to their targets with radio guide bombs, or with automatic homing devices. Further developments will certainly include rocket-launched satellites for Earth observations and astronomical studies, manned rocket flight, and also orbiting space stations with permanent human occupancy. In the long run, developments will provide opportunities to travel to the Moon and to planets.[13]

Among the Americans who debriefed the members of the rocket team was Major Robert B. Staver, chief of the jet propulsion section of Army Ordnance. In December 1945, he sent his superiors a rapturous report on how to use the newly acquired Germans. "The times call for some visionary planning," he said. If the Army utilized the Germans properly and mounted a major research and development program, "within twenty-five years this country will find itself about twenty-five years ahead of the rest of the world." Indeed, the military program would "result in one of the most exciting ventures in history."[14]

HIGH HOPES

The Army men who listened to von Braun were hooked. They did not care about von Braun's obsession with space stations and space travel, but they were reasonably certain that he and his men could develop advanced missiles that would give the United States an edge in the next war. In contrast, Cdr. Harvey Hall of the Navy's Bureau of Aeronautics was intrigued by the notion of manmade satellites serving as observation platforms. The oceans were wide and trackless. It was not an easy thing to keep up with who had what, and where, in the blue-water deep. Observation satellites would surely prevent future Pearl Harbor-style attacks and ensure victory in naval battles.

Commander Hall formed a Navy Committee for Evaluation of the Feasibility of Space Rocketry, which worked closely with consultants from Douglas Aircraft, North American Aviation, the Glenn C. Martin Company, and the aeronautical laboratory at Cal Tech. The consultants said a satellite would be technically feasible but expensive.

"Expensive" was the key word. Military budgets were slashed after the war. Might not the Navy and the Army, Hall asked, reach beyond their traditional rivalries and pool resources to launch a satellite? On March 7, 1946, representatives of the U.S. Army Air Forces and the U.S. Navy faced one another at a meeting of the War Department's Aeronautical Board. Yes, they were interested in the Navy proposal, the airmen said, but they wanted to think the proposition over. Another meeting was scheduled for May 14.

The "think-it-over" bit was a gambit. The Army Air Forces believed it should have primary responsibility for a military satellite, if one were ever built. Satellites, the reasoning went, would be way up there in the wild blue yonder—beyond it, for that matter. Given that, satellites and spaceships would be extensions of strategic air power.[15] Carl A. Spaatz, commanding general of the Army Air Forces, and Curtis LeMay, his deputy chief of staff for research and development, were determined to protect their turf by outflanking the Navy. The Air Forces, however, would have to do more than merely say "no" to the Navy at the May 14 Aeronautical Board meeting. A thumbs-down without proper explanation would seem churlish.[16]

Spaatz and LeMay knew where to find a quick fix to their interservice dilemma: the newly created Air Forces think tank, Project RAND. LeMay asked RAND to prepare a report that would demonstrate that the Army's air arm was not only up to speed but capable of pursuing satellite development on its own when the time was right. By May 2, the sixteen-member RAND team had produced a three hundred and twenty-one page study, *Preliminary Design of an Experimental World-Circling Spaceship.* It was the first report of the new organization and it is a space-lore classic.[17]

Unmanned orbiting satellites were feasible, the RAND team said, even with technology not much more advanced than that reached in the V-2 program. If the United States chose to do it, a five-hundred-pound satellite could be inserted into orbit within five years or so at a cost of about $150 million. The first manmade satellite "would inflame the imagination of mankind, and would probably produce repercussions in the world comparable to the explosion of the atomic bomb."

A couple of decades later, satellites would "be one of the most potent scientific tools of the twentieth century." They would be a boon for cosmic ray research, studies of gravitation, investigations into variations in the Earth's magnetic field, as well as the properties of the ionosphere. The vacuum of space would be useful in experiments requiring low pressures. Further, "biologists and medical scientists would want to study life in the acceleration-free environment of the satellite. This is an important prerequisite to space travel by man."

Satellites would open new worlds of knowledge to astronomers. "A telescope of even modest size could, at a point outside the Earth's atmosphere, make observations… which would be superior to those now made with the largest terrestrial telescopes." Weather forecasters also would be delighted.

"From a satellite at an altitude of hundreds of miles, circling the Earth in a period of about one and one half hours, observations of the cloud patterns on Earth, and of their changes with time, could be made with great ease and convenience." Weather observations, like astronomical observations, would be sent back "by television means."

Satellites would revolutionize global communications. Long-range radio, in which signals were bounced off the lower layers of the ionosphere to distant points, was notoriously unreliable because the ionosphere was always in flux, affected by "the time of day, the season, sunspot activity, and other factors." In contrast, communications satellites would offer predictability and thus reliability.

It is likely that the RAND experts had by then read a provocative article published in the October 1945 issue of *Wireless World,* which suggested that space stations in geostationary orbits could bring telephone, radio, and television to the entire planet. "Extra-Terrestrial Relays: Can Rocket Stations Give World-Wide Radio Coverage?" was written by Arthur C. Clarke, then a young British space-travel enthusiast who had worked with American scientists and technicians on glide-path radar systems during the war. His RAF colleagues called him "Spaceship."[18]

The bulk of the RAND study was a technical look at rocket engines, fuels, materials, and orbital mechanics. But late in the report, the authors wistfully wrote that it "must be confessed that in back of many minds of the men working on this study there lingered the hope that our impartial engineering analysis would bring forth a vehicle not unsuited to human transportation." Their analyses led them to believe that acceleration forces could be borne by the human body and that it might be possible to create a human-friendly environment in space. Most important, the belief that someday it would be possible to return satellites safely from space gave the RAND team "a note of assurance that the hope of an inhabited satellite is not futile."

Nonetheless, Project RAND was an Army Air Forces think tank and the military implications of Earth satellites could hardly be ignored. Although the Air Forces' bombers had contributed greatly to winning World War II, the report said, air defense systems would steadily improve and U.S. bombers would have a tougher go of it in future wars.

"Modern radar will detect aircraft at distances up to a few hundred miles, and can give continuous, precise data on their position." Meanwhile, the accuracy of the enemy's anti-aircraft guns would be improved and guided anti-aircraft missiles would become ever more deadly. "This being so, we can assume that an air offensive of the future will be carried out largely or altogether by high-speed pilotless missiles."

Today, warheads atop intercontinental ballistic missiles are said to be able to hit targets five or six thousand miles distant within yards of their aimpoints. Extraordinarily sophisticated onboard inertial guidance systems make that degree of accuracy possible. But in 1946, such precision in onboard guidance was not anticipated. Military satellites, however, might solve the accuracy problem, RAND said. After the missiles were fired, observations from space would enable missile controllers to analyze the trajectories of the missiles and then send them the "final control impulse" that would direct the missiles precisely to their intended targets.

Alternatively, RAND said, an unmanned satellite could be a weapon. "After observation of its trajectory, a control impulse can be applied in such direction and amount, and at such a time, that the satellite is brought down on its target."

The authors of the RAND study were keenly aware that they were working with an exceedingly foggy crystal ball in the spring of 1946. They emphasized that the wonders they described were not yet possible. A five-hundred-pound spaceship based on technologies then available would be a primitive affair, albeit awe-inspiring in public-relations terms. Nonetheless, the folks at RAND had high hopes:

> The craft which would result from such an undertaking would almost certainly do the job of becoming a satellite, but it would be bulky, expensive, and inefficient in terms of the spaceship we shall be able to design after twenty years of intensive work in this field. In making the decision as to whether or not to undertake construction of such a craft now, it is not inappropriate to view our present situation as similar to that in airplanes prior to the flight of the Wright brothers. We can see no more clearly all the utility and implications of spaceships than the Wright brothers could see fleets of B-29s bombing Japan and air transports circling the globe.[19]

With twenty years of intensive work, American spaceships—imagery, communications, and warning satellites—had become essential to keeping the Cold War peace. In another thirty years, new generations of imagery, signals-intercepting communications, geo-positioning, and weather satellites had become central to the prosecution of America's new way of fast-break war. The von Braun guardian-of-the-peace rhetoric, resurrected and refined, is now called "prompt global strike" from space.

9

The Right Question

At the end of World War II, Josef Stalin feared the United States. He was certain America would use the bomb to intimidate Moscow, which sought to consolidate its newly acquired holdings in Eastern and Central Europe and to expand its influence in the Mediterranean, the Middle East, and the Far East. "Hiroshima has shaken the whole world," Stalin reportedly said after the destruction of Hiroshima and Nagasaki. "The balance has been destroyed."[1]

Stalin had established a Soviet bomb program in February 1943. But in a nation in which scarce industrial resources were devoted to the immediate task of defeating Germany, the program made little progress. In late 1945, Stalin was determined to restore the global balance by greatly accelerating the bomb project. Lavrenti Beria, chief of the secret police and among the most feared men in the Soviet Union, was put in charge. In the war-ravaged Soviet Union, atomic scientists were among the few who had ample food, good housing, and other perks. The quid pro quo: they must produce a nuclear weapon quickly.[2]

The Soviet Union tested its atom bomb on August 29, 1949. The first scientist to venture onto ground zero (in a retrofitted tank) commented that the sandy soil around the bomb crater had turned to glass that "crackled eerily beneath the tracks of the tank. Molten lumps flew about in all directions like small pieces of shrapnel and radiated invisible alpha, beta, and gamma rays.... The steel girders of a bridge were twisted into a ram's horn."[3]

The twenty-fourth Soviet nuclear test took place on November 22, 1955. It was an air-dropped prototype hydrogen bomb. Being a test device, its explosive yield was intentionally cut in half—part of its expensive fusion fuel had been replaced with inert material. Nonetheless, the bomb exploded with the power of about 1.6 million tons of TNT.

THE EARTH CHANGED

Dwight D. Eisenhower did not assume the presidency at an easy moment in the nation's history. On January 20, 1953, inauguration day, things seemed unusually dicey. The Korean War had dragged on since June 1950 and many Americans thought it might be necessary to use nuclear weapons to end it. But if nuclear weapons were used in Korea, would that be the beginning of the end? The Soviet Union presumably had become a nuclear power by 1953, and the conventional wisdom was that Moscow had ordered the invasion of South Korea in a campaign to chip away at the "Free World." World War III might well begin in Korea.

And if not in Korea, World War III might possibly begin in Berlin, a divided city in a ripped-apart nation. Editorial cartoonists regularly depicted Berlin, located deep within the Soviet sector, as a wooden powder keg with a burning fuse. Or perhaps the flashpoint would be at the other end of the Eurasian land mass: Taiwan, then called Formosa. Red China coveted Formosa, to which the remnants of the old Chiang Kai-shek government had fled after losing China's long civil war. The United States supported Chiang even though he was hopelessly corrupt. If war came in the Taiwan Strait, could it be contained? On the other hand, war might begin merely because the Soviet Union and the United States were primed for it, *expecting* it.

By the time Eisenhower took the oath, authorities in a few major cities, including New York, San Francisco, and Seattle, had begun issuing metal identification tags to schoolchildren. (In Philadelphia, they could be purchased in stores.) The tags looked suspiciously like military dog tags. Meanwhile, children in large cities were learning to "duck and cover" in the event of an atomic flash. A cartoon character named Bert began to appear in short animated films:

> *There was a turtle by the name of Bert.*
> *And Bert the Turtle was very alert.*
> *When danger threatened him he never got hurt.*
> *He knew just what to do.*
> *He'd Duck and Cover. Duck and Cover.*
> *He did what we all must learn to do.*
> *You and you and you and you.*
> *Duck and Cover!*[4]

For adults, there was the enormously popular movie *The Day the Earth Stood Still*, still a staple of late-night TV. Klaatu, a mysterious, handsome, and awesomely courteous stranger, and his silent and indestructible robot companion, Gort, land their flying saucer on The Ellipse in Washington, D.C. Klaatu issues a chilling message to Planet Earth: Now that you earthlings have atomic weapons, you are being closely watched.

> The universe grows smaller every day and the threat of aggression by any group anywhere can no longer be tolerated. There must be security for all—or no one is secure.... It is no concern of ours how you run your own planet, but if you threaten to extend your violence, this Earth of yours will be reduced to a burned-out cinder.

On a higher intellectual plane, people puzzled endlessly over Ray Bradbury's new book, *The Martian Chronicles*, a collection of short stories and vignettes that was to become one of the most widely read science fiction works of the 1950s. *Chronicles* told of mordant, lyrical, fantastic, and just plain odd encounters between colonists from Earth and native Martians. Although the stories were set on Mars, a war-ravaged Earth was a background player. Eventually, Earth was consumed in nuclear fire, as depicted in a bizarre, offhand manner in the vignette, "The Off Season." Sam, one of the colonists on Mars, looks up one night in the year 2005:

> Earth changed in the black sky.
> It caught fire.
> Part of it seemed to come apart in a million pieces, as if a gigantic jigsaw had exploded. It burned with an unholy dripping glare for a minute, three times normal size, then dwindled.[5]

LOOSE CANNONS

Eisenhower's loathing of nuclear weapons is well documented. He would gladly abolish such weapons if feasible, he often said.[6] Nonetheless, by the time he took office, the Soviet Union was a nuclear power and its intentions toward the United States seemed hostile. The president had to reckon with those facts. His response was—in part—his "New Look" defense posture.

The New Look was essentially the Truman policy of containment and deterrence writ in starker and more systematic terms. The fact that Eisenhower, widely regarded at home and abroad as a man of peace, would use the threat of massive nuclear retaliation to preserve peace puzzles many. The doctrine had many nuances and contradictions. But in shorthand, it rested on these premises:

- Soviet leaders wanted to preserve their own power within the Soviet Union and Soviet satellite states. If they could expand Soviet influence elsewhere, they surely would, but not at the risk of war with the United States.
- The best way to ensure that the Soviet Union and the United States did not stumble into war by miscalculation was for the United States to emphasize that nuclear war would be destructive beyond measure.
- The United States must not allow itself to get sucked into further Korean-style "limited" or "brushfire" wars fomented by the Soviet Union. Brushfire wars would drain U.S. resources; more important, such wars could flare out of control and bring the United States and the Soviet Union into direct confrontation.
- The Cold War was likely to last for a long time, possibly decades. The United States, however, would eventually prevail if it remained true to its fundamental spiritual values and its democratic principles, and if it avoided spending itself into bankruptcy on armaments.
- Eisenhower's strategy for avoiding nuclear war was straightforward: Make it clear that war between the United States and the Soviet Union was unthinkable and therefore must not be fought. That was not a strategy for peace; at best, it promised an uneasy stalemate. His bolder plan was to propose concrete measures that would eventually bring the military competition—and thus the Cold War—to an end.

But first, the president had to ensure that nuclear war did not begin because of miscalculations or miscommunications, or as the result of missed opportunities. That meant putting a lid on some of his top military officers, many of whom believed that war with the Soviet Union was virtually inevitable. It would likely begin, they thought, with a Soviet bolt from the blue, a preemptive strike that could largely disarm America.

The first major public bolt-from-the-blue warning came in the July 5 and August 16, 1948 issues of *Life* magazine, then arguably the most popular and influential publication in the United States. The author of the two-part article was Carl Spaatz, the recently retired chief of staff of the Air Force. At present, said Spaatz, the Soviet Union was no match for the

United States, which was still the sole atomic power. That would change. The Russians were "working feverishly to break the American monopoly." As early as 1952, the Russians might have their own atomic bombs—and the bombers that could deliver them.

Soviet Tupolev bombers (copies of the American B-29) would lack the range to hurt the United States with conventional explosives, Spaatz said. Although they could reach U.S. cities, they would not have enough fuel to return to their bases. With conventional bombs, that wouldn't make sense; World War II-style bombing required return trips to the same targets. But once the Soviets had multiple atomic bombs, Soviet leaders might be tempted to stage a "flash blow."

> The atomic bomb is so powerful and the opportunities of surprise are so great that conservative military planners now accept the proposition that a nation's whole bomber force might with great profit be expended in a single paralyzing attack. From either Murmansk or eastern Siberia practically every U.S. industrial area of consequence falls within the Tupolev's one-way, no-return range. To be sure, all airplanes so dispatched would be lost, and the crews as well, although the latter might seek escape by landing at sea or in the Arctic wilderness. But with such stakes would the fatalistic Russians boggle?[7]

Although Eisenhower believed it highly unlikely that Soviet leaders would ever order a bolt from the blue on the United States, he could not be certain. The fear of a surprise attack, wrote science adviser James R. Killian, "haunted Eisenhower throughout his presidency."[8] Like most military men and national security analysts, the president believed that if the evidence were conclusive that the Soviet Union was about to launch a strike, American bombers ought to get into the air and—with luck—destroy some of the Soviet planes while they were still on the ground.

Where does one draw the line? How could one be certain beyond any possibility of doubt that the Soviet Union was just days or hours away from launching an attack? At what point might preemptive strikes become a wholly immoral preventive war? How does one maintain pressure on a hair trigger without inadvertently firing? And if the "other side" knows that you are ready to pull the trigger, might it be tempted to launch its own preemptive attack? And if you *believe* the other side is entertaining such thoughts… what do you do then?

Beginning during the Truman administration, at least a few American military men had devised a prescription for ending the mental agony that came from the endless worry about a Pearl Harbor-style strike on the United States as well as on American bases abroad: an *American* bolt from the blue.

Shortly after the end of World War II, Gen. Leslie Groves, the Manhattan Project chief, helped draft a U.S. plan that would have turned control of atomic energy over to an organization established by the United Nations. The plan didn't fly. That didn't surprise Groves, who had little confidence in the United Nations, the Soviet Union, or the plan itself.

In a confidential memo to a member of the U.S. delegation to the newly created U.N. Atomic Energy Commission dated January 2, 1946—more than five months *before* the U.S. plan was officially presented to the United Nations—Groves outlined an alternative strategy. If the international control approach failed, as he believed it would, the United States must consider something completely different: preemptive military action.

> If we were truly realistic, instead of idealistic, as we appear to be, we would not permit any foreign power with which we are not firmly allied, and in which we do not have absolute confidence, to make or possess atomic weapons. If such a country started to make atomic weapons we would destroy its capacity to make them before it had progressed far enough to threaten us.… With atomic weapons, a nation must be ready to strike the first blow if needed. The first blow or series of first blows may be the last.[9]

In April 1947, Adm. Ralph Ofstie, a heavyweight in Navy circles, said in a memo to the U.S. Navy General Board that he had no problem with striking first and "knock[ing] hell out of Moscow with atomic bombs." Meanwhile, an article in the Fall 1947 issue of *Air University Quarterly Review* said "the complexion of atomic war reemphasizes the old cliché that the best defense is a good offense and alters it somewhat: the best defense is the *first* offense in force." A year later in the same publication, an editorial argued that the public should be enlightened about America's options. Once informed, the public would support preventive war.[10]

General Orvil Anderson, commandant of the Air War College, a clout-heavy institution based in Alabama, was quoted in an August 1950 issue of the *Montgomery Advertiser* as saying: "Give me the order to do it and I could break up Russia's five A-bomb nests in a week. And when I went up to Christ I think I could explain to Him why I wanted to do it—now—before it is too late. I think I could explain to Him that I had saved civilization."[11] Anderson thought that portion of the newspaper interview had been off the record; he assumed too much and he was relieved of his command.

About the same time, Secretary of the Navy Francis Matthews said in a speech at the Boston Navy Yard that the United States must be ready "to pay any price" to achieve world peace, "even the price of *instituting a war to compel cooperation for peace*." (Italics added.) President Truman attempted to put an end to such loose-cannon talk. He fired Matthews and made it clear that he would not tolerate men who contemplated preventive war. In his *Memoirs*, Truman said of Matthews and others who had taken up the preventive-war chant: "There is nothing more foolish than to think that war can be stopped by war. You don't 'prevent' anything but peace."[12]

Now, on January 20, 1953, Eisenhower took over the chore of strapping down the loose cannons on the ship of state, the most vocal of which was Gen. Curtis LeMay, commander of the Strategic Air Command and later vice chief and then chief of staff of the Air Force. In 1957, LeMay, a long-time champion of preemptive attack, told one high-level defense analyst, Robert C. Sprague, that he was not worried that the Soviet Union could actually carry off an effective surprise attack. He said he "had airplanes flying secret missions over Soviet territory twenty-four hours a day, picking up all sorts of intelligence information." He would not have to rely on distant early warning radars to give him *tactical* warning of an attack; he would have plenty of *strategic* warning.

"If I see that the Russians are amassing their planes for an attack, I'm going to knock the shit out of them before they take off the ground."

"But general," Sprague said, "that's not national policy."

"I don't care," the general replied. "It's my policy. That's what I'm going to do."[13]

Itchy trigger fingers troubled the president. But the deeper problem was systemic: a lack of solid information about Soviet capabilities upon which to base rational policies and plans. Carl von Clausewitz, a Prussian Army officer, a veteran of the Napoleonic Wars and the most famous military theoretician since Sun-tzu, spoke of the "fog of war." He focused on the unpredictability of war, its accidental character, and the role of chance. Uncertainty adds to the "friction" of war. "Three-quarters of the factors on which action in war is based are wrapped in a fog of greater or lesser uncertainty.... Chance makes everything more uncertain and interferes with the whole course of events."[14] During Eisenhower's tenure, von Clausewitz's observations could have been amended to "the fog of the Cold War could be fatal in the nuclear age."

During the Cold War, U.S. forces had to be prepared for surprise attack. But in a time of high East-West tension—when hard information about Soviet capabilities and readiness would be sketchy and ambiguous—a miscalculation could lead to a tragic outcome. Near the end of his first year in office, President Eisenhower wrote in his diary, "As of now the world is racing toward catastrophe."[15]

Americans were not alone in fearing a surprise attack. At Moscow's highest levels, many Soviet officers, analysts, and policymakers were persuaded that the United States was building fleets of bombers and enlarging its stockpile of nuclear bombs precisely so it could launch a preventive war against the Soviet Union.

"[Stalin] lived in terror of an enemy attack," Nikita Khrushchev recalled in his memoirs. "For him foreign policy meant keeping the anti-aircraft unit around Moscow on a twenty-four-hour alert."[16] If war seemed imminent to Moscow's leaders, would they be tempted to launch their own preemptive strike during a time of high tension?

AN ACT OF WAR?

An American military attaché spotted a new Soviet all-jet bomber at an air base south of Moscow in 1953. The Myasishchev-4, later dubbed the "Bison" by the United States, was huge—roughly equivalent to America's B-52, which was then coming into production. More Bison sightings were reported in 1954 and 1955.

In May 1954, Nathan Twining, chief of staff of the Air Force, said on Armed Forces Day that the Bison had been developed for the sole purpose of "reaching important targets in the United States." He added that the Soviet air force had become "by far the biggest air force in the world"—it had "thousands more combat planes than the United States Air Force, Navy, Marines, and Army combined."[17]

The 1956 National Intelligence Estimate or "NIE" predicted that the Soviet Union might have five hundred Bisons capable of attacking the United States by the early 1960s. U.S. Air Force estimates were even higher—six to eight hundred Bisons. Both the NIE and the Air Force estimates were wrong, partly because they were based on sketchy evidence (very few sightings) and erroneous assumptions. But at the time, Eisenhower's critics said a "bomber gap" was developing and accused a budget-obsessed president of placing the United States in mortal jeopardy. After Sputnik, bomber-gap rhetoric was replaced by claims of a missile gap.

In the early days of the Eisenhower administration, the U.S. intelligence community could offer only crude guesses regarding Soviet missile capabilities. A National Intelligence Estimate given to Eisenhower in October 1954 said that "our best assessment" was based on "inadequate evidence" in a "largely unexplored field."[18] By 1957, another NIE had apparently made a quantum leap in certainty. It asserted that by the end of 1960 the Soviets would deploy some five hundred intercontinental ballistic missiles (ICBMs) and about a thousand by the middle of 1961, many times the number of missiles the United States would have.

The latter estimate became the foundation of the missile gap, which grew ever larger as Eisenhower's critics, especially Democrats with presidential aspirations such as Senators Stuart Symington of Missouri, Lyndon B. Johnson of Texas, and John F. Kennedy of Massachusetts, used it to hammer the sitting president.

Symington, Johnson, and Kennedy had plenty of company. The question that vexed most Americans in the 1950s was, "What *are* the Soviets up to?" For Eisenhower, that question was the wrong way around. The "answer" called for an exercise in long-distance mind reading, which meant the query was essentially unanswerable. The intentions of a nation's leaders are a matter of guesswork in the best of circumstances when diplomatic channels are relatively free of static. But diplomatic channels between the United States and the Soviet Union were ablaze with static; that had always been so, even during World War II when the two nations were allies of convenience.

Eisenhower was more interested in another question, the right question: What were the Soviet Union's actual capabilities? What was the hard evidence? From early in Eisenhower's tenure, the intelligence community had been aware that the Soviet Union had a long-range bomber program as well as a missile program. But how advanced were these programs? What kinds of bombers were they building? What was their range? Where were their bases? As for missiles, how far along was the Soviet program? Had Soviet scientists solved the reentry problem? (A nose cone, like most meteors, tended to burn up upon reentry into the atmosphere; the warhead inside the cone would be damaged or destroyed.) If the Soviets actually had operational missiles, where were their launch pads? What was their range? How many did the Soviets have?

The threat allegedly posed by Soviet bombers had been worrisome enough—but long-range Soviet missiles? The hair trigger of nuclear war would suddenly get a lot more sensitive if the Soviet Union had perfected ICBMs.

The president's intuition told him that a missile gap probably did not exist. He understood that the ability to insert sputniks into orbit did not automatically translate into a grave military threat. Putting a satellite into orbit was easy compared to the task of reliably putting a missile warhead on target after a fiery reentry.

Further, the president was wise to the perils of worst-case analyses, especially when they served the interests of one service over the others—in this case, the Air Force. He suspected that the missile gap was the product of such analyses by the Air Force and its friends in the booming aerospace industry.

The dynamic inside the Pentagon was also familiar: the more alarming the presumed threat, the more likely it was that a service—Army, Navy, or Air Force—could persuade Congress to fund newer and more expensive weapons in ever greater numbers. One historian says that "in the Oval Office, Eisenhower railed against the 'sanctimonious, hypocritical bastards' pushing the missile gap. 'God help the nation when it has a president who doesn't know as much about the military as I do.'"[19]

We now know that Eisenhower was right. Bomber and missile gaps existed all right, but the numbers were all in America's favor. But in the mid- and late 1950s, how could the president conclusively prove whether a bomber or missile gap did or did not exist?[20]

On-the-ground human intelligence—"HUMINT" in intelligence argot—was not good enough. Allen Dulles, director of central intelligence, was a partisan of cloak-and-dagger intelligence; Eisenhower was not, at least insofar as the Soviet Union was concerned. The Soviet Union was a police state tighter than any the modern world had ever known. It was not a HUMINT-friendly environment.

Eisenhower was faced with a numbingly dangerous choice when he took office. Soviet agents needed little more than a Rand McNally road atlas to locate nearly everything of importance in the United States. In contrast, the Soviet Union was such a tightly closed society and such a vast country that American planners had only vague ideas of what was going on there. Aerial reconnaissance of the Soviet Union seemed to be the only way to go.

And yet, according to international law it was unlawful to intentionally fly over the territory of another nation without first asking permission. To do so could be construed as an act of war. Nonetheless, uncertainty surrounding Soviet activities was itself dangerous; in a time of tension, uncertainty regarding Soviet capabilities could lead to war. Eisenhower had to do something to dispel the fog.

The Earth had changed immeasurably since the advent of atomic weapons, but it had not yet disintegrated into Ray Bradbury's nuclear fire. To help preserve the peace, uneasy as it was, Eisenhower needed hard data regarding Soviet capabilities. Guesswork, even when well informed, was not good enough. Aerial spying in which bombers and hangars and missiles could be located and counted was essential.

Aerial data would help the nation prepare for war by giving war planners the precise coordinates of Soviet targets. That's why Strategic Air Command favored it, and that's why the Soviet Union would try to shoot down American spy planes. But outweighing everything, from the president's perspective, was the fact that solid data gained from aerial spying could *diminish* the possibility of war by reducing the uncertainty about Soviet capabilities. In turn, that would allow him to confidently pursue an arms control agenda.

"Without [aerial reconnaissance] you would only have your fears on which to plan your own defense arrangements and your whole military establishment," Eisenhower told George W. Goddard, dean of America's aerial reconnaissance corps before and during World War II. "Now if you're going to use nothing but fear and that's all you have, you are going to make us an armed camp. So this kind of knowledge is vital to us."[21]

10

Open Skies, Space Spies

After the death of Josef Stalin in March 1953, President Dwight Eisenhower launched a peace offensive with an April 16 speech before the annual convention of the American Society of Newspaper Editors. The Cold War had "been tragic for the world and, for the Soviet Union," the president said. What could the world hope for "if no turning is found on this dread road?"

The worst to be feared and the best to be expected can be simply stated.

The worst is atomic war.

The best would be this: a life of perpetual fear and tension; a burden of arms draining the wealth and the labor of all peoples; a wasting of strength that defies the American system or the Soviet system or any system to achieve true abundance and happiness for the peoples of this earth.

Every gun that is made, every warship launched, every rocket fired signifies, in the final sense, a theft from those who hunger and are not fed, those who are cold and are not clothed.

This world in arms is not spending money alone.

It is spending the sweat of its laborers, the genius of its scientists, the hopes of its children.

The cost of one modern heavy bomber is this: a modern brick school in more than thirty cities.

It is two electric power plants, each serving a town of sixty thousand population.

It is two fine, fully equipped hospitals.

It is some fifty miles of concrete highway.

We pay for a single fighter with a half million bushels of wheat.

We pay for a single destroyer with new homes that could have housed more than eight thousand people.

This, I repeat, is the best way of life to be found on the road the world has been taking.

This is not a way of life at all, in any true sense. Under the cloud of threatening war, it is humanity hanging from a cross of iron.[1]

The moment had come, said Eisenhower, for "governments of the world to speak their intentions with simplicity and with honesty." For its part, the United States was prepared to enter into comprehensive disarmament negotiations that would, in the end, include "a practical system of inspection under the United Nations." Negotiations would be only a start. Neither the United States nor any other nation could properly claim to possess a perfect, immutable formula for disarmament.

"But the outcome of such a disarmament process would be clear. It would be a peace founded upon decent trust and cooperative effort among nations" and "fortified, not by weapons of war but by wheat and by cotton, by milk and by wool, by meat and by timber and by rice. These are words that translate into every language on earth. These are needs that challenge this world in arms."

The speech was well received in the United States and in many parts of the world, even in India where pro-Soviet sentiments were strong. But it seems to have impressed no one in the Kremlin hierarchy, whose top men were engaged in a post-Stalin power struggle of shifting alliances and intrigue, a contest that would not definitively end until the summer of 1957, when Nikita Khrushchev finally cemented his first-among-equals position. Meanwhile, the president's overtures were rebuffed.

Eisenhower's second major disarmament initiative came in July 1955, at a summit conference in the magnificently ornate Palais des Nations in Geneva, Switzerland. The cast of principals: Eisenhower; Anthony Eden, prime minister of Britain; Edgar Faure, prime minister of France; and Nikolai Bulganin, prime minister of the Soviet Union and chairman of the Soviet Council of Ministers. Nikita Khrushchev, first secretary of the communist party, and Vyacheslav Molotov, foreign minister, accompanied Bulganin.[2]

The conference would confront a host of difficult issues, the most troublesome being the perennial questions of how to promote disarmament and what to do about a divided Germany. The United States, Britain, and

France sought to reunify Germany; the Soviet Union, which believed it had ample reason to mistrust a unified Germany, wanted to make the division permanent. Meanwhile, disarmament, which everyone talked about in grand terms but no one was willing to do anything substantive to bring about, seemed to be a dead horse. The gulf between East and West was wide and deep.

On the fourth day of the conference, Eisenhower began his main speech. "Disarmament is one of the most important subjects on our agenda," he said. But "it is also extremely difficult." Verification was the principal problem. "No sound and reliable agreement can be made unless it is completely covered by an inspection and reporting system adequate to support every portion of the agreement." The United States had not yet been "able to discover any scientific or other inspection method" that could verify the elimination of nuclear weapons with certainty. "So far as we are aware no other nation has made such a discovery." Up to that point, the speech had been well-meaning boilerplate. But then Eisenhower took off his glasses, laid them on the table, turned toward Bulganin and Khrushchev, and said:

> I propose, therefore, that we take a practical step; that we begin an arrangement, very quickly, as between ourselves—immediately. These steps would include:
>
> To give each other a complete blueprint of our military establishments, from beginning to end, from one end of our countries to the other; lay out the establishments and provide the blueprints to each other.
>
> Next, to provide within our countries facilities for aerial photography to the other country—we to provide the facilities within our country, ample facilities for aerial reconnaissance, where you can make all the pictures you choose and take them to your own country to study; you to provide exactly the same facilities for us and we to make these examinations, and by this step to convince the world that we are providing as between ourselves against the possibility of great surprise attack, thus lessening danger and relaxing tension.
>
> Likewise, we will make more easily attainable a comprehensive and effective system of inspection and disarmament, because what I propose, I assure you, would be but a beginning.

Eisenhower's "Open Skies" proposal was electrifying.[3] "I wish," said France's Faure, "the people of the world could have been in this conference room to hear the voice of a man speaking from great military experience. Had this been possible, they would believe that something had changed in the world in the handling of this question of disarmament."[4] Even Bulganin, the presumed head of the Soviet delegation, said the proposal was sincere and worthy of study.

After adjournment, the delegates and their aides moved to a reception hall for drinks and chatter. Khrushchev quickly confronted the president. "I disagree with (Bulganin). The trouble is, this is just espionage. We do not question your motives in making this proposal, but who are you trying to fool?... This kind of plan would be fine for you because it would give your strategic forces the chance to gather target information and zero in on us."[5]

Eisenhower was dismayed and responded: "Mr. Khrushchev, surely your scientists and your generals are telling you the same thing ours are telling us. One of these bombs would devastate any major city, then stir up death-dealing dust that will blow with the winds around the world. As you know, these winds blow west to east; so if we ever cut loose with a lot of these nuclear bombs, it will be the virtual end of civilization north of the equator.[6]

The Soviets rejected Open Skies; whether Eisenhower truly believed they might accept it is an open question.[7] In any event, the president had a backup plan, which he had approved on November 24, 1954, some eight months before the Geneva summit. One way or another, the closed Soviet system would be opened for aerial inspection. That, Eisenhower believed, would help prevent World War III.

"RAVENS," "CROWS," AND "FERRETS"

U.S. spy planes had been routinely poking around the periphery of the Soviet Union since 1946. The sleuth planes were called "ferrets," a term that harked back to World War II, when British and American electronic-intelligence aircraft acquired the nickname. (British crewmen aboard ferrets were "ravens"; the Americans were "crows"—Americanized ravens.)

Ferreting was serious business. Strategic Air Command would need hard data about the characteristics of Soviet defensive radar systems so American bombers could take countermeasures, if a shooting war ever came. But the crows could not learn much about Soviet radar systems unless the Soviet crews manning the radars turned them on. The crows were endlessly inventive at provoking the Soviets. One crow later recalled: "One of the best tactics is to get right on the deck, at say, two hundred feet or less, and go in real close to the area that you're interested in, and then pop up, to five thousand or seven thousand feet.... This would cause them to turn things on they wouldn't normally turn on."[8]

Another trick was to throw chaff—metal strips—out of the plane. "The Russians would think we were a squadron and all hell would break loose." Senior officers soon banned that practice. "So we came up with another trick. We used to stack all the empty beer cans on the nose wheel hatch. When we got to the Soviet border we would drop the nose wheel for a moment and all the cans would drop. Again the Russians thought we were a squadron and up would come the defenses."[9]

At first, the Soviet leaders were humiliated with their inability to do anything about the American spy flights. "I would even say that the Americans were invincible at that time, and they flaunted this fact by sending their planes all over Europe," Khrushchev later recalled. "They violated the air space of the Soviet Union itself, mostly along the Baltic coast and in the north near Murmansk."[10] Beyond that, the flights frightened Soviet leaders. They feared the United States was probing their defenses in preparation for a surprise attack. One highly respected Soviet military analyst put it this way: "American theoreticians are frankly in favor of preventive war and surprise attack.... Public officials, even though they always speak of the 'incompatibility' of preventive war with the principles of American 'democracy' and 'morality,' in effect fully share these views.... It follows that the threat of unleashing preventive war by American imperialists against the Soviet Union and other countries of the socialist camp is quite real."[11]

The first shoot-down of a ferret flight, a Navy plane eavesdropping on Soviet naval facilities in the Baltic, came on April 8, 1950. Ten men were lost. Soviet officials claimed the aircraft had penetrated ten miles inside Soviet airspace. The United States said that the plane had been over international waters, that it had been fired upon without warning, and that it was not a spy plane. The true nature of the flight, however, quickly leaked out from U.S. sources.[12]

After the Korean War got under way in June 1950, the Strategic Air Command began to press for more than photographic and "signals" intelligence in peripheral areas of the Soviet Union. Pentagon officers and civilian hardliners were convinced that Stalin was putting his plan for world domination into high gear. China had fallen to the communists the previous year; now Korea might explode into World War III. If SAC were to successfully bomb targets deep within the Soviet Union in the event of war, its crews would require good data on where the targets were and what they looked like. Existing maps lacked precision; there were blank areas everywhere.

The lack of reliable up-to-date targeting data had long troubled SAC's war planners. In December 1946, the Air Force initiated Project Wringer in which thousands of German war prisoners repatriated by the Soviet Union were questioned in depth.[13] Other investigators mined wartime German intelligence archives for data. SAC even employed Hitler's senior intelligence officer on the Eastern Front, Reinhard Gehlen, and the remnants of his Nazi spy ring, to develop information on possible Soviet targets. Gehlen's information was often faulty, but SAC commander Curtis LeMay regarded it as better than nothing.

"Certainly what they [the German spy network] provided was far better than what we could have gathered on our own," LeMay recalled in 1971, "because at this time we were really babes-in-the-woods as far as intelligence was concerned."[14]

LeMay had to assume that if war came, SAC's bombers would be forced to attack at night or in rotten weather. Given that, his crews would have to rely on radar, not visual clues, to find their targets. Radar images, however, would not count for much unless the crews had photos of earlier radarscope images of the targets. The crews would also need radarscope images of the terrain that lay along their routes. Deep reconnaissance flights into the heart of the Soviet Union would provide the necessary target data and radarscope imagery.

The Truman administration had worked out an arrangement with Winston Churchill for Britain's Bomber Command to conduct a limited number of secret deep-penetration flights. SAC would supply the planes—high-flying, jet-powered B-45s equipped for radar spying; Bomber Command would provide the crews and the airbase, Sculthorpe, in Norfolk. U.S. Air Force markings were stripped from the B-45s and replaced by RAF insignia. The British crews were trained at airbases in Louisiana and Ohio.

The first long-range "RAF" flights over Soviet territory occurred in April 1952. One plane left England and headed for the Baltic states. Another was vectored toward Moscow. The third flew over industrial complexes in southern Ukraine. The crews, which carried fake flight plans, had been briefed to say they had been lost, if downed by the Soviets. "How much that [story] would have worn with all the equipment on the aircraft I don't know," said one crew member. "And if that [equipment] couldn't have been destroyed, we wouldn't have stood much of an argument with them at all."[15]

Virtually the same scenario was repeated two years later, in April 1954. The previous flight plans were followed, roughly speaking, although the southernmost route was longer and zigged and zagged more than the earlier flight. The Soviet air defense network detected the flights but failed to shoot down any planes. Defense units assumed the aircraft were on reconnaissance missions; nevertheless, according to a Russian historian, "Specialists of the day could not rule out that there were not nuclear weapons on board." The defense forces had mistaken the B-45s for America's new, state-of-the-art B-47 bombers.[16]

WE'RE GOING TO HAVE A STORM

Spy planes conducting aerial reconnaissance of the Soviet Union, Eastern Bloc states, and China were military aircraft retrofitted for snooping—B-17s, B-29s, B-50s, B-45s, B-47s, and even some fighter planes. These aircraft collected useful information and their crews were immensely brave. Dozens of crewmen were shot out of the sky. Some were rescued and eventually made their way back to the United States; the majority did not and their fate remains unknown. The converted military aircraft simply could not fly high enough to always escape Soviet defenses.[17]

As early as December 1946, Richard S. Leghorn, one of the Army Air Forces' brightest lights in World War II aerial reconnaissance, had begun promoting peacetime reconnaissance—or "pre-hostilities" reconnaissance, as he called it—of the Soviet Union. New kinds of planes, he said, should be expressly built for the task, "extremely long-range aircraft capable of flying at very high altitudes," perhaps as high as seventy thousand feet.

Leghorn said at a meeting attended by a who's-who in aerial reconnaissance that it would be possible to camouflage the aircraft against visual observation. It was even possible "that means of preventing telltale reflections of other electromagnetic wave lengths, particularly of radar frequency, can be developed." (Leghorn anticipated America's first radar-deflecting "stealth" combat aircraft: the F-117 fighter-bomber, which entered the Air Force inventory in the 1980s, and the B-2 flying-wing bomber, which began flight tests in the summer of 1989.) The Air Force brass rejected Leghorn's ideas. In an era of tight post-war budgets, the Air Force could not develop a new plane designed solely for reconnaissance. It had to make do with proven multi-engine bombers fitted out for reconnaissance.[18]

By the summer of 1952, however, the situation had changed. Leghorn had by then forged a close relationship with Col. Bernard A. Schriever, a former protégé of Henry "Hap" Arnold and a monumentally energetic, capable, and confident officer. "He may have been a colonel," said a man who knew Schriever well, "but he didn't act like one. Even when he was a lieutenant, he behaved like a general. I saw him tell generals what to do. He was a real visionary. He knew we needed new ideas."[19]

Schriever helped put together a team of civilian experts in the summer of 1952 to study America's vulnerabilities to surprise attack and how the Air Force could meet the challenge. Among the many recommendations of the Beacon Hill Study was that the Air Force develop a spy plane that could "operate in Soviet airspace with greatly reduced chances of detection and interception."[20] The MiG-17, then the most advanced Soviet fighter, had a useful ceiling of about forty-five thousand feet; a plane cruising at more than sixty thousand feet would be relatively safe.[21]

Once the Beacon Hill Study was delivered in June 1952, the Air Force moved quickly. It urged Martin Aircraft to adapt the B-57 bomber (an American version of the British Canberra) as an interim spy plane, and it asked Bell Aircraft and Fairchild Engine and Airplane to submit competitive proposals for a new single-purpose spy plane.

Arguably, the nation's best aircraft designer was Kelly Johnson at Lockheed Aircraft. Among his many credits were the 1943 Constellation, a graceful fish-like machine with three tail stabilizers that carried passengers coast-to-coast, non-stop, at the incredible cruising speed of 280 miles per hour; World War II's P-38 Lightning, the "forked-tail devil" that may have been the most versatile fighter of the war; the P-80 Shooting Star, America's first operational jet fighter; and the recently designed F-104 Starfighter (the "missile with a man in it"), which would set a world speed record of 1,404 miles per hour in May 1958 and a world altitude record of 103,395 feet in December 1959. Lockheed, however, was not asked to submit a proposal.

But word of the project was leaked to a Lockheed executive in November 1953 and the company asked Johnson to put together a preliminary concept, which he called the CL-282. Johnson took his concept to Washington in the spring of 1954. His plane would be slim, with an improbably wide wingspan, like a sailplane built around an extraordinarily powerful jet engine. To save weight, it would be neither armed nor armored. It would lack a pressurized cockpit; it would have no ejection seat. It would be so fragile by military standards that in a sharp evasive maneuver, its wings would snap off. It would have no landing gear; it would ride on a wheeled dolly at takeoff and skid to a landing on skis and a reinforced belly. The CL-282 was as unmilitary as an aircraft could be. On April 1954 Schriever's men briefed SAC's commander: "General LeMay stood up halfway through the briefing, took his cigar out of his mouth, and told the briefers that if he wanted high-altitude photographs, he would put cameras in his B-36 bombers and added that he was not interested in a plane that had no wheels or guns. The general then left the room, remarking that the whole business was a waste of his time."[22]

How the president chose the CL-282 over contenders favored by the Air Force is an oft-told story packed with a fair share of internecine intrigue.[23] Despite the convoluted nature of the tale, in the end, the choice came down to a simple but remarkable fact: Throughout his tenure as president, Eisenhower often valued the judgments of his civilian scientists over those of his top military men. James R. Killian, his chief science adviser, later expressed wonder at that.

"There was a faint echo of Jefferson in Eisenhower's cordiality toward scientists and his curiosity about scientific matters," Killian said.[24] Some of Eisenhower's "failures and inadequacies" in other areas troubled Killian, but the president always had an "easy relationship" with his many science advisers, all of them brilliant—and most of them Democrats.[25]

The president's candor regarding national defense matters was extraordinary, recalls Killian. "At almost every meeting" with his science advisers, "he spoke of his fervent hope to moderate the arms race and to advance the cause of peace." Further, he "repeatedly expressed dismay over the service rivalries in the Department of Defense and the power the military exercised over the Congress and public opinion."[26]

In the matter of aerial spying, the president increasingly turned to his science advisers, especially Killian and Edwin Land, president of Polaroid Corporation, a brilliant inventor, an industrialist, and a man long involved in aerial photoreconnaissance. The opinions of Air Force Chief of Staff Nathan Twining and SAC Commander LeMay were given lesser weight.

In late October 1954, Killian and Land met with the president about the CL-282. The meeting was so far off the record that it was not recorded on the president's official schedule. "After listening to our proposal [recommending the CL-282] and asking many hard questions," Killian recalled, "Eisenhower approved the development of the U-2 [CL-282] system, but he stipulated that it should be handled in an unconventional way so that it would not become entangled in the bureaucracy of the Defense Department or troubled by rivalries among the services."[27]

"An unconventional way" meant that the Central Intelligence Agency— not the Air Force—would develop and operate the plane. The president wanted the whole business to be as unmilitary as possible in an effort to minimize the affront to the Soviet Union, if Soviet officials became aware of the overflights.

Under the CIA, the CL-282 became the U-2—"U" for utility. The Air Force would cooperate with the CIA as needed, but the CIA would be in charge. It would be all right to use military pilots, but the planes themselves must be weaponless. The military pilots would be "sheep-dipped"; they would resign from their respective services before being hired by the CIA as civilians. Insofar as the public was concerned, the U-2 would be nothing more than a high-flying weather-research plane. But the U-2 would at least have wheels instead of skis—and it also wound up with an ejection seat.

Eisenhower's decision was formalized on November 24, 1954. Allen Dulles, who headed the CIA, was not happy. He was not sure he wanted to be in the aircraft development and piloting business. Meanwhile, Air Force Chief of Staff Twining was angry; he believed his service had been victimized by a CIA power grab. In an interview years later, he said that Allen Dulles and his men "were getting too big for their britches. They did not know how to handle this kind of operation."[28]

"Well, boys," John Foster Dulles recalls Eisenhower saying when he approved the U-2 program, "I believe the country needs this information, and I'm going to approve it. But I'll tell you one thing. Someday one of these machines is going to be caught, and we're going to have a storm."[29] The president was willing to risk the storm to get hard data regarding Soviet capabilities, although he was parsimonious in authorizing deep flights over Soviet territory—just twenty-four flights over a four-year period.[30]

The first U-2 flight over the Soviet Union was on July 4, 1956, a date dictated by weather conditions rather than symbolism. Eisenhower had been advised that the plane would fly so high that Soviet radar probably would not detect it. But the flight was detected; the U-2 flew over military sites in the north, as well as Leningrad, the cultural capital of the Soviet Union. The next day, another flight passed over Moscow.

Nikita Khrushchev was furious about the timing. As a show of goodwill, he had made an Independence Day visit to the U.S. embassy in Moscow. After learning of the flights, he told his son Sergei that he imagined the State Department and the White House were "laughing" at him because of the Soviet's inability to shoot down the intruder.[31] The general secretary would work on that problem.

SPRINGING THE TRAP

In November 1953, the Lockheed executive who first proposed that his company design a high-flying spy plane wrote a memo to his bosses suggesting that "if extreme altitude performance can be realized," the craft "should be capable of avoiding virtually all Russian defenses until about 1960."[32] It was May 1, 1960 when the Soviets finally shot down a U-2.

When downed, Francis Gary Powers was the most experienced U-2 pilot, having flown twenty-seven missions, including one over the Soviet Union and another over China. His May 1 mission, *Operation Grand Slam*, was the most ambitious of the U-2 series; it would take off from Peshawar, Pakistan, and land in Norway. The mission was designed to cover three thousand three hundred nautical miles in about nine hours. Along the way, Powers would photograph several military sites including a nuclear weapons complex at Chelyabinsk, a missile test site at Tyuratam, and a missile base at Plesetsk.

Powers's mission likely would have been the last deep overflight of Soviet territory. An April 9 flight had been nearly brought down by newly improved surface-to-air missiles, a fact apparently not brought to the president's attention. Soviet air defenses were getting very good.[33]

Four and a half hours into the May 1 flight, three new-generation surface-to-air missiles were fired at Powers. One missed; another missile destroyed a Soviet fighter chasing Powers; and the third detonated just behind the U-2. Hit by shrapnel, Powers's plane began to go out of control. Unable to use his ejection seat because of damage, Powers jettisoned the canopy and unfastened his safety harness. He was sucked out of the plane, which meant he was unable to reach the U-2's destruct mechanism. The plane crashed but did not fully disintegrate. Powers landed safely and was quickly surrounded by Soviet farmers and officials.

Unknown to the CIA, the Soviet Union had obtained both plane and pilot, a fact that led to one of the great fiascoes of the Cold War and to the aborting of a promising mid-May summit meeting in Paris. Ironically, Eisenhower had approved the flight largely because it would provide hard data that would be useful for successfully concluding the summit, which was designed to limit nuclear testing.

In a May 3, 1960 statement, the National Aeronautics and Space Administration said a joint NASA–Air Force weather research plane based in Adana, Turkey, apparently had gone down in the Lake Van area of Turkey. The mission had been to study "clear air turbulence." However, the statement said, the pilot had reported difficulties with his oxygen equipment. Later in the day, a State Department spokesman said it was "entirely possible that having a failure in the oxygen equipment, which could result in the pilot losing consciousness, the plane continued on automatic pilot for a considerable distance and accidentally violated Soviet airspace."[34] That bit of dissembling would "explain" the U-2 wreckage once it was found.

The wink-wink weather-research cover story was a standard Cold War chestnut, which scarcely any knowledgeable person on either side of the Iron Curtain believed. In January and February 1956, for instance, the Air Force launched five hundred and sixteen high-altitude "weather research" balloons from Western Europe. They were spy balloons designed to take photos as they jet-streamed eastward across the Soviet Union. Their camera-carrying gondolas would be cut loose over the western Pacific; C-119 "Flying Boxcars" would then snatch the gondolas as they floated down under parachutes. Many balloons were shot down over the Soviet Union; others malfunctioned; some simply vanished. Forty-six payloads were recovered by the Air Force, but only thirty-four had recognizable photographs. The photos didn't show much, other than a lot of trees. Soviet authorities scored a worldwide propaganda coup by displaying the remnants of "weather balloons" in Moscow, including their cameras.[35]

On May 5, Khrushchev announced in the course of a long speech to the Supreme Soviet that a U.S. spy plane had been shot down deep in Soviet territory. He denounced it as an "aggressive act"—one that had occurred on May Day, the Soviet Union's most important holiday. That struck Khrushchev as a particular insult.

"Just imagine what would have happened had a *Soviet* aircraft appeared over New York, Chicago, or Detroit," Khrushchev said. "How would the *United States* have reacted?" Khrushchev looked directly at the U.S. ambassador, who had been invited to the hall: "What was this? A *May Day* greeting?"[36]

Who sent the spy plane, Khrushchev asked. The president? "Or was this an aggressive act performed by Pentagon militarists without the president's knowledge?... Even now, I profoundly believe that the American people—except for certain imperialist and monopolist circles—want peace and friendship with the Soviet Union.... I do not doubt President Eisenhower's sincere desire for peace."[37]

The next day, the U.S. government repeated its cover story—an unarmed weather-research plane was missing and the pilot's name was Francis Gary Powers. The Soviets were asked to furnish the United States with the "full facts" of the investigation as well as information on the "the fate of the pilot." The CIA had assumed that if a U-2 were hit, the fragile craft would break apart and the pilot would be killed. For a time, pilots were provided with a fast-acting potassium cyanide ampoule to bite down on in the unlikely event of capture. After a pilot nearly killed himself when he mistook one for a lemon drop, pilots were given a needle containing concentrated algal, a shellfish toxin. The willingness to commit suicide was not, however, part of the job description.[38]

Finally, Khrushchev sprung the trap before the members of the Supreme Soviet. "Comrades, I must let you in on a secret. When I made my report two days ago, I deliberately refrained from mentioning that we have the remnants of the plane—and we also have the pilot, who is quite alive and kicking." The reason he had not been wholly forthcoming in his first report, Khrushchev said, was because if he had been, "the Americans would have thought up still another fable."

The next American response, issued hours later, said "as a result of the inquiry ordered by the president it has been established that insofar as the authorities in Washington are concerned there was no authorization for any such flight as described by Mr. Khrushchev." However, it appeared that "in endeavoring to obtain information now concealed behind the Iron Curtain a flight over Soviet territory was probably undertaken by an unarmed civilian U-2 plane." The "excessive secrecy practiced by the Soviet Union in contrast to the free world" made such flights necessary.

Insofar as the authorities in Washington are concerned there was no authorization.... What did that mean? What could it possibly mean? The situation had become intolerable. Who was running the show in the United States? Rogue intelligence agents? Out-of-control generals? Paranoid pranksters? Or the president? If the president were not in charge, it would be proof of presidential inattention if not incompetence. And if intelligence agents or generals had truly gone off the reservation, things did not look good for the Free World, which almost invariably turned to the president of the United States for leadership.

Eisenhower ordered the State Department to issue a new statement noting, among other things, that the president *had* authorized spy flights over the Soviet Union, although not "specific missions," a disingenuous phrase that preserved a bit of space between the president and the May 1 flight, in the hope of salvaging the Paris summit, scheduled to begin on the 16th. Shortly after the statement was issued, the president spoke at a news conference.

"No one wants another Pearl Harbor," Eisenhower said. "This means that we must have knowledge of military forces and preparations around the world, especially those capable of massive surprise attack. Secrecy in the Soviet Union makes this essential. In most of the world no large-scale attack could be prepared in secret. But in the Soviet Union there is a fetish of secrecy and concealment. This is a major cause of international tension and uneasiness today. Our deterrent must never be placed in jeopardy. The safety of the whole free world demands this."

Intelligence-gathering activities, the president added, "have a special and secret character. They are, so to speak, 'below the surface' activities" with "their own rules and methods of concealment, which seek to mislead and obscure." It was a "distasteful" but necessary business. "This was the reason for my Open Skies proposal in 1955, which I was ready instantly to put into effect, to permit aerial observation over the United States and the Soviet Union which would assure that no surprise attack was being prepared against anyone."[39]

The American people were relieved to hear the president was in charge; they were happy to learn that he apparently had a factual basis for having assured them time and again that the United States was not in imminent danger of a Soviet sneak attack. But they were dismayed to learn that America's ability to actually *see* behind the Iron Curtain would probably end.

Given the diplomatic furor, spy flights over Soviet territory surely would not continue.[40]

An extraordinary coda to the U-2 affair was offered years later by George B. Kistiakowsky, the president's chief science adviser when Francis Gary Powers was shot down. "I was alone in the president's office on some unrelated matter," Kistiakowsky recalled, "when [Eisenhower] said, referring to the U-2, that we scientists had failed him. I responded that the scientists had consistently warned about the U-2 eventually being shot down and that it was the management of the project that failed."

> The president flared up, evidently thinking I accused him, and used some strong uncomplimentary language. I assured him that my reference was to the bureaucrats that ran the show. Cooling off, the president began to talk with much feeling about how he had concentrated his efforts the last few years on ending the Cold War, how he felt that he was making big progress, and how the stupid U-2 mess had ruined all his efforts. He ended very sadly that he saw nothing worthwhile left for him to do now until the end of his presidency.[41]

ADAM AND EVE

Francis Gary Powers was to be the last U-2 pilot to intentionally overfly Soviet territory. Nevertheless, the ability of the United States to see what was going on inside the Soviet Union would continue; Eisenhower's peace-oriented "open skies" concept would now move into space. Photographic technologies developed for the U-2 had been enormously useful to a deep-black spy satellite program called Project CORONA. ("CORONA" is not an acronym; according to spy lore, the name came from a key directive typed on a Smith-Corona typewriter.)

On February 28, 1959, the first attempt to insert a CORONA satellite into orbit took place. It failed. Twelve more attempts also failed. "Let's not worry about it [the failures]," Eisenhower said. "Let's stay with it. It's so important, and we need it. We need to just keep going with it."[42] The first success came on August 10, 1960, one hundred and two days after Powers's U-2 had been shot down.

The first successful CORONA satellite passed over the Soviet Union seven times and provided more photographic coverage of that closed nation than all twenty-three successful U-2 flights combined. The CORONA program ended in May 1972 after many successes, including detection and surveillance of all Soviet medium-range, intermediate-range, and long-range missile launch sites; photographing all classes of Soviet submarines and their bases; tracking the Soviet surface fleet; identifying and counting Soviet fighters and bombers; revealing the presence of Soviet missiles in Egypt; documenting Soviet assistance to China's nuclear program; and uncovering the Soviet antiballistic missile program. All subsequent national security satellites trace their lineage to CORONA. On March 16, 1967, President Lyndon B. Johnson said in off-the-record remarks, which have nonetheless been widely distributed:

> I wouldn't want to be quoted on this, but we've spent thirty-five or forty billion dollars on the space program. And if nothing else had come out of it except the knowledge we've gained from space photography, it would be worth ten times what the whole program has cost. Because tonight we know how many missiles the enemy has and, it turned out, our guesses were way off. We were doing things we didn't need to do. We were building things we didn't need to build. We were harboring fears we didn't need to harbor. Because of satellites, I *know* how many missiles the enemy has.[43]

Development of the U-2 and the CORONA program was overseen by many of the same men—Eisenhower's key scientists, engineers, and intelligence personnel. They knew that the U-2 would suffice for a time, but sooner or later CORONA would have to take over the open-skies task. If the U-2 was Adam, CORONA was Eve. They were conceived to help preserve the peace and together they begat an ever widening spectrum of national security space satellites.

11

Freedom of Space

What *were* the Soviets up to? That was a largely rhetorical question in the minds of millions of Americans after Sputnik—"rhetorical" because most Americans thought they already knew the answer: Soviet leaders sought global domination. They intended to force the United States and the Western world to kowtow to Moscow or risk destruction.

Eisenhower was not so sure. Although he mistrusted the Soviet leaders, he was reasonably certain that the Soviet Union lacked the raw military power—or even the potential military power—to have its way with the West. The man who had overseen the largest and most complex invasion plan in modern history while riding herd on the most flamboyant prima donnas in the European theater, Gen. George S. Patton and Field Marshal Bernard L. Montgomery, was not easily spooked.

The president believed that Nikita Khrushchev was a canny fellow as well as a master of bluff and bluster. Khrushchev claimed in a variety of post-Sputnik forums that the Soviet Union was churning out ocean-spanning missiles "like sausages." That played well in many parts of the world—and even in the United States sophisticated people who should have known better took the bait.

The Alsop brothers, Joseph and Stewart, wrote in the August 1, 1958 issue of the *New York Herald-Tribune* that officers at the Pentagon "shudder" at the danger that a complacent president had let the nation fall into. "They shudder because in [coming] years, the American government will flaccidly permit the Kremlin to open an almost unchallenged superiority in the nuclear striking power that was once our superiority."[1]

John F. Kennedy, a close friend of Joe Alsop and a man whose accomplishments in the Senate were meager compared to his political ambitions, eventually rode the alleged missile gap to the White House. "We are rapidly approaching that dangerous period which… others have called the 'gap' or the 'lag' period," Kennedy said on the Senate floor on August 14, 1958. "[Soviet] missile power will be the shield from behind which [the Soviet Union] will slowly but surely advance—through Sputnik diplomacy, limited brushfire wars, indirect non-overt aggression, intimidation and subversion, internal revolution, increased prestige or influence, and the vicious blackmail of our allies."[2]

As the American people learned years later (and as Eisenhower suspected at the time), there was no missile gap; the Soviet Union was always playing catch up. Khrushchev's post-Sputnik grand strategy was simple in outline if difficult to pull off: build up Soviet agriculture and industry at home; promote "liberation" in the impoverished Third World; and scare the pants off of Western leaders by reminding them that the Soviet Union had the largest missiles topped by the world's biggest, baddest, most powerful nuclear warheads.

In a rambling day-long conversation on June 23, 1959, Khrushchev managed to be cordial with one of his favorite capitalists, Averell Harriman, a former ambassador to the Soviet Union who was then the governor of New York, while simultaneously conveying a tough-guy message. The meeting began in the Kremlin and continued at Khrushchev's rural dacha, where glasses of cognac may have played a role in the tone of some of Khrushchev's conversational gambits. At one point, Khrushchev said:

> Please understand, we want friendship. Within five to seven years we will be stronger than you.… If we spend thirty billion rubles on ballistic missiles in the next five to six years, we can destroy every industrial center in the United States and Europe. Thirty billion rubles is no great sum for us.… I am frank because I like you as a frank capitalist. You charm us as a snake charms rabbits. I am talking about potentialities. Of course, we will make some missiles but we won't use them. We know if you use yours, it would be silly. Who would lose more? Let us keep our rockets loaded and if attacked we will launch them.[3]

Those remarks were vintage Khrushchev. Gruff, boastful, crude, and at times disarmingly candid. Forests were felled during the Eisenhower years to make the paper on which were printed analyses of the temperament and intentions of Khrushchev and his close colleagues.

The president's private assessment of the temperament of Soviet leaders was direct: they did not want war with the United States. "These Communists are not early Christian martyrs," Eisenhower wrote on one occasion. "Make no mistake, they like their jobs." At another time, he said of Soviet leaders, they "know the lesson of Napoleon, of Hitler, of Mussolini.... I cannot see them starting a war merely for the opportunity that such a conflict might offer their successors to spread their doctrine." Moscow would not initiate a war; rather, it would work in the background, probing, subverting, "poisoning men's minds" with "lying propaganda" and "false promises."[4]

Hard data gathered by satellites about Soviet capabilities would—presumably—bolster the president's intuitive opinion that Moscow was not preparing a surprise attack. Eisenhower's actions regarding space were sophisticated and far-sighted. He persisted in the development and deployment of Project CORONA, which would prove to be instrumental in clearing away the fog that enveloped Soviet military capabilities. The data provided by CORONA arguably helped his successors avoid nuclear war. But the president's most profound contribution regarding national security space was the development of two complementary concepts: space for peaceful purposes and "freedom of space."

SPACE BATTLES

Bernard A. Schriever, the early proponent of a high-flying spy plane mentioned in the last chapter, was one of the most brilliant and influential men in the history of the Air Force. On August 2, 1954, at forty-four years of age, Schriever found himself in charge of an operation that rivaled the wartime Manhattan Project in scope. It was blandly called the Western Development Division and its headquarters were in a former school on Manchester Avenue in Inglewood, California.

Schriever eventually oversaw the work of some seventy thousand people, including eighteen thousand scientists, seventeen prime contractors, two hundred subcontractors, and thirty-five hundred suppliers. Their mission: create America's first intercontinental ballistic missile, which would be called the Atlas.[5]

As smart as any top-drawer scientist, Schriever was also energetic beyond reason, regularly working sixteen-hour days. And like many of his Air Force colleagues, he was convinced that President's Eisenhower's space-for-peaceful-purposes policy, established in 1955, was a mistake. During a pre-Sputnik speech in San Diego in February 1957, Schriever suggested that, "in the long haul, our safety as a nation may depend upon our achieving space superiority. Several decades from now, the important battles may not be sea battles or air battles, but space battles, and we should be spending a certain fraction of our national resources to insure that we do not lag in obtaining space superiority."[6]

The speech came nearly eight months *before* Sputnik and it is still cited in space-warrior circles as an example of Schriever's prescience.[7] But there was a problem. President Eisenhower had been publicly promoting a space-for-peaceful-purposes policy for nearly two years by the time Schriever made his remarks. Official Washington understood that no one in a high government or military position was supposed to link the word "space" with something as ominous as "battle." Schriever received a wire from the office of the secretary of defense, the gist of which was: "Do not use the word 'space' in any of your speeches in the future."[8]

Then, after Sputnik, the lid came off. Everyone, it seemed, was talking about military space, and much of the commentary focused on the presumed incompetence of President Eisenhower and his administration. They had let the godless Communists surge ahead, and now the United States was in big trouble. The need for America to militarily dominate space was axiomatic to countless editorialists, columnists, politicians, and ordinary people.

Space would become the new venue in which the great East-West drama would continue to play out; U.S. control of space, these early space warriors said, was essential to survival as a free nation. As noted in Chapter One, Thomas Dresser White, chief of staff of the Air Force, preached that control of space "should be the goal of all Americans." White elaborated his view in preparedness hearings conducted by Sen. Lyndon B. Johnson from November 1957 to January 1958.

"I actually foresee the use of weapons in space, both on offensive and defensive," General White testified. "I can imagine a satellite being a missile-launching platform. It is possible to put one of those things in space, and have it go over any given spot on Earth and at a given signal... have that fire a missile at a given point on Earth, a certain city, for example." Moments later, Johnson asked Schriever, who was sitting next to White, if he considered "control of space extremely important to the free world." Schriever's answer: "Well, I certainly do, although I would not be able to give you exactly why in tangible terms."[9]

"It is strange now to recall the fantasies that Sputnik inspired in the minds of many able military officers," Eisenhower's science adviser, James R. Killian, later noted. "It cast a spell that caused otherwise rational commanders really to become romantic about space. No sir, they were not going to fight the next war with the weapons of the last war; the world was going to be controlled from the high ground of space."[10]

Early space warriors were generally pleased with Project CORONA, the first U.S. spy satellite program. Air Force officers had long valued aerial reconnaissance because it identified targets and provided relatively precise geographical coordinates for bomb crews, should war come. Space reconnaissance would continue that targeting function.

What early space warriors, such as Generals White and Schriever, failed to fully credit was that Eisenhower was so deeply dedicated to his peaceful-purposes policy and its fraternal twin, freedom of space, that he was not going to be swayed. To be sure, Eisenhower expected space-for-peaceful-purposes to play well with the leaders of other nations, especially "neutral" nations, thus scoring a propaganda coup for the United States. Nonetheless, the policy was not a ploy.

Military men valued space reconnaissance because it could help them fight the Reds more efficiently and decisively, if and when war came. Eisenhower was much more interested in ensuring that war did not come. He was loath to extend the arms race into space; he believed that space must be preserved as neutral territory, a sanctuary where all manner of satellites could roam as long as they were not weapons—"freedom of space." Establishing that principle would make it less likely that the United States and the Soviet Union would blunder into a civilization-destroying war.

BIRTH CERTIFICATE

Since their path-breaking 1946 study, *Preliminary Design of an Experimental World-Circling Spaceship*, analysts at RAND had continued to refine the idea and purposes of military satellites. A 1949 RAND study said a satellite built as a "surveillance instrument" could serve as a major element of political strategy. "No other weapon or technique known today offers comparable promise as an instrument for influencing Soviet political behavior."[11]

In the early 1950s, RAND put together a series of ever more sophisticated satellite studies, "Project Feed Back."

By the mid-1950s, a few Air Force officers had begun to believe that spy satellites would someday be useful. But the heavy emphasis was on "someday." Certainly it would be possible to orbit a small scientific satellite before the decade ended, if the nation chose to do so. Such a satellite would send data back by telemetry. But a *spy* satellite? The Soviet Union was roughly two and half times the size of the United States. Even with the U-2 flights, much of the Soviet landmass was terra incognita. How, exactly, could one capture images of the Soviet Union from hundreds of miles overhead that would be crisply sharp enough to be useful? With multiple passes, a satellite would be able to see all of the Soviet Union; but how could it reveal enough detail to pick out launching pads, fuel tanks, radars, and command-and-control bunkers?

And even if sharply focused images could be captured, how would they get from orbital space to the desks of analysts? Theoretically, it might be possible to beam detailed images back to Earth by television. But that would not be possible for many years—perhaps the mid-1960s, perhaps later. That wasn't good enough. Sooner rather than later, Eisenhower believed, the Soviets would shoot down a U-2. The United States would need a ready-to-launch satellite backup plan.

If the technical problems of developing useful spy satellites could be overcome, the nation would still face a huge political challenge. Would not Soviet leaders—and much of the world—view spying from space during peacetime as an ominous act—perhaps as "pre-hostilities" reconnaissance, as it was often called in Air Force circles? That was not an unreasonable concern. Since the completion of an international agreement in 1944, international law had declared that the airspace over a nation and its colonies as sovereign territory, which it had the right to protect. The aircraft of other nations were required to request permission to fly over a nation's territory in peacetime or risk an incident. The Soviet Union and its captive states routinely denied flyover rights.

In contrast to airspace, outer space in the 1950s was virgin territory untouched by law or custom. When it came time to formulate space law—and that time was approaching—the international legal community might resort to precedent, as lawyers were wont to do, and extend the principle of national sovereignty to orbital space. If that happened, a nation would have the right to deny overflight privileges to the satellites of other nations. If satellites were orbited anyway, the protesting nation presumably would then have the legal right to destroy it just as surely as it had the legal right to shoot down an aircraft (as a last resort) that was intentionally intruding on its airspace.

The possibility that national sovereignty might be extended to space troubled the Eisenhower administration. How, exactly, would Washington go about asking Moscow for permission to overfly Soviet territory with *spy* satellites? If the United States had launched spy satellites during that unsettled period in international space law, and if these satellites had then passed over the Soviet Union, Moscow presumably would be in a position to mount an effective international protest that would capture the sympathies and support of much of the world.

A possible answer to the dilemma had been proposed by a prescient RAND study, which had been presented to the Air Force on October 4, 1950, seven years to the day before Sputnik was launched. In essence, the study suggested that the United States establish the principle of freedom of space with non-threatening research satellites before launching spy satellites. "That RAND document," writes historian Walter A. McDougall, "deserves to be considered the birth certificate of American space policy."[12]

In that respect, the International Geophysical Year, or "IGY"—the multifaceted scientific research project that would eventually involve more than five thousand scientists and technicians from sixty-four nations—was a fortuitous break for the Eisenhower administration. The eighteen-month "year" would begin July 1, 1957 and end December 31, 1958.

KAPUTNIK

Preliminary ideas for the IGY were put together at an informal meeting of scientists in April 1950, in Silver Spring, Maryland. Data regarding the major phenomena of the Earth would be gathered and studied more or less simultaneously during the year. The data would help scientists pursue countless questions: Was the Earth's climate changing? If it were getting warmer, would the polar ice melt, flooding coastal cities? Might it be possible to learn enough about weather patterns to accurately predict local weather—even hurricanes? Were continents "drifting," as some suspected? What was the origin of the cosmic rays that bombard the Earth? Might it be possible to someday safely travel in space?

Although IGY projects were set up all over the world, the most dramatic venues would be the Antarctic and orbital space. Little was known about either. The 1957–1958 timeframe was chosen to coincide with an expected peak in sunspot activity; the next such peak was not expected until 1970. ("Sunspots"—what they were and what impact, if any, they had on Earth— had tantalized scientists since they were first seen in 1610.)

On April 15, 1955, the Soviet Union announced it would launch a scientific satellite during the IGY; the United States made a similar announcement on July 29, 1955. Press Secretary James C. Hagerty said the president had expressed "personal gratification that the American program will provide scientists of all nations this important and unique opportunity for the advancement of science."

Hagerty, however, did not note that the American satellites were essential to establishing the principle of freedom of space—the concept that national sovereignty ends where space begins—as well as the principle that space ought to be used for peaceful purposes. The scientific IGY satellites would be stalking horses for the later "spysats." Freedom of space and peaceful purposes had become national space policy on May 27, 1955. "It should be emphasized that a [research] satellite would constitute no active military offensive threat to any country over which it might pass," the policy document said. Those fraternal-twin principles would pave the way for spysats.[13]

Determining how America's first satellite would be launched into space was not easy. Wernher von Braun and his Army missile team were eager to do it, as was the Air Force, with a variant of its long-range missile, the Atlas, then under development. The Air Force proposal didn't have a chance; producing an intercontinental ballistic missile was the nation's highest military priority at the time, and the administration didn't want to do anything that might take time or energy away from the Atlas team. The Army proposal— based on its Redstone–Jupiter C intermediate-range missile program—was given heavy-duty consideration, along with a Navy proposal rooted in previous work on the Navy's Viking rocket.

Although the von Braun-Army proposal was immensely intriguing, the Navy proposal had an edge from the get-go: the Viking program was civilian in character. The Naval Research Laboratory, in cooperation with civilian scientists, had been launching instrumented high-altitude "sounding" rockets into the lowest reaches of space since 1947 to gather scientific data. The Viking rocket had no military antecedents; the von Braun-Army proposal had a lineage that began with the German V-2 rocket. The Navy program got the nod and became Project Vanguard.

Wernher von Braun, the chief advocate of space satellites and the most experienced rocket scientist in the United States, was virtually frozen out of the IGY satellite race, though his Jupiter C project was generally regarded as a backup if Vanguard should fail. Even after the Navy proposal was chosen, von Braun and his Army allies lobbied strenuously for the opportunity to launch the first satellite, even to the point of engaging in behind-the-scenes intrigue. At one point the administration felt compelled to notify the von Braun camp that it must not "inadvertently" orbit a satellite during one nose-cone reentry test.

Eisenhower and his advisers were determined that America's first satellite would be seen as wholly peaceful in origin; an Army missile directly descended from the V-2 may have been beyond the pale. (Von Braun, technical director of the V-2 project, had not only joined the Nazi party, he had also become—reluctantly, he said—an officer in the SS. In Huntsville, his inner circle was largely composed of veterans of the V-2 project. It is at least imaginable that Von Braun and his colleagues simply had the wrong accents for America's peaceful IGY satellites.) Nonetheless, von Braun was furious when he learned of the Sputnik launch.[14]

The Soviet IGY satellite program was shrouded in secrecy insofar as the public was concerned. In contrast, Project Vanguard was open, even embarrassingly so. The first satellite attempt, a launch that its designers believed had a low probability of achieving orbit, came shortly before noon on December 6, 1957. The event had been highly publicized and the world's press was there with paper and pencil—and, devastatingly, with newsreel and TV cameras.

A key member of the Vanguard team, apparently a poet at heart, described the launch from a vantage point in a nearby bunker. "The engine started with a heart-rending, hoarse, whining moan like that of some antediluvian beast in birth pain." Flame—"brilliantly white and streaked with black"—howled from the nozzle. The "vehicle shook itself momentarily like a wet dog" and then "ripped itself loose from its iron womb and rose slowly." And then...

It seemed as if the gates of hell had opened up. Brilliant stiletto flames shot out from the side of the rocket near the engine. The vehicle agonizingly hesitated for a moment, quivered again, and in front of our unbelieving, shocked eyes, began to topple. It sank, like a great flaming sword into its scabbard, down into the blast tube. It toppled slowly, breaking apart, hitting part of the test guard and ground with a tremendous roar that could be felt and heard even behind the two-foot concrete wall of the blockhouse and six-inch bulletproof glass.[15]

The *New York Times* called the American attempt, "Sputternik"; the *New York Herald-Tribune*: "Goofnik." Other catchy names included "Flopnik," "Dudnik," and "Kaputnik."[16] Nikita Khrushchev had great sport with Kaputnik wherever and whenever possible, likening it to an orange that blew up in front of a global audience.[17]

Khrushchev's gloating was premature. It was true that the Americans had been embarrassed; in retrospect, "Project Vanguard" had been a poor choice of names for the IGY satellite effort.[18] But Khrushchev was wrong to assume that the Soviet Union was somehow the leader in either missiles or satellites. The Eisenhower administration was progressing rapidly on the rocketry front, thanks in large measure to General Schriever's extraordinary management of the missile program. Even as Eisenhower's critics savaged the president over space issues, the United States had an ultra-secret satellite program under way that was far more sophisticated than anything the Soviet Union was working on; it eventually led to Project CORONA.

By the mid-1950s, the folks at RAND had come up with a multifaceted satellite program for the Air Force called WS-117L. The program embodied several different concepts, including a satellite with infrared sensors that would warn of a Soviet attack and satellites that would collect electronic signals, much like ferret aircraft.

The imagery part of the program focused on sending pictures back to Earth by television. A camera would take the pictures and the film would be developed in space. The negatives would be electronically scanned and beamed to Earth. The pictures were expected to be pretty fuzzy at first; the Air Force assumed it would take a decade or longer to refine the system.

But one of the concepts in the WS-117L program was radically different. The camera in space would take photos; then a "bucket" containing the exposed film would be "deorbited" and sent back to Earth where it could be recovered, developed, and analyzed. If the system worked, the pictures would be sharp enough to provide solid information.

After the launch of Sputnik, the film-recovery idea captured the imagination of many of the scientists who had been involved with the U-2. The film-recovery concept was detached from the WS-117L program and called CORONA. Much like the U-2 program, it would be led by the CIA, with the Air Force in a supporting role.

CORONA, like the U-2, was assumed to be an interim system, a stopgap to be used until more sophisticated electronic-based systems came on line. In fact, it worked far better than expected. Over a span of fourteen years, there were one hundred and forty-five CORONA launches, one hundred and twenty of which were total or partial successes. CORONA satellites photographed a total land area of five hundred and fifty-seven million square miles and used nearly four hundred miles of special large format film. Details of the program were not declassified until September 1996, and they can be found in the intriguing and comprehensive *Eye in the Sky*, published in 1998 by the Smithsonian Institution.[19]

THE SOVIETS HAVE PROVED VERY HELPFUL

On January 31, 1958, the United States finally orbited its first IGY satellite, Explorer I, with one of von Braun's rockets. Explorer I weighed just thirty-one pounds, including eighteen pounds of instrumentation. It was widely ridiculed at the time; Sputnik II, weighing one thousand, one hundred and twenty pounds, had been launched on November 3, 1957 with a dog named Laika aboard, who died in space as planned, thus enraging America's dog-loving public.[20] In contrast, Explorer's instruments provided a wealth of scientific data including radiation readings that enabled James van Allen, one of the originators of the IGY idea, to describe a radiation belt encircling the Earth. Readings from later Explorers determined that there were an inner and an outer belt.

The United States was altogether serious when it said its IGY satellite program was designed to gather scientific data that would be shared with the rest of the world. What the United States did not say was that the United States also had a secret spy satellite program under way.

The IGY and spysat programs were separate, but the spysat had the higher priority and was thus better funded. Nonetheless, the IGY program was in a fundamental sense more important. It was essential to Eisenhower's freedom-of-space policy. By launching the first Earth satellite, Eisenhower believed that the United States would show its continuing technological wizardry to the world while demonstrating that satellites could freely and legally fly over any nation.

As it happened, the United States was not first in space, but that was hardly tragic from the administration's point of view. Four days after Sputnik, a high-level group of advisers met with the president. Early in the meeting, Donald H. Quarles, assistant secretary of defense for research and development and one of the administration's savviest men regarding science and technology, famously noted:

> Our government had never regarded this [IGY] program as including as a major objective that the United States should launch an Earth satellite first, though, of course, we have always been aware of the Cold War implications of the launching of the first Earth satellite.
>
> Another of our objectives in the Earth satellite program was to establish the principle of the freedom of outer space—that is, the international rather than the national character of outer space. In this respect the Soviets have now proved very helpful. Their Earth satellite has overflown practically every nation on Earth, and there have thus far been no protests.[21]

While generals, politicians, and pundits argued passionately and publicly for U.S. dominance in space, Eisenhower was not interested in that sort of muscle flexing. Rather, he would work with Soviet leaders to guarantee freedom of space for all satellites, no matter their purpose—as long as they were not weapons. Regarding aerial spying, Eisenhower had always urged caution. In May 1956, for instance, he told his inner circle that it was vital "to be wise and careful in what we do" because he wanted "to give the Soviets every chance to move in peaceful directions and to put our relations on a better basis."[22] He felt the same about spysats.

THIS NEW OCEAN

President Eisenhower was committed to space for peaceful purposes, but would a new president develop a bolder and more assertive policy—perhaps a policy of space dominance? Early space warriors were hopeful.[23] Senator Stuart Symington of Missouri and Senate Majority Leader Lyndon B. Johnson of Texas campaigned vigorously on the missile gap and space issues in their respective attempts to capture the Democratic nomination for president, as did Sen. Jack Kennedy. With the election of Kennedy in November 1960, space warriors had renewed hope.

In July 1961, a few months after Yuri Gagarin's first orbital flight—another Soviet first—General Schriever, who had built a stellar reputation for the extraordinarily efficient way he had directed the Air Force's missile programs, testified before the Senate Preparedness Investigating Subcommittee about the need for a new space policy. "I think we have been inhibited in the space business through the 'space for peace' slogan," Schriever said.[24] The general hammered at that theme until retirement in 1966, gaining widespread support among his colleagues.[25]

In retirement, Schriever became *the* elder statesmen of the space-warrior community. At a space conference in 1995, he noted, with satisfaction, that he knew a lot of the younger Air Force officers and they were "on the right track. I have no doubt that they will get us [into space] in the future, and that we will achieve a survivable, real wartime capability in space."[26]

By mid-1962, the Kennedy team, chastened by the actual task of governing while avoiding war with the Soviet Union, began to put the brakes on Air Force space proposals. Kennedy had apparently decided that Eisenhower had got it right, after all. Spy satellites, communications satellites, warning satellites, geo-positioning satellites, and so on were fine. They were passive devices that helped bring some degree of fog-lifting stability to the Cold War. But space control? Weapons in space? The *Air Force* in space? That wasn't going to happen. Insofar as possible, the manned Moon mission—which Kennedy proclaimed to the world May 25, 1961—would be a civilian affair. Military pilots could train as astronauts, but their mission would be non-military.

Kennedy believed that beating the Soviets to the Moon would reclaim some of the prestige the United States had lost to the Soviet sputniks. A Moon landing would provide striking evidence of American techno-power, and that was thought to be geopolitically important; the United States and the Soviet Union were then locked in a battle for Third World hearts and minds.

Winning the Moon race also would send a not-so-subtle military message to the Soviets: any nation that could put men on the Moon and get them back could also hit an earthly target with accuracy. Nikita Khrushchev understood the importance of accuracy. "It always sounded good," Khrushchev said years later, "to say in public speeches that we could hit a fly at any distance with our missiles." But, he added, the Soviets lacked the guidance systems to actually do it in those early years. "Despite the wide radius of destruction caused by our nuclear warheads, pinpoint accuracy was still necessary—and it was difficult to achieve."[27]

Another benefit to the Moon race: dollars poured into the Moon mission would help build up the aerospace industry and that would have positive implications for the American ballistic missile program, which Kennedy believed required a robust aerospace industry. Finally, the Moon mission would show the world and the American public that the United States was on the move again. That would buck up the nation's collective morale and it might even help ensure Kennedy's re-election in 1964. In a September 12, 1962 speech at Rice University in Houston, Kennedy explained his space policy in words worth recalling today.

> [S]pace science, like nuclear science and all technology, has no conscience of its own. Whether it will become a force for good or ill depends on man, and only if the United States occupies a position of pre-eminence can we help decide whether this new ocean will be a sea of peace or a new terrifying theater of war.
>
> I do not say that we should or will go unprotected against the hostile misuse of space any more than we go unprotected against the hostile use of land or sea, but I do say that space can be explored and mastered without feeding the fires of war, without repeating the mistakes that man has made in extending his writ around this globe of ours.[28]

"Without feeding the fires of war." Kennedy and his successor, Lyndon B. Johnson, practiced considerable restraint regarding the military uses of space. Johnson, who a few years earlier had condemned Eisenhower for letting the Soviet Union surge ahead in space, worked with Soviet leaders to create the Outer Space Treaty of 1967, which banned weapons of mass destruction from space. To the dismay of General Schriever and his fellow space warriors, Kennedy and Johnson made Eisenhower's space-for-peaceful-purposes their policy, too.

12

The Road Not Taken

In the late 1990s, U.S. Space Command asked Jim Oberg to help develop a theory of space power. Oberg was a good choice. He had been a top NASA engineer for more than two decades and he was thoroughly familiar with military-space projects in both the United States and the Soviet Union. He was—and is—an exceptionally thoughtful and well-informed space warrior.

Oberg's *Space Power Theory*, published in 1999, was lukewarm toward weaponizing space. Weapons in space would not necessarily be a good thing, Oberg said, for reasons ranging from cost to the adverse impact they would likely have on America's foreign relations. And yet, Oberg believed that the weaponization of space was inevitable simply because of the "irrationality of human conflict." Arguments about the "incorrigible nature of humanity," he wrote, "have a rationality of their own" that would lead, sooner or later, to space-related weapons.

> [I]n a circular type of logic, the argument for fielding space-based weapons becomes self-justifying. The need to place weapons in space as a defense against weapons in space begets the scenario from which the original contention was based. Against this paradox, those who support the sanctity of space have no recourse. As a result, despite every conceivable argument that can be thrown against [weaponization], the simple historical inevitability of war, warfare, and arms cannot be overthrown.

At its core, Oberg writes, "the notion of weapons in space is one that pits military pragmatists against idealistic futurists. Or, put another way, it is a conflict between those that espouse the immutable nature of human beings against those that believe they are slowly, but definitely and irreversibly, moving toward an era of greater cooperation and unity; it is the idealists versus realists, the political hawks versus the doves, and it is an argument probably as old as humanity."[1]

Oberg could be right. Those of us who believe that President Eisenhower's space-for-peaceful-purposes policy must be retained and honored in the twenty-first century need to face facts: Human history does not give a lot of support to the idea that space should be treated differently from land, sea, and air when it comes to conflict and war. As Oberg suggests, the weaponization of space may be inevitable because of man's warlike nature. A dark view, surely, but one that can be reasonably argued.

A couple of years after Oberg's book was published, the inevitability idea was echoed by Donald Rumsfeld's Space Commission. "We know from history that every medium—air, land and sea—has seen conflict. Reality indicates that space will be no different. Given this virtual certainty, the U.S. must develop the means both to deter and to defend against hostile acts in and from space."[2] Inevitability of conflict; that's the defining belief of the space-warrior community.

Can such an oft-repeated idea be misleading? The answer is almost surely "yes." Space *is* different from land, sea, and air, a fact recognized by virtually every nation save the United States and Israel. Combat on land and on the seas is as ancient as humankind. As for war in the air, we might as well cite Harriet Beecher Stowe's Miss Topsy, who "just grow'd." The first aerial bombardment was in 1849, the year that Pavlov was born, Chopin died, and the "Forty-niners" were heading to California in covered wagons, dreams of gold ricocheting within their heads. The target of that mid-nineteenth-century aerial bombardment was the coastal city of Venice, then in rebellion against Austria's Hapsburg Empire. The Austrians rigged unmanned hot-air balloons to drop bombs on the city.[3]

Before the Great War of 1914–1918 began, thoughtful people believed that in the natural course of things airships—dirigibles—would find terrifying military uses.[4] Delegates to the Second Hague Conference in 1907, fearful of bomb-carrying dirigibles, added a clause to the Convention on Land Warfare that said: "It is forbidden to attack or bombard by any means whatsoever, towns, villages, dwellings or buildings that are not defended." It was a feel-good clause, but worthless; there was no enforcement mechanism—and no intention of enforcing it. Most great powers rejected the ban.[5]

Then came airplanes. On Sunday, July 25, 1909, Louis Bleriot, a French-man, took off from Pas de Calais at 4:30 a.m. in a monoplane of his own design. Forty minutes later, he landed at Dover Castle on Britain's southeast coast. He was feted on both sides of the English Channel as a hero, which he surely was. But a British newspaper, the *Daily Graphic*, dryly noted:

> M. Bleriot has guided an aeroplane in a given direction, and un-der not too favorable conditions, over the strip of water which makes England an island. There is no need to labor the point. The lesson is for all to read. What M. Bleriot can do in 1909, a hundred, nay a thousand aeroplanes may be able to do in five years' time.... A machine which can fly from Calais to Dover is not a toy, but an instrument of warfare of which soldiers and statesmen must take ac-count.[6]

In the early years of the twentieth century, Europe's national leaders sim-ply gave no systematic thought to preserving the air as a sanctuary free of conflict. They were certain that airships and aircraft would evolve into war machines, which meant they would be fair game during conflict.[7] In the twenty-first century, why should the fate of military-oriented spacecraft be any different?

Diplomatic history provides an evocative answer. National leaders throughout the world have given systematic thought for more than forty years as to how space might be preserved as a conflict-free sanctuary. Gov-ernments everywhere, following President Eisenhower's lead, have repeat-edly gone on record as asserting that space *is* different from the land, sea, and air and must be reserved for peaceful purposes.

Is that possible? Can space, unlike the envelope of air that surrounds the Earth, remain a sanctuary free of conflict? Possibly. But only if the United States, the indispensable nation regarding space, boldly and without cyni-cism takes the lead in making it happen. America is the only nation powerful enough in space to make a new and fully verifiable space treaty a reality.

FATHER KNOWS BEST

Space warriors suggest that Eisenhower's peaceful-purposes principle is an outdated relic of the early Cold War. Steven Lambakis, a senior national security and international affairs analyst at the National Institute for Public

Policy and a leading space warrior, lays out that view in his comprehensive space-policy book, *On the Edge of Earth*. "I believe that Americans share a common vision for space and that it centers on the idea of freedom."

> Freedom for all governments and private interests to come and go as they please, to function in space as they please, to stay as long as they please—provided that these activities pose no harm to U.S. interests or security—fairly characterizes the United States's vision for space as expressed in more than forty years of declared policy. That said, there has not been clear agreement on how to realize that vision.

That assessment is a fair and accurate description of America's stated policy. The problem, as Lambakis says, is that there is no "clear agreement" as to *how* to ensure freedom of space. Eisenhower's idea regarding freedom of space was that a live-and-let-live policy was best. Satellites, even those that served military purposes, ought to enjoy free passage in space if they were not themselves weapons. Full stop.

In contrast, Lambakis and his colleagues in the space-warrior community prefer a more assertive stance. "The past," Lambakis writes, "teaches us that power, strength, endurance, versatility, and flexibility are all good qualities within a national security strategy, qualities that befit the global responsibilities of the United States and help ensure its freedom to act in the other environments."

> *...It is a desirable goal, therefore, to propel the United States generations ahead in military technology, and to use that technology within sound strategic and institutional frameworks to achieve vision-inspired ends.*
>
> Consonant with this understanding, *the United States should strive to remain the preeminent military power in space.* This is a laudable and noble end. To be powerful in space does not mean to act imperialistically. It does mean being mentally and physically capable of acting freely in space, if need be in order to control specific orbits. Being in a position of dominance will be important.

The United States, says Lambakis, might even declare a "Monroe Doctrine" for space. The original nineteenth-century Monroe Doctrine "did not reflect an attempt by the United States to colonize or even control the Western Hemisphere." It was simply an "unambiguous statement" about how important this region of the world was to the United States. Similarly, the United States should let the world know that it would "consider any attempt on their part [foreign powers] to extend their system to any portion of *outer space* as dangerous to our peace and safety." This would "not imply a desire to be a global constabulary or achieve an all-encompassing domination of the space environment." But such a declaration would "reinforce the idea that *Washington should oppose all attempts by foreign powers to establish permanent, or even situational control over any of Earth's orbits.*"[8]

The Monroe Doctrine is an inappropriate analogy. That doctrine, first promulgated in 1823, later evolved under President Theodore Roosevelt into an assertion of hegemony over a particular region—*our* part of the world, as American nationalists put it. Does it make sense to speak of an artifact that is more than a century old as a guide for national security space policy in the twenty-first century? The quick answer is "no." And yet, according to the 2006 U.S. National Space Policy:

> The United States considers space capabilities—including the ground and space segments and supporting links—vital to its national interests. Consistent with this policy, the United States will: preserve its rights, capabilities, and freedom of action in space; dissuade or deter others from either impeding those rights *or developing capabilities intended to do so*; take those actions necessary to protect its space capabilities; respond to interference; and deny, if necessary, adversaries the use of space capabilities hostile to U.S. national interests." (Emphasis added.)

At first reading, these words seem sensible enough. We'll protect that which is ours. But upon reflection, the italicized clause surely sounds like a Monroe Doctrine for space, a domain that, in the words of the U.S.-inspired Outer Space Treaty of 1967, is the "province of all mankind." The United States is rapidly moving ahead with the development of a doctrine of space control and hardware designed for dominance—the very things that it says other states must not do.

On the Edge of Earth proposes a benign "Father Knows Best" approach, with the United States as father and the rest of the world as an enormous extended family. (Britain, of course, would be the savvy and loyal helpmate.) The United States would be the "global constabulary"—ready, willing, and able to "control specific orbits," as required.

METEORS AND DRAGONS

The alternative to a U.S. hegemonic capability would be a new space treaty, one that would decisively and verifiably prevent any state from exercising "situational control"—or any other kind of control—over space. The U.N. General Assembly has voted every year since 1981 with near unanimity to begin a process that would ultimately lead to the banning of *all* space-related weapons—not just space-based weapons of mass destruction, which is the case with the Outer Space Treaty of 1967. The effort goes under the awkward title, "Prevention of an Arms Race in Outer Space" or PAROS.[9]

Democratic as well as Republican administrations have systematically prevented PAROS negotiations from getting under way.[10] The official U.S. position has been—and still is—that there is no arms race in space; therefore there is no reason to negotiate a treaty. Consider this June 2006 speech to the Conference on Disarmament in Geneva by John Mohanco, deputy director of the Office of Multilateral Nuclear and Security Affairs.[11]

Over the years, the United States as well as other nations, said Mohanco, have attempted to figure out ways to ban "antisatellite weapons or other space-related weapon systems." It has proven impossible. Many proponents of such bans "assume that it is easy to identify what is or is not a weapon in outer space. This certainly is not the case… as anything in outer space with the ability to alter its trajectory could be a weapon. This includes any of the current meteorological, communications, remote sensing, or navigation satellites currently in orbit. Any of these could, in principle, have its orbit altered so as to collide with another satellite."

Mohanco was correct; satellites able to change their orbits could "in principle" be aimed at other satellites. But that would be a clunky and extraordinarily expensive way to go. Orbital mechanics are such that it is a tricky business to hit a satellite with a satellite. One does not simply aim at a target in space and shoot, as in *Star Trek* and *Star Wars* movies. Both satellites would be moving at many thousands of miles per hour and on different trajectories and planes. (Imagine a hunter shooting a goose in flight while he is on a moving platform traveling just as fast as the duck, but at a cross angle.)

If a nation hopes to have any chance of success in hitting satellites with other satellites, it had better use built-from-scratch "killer satellites." (As noted in Chapter Five, the United States is working on close-inspection smallsats that could, presumably, be adapted to disable or even destroy another satellite, if commanded to do so.)

Mohanco added that "any space-based object with sufficient fuel also can be de-orbited to strike the Earth. Delegations no doubt remember the concern occasioned when Skylab de-orbited, when the Kosmos satellite crashed in Canada, and the care taken with the de-orbiting of the *Mir* space station."

Fair enough. Most satellites are small enough to burn up in the atmosphere when their working lives end and they are commanded to commit suicide by fire.[12] Large satellites, however, are too big to burn up completely; if their remnants crash willy-nilly onto land, they could cause a lot of damage. That is why extraordinary care is taken when de-orbiting large satellites.

Mir was de-orbited in March 2001. The decision to bring it down was controversial in Russia. At one hundred and thirty-five tons, it was then the heaviest manmade object in orbit. Russians were proud of *Mir*; it had circled the Earth for fifteen years, racking up more than two billion miles in space. One hundred and four cosmonauts and astronauts had visited it at one time or another. And yet, Russia could no longer afford to keep it in operation.

Russian scientists predicted that upon reentry into the atmosphere, *Mir* would break up and most of its mass would burn up. They were right. They also said chunks of it would strike the Earth. They were right about that. Despite the loving care that went into the de-orbiting, Russian scientists could not specify precisely where the debris would hit. They could only say that parts of *Mir* would fall over a swath of the Pacific from New Zealand to Chile. Again, they were correct.

Could satellites be used as weapons by de-orbiting them? One usually wants to hit the target one aims at; a de-orbiting satellite could not meet that test. But as nutty as the de-orbiting satellite idea was, Mohanco went even further. "Indeed, any large object in orbit, whatever its peaceful purpose, can cause great harm by falling from orbit," he said. "We have merely to look at the impact crater in Arizona, the mass extinction at the end of Cretaceous Era, or the 1908 event at Tunguska to see the damage that simple rocks and balls of ice can cause when they fall from orbit."

That last sentence is breathtakingly cynical. A report issued by the RAND Corporation described the Tunguska event that took place on June

30, 1908 thusly: "An asteroid weighing about one hundred thousand tons exploded at an altitude of between 2.5 and 9 kilometers with a yield equivalent to forty megatons of TNT.… Had this explosion taken place over an urban area in Europe, it might have produced five hundred thousand human casualties."[13] So much for the "simple rocks and balls of ice" rhetoric.

The extinction of the dinosaurs at the end of the Cretaceous Era was another Earth-shattering event caused by an asteroid. Here's the lead paragraph of an article on the hit—an article that originated at Los Alamos National Laboratory, one of the nation's premier research laboratories:

> What would happen if a ten-kilometer-diameter asteroid penetrated Earth's crust at a speed of fifteen to twenty kilometers per second? The kinetic energy of such an asteroid (more than six miles in diameter) would equal the energy of three hundred million nuclear weapons and create temperatures hotter than on the sun's surface for several minutes. The expanding fireball of superheated air would immediately wipe out unprotected organisms near the impact and eventually lead to the extinction of many species worldwide.[14]

Compared to that asteroid, the meteor that hit in what is now northern Arizona fifty thousand years ago was a little guy. Before entering the atmosphere, it probably weighed about three hundred thousand tons; it may have lost about half that mass by the time it hit. Even so, its impact crater is five hundred and seventy feet deep and more than four thousand feet across.[15]

Little guy or not, the Arizona meteorite was incomparably heavier than anything the United States or any other nation has ever launched into space or intends to launch into space. In contrast to the objects cited by Mohanco that caused calamitous events, America's Space Shuttle (the airplane-like "orbiter" that carries both people and payload) weighs in at around a hundred tons, fully loaded. The International Space Station, which has been assembled bit-by-bit over the years, "weighs" more than twice as much as the orbiter.[16]

The inherent "dual-use potential of any space object," Mohanco asserted, "is a basic barrier to any attempt even to discuss bans on space weapons in any meaningful way. Delegations nonetheless could spend a great deal of time speculating about the kinds of exotic outer space weapons that might be developed years, or even centuries from now." He continued, with words that had no purpose other than to mock: "However, this would place us in the same position as the fictional scientist who, dissatisfied with the fact that dragons do not exist, devoted a year of study to the topic and determined that there were three types of dragons, each of which failed to exist in an entirely different manner."

Moments later, Mohanco once again restated the traditional U.S. position regarding space: "The United States remains committed to the peaceful exploration and use of space by all nations for peaceful purposes. 'Peaceful purposes' includes appropriate defense activities in pursuit of national security and other goals.... The Cold war is over... and there is no arms race in space. Thus, there is no—repeat, no—problem in outer space for arms control to solve."

THE HUMPTY DUMPTY RULE

The United States says that negotiations for a new space treaty would be a hard slog and would eventually come to nothing. Further, the mere attempt to negotiate a new treaty would be pointless because there is no arms race in space. Both "reasons" are misleading. As men and women in national security circles understand, the underlying reason why American diplomats systematically veto negotiations is that the United States seeks to keep its military-space options open. That has been true since the conclusion of the Outer Space Treaty of 1967.[17] The keep-our-options-open stance was candidly spelled out in the January 2001 report of the Space Commission. "There is no blanket prohibition in international law on placing or using weapons in space, applying force from space to Earth or conducting military operations in and through space."

The commission further asserted that "other states and international organizations" were intent on countering "U.S. advantages in space" by seeking "agreements that would restrict the use of space." Therefore, the "U.S. should seek to preserve the space weapons regime established by the Outer Space Treaty, particularly the traditional interpretation of the Treaty's 'peaceful purposes' language to mean that both self-defense and non-aggressive military use of space are allowed.... The U.S. must be cautious of agreements intended for one purpose that, when added to a larger web of treaties or regulations, may have the unintended consequence of restricting future activities in space."

The commission also said that by "specifically extending the principles of the U.N. Charter to space, the Outer Space Treaty (Article III) provides for the right of individual and collective self-defense, including 'anticipatory self-defense.'"[18] Men and women in the arms control field generally believe that interpreting the U.N. Charter and the Outer Space Treaty as allowing for "anticipatory self-defense" is a crock. The U.N. Charter says nations have a right to defend themselves when attacked; no one disputes that. But *anticipatory* self-defense? Scarcely anyone buys that outside of the borders of the United States.

Under the Space Commission's theory, which is shared by most space warriors, developing and deploying a comprehensive space-control system and placing weapons in space would be "non-aggressive" and thus "defensive" in character.[19] Football fans know what is going on here: "defensive" and "offensive" are highly subjective concepts. When a football team plays "defense," its linemen, who happen to be really big guys, go on the offense; their goal is to sack the other team's quarterback. But when the same team is on "offense," the chief responsibility of its linemen, who are also really big guys, is to defend their quarterback.

In football, teams have to wait until the ball is put into play before engaging in their offense/defense mayhem. In the military, where a "good offense" is often described as the "best defense," waiting for the other side to strike is considered a sucker's game. "Anticipatory self-defense" simply means shooting first.

Nearly a century and a half ago, while talking to a little girl named Alice who had fallen down a rabbit hole, a certain Mr. Dumpty scornfully said that when he used a word, "it means just what I choose it to mean—neither more nor less." But the real question, replied Alice, "is whether you can make words mean so many different things." No problem, said Mr. Dumpty. "The question is, which is to be master—that's all."

RULES OF THE ROAD

There have been many proposals for new space treaties over the past two decades.[20] The states most active on the treaty front are China and Russia, and that does not play well in the United States where a lot of people think of the Russian Federation as Evil Empire Lite and the People's Republic of China as the Next Great Threat.[21] Any new space treaty remotely like the

Sino-Russian proposal, space warriors say, would be disastrous.

"Russia and China clearly see a role for an international framework to govern space," said a July 2005 policy paper issued by the George C. Marshall Institute. "Arms control advocates are using the renewed interest in space issues to repeat the mantra that the U.S. is hell-bent on deploying weapons, that such actions are dangerous and unnecessary, and that only a treaty can restrain our aggressive tendencies. Fortunately, all those claims are flat wrong."

> The U.S. should resist calls for a new international treaty prohibiting the deployment of weapons in space, as Russia and China demand. Such a treaty is unenforceable and compliance to its strictures virtually unverifiable. The ignominious record of enforcing and verifying treaties prohibiting activities on Earth is proof enough to give pause to any conversation about a treaty governing activities in space.

"A treaty," says the institute, "would fail to address the chief reason an adversary would seek access to space in the first place—namely, the potential for inflicting a crippling blow against U.S. military and economic might by decapitating our surveillance and communications abilities. Instead, a treaty would eliminate the U.S.'s ability to defend against or deter such threats by precluding the necessary development of space systems and doctrine."[22]

The institute's analysis was conventional space-warrior rhetoric. In fact, a reasonable case can be made that a new space treaty that banned *all* space-related weapons while allowing the traditional military uses of space—mainly warning, reconnaissance, communications, and geopositioning satellites—would be both feasible and verifiable.

To be sure, the arms control community is not of one mind about the need for a "new" treaty. Some believe that the venerable Outer Space Treaty of 1967, which simply prohibits the stationing of weapons of mass destruction in space, can be reworked into a more comprehensive agreement. This strategy makes many arms controllers uneasy. The rule of thumb: It is always risky to re-open an existing treaty. Once a treaty is re-opened, all sorts of good features could be lost or muddied in the ensuing diplomatic melee. It is generally better, goes the conventional wisdom, to construct a new treaty that builds on the previous treaty.

On the other hand, there are options that don't involve any kind of a formal treaty. Arms controllers and even a few space warriors often speak of "confidence-building measures," particularly the possibility of "rules of the road" or a "code of conduct for space." Rules of the road would embrace agreements by spacefaring nations to avoid actions that could be perceived as provocative or injurious to the rights of other nations.

A mutual commitment to refrain from smashing satellites in orbit—such as the kinetic-kill ASAT tests by the United States in 1985 and by China in January 2007—would be a no-brainer; it would surely qualify as one "rule." After all, kinetic-kill ASATs have no other purpose than destroying satellites.

There are many other possible "rules" for a code of conduct. Specific agreements might include "keep-out zones." Such zones would prohibit spacefaring nations from inserting satellites into orbits that would come close to (or intersect with) the orbits of other satellites. Rules of the road, writes Zhang Hui, a research associate at Harvard's Managing the Atom project, would be intended to reduce suspicion and encourage the orderly use of space. They would formalize "cooperation on reducing space debris, notification of space launch, development of safe traffic management procedures, and building a hotline between major missile and space powers." And yet, rules of the road—which would not have the legally binding force of a treaty—are not likely to be enough, says Zhang, to prevent conflict in space in the absence of "strengthened international agreements on space activity."[23]

That's a generally accepted observation in the arms control world; the Center for Defense Information and the Henry L. Stimson Center—both leaders in the rules-of-the-road movement concede that. As a Stimson Center monograph notes, a rules-of-the-road effort "would need to surmount many challenges, including how to define what constitutes dangerous military practices in space and how to devise suitable transparency measures to provide assurance of compliance or to warn of possible noncompliance." Compared to a treaty, rules of the road or a code of conduct for space would be a limited thing. Nevertheless, a code would be a positive step toward something more far-reaching and binding.

[A] possible argument against constructing rules of the road for space assurance is that such efforts might substitute for or displace treaty negotiations on preventing the weaponization of space. To the contrary, work to codify rules of the road could precede stalled treaty negotiations, facilitate them, or proceed in tandem. Much of the analysis required to construct rules of the road for responsible space conduct also has applicability for treaty negotiations. Progress on one track need not stall, and could accelerate, progress on another.[24]

AN ASAT BAN?

A different but complementary track to rules of the road would be to negotiate a formal ban on antisatellite weapons. ASATs have the potential to fuel an expensive arms race that, in turn, would contribute to ever greater levels of mistrust among nations. The latter is no small problem. Excessive mistrust eventually could lead to "crisis instability," a state of affairs that no one really wants in a world in which great powers are armed with nuclear-tipped long-range missiles.

Suppose that two powerful states had come to loggerheads on a variety of profoundly important issues. Suppose further that at a time of high tension that Nation A disables or destroys the reconnaissance satellites of Nation B—the eyes and ears with which Nation B keeps track of certain developments in Nation A. Would Nation B regard that "blinding" as an act of war? Bet on it. Would Nation B retaliate—perhaps by disabling the satellite eyes and ears of Nation A? Another solid bet. And what would Nation A do about *that*?

It does not require an overactive imagination to recognize that the outcome of such satellite-blinding attacks could have a brutally unfortunate outcome. This is not a new concern; it dates back to the 1960s. To help prevent the nuclear arms race from devolving into a true death spiral, the United States and the Soviet Union began negotiating a series of arms control treaties designed to lessen the chance of nuclear war. Close to the heart of these treaties were mutual agreements not to interfere with the "national technical means" of the other nation. "National technical means" is a catchall term that embraces various surveillance satellites.[25]

As sensible as it seems, a formal ASAT ban would be an iffy thing to negotiate. As outlined in Chapter Five, the United States has a variety of existing or potential ASAT technologies ranging from kinetic-kill interceptors in its national missile defense system to robotic smallsats that could be adapted as antisatellite weapons. The fact that the United States is so far ahead of everyone else in antisatellite technology creates a huge problem for treaty proponents.

Conceivably, the United States might agree on a ban of kinetic-kill ASATs. Why not? America has more sophisticated ways to counter the satellites of other nations than pulverizing them. But why would other nations go along with such a limited ASAT ban, knowing that the United States could employ a variety of alternative antisatellite techniques?

The best way to sell the idea would be to persuade other spacefaring nations that a ban on kinetic-kill antisatellite weapons would be a good thing in itself—simply because testing such weapons, much less using them, is bad for everyone. The debris created by testing could eventually render orbital space very nearly unusable.

A simple desire, such as protecting the utility of space for future generations, is the kind of motive that is seldom persuasive in the tough, skeptical, and often cynical world of arms control in which parties to negotiations tend to mistrust one another, always assuming that the other party is angling for an advantage.

UNVERIFIABLE, INEFFECTIVE, EXTREMELY DANGEROUS

A rules-of-the-road approach or an ASAT treaty is anathema to many hardliners. An April 2007 "Report on U.S. Space Policy," compiled by the International Security Advisory Board, an official body that "provides the [State] Department with independent insight and advice on all aspects of arms control, disarmament, international security, and related aspects of public diplomacy," put it this way:

> The United States is constantly pressed by other governments, by NGOs [non-governmental organizations], and by individuals to engage in arms control processes (sometimes disguised as "codes of conduct" or "rules of the road") aimed at agreements to ban certain activities in space. Unfortunately, many such proposals would include unhelpful restrictions on the United States. Almost all contain provisions that are unverifiable and unenforceable. While these provisions would hinder the United States, they would have no sig-

nificant impact on nations determined to cheat and circumvent the proposed agreements.[26]

Even a ban on ASATs is not possible because "there is no way to verify whether a space system is designed for ASAT applications, has significant but latent ASAT capabilities, or only minimal ASAT capabilities because every space system that can maneuver or transmit has some ASAT potential. Direct ascent ASAT weapons—kinetic, explosive, or directed energy— cannot be prevented as long as there are ballistic missiles."

There is some truth to the latter observation. Direct-ascent ASATs require ballistic missiles to boost them into space—that's the easy bit. But once the ASAT reaches space, it must disconnect from its booster and find and hit the target satellite. That is a technologically daunting task. Only the old Soviet Union, China, and the United States have tested ASATs. An ASAT that has not been thoroughly tested against actual satellites is, at best, a wannabee.

The advisory board also notes that "mini- and micro-satellites are being developed that can be launched in large numbers and remain in space for a year or more, their ultimate mission and capabilities completely unknown and unverifiable." That requires a second take. While it is true that a few other nations have tested science-oriented smallsats, as noted in Chapter Five, the United States is far ahead of everyone else in testing robotic seek-and-find maneuverable smallsats that could be, in theory, adapted as anti-satellite weapons.

Indeed, the advisory board is leery of *any* process that might limit America's range of action in space, and it is forthright about it. "Space weapons are nearly impossible to identify and define sufficiently for the purposes of arms control agreements.... Moreover, international agreements, *or the very negotiation of them*, that attempt to ban such unidentifiable 'weapons' can have damaging consequences, intended or unintended, on U.S. rights in space and freedom of access to and use of space." (Emphasis added.)

> Ironically, some states that are leading the call for a ban on the so-called weaponization of space are at the forefront of developing capabilities that threaten peaceful uses of space by the United States. Limiting U.S. capabilities through an arms control regime that is unverifiable and ineffective would be extremely dangerous to our national security interests.

For these reasons, the United States should continue to oppose such arms control initiatives in the international arena, including most particularly the Prevention of an Arms Race in Outer Space (PAROS). Mindful of its growing need to protect its space assets, the United States should also insist upon the freedom to develop and deploy defensive ASATs.

A few pages on, the advisory board adds an emphatic coda: "A strong effort should be made to shift the [domestic] space debate from the prevailing arms control paradigm to the national security and economic areas."[27]

Hardliners downplay the value of arms control treaties, arguing that in an essentially anarchic world, the "security" offered by treaties is more illusion than fact.[28] Insofar as great powers are concerned, goes the refrain, only military and economic power guarantee security—whether that power is possessed mainly by the state itself or whether its power is amplified by acting in concert with other states with congenial interests. A bromide commonly proffered by treaty skeptics is that arms control treaties "work" only when they are not needed and they do not work when they are needed.

MIND EXPERIMENT

Michael E. O'Hanlon, a highly respected Brookings Institution military analyst and frequent talking head on cable news channels, writes in his book *Neither Stars Wars Nor Sanctuary: Constraining the Military Uses of Space* that by "racing to develop its own space weapons, the United States would provoke two unfortunate sets of consequences."

> Militarily, it would legitimate a faster space arms race than is otherwise likely—something that can only hurt a country that effectively monopolizes military space activities today. Second, it would reinforce the current prevalent image of a unilateralist United States, too quick to reach for the gun and impervious to the stated will of other countries (as reflected in the huge majority votes at the United Nations in favor of negotiating bans on space weaponry).

I have cherry picked from among O'Hanlon's statements here. O'Hanlon is not a proponent of a new space treaty; a new treaty "would be generally unverifiable," he says. Also, a new treaty would be "incapable of changing the simple fact that many ballistic missile defense systems have inherent antisatellite potential that would allow them to be transformed into antisatellite weapons with relatively modest adjustments." Further, although the United States does not need antisatellite weapons now, America should not "permanently forswear the need for antisatellite capabilities." The United States, he asserts, might need them someday.[29]

I quote O'Hanlon because his book lays out a middle-ground argument with admirable brevity and clarity. His is a voice of moderation and *Neither Star Wars Nor Sanctuary* can be profitably read by anyone with an interest in military space issues. O'Hanlon makes telling points regarding arms control efforts as applied to space, including the certainty that negotiating a new space treaty would be excruciatingly difficult.

He is right about that. But would an attempt to negotiate a new treaty be as pointless as he suggests? Of the eight hundred-plus satellites of all kinds circling the Earth, more than half belong to the United States. In the event of a conflict in space, the United States has more to lose than any other nation.

Conflict in space may be inevitable, but not precisely for the reasons Oberg, the Space Commission, and many others suggest. It may be inevitable because, in the words of O'Hanlon, if the United States develops and deploys space-related weapons, "it would legitimate a faster space arms race than is otherwise likely—something that can only hurt a country that effectively monopolizes military space activities today." That's speculative, of course, but it's not unreasonable speculation.

Political science realists talk endlessly of the "security dilemma," a zero-sum business in which a state that becomes extraordinarily powerful is seen by other states as diminishing their own security, thus prompting fear-driven countervailing reactions. Realists—and O'Hanlon is a realist—have a point. The desire to enjoy freedom of action in world affairs is not a uniquely American aspiration. Governments, whether democratic, authoritarian, totalitarian, monarchical, or theocratic, do not want to be hemmed in; they want to maximize their own freedom of action vis-à-vis other states.

In a world based on the principle that nations are sovereign entities, an American decision to develop and deploy a unilateral space-control capability would raise profoundly troubling questions regarding the meaning of sovereignty. It would be regarded by many states as an intolerable violation of global norms—and of their sovereignty.

"He who controls space controls the Earth" is an assertion that began popping up in the wake of Sputnik.[30] The assertion is not intuitively false; indeed, it is widely believed. What would we Americans do if we thought that another state, even a democratic state, was about to develop and deploy a comprehensive space-control capability and place weapons in space?

Imagine that China, which had already blasted a satellite in orbit, announced that it planned to develop and deploy a variety of advanced anti-satellite weapons so that it could militarily "control" space within, say, fifteen or twenty years, if needed. Or entertain the idea that Russia, or India, or Indonesia said that it planned to deploy space weapons—unmanned orbiting bombers, perhaps. Picture a document issued by any nation that included a four-color illustration of an orbiting space laser, its beam striking the Earth.

Imagine the nearly unimaginable—that the nominated country was thought to have the scientific, technical, and financial resources to actually pull it off. Many nations, including China, have the potential to conduct limited military operations in space, but only the United States has the financial ability and the technical ingenuity to aspire to full-blown control of space.

But we are suspending disbelief here. Would you be surprised if China or Russia or any other nation announced that it planned to unilaterally develop and deploy a capability to dominate space? Worried? Alarmed? Angry? Of course we Americans would be worried, alarmed, angry. What right would any nation have to unilaterally develop the capability to "deny" access to space to others—potentially *at a time of its own choosing*?

If any nation, even a friendly nation, announced such plans, Americans would demand that Washington lean on the offender. Meanwhile, the United States would call on the international community to impose draconian economic and political sanctions until the state's policies were reversed. But if such measures failed, the world would have a new space race. Military dominance of near-Earth space rather than sending men and women to the Moon and Mars would become the goal.

The new space race would be outrageously expensive; it would siphon intellectual resources and scarce capital into black holes of mutual suspicion; it would compromise the ability of nations to meet everyday human needs. Worse, it would undermine international cooperation on solving or at least mitigating a host of pressing global problems. But the United States would not let Country X or Nation Y develop a comprehensive and demonstrated capability to control space.

Reasonable people in Boston or Chicago or Seattle do not fret over Chinese or Russian or Indian satellites sliding overhead, unseen and unheard. Whatever the purpose of these satellites may be—and they have many functions—they are not weapons.

The mere idea that another nation might someday develop and deploy a substantial and systematic capability to disrupt, disable, damage, or destroy a significant number of U.S. satellites with space-based weapons—or even land-, sea-, or air-based weapons—would be intolerable. It would impel the United States to take immediate and decisive action. Any U.S. president who failed to act with martial vigor in the face of hard evidence that another nation was about to place weapons in space would court impeachment.

In the real world, the United States is the only nation that openly speaks of achieving dominance of space. So far it has not fully matched its actions to its rhetoric. But if the United States definitively chooses to go full tilt toward the goal of space dominance, it would do so with the best of intentions. The United States would say that it would never deny access to space to another country except *in extremis*.

But what nation would willingly rely on the good intentions of another powerful nation, even one as relatively decent as the United States?[31] Would the United States *always* use its space power for the good of all, as it asserts? Or might it someday use that system to enforce uniquely American commercial interests? Further, what other nation could reliably bet that the United States would simply *fail* in its efforts to develop a robust space-dominance weapons capability because of overwhelming technical difficulties and horrendous costs? Americans, after all, are in the habit of making the impossible look easy when it comes to the technology of war.

China's ASAT test in January 2007 may have given us at least one answer to those questions. Although the Middle Kingdom says it wants to negotiate a new space treaty with the United States, it also stands ready to challenge an attempt by the United States to apply full spectrum dominance to space. Unless the United States changes course, its insistence on achieving the capability to control space in a time of conflict will almost surely ignite a space arms race, and arms races nearly always increase the possibility of conflict.

What better way to change course than to take the lead in pursuing a new and unrelentingly tough space treaty that would ensure that no nation, including the United States, could militarily dominate space?

ECHOES OF THE 1940S

If the United States were to pursue a treaty that would effectively ban space-related weapons, it would have to decisively switch gears in its national space policy. That would take guts. Few nations with a commanding military lead in one field or another willingly choose to give it up. The United States tried it once, although (perhaps) in a half-hearted way.

At the end of World War II, the United States had an intact industrial base, some twelve million men under arms, and a monopoly on atomic weapons. The Soviet Union also had a huge army, most of it in Europe, but otherwise it was a ravaged and crippled nation that had no atomic weapons. The Truman administration could have played major-league hardball with Josef Stalin immediately following the war; instead, the administration called the men home and began scrapping tanks and bombers and warships with startling abandon. Although the administration mistrusted Soviet leaders and reminded them from time to time that Uncle Sam had an atomic bomb in his hip pocket, it nevertheless said it would ultimately give up its nukes if certain conditions were met.

In October 1945, the Truman administration said it would seek "international arrangements" leading toward the "renunciation of the use and development of the atomic bomb." With the president's blessing, Dean Acheson, undersecretary of state; David E. Lilienthal, chairman of the newly created Atomic Energy Commission; and J. Robert Oppenheimer, the scientific head of the Manhattan Project, took the lead in developing a step-by-step plan designed to eventually cede control of atomic energy to a new U.N. agency—if the plan were accepted by the Soviet Union.[32] The United States would give up its atomic monopoly.

Truman chose Bernard M. Baruch, a seventy-six-year-old Wall Street speculator with a perhaps undeserved reputation for sagacity, to refine and toughen the Acheson-Lilienthal-Oppenheimer plan and present it to the world. "We are here," Baruch told the newly established U.N. Atomic Energy Commission on June 14, 1946, "to make a choice between the quick and the dead. That is our business. Behind the black portent of the atomic age lies a hope which, seized upon with faith, can work our salvation. If we fail, then we have damned every man to be the slave of fear."

Neither the dramatic wording of Baruch's speech nor the lengthy negotiations that followed had much impact. Revisionist historians generally dismiss the Baruch version of the Acheson-Lilienthal-Oppenheimer plan, saying that in Baruch's hands, it became little more than a propaganda ploy to embarrass the Soviets. The Truman administration, they allege, was sure that the Soviets would reject it because the plan called for rigorous on-site inspections, something a paranoid society built on secrecy could not accept. Further, the plan called for "serious" penalties against transgressors, a veto-proof provision that was unacceptable to the Soviet Union, which already regarded the United Nations as an Anglo-American tool. In a March 5, 1947 speech at the United Nations, the Soviet delegate, Andrei Gromyko, described the plan as based on "fundamentally vicious premises" that were "incompatible" with state sovereignty.[33]

The Baruch Plan may have been a ploy. The proposal was structured so that the United States could retain its edge in nuclear technology for a very long time, note many critics, thus assuring that it could quickly convert that technological prowess "into military capabilities in the event that the underlying agreement broke down."[34] Dean Acheson, surely no fan of Stalin, communism, and the Soviet Union, didn't like Baruch's version of the plan, either. The "swift and sure" punishment provision that Baruch added to the plan, he said, "could be interpreted in Moscow only as an attempt to turn the United Nations into an alliance to support the United States threat of war against the USSR unless it ceased its efforts, for only the United States could conceivably administer 'swift and sure' punishment to the Soviet Union." That, said Acheson, "seemed uncomfortably close to war."[35]

A more generous interpretation of the Baruch Plan would be that it was a well-intentioned initiative infused with characteristic run-it-up-the-flagpole American idealism. Would any other nation that had found itself at the end of a great war as the sole proprietor of the "ultimate weapon" have offered to give up that advantage, no matter how artfully the plan was structured? Not likely. (A counterfactual worth pondering: What if Stalin had ended the war with atomic weapons rather than the United States?)

In any event, the United States hedged by conducting atomic tests in the Pacific about the time the Baruch Plan was introduced. If the Baruch Plan was a carrot, Operation Crossroads—two plutonium bombs detonated at Bikini atoll in front of newsreel cameras and reporters from all over the world—was surely a stick, and a very heavy one at that. The tests told Stalin that the United States had so many atomic bombs that it could afford to "waste" two. In reality, the United States had just a handful in 1946.[36]

It was a year of mixed messages. The Baruch Plan, despite its flaws, was at least in part a product of American generosity, of a stated willingness to short-circuit an arms race before it began. Meanwhile, Crossroads was an unqualified demonstration of America's raw unilateral power. Combined with the earlier Anglo-American refusal to at least notify Stalin of the Manhattan Project, Crossroads was an unmistakable signal to the Soviet Union: If an arms race occurs, the United States will win it.

Unlike some "revisionist" historians, I can't buy the notion that the United States was largely responsible for launching the Cold War because of its belligerence toward the Soviet Union. Josef Stalin and his thuggish henchmen were a bad lot; some sort of Cold War was probably inevitable, although it clearly got out of hand, as noted in Chapter Four.[37]

If you believe that the leaders of modern China are as vile as Stalin and his crew, then developing and deploying a comprehensive space-control system probably makes a good deal of sense. But if you think—as I do—that China's leaders have no intention of competing militarily with the United States in space, if they can help it, then a tough new space treaty is the way to go.

The Chinese government is neither democratic nor is it particularly enlightened. But the attempt by hardliners to cast it as the Next Great Threat to America is a grotesque misreading of current trends in China. The Middle Kingdom needs a reasonably friendly United States as much as America needs a reasonably cooperative China. As I argue in Chapter Fifteen, the United States and China are engaged in a long-term symbiotic relationship and it would be a losing proposition for both if they were to break that bond.

A SELF-FULFILLING PROPHECY

America's current space policy, quoted a few pages back, says that America will "preserve its rights… [and] dissuade or deter others from either impeding those rights *or developing capabilities intended to do so.*" (Italics added.)

That italicized phrase is problematic because it suggests an American Monroe Doctrine for space. Beyond that, the paragraph implies a degree of unilateralism that is broadly inconsistent with the spirit of an international treaty. The essence of a treaty is that it substitutes collective judgments and actions for unilateral judgments and actions. Signatories to a treaty cede a measure of sovereignty in return for achieving a mutually useful goal—in this case, a world in which there are no dedicated space-related weapons. A new treaty would preserve America's freedom of action in space along with the freedom of action for everyone else.

That's a profoundly scary idea to many Americans who believe that America's military might is the *sine qua non* of national security. To successfully conclude a treaty, the United States would have to endorse provisions that would permit other nations to develop and deploy reconnaissance, communications, and geo-positioning satellites. Such satellites, in theory, might give them a rough parity with the United States in space. In reality, such space hardware is expensive and presumably few, if any, states would go the near-parity route.

The flip side, of course, is that any state, such as China, that seeks to challenge the United States regarding military space capabilities *already has the legal right to do so*, no matter what the official statement of U.S. space policy says. The Outer Space Treaty of 1967 bans nuclear weapons and weapons of mass destruction in space. But all nations are legally free to develop non-nuclear antisatellite weapons, space bombers, space lasers, or whatever.

A properly constructed PAROS treaty would eliminate those possibilities. The United States would be forced to give up the notion that it—and only it—has the right to seek military dominance in space. For any arms control treaty to work, all signatory states must be willing to limit their freedom of action. That's what arms control is all about: leveling the playing field in a systematic and mutually acceptable way. From a space-warrior point of view, such a treaty would be dangerous.

To the extent that America's space warriors favor unilateral full spectrum dominance in space, I suggest that they are involved in a classic self-fulfilling prophecy reminiscent of the action-reaction arms race of the Cold War. Space warriors insist that U.S. space dominance is needed because some nations will eventually develop their own sophisticated military space capabilities, thus threatening American interests. That's the dynamic Jim Oberg cited: "The need to place weapons in space as a defense against weapons in space begets the scenario from which the original contention was based. Against this paradox, those who support the sanctity of space have no recourse."

But there is a possible recourse. A new international space treaty would short-circuit that dynamic—if it is hardheaded enough, if it is fully verifiable, if it incorporates tough and certain sanctions against violators—the difficulty would come in finding ways to penalize delinquent states and not their subjects—and if the treaty is negotiated by some of the most skeptical realists the nation produces.

PROFOUND INTRUSIVENESS

One of the problems with arms control treaties, goes a pervasive anti-treaty argument, is that they are often difficult if not impossible to verify. Over the years, bad-faith nations have clandestinely violated treaty terms almost at will. Germany did that in the 1930s by secretly (and then openly) rearming, in violation of the Treaty of Versailles. More recently, Iraq and North Korea and (possibly) Iran demonstrated in the 1980s and 1990s that it was possible to mount clandestine nuclear bomb programs in violation of the terms of the Nuclear Non-Proliferation Treaty.

Compared to the difficulty of verifying bans against nuclear, chemical, or biological weapons, however, verifying a space-weapons treaty would be relatively straightforward, at least in a technical sense. Chemical and biological weapons can be developed and manufactured secretly at virtually any industrialized location. Nuclear weapons programs can be hidden in their early stages, although a program advanced enough to be much of a threat cannot be hidden for long.[38] Few arms control treaties can guarantee that *all* cheating will be detected in a timely manner; perhaps no treaty can do that. Treaties, however, can make it very tough to cheat, which in the long run handicaps the bad actors.

But an antisatellite program—the "threat" space warriors focus on—is a different animal. It is not a they-can-hide-it-until-it's-too-late sort of thing. A large and reliable ASAT program, the only kind of program that could present a substantive threat to America's space assets, would require tests in space. Repetitive tests. Tests that would be "seen" by existing U.S. observation satellites and land-based telescopes and radars. Donald Rumsfeld's Space Commission said, with candor, that even the United States would need to conduct "live-fire events" in space to perfect its ASAT capabilities. And that, in turn, would require "testing ranges in space."[39]

Admittedly, to make a detection system reasonably foolproof, space surveillance technology would have to be upgraded so that an international monitoring agency, created by the treaty, could track all satellites from the moment they are deployed to the moment they die. There is ample down-to-Earth precedent for that sort of thing. The Comprehensive Nuclear Test Ban Treaty, for instance, employs an international monitoring system composed of a global network of seismological, radionuclide, hydroacoustic and infrasound detectors. Even a minuscule underground nuclear test, even the "fizzle" test conducted by North Korea in October 2006, shows up on these instruments.[40] Suspicious orbital behavior by a satellite, such as changing its orbital plane to match the orbital plane of a potential "target" satellite, would be *prima facie* evidence of bad intent.

The difficulties of working out a new Outer Space Treaty should not be minimized. They are enormous, especially the details of verification. In negotiating arms control treaties, nations generally say they want verification—but do they mean it? In working with the Soviet Union on nuclear arms control, President Reagan repeatedly said, "Trust, but verify." That's a good dictum and to his credit, he meant it. The problem is not the concept of verification but how to do it in a way that is intrusive enough to be reliable, but not so intrusive that nations can't live with it.

It would not be insurmountably difficult to design an international space surveillance system, but it would require substantial cooperation among spacefaring nations and large infusions of technical expertise and money. Eventually, the system, featuring a variety of land and space-based optical and radar components, could provide a great deal of real-time information about objects already in orbit while remotely monitoring all of the world's spaceports. (There are not many spaceports; forty-plus years into the Space Age, there are fewer than two dozen, plus the nominally clandestine test facility near the town of Nodong in North Korea. Further, the majority of spaceports are operated by the United States or its friends or allies.)

New spaceports able to support rockets capable of boosting killer satellites into *high* orbits could not be built and operated in secrecy. Because of the nature of their mission, spaceports are large open-air facilities easily seen by observation satellites. Would it be possible for a rogue nation to launch killer satellites from previously unknown and perhaps temporary locations? Probably. Such launches, however, would be immediately visible to infrared-sensitive satellites stationed in space.[41]

"High" is emphasized in the preceding paragraph for a reason. Boosting a satellite-killer into *low*-Earth orbit is not difficult. China used a mobile medium-range ballistic missile for its ASAT test in January 2007, and mobile launchers are not easily found, at least before the launch. In contrast, a missile's fiery plume is quickly and easily spotted by America's infrared-equipped warning satellites. Nonetheless, as noted in Chapter Four, launching a missile and hitting a satellite are two different things. The first is easy; the second incredibly difficult. A nation that hopes to launch a "Pearl Harbor" strike against American satellites in *low*-Earth orbit would have to conduct many preliminary tests. Those tests would not go unseen.

It would not be enough to watch spaceports from afar. Antisatellite weapons could be disguised as scientific or commercial satellites. Highly intrusive on-site inspections would be needed to take care of that problem. *On-site inspections*? As Shakespeare might put it if he were around, "Ay, there's the rub."

Although Russia and China have been the chief proponents of a new space treaty, they have expressed wariness regarding intrusive inspections. A joint Sino-Russian working paper submitted to the Conference on Disarmament on May 22, 2006 says, in part:

> Politically, verification touches upon the issue of the protection of a nation's advanced technology and militarily sensitive information. This is especially true with the fact that, because of the relatively profound intrusiveness of on-site verification, few States with outer space capability will allow personnel from other States to inspect their laboratories, or to stay permanently at their launching sites.[42]

Translated, the Russians and the Chinese talk the talk, but they may not be willing to walk the walk. Would the Chinese and the Russians actually sit down with the United States and make a fully verifiable treaty happen? A new space treaty without foolproof verification measures would be a nonstarter for the United States, as it should be.

If, however, the United States ever sat down at the negotiating table, the most contentious issue might be missile defense. As noted in Chapter Four, it is not easy to find a scientist familiar with missile defense technology who believes it would work well if the United States were ever attacked. No matter. The word "defense" is an emotion-laden word and "leaving the nation defenseless against missile attack" is a phrase made in paradise for demagogues. The United States is not likely to give up its missile defense efforts short of an attack of mass rationality.

The problem is easily understood. Any nation with a reasonably sophisticated missile defense system—even one that is unlikely to work in a crisis—has a potentially workable antisatellite system. If a new space treaty is to be realized, all nations must be free to develop their own missile defense systems—*if* they are land-, sea-, or air-based systems, as are the American systems now under development. While such systems are de facto ASATs, they are *limited* ASATs; they can intercept satellites in low-Earth orbit but not satellites in higher orbits.[43]

In contrast, a PAROS treaty cannot permit *space*-based anti-ballistic missile systems. While even a space-based system probably would be largely ineffective against missiles fired in anger or by accident, some kinds of space-based systems could potentially threaten satellites in any orbit. That's not a certainty; but opening that particular Pandora's Box would almost surely be a deal breaker for any nation.

Yet another Pandora's Box: robotic smallsats, such as those described in Chapter Five. Because of their potential to seek, find, disable, or even destroy satellites in any orbit, they would require very rigorous pre-launch inspection, which would put proprietary secrets at risk. That presents an intriguing conundrum. Which is the greater value: protecting proprietary secrets, or ensuring that there are no space-related weapons?

Idealistic? Pie in the sky? Fuzzy-headed? Perhaps. But a new space treaty, even with expensive verification measures, would be a small price to pay for avoiding a space-related arms race and a new cold war. Humankind faces fearsome global problems in this century—wars within failed states that have global consequences; persistent poverty in much of the world; the war on terrorism; natural disasters; fiscal, monetary, and energy crises; and on and on and on. Do we really need an arms race in space?

PUT UP OR SHUT UP

The scope of arms control treaties is always difficult to work out, as are definitions and technical issues related to verification. But with a new space treaty, the greatest barriers likely would be political rather than definitional or technical, especially for the United States. A new treaty would prevent the United States from developing a space-dominance capability, an idea that has energized space warriors for more than forty years.

If all of the world's spacefaring nations, save the United States and Israel, say they favor a new space treaty, why not pursue a put-up-or-shut-up strategy? If these nations truly mean it when they say they want a new treaty, effective verification systems for such a treaty presumably could be designed.

In contrast, enforcement provisions would be far more difficult. Signatories to the treaty would have to be unfailingly willing, if preliminary sanctions fail, to disable, damage, or destroy the spaceport facilities of a nation found to be in clear violation of the terms of the treaty. Every effort must be taken, of course, to spare innocent life.

Draconian? Yes. But a new, enforceable space treaty might be needed to prevent a global arms race in space, the consequences of which would be unpredictable and likely dangerous. In the modern world, an intrusive treaty, even with harsh sanctions, is a necessary evil. Here we have a clash of worldviews more profound than anything even Jim Oberg imagined. He wrote that "the notion of weapons in space is one that pits military pragmatists against idealistic futurists. Or, put another way... it is the idealists versus realists, the political hawks versus the doves."

To make a treaty workable, perhaps, hawks must *also* be doves and doves must *also* be hawks. In the animal world, that's impossible. But the human mind is a wonderfully adaptable thing, isn't it, fully capable of holding seemingly contradictory ideas at the same time. A treaty that lacks the mechanism to dish out swift and sure punishment to violators would not be worth much. So those of us who want a treaty must accept the notion that it *must* be able to deal harshly—and with certainty—with violators.

Is that requirement a deal breaker? One of the most profound lessons of the twentieth century was that international organizations, including the old League of Nations and the United Nations, can be endlessly pusillanimous when it comes to enforcing tough words with tough actions. That twentieth-century experience can be interpreted in two ways. The first is simply to say that the idea of swift and sure punishment through an international treaty will not work, so why pursue such a treaty in the first place?

But another approach is to simply recognize the dark historical reality of the recent past. The twentieth century was the bloodiest in the history of humankind, and one reason for that was that international organizations failed to act decisively in the interests of humanity as they were expected to do. In the twenty-first century, a new, enforceable space treaty has a real chance to succeed where such organizations failed. Is humankind ready for such a treaty?

A TIME FOR BOLDNESS

Perhaps the strongest argument for a space treaty is that it would be consistent with the American belief in the rule of law. To be sure, many space warriors seem enamored of a Monroe Doctrine for space. But even in America, the original Monroe Doctrine is now regarded by everyone, save unreconstructed nationalists, as an anachronism, an artifact of a lawless era of gunboat diplomacy.

In September 2000, Robert T. Grey, then U.S. ambassador to the Conference on Disarmament in Geneva, said: "The United States agrees that it is appropriate to keep [PAROS] under review.... On the other hand, we have repeatedly pointed out that there is no arms race in outer space—nor any prospect of an arms race in outer space, for as far down the road as anyone can see."[44] Ambassador Grey was not altogether happy with that formulation at the time, but being a representative of the United States, he had to adhere to national policy. Now that he has retired from government service, he has a different take on the matter. In May 2007, Grey offered a short history of space-related arms control, and said:

> Beginning in the Eisenhower administration and concluded during the Kennedy administration, the international community, with strong and positive American leadership, concluded the Outer Space Treaty, which calls for using space to promote the common interest of all mankind. The leaders and governments who negotiated this treaty were determined to create a new international order in which multilateral cooperation and the peaceful resolution of disputes was to be the new order of the day.

Since the 1960s, said Grey, the uses of outer space have greatly expanded. "It is used not only for commercial services such as communications and for scientific exploration, but for military surveillance, navigational assistance, weather forecasting, and a host of other useful and necessary activities."

> Weaponization of space would put all of these activities at risk. Defensive military deployments anywhere always run the risk of being overwhelmed by new or existing offensive capabilities that are frequently cheaper to develop. This is no less true in space than it is on land, or on or under the sea. Any sensible person would conclude that no nation could achieve space dominance—it is simply not possible.

Slogans filched from the days of wooden ships and iron men are simply not relevant to outer space. Yet one nation acting alone is moving relentlessly forward. Every government in the world, except for the Bush administration, is willing to negotiate drafting a regime that will ban weaponization of outer space and promote international cooperation.[45]

Grey's words came during the waning years of a particular presidential administration. But the principle he spoke of extends beyond any given administration. Since 1958, space warriors have argued the necessity for American military dominance of space, dominance that, they say, would be exercised for the good of humankind.

A great nation, a law-abiding power that seeks to influence the world by example, can do better than to offer up the old military-dominance paradigm, which has roots that extend back into the mists of time. A great nation founded on the rule of law can afford to be generous, visionary, and bold. And what could be bolder and more visionary than leading the world to a treaty that would ensure that space remains free of conflict?

13

The Americanization of the World

The United States is so many years ahead of everyone else in the military uses of space that it can safely afford to spend some time exploring whether a new space treaty is both feasible and verifiable. If it becomes clear after two or three years that negotiations aren't going anywhere, the United States would still have the option of going its own way in space. Yes, the United States is *that* far ahead.

The reason space warriors so cavalierly dismiss the treaty route seems obvious to some: the United States is a new kind of imperial nation and a policy of space dominance would serve that new imperium. A 2004 videotape produced by one activist organization, for instance, begins with a montage of American rockets blasting into space, most of which were launched by NASA, the civilian space agency. The narrator asserts that the "glory days of NASA are over. Today, the military-industrial complex is marching toward world domination in space technology on behalf of the global corporate interests."[1]

Later in the presentation, we learn that these corporate interests already "control" the White House and the Congress, and that corporate goals include controlling Earth from space for multiple reasons ranging from securing the lion's share of the world's oil to mining asteroids for their (presumed) mineral riches.

World domination? A bit much. Space warriors are as dedicated to defending the nation as you and I; the salient question is how those interests are best defended. I have yet to run into a twenty-first century space warrior who has world domination in mind. I do, however, wonder what Wernher von Braun was thinking of more than a half century ago when he promoted his nuclear-armed guardian-of-the-peace satellite scheme.

Nonetheless, debating the question of whether or not the United States is an empire, or is becoming one, is a growth industry. At least writing books on the subject is. Consider just a few of dozens of recent titles: *American Empire: The Realities and Consequences of U.S. Diplomacy* by Andrew J. Bacevich; *The Empire Has No Clothes* by Ivan Eland; *Colossus: The Rise and Fall of the American Empire* by Niall Ferguson; *Nemesis: The Last Days of the American Republic* by Chalmers Johnson; *The Folly of Empire: What George W. Bush Could Learn from Theodore Roosevelt and Woodrow Wilson* by John B. Judis; *Sands of Empire: Missionary Zeal, American Foreign Policy, and the Hazards of Global Ambition* by Robert F. Merry; and, for that matter, virtually any book by Noam Chomsky, including *Hegemony or Survival: America's Quest for Global Dominance*.

In 1998, Hubert Vedrine, then foreign minister of France, dubbed the United States the global "hyperpower." Among all countries in the world today, Vedrine later wrote, "one constitutes a category all by itself, notwithstanding the formal equality of the states of the United Nations.... The United States is predominant in all areas: economic, technological, military, monetary, linguistic, cultural. This situation is unprecedented: What previous empire subjugated the entire world, including its adversaries?"[2]

The America-as-empire debate is both old and vital. (In late June 2007, I googled "American empire" and got about 1,080,000 hits in 0.17 seconds.) But in the end, the question is value laden and cannot be resolved. It isn't even possible to agree on what the word "empire" means. Does it mean a brutally exploitive regime like many of the nineteenth-century European colonial empires? Or does it suggest a somewhat more benign and collaborative arrangement, a bit like the old British empire? Or does empire denote dictatorial control of subservient states through political puppets, as with the Soviet empire?

None of those definitions fits the United States. Perhaps journalist Martin Walker got it right a few years ago in a provocative essay in which he simply observed that "America is a virtual empire, whose power is so evident and so sweeping that it does not need to be formally exercised."[3]

Walker and others who argue that the United States is a new kind of empire score impressive points. But in the end, the empire debate resembles a preaching-to-the-choir sort of thing. Just as surely as *National Review* and *The Nation* will never agree on the true meaning of federalism, we Americans will never reach a consensus on empire. In the end, the most illuminating question regarding American empire may be: Are we looking at the *right* "e" word?

We Americans will never fully agree on many important matters, nor should we. The genius of America is that it brings together a broad spectrum of people with disparate values under a single secular umbrella, the Constitution. That makes for a yeasty and culturally rich environment that ensures constant disputation. But we can surely agree that the United States has a long collective history of describing itself as the most *exceptional* nation in the history of the world. That idea, which may well be the overarching American paradigm, has immense consequences within the United States and virtually everywhere else, including space.

International law declares that space is the "province of all mankind." But the underlying spirit of American exceptionalism may, sooner rather than later, persuade the government of the United States that it alone should develop and deploy a comprehensive capability to control near-Earth space and to place weapons in space. It is the pervasive belief in America's exceptional mission, rather than an imperial mission, that underlies the rejection of space-treaty negotiations.

MONSTERS TO DESTROY

Long before there was a United States, the English colonies in the New World were widely seen in Europe by liberal thinkers as a promised land where spiritual and civic regeneration was possible, even likely. Moral and material Progress with a capital P would be worked out to its fullest extent in the New World rather than in the tired and corrupt Old World. A phrase uttered by John Winthrop in 1630 is recited nearly four hundred years later, thanks in part to Ronald Reagan's revival of Winthrop's city-on-the-hill image.

Winthrop, governor of the new Massachusetts Bay Colony, told his band of English émigrés, mostly Puritans, that life would be rigorously hard in America. But if they loved God and one another; if they worked together with meekness, gentleness, patience, and liberality; and if they rejoiced together, mourned together, labored together, and suffered together, they would find that God would dwell among them and their community "shall be as a Citty upon a Hill, the Eies of all people are uppon us."[4]

Those observations about divine destiny were among the first expressions of American exceptionalism. The Founding Fathers were exceptionalists too, as one would expect of men willing to die for an idea. If the American experiment should fail, wrote Alexander Hamilton in *The Federalist* No. 1, that failure would deserve "to be considered as the general misfortune of mankind." After retiring as president, Thomas Jefferson described the United States as the world's "sole depository of the sacred fire of freedom and self-government."[5]

It makes no difference whether the United States was actually singled out by God for greatness or whether it was merely a nation blessed with abundant natural resources, good and deep topsoil, a relatively benign climate, energetic immigrants from the Old World, and a lot of room to fill, once the original inhabitants had died of smallpox or had been otherwise removed. What *is* relevant is that so many opinion shapers and policymakers have preached American exceptionalism.

During America's formative years, exceptionalism was generally expressed in the idea that the people of the United States would build a new kind of nation that would become a model to the world. Otherwise, the United States would practice a live-and-let-live policy toward other nations. That was prudent. European history was one of war interrupted by short and uneasy periods of fragile peace. Why get caught in the middle of a European conflict by taking sides? That was the genesis of the early U.S. foreign policy as described by President George Washington in his Farewell Address: The United States should not become entangled in the intrigues, alarums, and wars of the Old World; it must "observe good faith and justice toward nations"; it should extend "commercial relations" with them but otherwise have "as little political connection as possible."[6]

Washington (and his ghostwriter-in-chief, Alexander Hamilton) offered sensible advice. The United States, like any newborn, was weak; it needed time to grow stronger. Neutrality was basic survival strategy. Although the policy is sometimes called isolationism, it was far from that. America's merchant ships plied the Caribbean, the Atlantic, and the Mediterranean by the thousands. The War of 1812 was fought in large measure to underscore American rights in the lucrative shipping trade. America's neutrality was an *armed* neutrality.

John Quincy Adams famously summed up America's neutralist policy in 1821 while serving as James Monroe's secretary of state. "What has America done for the benefit of mankind?" Adams rhetorically asked. Well, she had "proclaimed to mankind the inextinguishable rights of human nature" as the "only lawful foundation of government." She had consistently held forth to all nations the "hand of honest friendship." She had spoken, though often to "disdainful" ears, "the language of equal liberty, of equal justice, and of equal rights."

For nearly a half century, Adams said, America had "respected the independence of other nations while asserting and maintaining her own." She did not interfere in the "concerns of others." Indeed, "wherever the standard of freedom and independence has been or shall be unfurled, there will her heart, her benedictions and her prayers be. But she goes not abroad in search of monsters to destroy."[7]

THE GREAT NATION OF FUTURITY

It is hardly possible to exaggerate the importance of John L. O'Sullivan in giving voice to American expansionism in the nineteenth century. O'Sullivan, editor of the nationalistic publication, *The United States Magazine and Democratic Review*, did not invent the idea that the United States had an inherent, God-given right to expand far beyond its original Atlantic-coast borders. That idea had been around for a long time.[8]

In June 1803, for instance, Alexander Hamilton's newspaper, the *New York Evening Post*, got wind of a secret land deal with France, now known as the Louisiana Purchase. The *Post* favored the acquisition and editorialized that the United States had a divine right "to regulate the future destiny of *North America. The country is ours*; ours is the right to its rivers and to all the sources of future opulence, power, and happiness, which lay scattered at our feet."[9]

But it was O'Sullivan, not Hamilton, who eventually made "manifest destiny" a kind of national religion. In 1839, he published a remarkable editorial ("The Great Nation of Futurity") that put a name to an ideology that still informs American actions in the twenty-first century, including space-warrior attitudes toward national security space.

> The far-reaching, the boundless future will be the era of American greatness. In its magnificent domain of space and time, the nation of many nations is *destined* to *manifest* to mankind the excellence of divine principles; to establish on Earth the noblest temple ever dedicated to the worship of the Most High—the Sacred and the True.

All this will be our future history, to establish on Earth the moral dignity and salvation of man—the immutable truth and beneficence of God. For this blessed mission to the nations of the world, which are shut out from the life-giving light of truth, has America been chosen; and her high example shall smite unto death the tyranny of kings, hierarchs, and oligarchs, and carry the glad tidings of peace and good will where myriads now endure an existence scarcely more enviable than that of beasts of the field. Who, then, can doubt that our country is destined to be the great nation of *futurity*? (Italics added.)[10]

In an 1845 editorial advocating western expansion, O'Sullivan finally got the word sequence right. It was America's "manifest destiny to overspread the continent allotted by Providence for the free development of our yearly multiplying millions."[11] It was an exceptionalist sentiment, all right, but it was something more—a quintessential expression of nationalism, an ethos that tends to ignore or denigrate the contributions and achievements of other groups that are also part of the rich human tapestry.

The spirit of nationalism has waxed and waned in the United States. The years surrounding the turn of the twentieth century were a high point—as were the years surrounding the turn of the twenty-first century.

THE SPLENDID LITTLE WAR

In 1898, the United States abandoned its neutralist foreign policy and went abroad to smite a monster—the colonial empire of Spain, which was indeed pretty rotten. The most "problematic" feature of this foray into colonialism was not the colonialism itself, according to the distinguished historian Walter A. McDougall. It was the "moral progressivism" that most people now applaud. "The United States went off the rails, in terms of its honored [neutralist] traditions, when it *went to war with Spain in the first place*," he writes.[12]

The proximate cause of the Spanish-American war was that the battleship *Maine* had blown up on February 15, 1898 in Havana harbor while on an extended "courtesy" call. Two hundred and ninety-eight men were killed. Although the explosion was probably accidental, and many newspapers counseled patience while the cause of the explosion was investigated,

Spanish provocateurs were widely blamed and a "yellow" press beat the war drums incessantly.[13]

The United States freed Cuba from Spain in the spring of that year, although it reserved extensive rights of future intervention, converting it into a quasi-colony. It also gained control of Puerto Rico, Guam, and Manila, the principal city of the Philippine Archipelago. From an American standpoint, the Spanish–American War was a tidy affair with outcomes measured in days and weeks, not months or years. Three-hundred and thirty-two Americans died as a result of combat, although nearly three thousand eventually succumbed to disease, mainly malaria and yellow fever. Secretary of State John Hay characterized it as "a splendid little war begun with the highest motives, carried on with magnificent intelligence and spirit, favored by that fortune which loves the brave."[14]

Americans had been ready for the conflict, having been "keyed up" by a nationalistic press to a "high pitch of nervous and wrathful excitement," according to a contemporary account in the 1899 edition of *Encyclopaedia Britannica*. Helping Cuban freedom fighters—*insurrectos*—drive the loathsome Spaniards from the Caribbean was widely thought to be morally just. Spain had raped, pillaged, and exploited native peoples for centuries and it had even established concentration camps in Cuba as a means of isolating the *insurrectos*. The camps, ridden with disease and stalked by death, were a particular affront to the American people, most of whom had apparently given little thought to the meaning and purpose of America's newly established Indian reservations.

Following the American declaration of war, the cover of the April 30, 1898 *Harper's Weekly*, the self-styled "journal of civilization," captured the prevailing mood. Standing tall on the cover was a lithe, handsome, dark-haired Cuban woman wrapped in the Stars and Stripes, face uplifted, arms stretched heavenward, palms turned upward in joy, the just-broken shackles of tyranny and enslavement falling away. The caption: *"Cuba Libre!"*

"I HAVE READ THE CONSTITUTION"

That the Caribbean should become an American lake after the liberation of Cuba and Puerto Rico was not an especially contentious issue in the United States. Geography and the ever-present threat of great-power depredations in the Western Hemisphere made it seem both inevitable and proper. But the Philippines, where the Spanish fleet had fallen with immoderate speed to the Asiatic Squadron commanded by George Dewey, was another matter.

Dewey had been readied for war by Assistant Secretary of the Navy Theodore Roosevelt, who had—on his own initiative—ordered the commodore to stand by in Hong Kong, his fleet fueled and provisioned, so he could do battle as soon as war was declared. Dewey's success was a prideful thing to most Americans—*Dewey! Dewey! Dewey!/ Is the hero of the day/ And the Maine has been remembered/ In the good, old-fashioned way.* Nonetheless, the ultimate disposition of the Philippines became a vexatious matter.

The Philippine Archipelago was *terra incognita* to most Americans. London was closer to San Francisco than San Francisco was to Manila. The United States had demonstrated that it had the military power to take over the entire archipelago, if it so chose. But did it have the moral and constitutional right to retain the Philippines as a colony? After all, the Filipino *insurrectos* had been fighting for their freedom, however ineptly and sporadically, long before the Americans intervened. Between the formal end of hostilities with Spain in August and peace-treaty negotiations scheduled for December, President William McKinley had to decide what to do.

The decision was not easy, according to McKinley. He was not an *a priori* imperialist. He knew the *insurrectos* had joined forces with Dewey, at Dewey's express or implied invitation, to help bring the Spanish down. Further, the leader of the *insurrectos*, Emilio Aguinaldo, clearly believed the Filipino independence movement had Dewey's support—and therefore the support of the United States, the world's most outspoken champion of liberty.

Aguinaldo may have misunderstood or he may have been misled. Joseph L. Stickney, an aide to Dewey, noted that Aguinaldo was a "man of intelligence far beyond that of most of his people" who spent considerable time probing the intentions of the American government.[15] At one meeting with Gen. Thomas M. Anderson, who led the initial ground invasion, Aguinaldo asked whether "the United States had any intention of treating the Philippines as colonies."

Anderson replied that he could not speak for the government. But he added that the United States had been a nation for more than one hundred and twenty years without colonies, and Aguinaldo could judge for himself whether the U.S. government would try to colonize a distant territory at this late date.

"That is true," Stickney recalls Aguinaldo as saying, "and besides I have read the Constitution of the United States very carefully, and I cannot find in it any provision for colonies."[16]

GOD'S GUIDANCE

Back in Washington, McKinley dithered over what to do for weeks, then months, saying he was unsure as to the right course. Should the Filipinos be granted independence after a suitable tutorial in self-government? Should the Philippines become a protectorate complete with American naval bases? Or should it become an outright colony?

McKinley listened to the arguments of self-described imperialists Teddy Roosevelt and Henry Cabot Lodge and he carefully probed public opinion by having aides measure audience reaction to pro-annexation phrases in his speeches, something like the focus groups used by today's ad agencies. McKinley, a pious Methodist, also prayed for divine guidance. Eventually the Lord spoke.

"One night it came to me this way," McKinley later explained. "We could not turn them [the Philippines] over to France or Germany, our commercial rivals in the Orient—that would have been bad for business and discreditable." Nor could the United States "give them back to Spain—that would be cowardly and dishonorable." And yet, America could not let the Filipinos rule their homeland because they were manifestly "unfit for self-government—and they would soon have anarchy and misrule."

The divinely inspired answer: Keep the Philippines and "educate the Filipinos and uplift and Christianize them as our fellow-men, for whom Christ also died." McKinley then went to bed and "slept soundly."[17] (Ironically, the Filipinos had long ago been Christianized by Catholic missionaries, a fact that may have escaped McKinley's notice. But why didn't God remember it?)

The decision to convert the newly freed Philippines into an American colony did not go down well with everyone in the States. An extraordinary anti-imperialism movement took shape and nearly carried the day. Mark Twain, the most popular author of the day, said the United States might as well produce a flag for the new "Philippine Province." It would be based on the stars and stripes, but "with the white stripes painted black and the stars replaced by a skull and cross-bones." William James, philosopher and psychologist, characterized the administration's ultimatum to the *insurrectos* as: "We are here for your own good; therefore unconditionally surrender to our tender mercies, or we'll blow you into kingdom come."[18]

The *insurrectos* did not surrender. The war that followed was nasty, brutish, and not short. Early on, U.S. troops were outnumbered but had superior firepower. The *insurrectos* turned to guerrilla tactics, which the Americans were hard-pressed to counter. Both sides engaged in torture and committed atrocities.

By the time the war wound down in the spring of 1902, 4,234 American soldiers had died, as had about sixteen thousand Filipino soldiers and irregulars. Perhaps as many as two hundred thousand Filipino civilians also died, mostly from war-related disease and malnutrition.[19] In some respects, the war was a preview of Vietnam, sans helicopters and gunships.

William McKinley—a man chiefly remembered today for having been killed by a deranged anarchist—had become, in the aftermath of a short and decisive war, a partial convert to a new vision of America, a truly *exceptional* vision. No longer would the United States simply be a model for the nations of the world; rather, it would go abroad from time to time to remake the world.

A REGENERATING IDEA

Albert J. Beveridge, a thirty-five-year-old lawyer from Indianapolis delivered an impassioned plea for the annexation of the Philippines at the Indiana Republican convention on September 16, 1898, before McKinley had made up his mind. Some two hundred Republicans with "torches and red lights" accompanied by a marching band came to his home the night of the speech and escorted him to the hall.

The talk, a full-blown oration, was a foot-stomper. The cadences, the repetition, the syntactical drive, the *power* of Beveridge's words are hard to grasp in our modern sound-bite-constricted world. But the tightly packed crowd, numbering in the thousands, was soon "cheering sentences, not waiting for the climaxes."[20]

> It is a noble land that God has given us; a land that can feed and clothe the world; a land whose coastlines would enclose half the countries of Europe; a land set like a sentinel between the two imperial oceans of the globe, a greater England with a nobler destiny.

It is a mighty people that He has planted on this soil; a people sprung from the most masterful blood of history; a people perpetually revitalized by the virile man-producing working-folk of all the Earth; a people imperial by virtue of their power, by right of their institutions, by authority of the Heaven-directed purposes—the propagandists and not the misers of liberty.

Having established that God looked upon the United States with favor, Beveridge turned to the country's duty to govern those who were unfit to govern themselves. "The Opposition tells us that we ought not to govern a people without their consent," he asserted. "I answer, the rule of liberty that all just government derives its authority from the consent of the governed, applies only to those who are capable of self-government. We govern the Indians without their consent, we govern our territories without their consent, we govern our children without their consent." He then turned to Manifest Destiny, by now a familiar concept.

The march of the flag! In 1789 the flag of the Republic waved over four million souls in thirteen states, and their savage territory which stretched to the Mississippi, to Canada, to Florida. The timid minds of that day said no new territory was needed, and for the hour, they were right. But Jefferson, through whose intellect the centuries marched; Jefferson, who dreamed of Cuba as an American state; Jefferson, the first Imperialist of the Republic—Jefferson acquired that imperial territory that swept from the Mississippi to the mountains, from Texas to the British possessions, and the march of the flag began.[21]

The speech was a coast-to-coast sensation; it was widely reprinted in the national press and three hundred thousand copies were distributed by the Republican Party throughout the country. Beveridge's new fame took him to the U.S. Senate.

After taking his senatorial seat in January 1900, Beveridge was invited to make his maiden speech on the floor. Not surprisingly, it dealt with the Philippines. In those days, freshman senators were expected to sit and observe and keep their mouths shut. If they spoke at all on the floor of the Senate, it was with diffidence. In contrast, Beveridge's speech astounded the political world for its length, its confidence, its fire. Near the end, the junior senator from Indiana said that God had "marked the American people as His chosen nation to finally lead in the *regeneration of the world*. This is the divine mission of America, and it holds for us all the profit, all the glory, all the happiness possible to man. We are trustees of the world's progress, guardians of its righteous peace. The judgment of the Master is upon us: 'Ye have been faithful over a few things; I will make you ruler over many things.'"[22] (Italics added.)

Despite the powerful anti-imperial backlash at the turn of the century, the regeneration idea expressed by Beveridge and others excited the nation. Orators and editorialists repeated it endlessly. In February 1902, while the guerrilla war in the Philippines still raged, Alfred Thayer Mahan, the nation's premier naval strategist and one of the nation's leading imperialists, spoke of the "conversion of spirit and ideals—the new birth—that has come over our own country" as a result of the Spanish-American War. "What the nation has gained in expansion is a *regenerating* idea, an uplifting of the heart, a seed of future beneficent activity, a going out of self into the world to communicate the gift it has so bountifully received."[23] (Italics added.)

Regeneration was a notion that America's founders had been familiar with. Their new nation would be a model to the world, a nation in which sovereignty was vested in the people. In contrast, turn-of-the-century imperialists like Beveridge and Mahan had a different take. American regeneration would be interventionist; it was not merely a model. Progressive thinkers of the day loved this new, muscular exceptionalism.

Josiah Strong, a popular and influential American preacher and a key figure in the Protestant "social gospel" movement, asserted time and again that God had "honored" the Anglo-Saxon race in general and Americans in particular for a reason: America's destiny was to save the world. The United States, he said, "has been made powerful, and rich, and free, and exalted—not to make subject, but to serve; rich, not to make greater gains, but to know the greater blessedness; free, not simply to exult in freedom, but to make free; exalted, not to look down, but to lift up."[24]

Brooks Adams made a secular case for exceptionalism in his slim little volume, *America's Economic Supremacy*, published in 1900. Adams—the brother of Henry Adams, the son of Charles Francis Adams (a diplomat who helped keep Britain neutral in America's Civil War), the grandson of John Quincy Adams, and the great-grandson of John Adams—was obsessed with the ebb and flow of historical and economic forces.

Britain was in decline, Adams said. "For nearly a hundred years," he wrote, Britain had "acted as the containing power, or balance wheel, of the world." But now that country was "losing her vitality" and "she could no longer be relied upon to perform that function." Until "a new equilibrium can be attained each community must fight for itself in every corner of the globe." The nation most likely to restore global equilibrium was the United States.[25]

> From this inexorable decree of destiny [the United States] cannot escape. The center of the economic system of civilization is in motion, and until it once more comes to rest, tranquility cannot return. All signs now point to the approaching supremacy of the United States, but supremacy has always entailed sacrifices as well as its triumphs, and fortune has seldom smiled on those who, besides being energetic and industrious, have not been armed, organized, and bold.[26]

Oddly, American exceptionalism found some of its most exuberant enthusiasts in Britain. Rudyard Kipling, Britain's poet laureate of imperialism, wrote "The White Man's Burden" to help persuade the United States to stay the course in the Philippines and to join the British in doing good works in the benighted areas of the world. Published in *McClure's Magazine* in February 1899, "Burden" was wildly popular in the United States. *Take up the White Man's burden/ Send forth the best ye breed—/ Go, bind your sons to exile/ To serve your captives' need;/ To wait, in heavy harness,/ On fluttered folk and wild —/ Your new-caught sullen peoples,/ Half devil and half child.*[27]

William Thomas Stead, a man last seen smoking his pipe on the deck of the *Titanic* in the early morning hours of April 15, 1912, was one of Britain's most influential and best-loved journalists and an archetypal turn-of-the-century British liberal—which meant that he was a social reformer at home and an imperialist abroad. He, too, was bullish about the American global role in the twentieth century.

As the twentieth century began, said Stead, British power—based on its dominant navy—was at its peak. Most of his countrymen thought Britain would rule the seas more or less forever, which meant that Britain would remain at the head of the greatest empire the modern world had ever known.

Stead disagreed. His *The Americanisation of the World or The Trend of the Twentieth Century*, published in 1902 in Britain, began with an extraordinary statement: "The advent of the United States of America as the greatest of world-Powers is the greatest political, social, and commercial phenomenon of our times." The ascendancy of America, however, was no cause for despair. It was an opportunity. But if Britain blew the opportunity, it was likely to "descend slowly but irresistibly to the position of Holland and of Belgium." In contrast, if Britain fell in wholeheartedly with the Americans, then it "would be able to continue its providential mission which has been entrusted to the English-speaking Race, whose United States will be able to secure the peace of the World."[28]

A MESSIANIC MISSION

Theodore Roosevelt vaulted into the presidency in September 1901 after the death of McKinley at the hands of an assassin. Roosevelt's guiding principle was the regenerative power of personal and national righteousness combined with vigorous action. He also believed that geography and national character played pivotal roles in determining a nation's destiny. In Europe, the major powers—especially Britain, France, Germany, Russia, and Italy—would balance one another's ambitions, thus preserving peace. In northeastern Asia, Russia and Japan would presumably balance one another. Meanwhile, the major European colonial states (plus Japan) would exercise collective hegemony over the less developed world.

But in the Caribbean and in Latin America, Roosevelt decided that the United States, acting alone, should exercise hegemony. The United States did not want nor did it require anyone's assistance. The isthmus canal, not yet built, was Roosevelt's central concern. He believed the United States must not tolerate any local instability that might somehow threaten the canal, the completion of which would at last make the United States a global power.

Roosevelt was worried that predatory (if righteous) European states might be tempted to poach on his country's natural sphere of influence in Latin America. The chief worry was Germany, whose ambitions had grown under Kaiser Wilhelm II. Roosevelt was enamored of Germany's culture and "Teutonic vigor," but he mistrusted the Kaiser, who had built the largest land army on the continent and was putting together a formidable navy.

In the last month of 1902, a nasty dispute flared between Germany and Venezuela, whose extravagantly corrupt dictator had ravaged the national treasury, causing Venezuela to default on loans obtained mostly in Germany, Britain, and Italy. Britain and Germany blockaded Venezuelan ports, as was the imperialist custom of the day when a weak nation defaulted. Britain wanted to settle the matter amicably; the German mood was not so pacific. Roosevelt believed, not unreasonably, that Germany had territorial designs on Venezuela. The dispute was resolved mostly because Roosevelt, invoking the Monroe Doctrine of 1823, declared secretly and with an admirable degree of diplomatic skill, that he would take the United States to war over the issue if Germany failed to back off.[29]

Although the showdown with Germany ended peacefully, Roosevelt believed that the profligate ways of Latin American leaders would lead to further defaults on their European debts, thus provoking future interventions in the Western Hemisphere by European powers, particularly Germany. Indeed, if Latin American leaders were persuaded that the United States would protect them from European reprisals, the default rate might go up.

In December 1904, Roosevelt changed the rules of the game. He put both the Old World and Latin America on notice that the United States, acting alone, would maintain law and order—mainly fiscal order—in the Western Hemisphere. That was a bold expansion of the earlier Monroe Doctrine, which had a distinctly passive tone: The 1823 doctrine said, in effect, that as long as European powers refrained from grabbing new territory in the New World, the United States would leave European interests in the New World alone.

In his "amendment" to the Monroe Doctrine, Roosevelt said the United States, and *only* the United States, would look after the welfare of its southern neighbors. As long as a "nation shows that it knows how to act with reasonable efficiency and decency in social and political matters, if it keeps order and pays its obligations, it need fear no interference from the United States."

But "chronic wrongdoing, or an impotence which results in a general loosening of the ties of civilized society" may "ultimately require intervention by some civilized nation." That nation would be the United States. "In flagrant cases of such wrongdoing or impotence" America would be forced—"however reluctantly"—to exercise an "international police power."

Roosevelt's new initiative was not altogether popular among the sovereign states of Latin America, many of whose national leaders and intellectuals feared that U.S. interventions would promote American corporate interests rather than the interests of their respective nations. Nevertheless, the "Roosevelt Corollary," as it came to be called, was more of an expression of *Realpolitik* than of flat-out imperialism. The possibility of European intervention was an ever-present threat and the United States was staking its claim to regional hegemony, something great powers had done for centuries. What was most intriguing about the corollary was its moralistic language.

> The steady aim of this Nation, as of all enlightened nations, should be to strive to bring ever nearer the day when there shall prevail throughout the world the peace of justice.... The peace of tyrannous terror, the peace of craven weakness, the peace of injustice, all these should be shunned as we shun unrighteous war. The goal to set before us as a nation, the goal which should be set before all mankind, is the attainment of the peace of justice, of the peace which comes when each nation is not merely safe-guarded in its own rights, but scrupulously recognizes and performs its duty toward others.[30]

Strong, Stead, Beveridge, Mahan and Roosevelt—what a corporate name *that* would have been!—were thoroughgoing imperialists, although even Roosevelt soon grew weary of the arduous task of running the Philippines. More fundamentally, they offered a profoundly messianic vision of America. The United States was destined to help secure the "peace of the world" by example, when possible, and by force of arms, when required.

The endless assertions of America's global mission by turn-of-the-century American exceptionalists and their British cousins may strike the modern ear as crude, flag-waving celebrations of raw unilateral military power and economic rapacity. That would not be altogether fair. Teddy Roosevelt, in particular, had a subtle mind, a keen grasp of history, and he understood the workings of the international system. He set a standard for presidential energy and intellectual brilliance that seldom has been matched in the history of the presidency. It would be the idealist Woodrow Wilson, not the realist Roosevelt, who would put the capstone to America's turn-of-the-century regenerative, messianic, and nationalistic exceptionalism.

14

The New Utopians

When the United States finally entered the Great War in 1917, it would have been sufficient for Woodrow Wilson to tell Congress that he was asking for a declaration of war because German submarines were sinking American ships without warning, even though the United States had remained officially, if not actually, neutral. He would have got his declaration; U-boat attacks were intolerable. But Wilson had nobler purposes.

"We have no selfish aims to serve," he said in his war message to Congress on April 2, 1917. "We desire no conquest, no dominion. We seek no indemnities for ourselves, no material compensation for the sacrifices we shall freely make." The United States would not fight merely to defeat the Central Powers; it would fight "for the ultimate peace of the world and for the liberation of its peoples." In the most memorable phrase of his presidency, he asserted that the "world must be made safe for democracy."

The United States, Wilson said, sought to lay the foundation for a new world order that would be supervised by his proposed League of Nations—a "general association of nations" that would guarantee "the political independence and territorial integrity to great and small states alike." As for America's quarrel in the Great War, it was with imperialism, militarism, and the failed European balance-of-power system, not with the German people.

American exceptionalism has many faces. One year it justifies colonialism in the Philippines; in another year, it provides the rationale for an anti-imperial policy. European leaders understood America's experiment in the far Pacific; colonialism was what great powers did. But the unrelenting self-righteousness of Wilson's new brand of exceptionalism—his moralisms, his sermons and sermonettes, his messianic fervor—annoyed European leaders intent on carving up the empires of Germany, Austria-Hungary, and Turkey as they converted the armistice of November 11, 1918 into a peace treaty. "Talking to Wilson," Premier Georges Clemenceau of France quipped at one point, "is something like talking to Jesus Christ."[1]

Nonetheless, Wilson's ideas—especially his commitment to obtaining a covenant for a peace-enforcing League of Nations—were wildly popular among ordinary people in France, Britain, Italy, and America. Upon arriving in France in 1919, where the peace conference was to be held, the American president was greeted with banners—*Hail the Champion of the Rights of Man* and *Honor to the Founder of the Society of Nations*. Two million people were said to have turned out in Paris for a parade in his honor. One journalist described the cry from the crowd as so loud as to be "inhuman—or superhuman."[2]

Allied leaders, especially the French (who wanted to punish Germany) and the Italians (who sought to pick up the South Tyrol, Trentino, the Dalmatian coast, and the port of Fiume from Austria-Hungary and part of Turkey from the Ottoman Empire), were dismayed by the public displays of enthusiasm. Among themselves, they spoke of how Wilson had refused for more than two years to lead the United States into the war, leaving European men to die by the millions in the mud.

America deserved the "respect due to a great nation which had entered the war somewhat late, but had rendered great service," said Australia's Prime Minister William Hughes. But it would be intolerable for the American president to "dictate to us how the world was to be governed." In his most unkind observation, Hughes added, "The League of Nations was to [Wilson] what a toy was to a child—he would not be happy till he got it. His one idea was to go back to America and say that he had achieved it, and that everything else could then be left for the League of Nations to complete."[3]

Things did not work out in Paris as Wilson had planned. Too often he mistook his belief in what should happen with what could be made to happen in the real world of conflicting passions and agendas. In the end, Wilson won some battles, lost many, and compromised on others. His proposed Covenant for the League was hacked and mutilated. But even in its savaged form, the Covenant was not acceptable to Republicans in the Senate, many of whom believed that joining the League would compromise American sovereignty.

How Wilson ultimately failed in achieving his vision is an oft-told tale of cynical Old World politicians who regarded Wilson's ideas as dangerously delusional, of Senate Republicans who were endlessly skeptical of Wilson's internationalism, and of how Wilson himself aggravated matters with his tendency to preach rather than negotiate. Wilson, wrote Walter E. Weyl in the June 7, 1919 issue of *The New Republic,* "seems to see the world in abstractions."

> To him railroad cars are not railroad cars but a gray, generalized thing called Transportation; people are not men and women, corpore-al, gross, very human beings, but Humanity—Humanity very much in the abstract. In his political thinking and propaganda Mr. Wilson cuts away all the complex qualities which things possess in real life in order to fasten upon one single characteristic, and thus he creates a clear but over-simple and unreal formula. As a consequence he is tempted to fall into inelastic categories; to see things black and white; to believe that similar things are identical and dissimilar things opposite.[4]

For Teddy Roosevelt, America's global mission centered on the need to exercise a manly vigor in the conduct of a righteous foreign policy, a world-view that would have the United States join with the other great powers in the task of policing the world for the good of all humankind. For Wilson, America's primary but still righteous mission was to fix the world. Wilson is often said to have been an "internationalist," which is true. But it was an oddly nationalistic internationalism. The model for the new international order would be the United States and its values.

A RENDEZVOUS WITH DESTINY

During the six decades following the Great War—decades of disillusion-ment, economic turmoil, and war—the Wilsonian mission was widely thought to be too grand, the realities of total war too grim, and the perils of the Cold War too ghastly to permit much rhetorical clarity and purity in foreign policy.[5] Foreign policy became a stew of balance-of-power maneu-vering and idealistic speeches, isolationism and engagement, multilateral-ism and unilateralism, forbearance and intervention, moral concerns and moralistic posturing, crusades in the name of human progress as well as in the bald pursuit of narrow U.S. interests.

It was Ronald Reagan who restored Wilson's grand vision—America's divinely sanctioned regenerative purpose to save the world—to a central place in the White House. To be sure, Reagan was not Wilson's ideological twin. Wilson favored multilateralism; Reagan was at heart a unilateralist. But, like Wilson, Reagan believed that American values were the values of humankind, even though individuals in other lands had yet to realize it.

In saving the world from communism, America would liberate humankind from bondage and the American people would themselves experience a spiritual rebirth. Reagan resurrected the turn-of-the-century regenerative and profoundly nationalistic idea with flair. In 1976, when he was governor of California, Reagan challenged the incumbent president, Gerald Ford, for the Republican presidential nomination. In a nationally broadcast speech, "To Restore America," the future president said:

> Call it mysticism, if you will, but I believe God had a divine purpose in placing this land between the two great oceans to be found by those who had a special love of freedom and the courage to leave the countries of their birth. From our forefathers to our modern-day immigrants, we've come from every corner of the Earth, from every race and every ethnic background, and we've become a new breed in the world. We're Americans and we have a…rendezvous with destiny.[6]

Reagan's successor, George Herbert Walker Bush, lacked, as he admitted, the "vision thing." In foreign policy, he reverted to the more traditional styles of Franklin D. Roosevelt, Harry S. Truman, Dwight D. Eisenhower, John F. Kennedy, Lyndon B. Johnson, Richard M. Nixon, and Jimmy Carter. That is, he pursued the policies of most twentieth-century American presidents, elegantly summed up a few years ago by Eugene W. Rostow, legal scholar, historian, diplomat, and hard-nosed Cold Warrior:

"We embrace contradictory principles with equal fervor and cling to them all with equal tenacity. Should our foreign policy be based on power or morality? Realism or idealism? Pragmatism or principle? Should its goal be the protection of interests or the promotion of values? Should we be nationalists or internationalists? Liberal or conservatives? We blithely answer, 'All of the above.'"[7]

PEOPLE WITH NEW IDEAS

Regenerative Rooseveltian-Wilsonian exceptionalism has been reborn in recent years, midwifed by a coalition of American triumphalists, neoconservatives, and right-wing evangelical Christians. In fairness, many evangelicals,
perhaps the majority, are not highly political. Although they tend to vote in
large numbers for socially conservative candidates, they are more keenly focused on doing good works and saving souls than in engaging in right-wing
political activism.[8] Neoconservatives provided the heaviest load of intellectual fuel for the renascence of exceptionalism.

Neoconservatism did not spring full grown, like Venus rising from the
sea, in the 1990s. It had deep roots. The neoconservative label was pinned
on a disparate collection of American intellectuals in the 1970s by Michael
Harrington, author of *The Other America* and America's leading democratic
socialist.[9] The description was intended to be unkind. Neocons were not
wildly popular with Eisenhower-style conservatives, either, men and women
who valued the old Calvinist virtues of thrift, good management, balanced
budgets, and businesslike prudence in all matters. Neoconservatives were
far less concerned with balanced budgets and less critical of social programs.
They were flamboyantly argumentative and reckless risk-takers by the standards of old-guard conservatives.

Neoconservatism is a tricky word, in part because so many men and
women commonly identified as "neoconservatives" now reject the term,
particularly after the invasion and occupation of Iraq turned sour. Today
they often prefer to call themselves "conservatives" or "realists" or even, in
a few cases, "true liberals." Irving Kristol, the man most closely identified
with early neoconservatism, famously defined "neoconservatives" as liberals
who had been "mugged by reality."[10]

Nonetheless, neoconservatives became immensely important in the intellectual life of the United States. In the 1960s and 1970s, they were, as
the cliché went, "people with new ideas." Many first-generation neoconservatives had been liberal Democrats or socialists, even Trotskyists. They
were the sort of men and women who had admired John F. Kennedy and
who had not voted for Barry Goldwater. But in the mid- and late-1960s,
they became progressively disenchanted with the way things were going.

America had lost its way, they said; its culture had become disorganized, unstable, intolerant, vulgar.

Neocons came to believe that the classic liberal values of the republic—private enterprise, indirect self-government, religious belief, and individual liberty tied to individual responsibility—had been undermined by an intellectually constipated liberal elite, by a doctrinaire New Left, by a hedonistic counterculture, by interest-group politics, by mindless egalitarianism, and by intolerant left-leaning academics who seemed never to have met a social-engineering scheme they could not embrace.

Neoconservative visions and disputations regarding domestic matters were supremely valuable, if only in the old marketplace-of-ideas sense. Neoconservatives aggressively challenged liberal fancies, conceits, and shibboleths, reminding liberals and policymakers that even the best-intentioned policies usually had unintended consequences. Policies and plans based on utopian visions, they said, seldom work as planned. Neoconservatives never tired of reminding liberals that the root meaning of utopia was "no place."

GEORGE WILSON BUSH

On the home front, neoconservative critiques of liberal policies were often cogent, realistic, and consistent with the insights of social science. Racial integration and open housing, for instance, were admirable goals, but busing children across town to achieve school integration was problematic. In the 1970s, that struck many liberals as racist; today, the unintended consequences of busing are hard to dispute: sleepy and overstressed children, the accelerated disintegration of neighborhoods in which ties to local schools were weakened or sundered; and in many large northern cities, white flight and resegregation.

If anything united the diverse array of neoconservative intellectuals in the late 1960s and 1970s, it was their self-described realism rooted in a no-nonsense interpretation of persuasive data accumulated in the social sciences—as well as their devotion to the Law of Unintended Consequences. Neoconservatives were in favor of social justice, but they were not utopians, as many liberals seemed to be. Indeed, neocons routinely described themselves as *anti*-utopians.

The unswerving contempt neocons had for the utopian schemes of "statist" liberals helped define who they were. Equal opportunity was right and proper and long overdue, but affirmative-action quotas were wrong, divisive, and stigmatizing. History had taught us that there were limits to what governments could accomplish in remaking society, went the neocon refrain. Liberal utopianism had created or exacerbated many of the nation's social, political, and economic problems.

But in world affairs, there were virtually no limits to what the United States government could do, according to many neocons. In the neoconservative vision of foreign policy, utopianism ruled. America had emerged from World War II as a nation with a new mission: to defeat the Soviet empire and remake the world.

During the Vietnam War, many neocons were fearful that the "liberal elite," horrified by the Vietnam experience, would attempt to pull the nation back into a new isolationism. They were equally alarmed by the Nixon-Kissinger policy of détente with the Soviet Union, said by neocons to be a morally corrupt empire. Perhaps most of all, they were dismayed by the possibility that the United States, in an attempt to preserve a steady supply of Persian Gulf oil, might renege or tone down its security commitments to Israel, the only democratic state in a sea of totalitarian sand, and "tilt" toward Israel's enemies.

Secretary of State Henry Kissinger "often sounds like Churchill and just as often acts like Chamberlain," said Norman Podhoretz in an influential 1976 article, "Making the World Safe for Communism." A new kind of pusillanimous liberalism was threatening America. "If it should turn out that the new isolationism has indeed triumphed among the people as completely as it has among the elites, then the United States will celebrate its two-hundredth birthday by betraying the heritage of liberty which has earned it the wonder and envy of the world."[11]

Men and women commonly labeled as "neoconservatives"—along with their kissin' cousins, post–Cold War triumphalists like Dick Cheney and Don Rumsfeld—have been greatly influential in reshaping American foreign policy in recent years. They were, for example, promoters of and chief cheerleaders for the Anglo-American invasion of Saddam Hussein's Iraq, the consequences of which may haunt America and the Western world for decades.

An editorial titled "George Wilson Bush" was published in the *Wall Street Journal* in mid-2002, some nine months before the invasion of Iraq.[12] The author was Max Boot, a neocon star of the first magnitude and then one of the *Journal*'s top editors. It was not an idiosyncratic essay; it expressed the common wisdom of the neoconservative world at the time. In it, Boot celebrated President George W. Bush's call for the overthrow of the Palestinian Liberation Organization's Yasser Arafat, a call that seemed to represent the "triumph" of "Wilsonians over realpolitikers, a development of considerable long-term consequence."

> Wilsonians, who long predate Woodrow Wilson, believe that both morality and self-interest should lead the U.S. to champion liberal values abroad. While often portrayed as a soft, fuzzy doctrine, Wilsonianism often requires the use of force. Wilson himself was one of our most interventionist presidents, dispatching troops not only to France but also to Mexico (twice), Haiti, the Dominican Republic, and Russia. Wilson was discredited by his post–World War I failures, but the ideas he championed have been one of the sturdiest strains in American foreign policy thinking.[13]

In contrast, "realpolitikers" have little use for "intrusions by morality into foreign policy," said Boot. "They believe that nations are governed by immutable geostrategic imperatives and that ideology counts for little in international relations. Realpolitikers preach stability; Wilsonians prefer revolution."

> Ronald Reagan, while more adroit in the use of power than Wilson himself, was essentially Wilsonian in his orientation. Not only did he bring down the "evil empire," he also helped nudge aside friendly dictators in the Philippines, South Korea and elsewhere. The first Bush administration, by contrast, was the embodiment of realpolitik. George H. W. Bush was devoted to stability above all else.[14]

The second President Bush might well be a different kind of guy, Boot suggested, although it was still too early in July 2002 for a definitive answer. Would Bush II be just another "realist" like his secretary of state, Colin Powell, or his national security adviser, Condoleezza Rice? Or would he be a true Wilsonian? There was reason to hope.

The test of the "nascent Bush Doctrine will occur in Iraq," Boot wrote. "There are still many within the administration who think that the ideal outcome would be for some Baathist colonel to knock off Saddam Hussein and establish a pro-American dictatorship." That would merely be a repeat of the "unrealistic 'realism'" that had for so long corrupted American foreign policy.

> The Wilsonian alternative is clear: We will settle for nothing less than the establishment of liberal democracy in Iraq within a federalist framework that allows a great deal of autonomy to the Kurds and Shiites. And if this requires American and allied troops to undertake occupation duty, so be it. Yes, this is an ambitious agenda, but no more ambitious than transforming Germany, Italy or Japan after World War II; in fact a great deal less so, because Iraq is a smaller country led by a thug less popular among his own people than Tojo, Hitler and Mussolini were.[15]

Boot was describing—yearning for—a Wilsonianism decked out in combat boots, Abrams main battle tanks, and F-16 Fighting Falcons. But he was also expressing a way of thinking that flowered profusely in the 1990s after the collapse of the Soviet Union and the quick victory in the first Gulf War. It was a foreign-policy stance that could be reasonably described as "New Utopianism."

THE AMERICAN LEAGUE

After the fall of the Soviet Union, neoconservatives were among the first to proclaim the joys, the challenges, and the opportunities of a "unipolar world." The "center" of world power was now the United States, Charles Krauthammer wrote in a special issue of *Foreign Affairs*. The United States, he said, was "the only country with the military, diplomatic, political and economic assets to be a decisive player in any conflict in whatever part of the world it chooses to involve itself."[16] As provocative as Krauthammer's essay was, the most distinctive neocon anthem appeared in the July/August 1996 issue of *Foreign Affairs* during the Bill Clinton–Bob Dole presidential campaign. It was called "Toward a Neo-Reaganite Foreign Policy."

"In foreign policy, conservatives are adrift. They disdain the Wilsonian multilateralism of the Clinton administration; they are tempted by, but so far have resisted, the neoisolationism of Patrick Buchanan; for now, they lean uncertainly on some version of the conservative 'realism' of Henry Kissinger and his disciples."[17]

Adrift? Uncertain? What, then, should America's role be in this chaotic post–Cold War world? According to authors William Kristol and Robert Kagan, it should be "benevolent global hegemony."

> Having defeated the "evil empire," the United States enjoys strategic and ideological predominance. The first objective of U.S. foreign policy should be to preserve and enhance that predominance by strengthening America's security, supporting its friends, advancing its interests, and standing up for its principles around the world....
>
> In a world in which peace and American security depend on American power and the will to use it, the main threat the United States faces now and in the future is its own weakness. American hegemony is the only reliable defense against a breakdown of peace and international order. The appropriate goal of American foreign policy, therefore, is to preserve that hegemony as far into the future as possible. To achieve this goal, the United States needs a neo-Reaganite foreign policy of military supremacy and moral confidence.

The Kristol and Kagan message was that a regenerative Reaganite foreign policy would be good for conservatism, good for America, and good for the world. The "most successful Republican presidents of this century, Theodore Roosevelt and Ronald Reagan, both inspired Americans to assume cheerfully the new international responsibilities that went with increased power and influence. Both celebrated American exceptionalism."

Even after the Iraq debacle, neoconservatives retain a full-blooded faith in the ultimate and exceptional righteousness of America's cause, in the Mideast and elsewhere. To their great credit, neocons have largely purged the Kiplingesque white-man's-burden brand of racism from their exceptionalism, a cleansing worth many cheers. Similarly, neocons seldom speak of divine destiny, although a goodly number of their allies on the Christian right seem enamored of bringing on the End Times sooner rather than later. For neoconservatives, a belief in America's absolute *civic* virtue as embodied in the Constitution stands in for providential direction.

In their ideological purity, neoconservatives are, just as Boot and others have often said, Wilsonians. Like Wilson, they would save the world; unlike Wilson, their peacemaking mechanism would be an interventionist America, not a League of Nations. They would apply the Roosevelt Corollary to the Monroe Doctrine to the rest of the world. A *Pax Americana*, they suggest—or, if you prefer, "benign global hegemony"—would promote democracy worldwide and thus enhance U.S. security.

The problem with Wilson, according to many neocons, was not his passion for spreading America's exceptionalist gospel; it was his unbending faith in *multilateral* initiatives (albeit under American direction) to keep the peace. Multilateralism was—and is—too often a dead end, according to the New Utopians. The United States is far better suited, temperamentally and militarily, to take on the peacemaking role than Wilson's feckless League of Nations or today's hapless United Nations. Given the political will, the United States, acting alone or with ad hoc "coalitions of the willing," could and should take on the League of Nations/United Nations peacemaking role. Call it the American League.

In his January 20, 2005 State of the Union address, President George W. Bush defined the American League for everyone, by saying that the "survival of liberty in our land increasingly depends on the success of liberty in other lands. The best hope for peace in our world is the expansion of freedom in all the world."

> America's vital interests and our deepest beliefs are now one. From the day of our Founding, we have proclaimed that every man and woman on this Earth has rights, and dignity, and matchless value, because they bear the image of the Maker of Heaven and Earth.
>
> Across the generations we have proclaimed the imperative of self-government, because no one is fit to be a master, and no one deserves to be a slave.
>
> Advancing these ideals is the mission that created our Nation. It is the honorable achievement of our fathers. Now it is the urgent requirement of our nation's security, and the calling of our time.
>
> So it is the policy of the United States to seek and support the growth of democratic movements and institutions in every nation and culture, *with the ultimate goal of ending tyranny in our world.*[18] (Italics added.)

"Ending tyranny in our world." A righteous, messianic, and nationalistic mission indeed. America's tragically wrong-headed preventive war, the "Liberation of Iraq," may have temporarily chastened the most assertive neocons and triumphalists, but that is far from certain. They are a farsighted bunch who are not easily dissuaded from pursuing the Right Course. As the Statement of Principles for the neoconservative Project for the New American Century put it more than a decade ago, the United States needs "to accept responsibility for America's unique role in preserving and extending an international order friendly to our security, our prosperity, and our principles."[19]

"Accept[ing] responsibility for America's unique role" is worth examination. Throughout the Cold War, many nations (collectively called the "Free World") looked to the United States for leadership. But in the post–Cold War context, "accepting responsibility" seems far more questionable; it suggests that the world is eagerly presenting this "unique role" to the United States like a Hollywood celebrity thrusting an Oscar into the hands of the year's "best" actor or actress, who graciously accepts. The reality is different.

Many nations do not particularly desire American save-the-world leadership, or America's messianic mission. They deeply resent the fact that the United States uses its considerable economic and military muscle in an attempt to create an international order that, despite feel-good phrases, largely promotes a world order congenial to American security, American prosperity, and American principles.

I, for one, cherish American security and prosperity, and especially America's principles, one of which was summed up by George Washington in his Farewell Address: "Observe good faith and justice toward all Nations. Cultivate peace and harmony with all."[20] To that I would add, "Even if they have different beliefs and cultures and deities."

HIS CHOSEN NATION

Not much has been said much about "space" in this or the preceding chapter. Nonetheless, the old spirit of American exceptionalism and its progeny, the New Utopianism, are the keys to understanding the persistent passion space warriors have for a policy of unilateral space dominance.

Control of space and weapons in space are old and powerful space-warrior desires, but they pale in comparison to the exceptionalist paradigm, the regenerative conviction that the United States can do as it pleases because it is righteous and selfless. Who needs a new space treaty when one already knows that one's own way is best?

Should the United States occupy the "ultimate high ground of space," as space-warrior boilerplate suggests? Should the United States prepare for the "ownership" of space, as Air Force Space Command says? Should space control be the "goal of all Americans," as Air Force Chief of Staff Thomas Dresser White urged during the Eisenhower years? Should America become the "guardian of the peace" from space, as Wernher von Braun argued in 1952? Or are these goals simply American exceptionalism carried to a loftier and more dangerous plane?

Pride in one's nation is as natural as the pride grandparents take in the sheer wonderfulness of their grandchildren. But to obsessively assert that one's nation is incomparably more virtuous than every other nation in the world is as bizarre as it is self-defeating. Yet in the end, that is the meaning and the message of American exceptionalism—and ultimately of the drive for U.S. dominance of space.

15

The Next Cold War?

Under Secretary of Defense Andrew Marshall was seventy-eight in the summer of 1999 when the Office of Net Assessment, which he headed, issued a vintage briefing book titled *Asia 2025*. In the world of hardline foreign policy, describing favorite warriors as "legendary" is commonplace. But Marshall was a legend, the real thing.

As a RAND analyst in the 1950s, Marshall worked closely with Herman Kahn and Albert J. Wohlstetter, gurus of nuclear strategy in the early years of the Cold War. He was an adviser to Jack Kennedy, himself a hardliner, in the "missile gap" presidential campaign of 1960. (Marshall played a key role in promoting the idea of a gap, perhaps the pivotal issue in that narrow victory.) In 1972, Henry Kissinger drafted Marshall to serve on President Nixon's National Security Council. Marshall soon became head of the Pentagon's newly created Office for Net Assessment and he was still running the shop when *Asia 2025* appeared.

Asia 2025 offered several complex "speculative" scenarios, all of which suggested that the United States might be in for a tough time in the Western Pacific, mostly because of China. The grand strategic plan of the Middle Kingdom, said one scenario, was to dominate East Asia as well as the maritime states of Japan, Philippines, Indonesia, and Taiwan, the latter being a renegade province, insofar as China was concerned.

Unless the United States actively prepared for a future confrontation with China, the scenario said, U.S. military forces eventually could be forced out of East Asia by Chinese-inspired anti-Americanism in South Korea and Japan. Taiwan would remain pro-American; nonetheless, by 2015 or 2025, China would have become so militarily powerful in East Asia (and the United States so constrained by Chinese power) that Taiwan and the rest of East Asia would fall under Chinese domination. (Russia would remain too weak to contest Chinese domination of the area.)

Meanwhile, India was likely to assert its power in South Asia and beyond—into China's sphere of influence. Nonetheless, according to yet another scenario, China and India might choose cooperation over confrontation and work out a condominium arrangement in which each state would remain dominant in its region. According to *Asia 2025*, the United States would still be the world's greatest military power, but it would no longer be able to significantly influence events in Asia.[1]

Marshall and his Office for Net Assessment were not alone in the 1990s in imagining a powerful and assertive China as the Next Great Threat. The "China threat" became an urgent theme among hardliners the moment the Berlin Wall fell in November 1989. By the mid-1990s, it was conventional wisdom among unreconstructed Cold Warriors that the United States must contain China's regional aspirations much as it had once constrained Soviet ambitions. In Pentagon war games, China was often the unnamed adversary—the not-so-mysterious "Far Eastern near-peer competitor." In a 1997 "Memorandum to Opinion Leaders," Gary Schmitt of the neoconservative Project for the New American Century wrote: "China is, as we all know, a rising power in a critical region of the world."

> Since the demise of the Soviet Union, China has made no secret of its long-term strategic goal of creating in East Asia a new security order which would no longer rest on American military and economic power.... The competition is a strategic fact and the U.S. should address it directly and firmly; ignoring it will only generate more dangerous problems in the future. As history demonstrates, appeasing the ambitions of a rising power rarely results in a diminution of those ambitions.[2]

John J. Mearsheimer, a University of Chicago political scientist and one of world's most highly regarded academic balance-of-power realists, ended his 2001 blockbuster, *The Tragedy of Great Power Politics*, by noting that trouble lay ahead for the United States if China's economy continued to grow at the rapid rate it had enjoyed in the 1990s.

For "sound strategic reasons" China would pursue regional hegemony just as the United States did in the Western Hemisphere in the nineteenth century, Mearsheimer asserts. A surging China would attempt to dominate

Japan and Korea and it would likely develop its own version of the Monroe Doctrine. "Just as the United States made it clear to distant great powers that they were not allowed to meddle in the Western Hemisphere, China will make it clear that American interference in Asia is unacceptable." China could become the most "formidable superpower" the United States has *ever* faced.[3]

A CURIOUS RELATIONSHIP

On the surface, such a threat estimate seems reasonable. Even a casual look at the literature of the People's Liberation Army since Gulf War I in 1991 suggests an obsessive pursuit of ways to counter U.S. high-tech military power, including U.S. assets in space. America's high-tech "revolution in military affairs" and its new way of precision war haunt the leaders of the PLA, a force that had long relied on sheer numbers of troops to prevail in conflict. Today the PLA is attempting to modernize by cutting back manpower and making the "informationalization" of its forces—its version of the revolution in military affairs—its highest priority.[4]

Hardliners in the Chinese government and the PLA assume that a military confrontation short of all-out war with the United States is virtually inevitable; similarly, U.S. hardliners believe that a future military showdown of some sort with China is likely, particularly if China's economy continues to boom.[5] Frank J. Gaffney, Jr., for nearly three decades one of the nation's most influential hardliners, testified in 2005 before the U.S.-China Economic and Security Review Commission that "China is systematically pursuing a strategy that should alarm freedom-loving people in this country and around the world. Its aim is, I believe, to displace the United States as the world's preeminent economic power and, if necessary, *to defeat us militarily*."[6] (Italics added.)

Are China's hardliners winning the battle to shape China's official policy toward the United States, as Gaffney suggests? That's an uncertainty that bedevils analysts in Washington and perhaps even in Beijing. In the bad old days, before President Richard Nixon began to patch things up with China in 1972, the Middle Kingdom spoke relentlessly of U.S. "hegemonism" in melodramatic terms, much as Christian fundamentalists discuss Satan. But China greatly moderated its official rhetoric in the post-Nixon years, in part because the Beijing government came to realize that communism was not working as an economic system.

During Mao's Great Leap Forward as many as thirty million Chinese may have died during the Great Famine from the spring of 1959 through 1961, triggered largely by Mao's misbegotten policies.[7] Mao's Cultural Revolution, launched in 1966, did not lead to that scale of death, but it did produce a near-total breakdown of society. By the early 1970s, China was effectively bankrupt and the machinery of the Communist Party was in turmoil. The eventual solution: the initiation of a policy of free enterprise with "Chinese characteristics"—or as Deng Xiaoping declared, "To get rich is glorious!"[8]

The changes in China over the past couple of decades have been dizzying. Although hundreds of millions of peasants in rural areas barely make it from day to day, the boom in the coastal cities as well as in many inland cities continues to be as astonishing as anything Deng could have imagined. What citizen of Chicago or New York, where skyscrapers were invented, can see the outrageous yet weirdly beautiful sci-fi skyline of Shanghai's "Pudong New Area" without experiencing a moment or two of slack-jawed awe?

The Chinese government may be corrupt and repressive but it is not collectively stupid. China learned a live-or-die lesson from the collapse of the Soviet Union: In a direct arms competition with the United States, the United States wins. The Soviet Union sought to create an alternate universe, a socialist paradise with Muscovite characteristics. It failed. In contrast, China has chosen, cautiously, to join the global community, and it expects the payback for that will be at least a modest degree of national prosperity.

Does China actively seek to initiate a Cold War–style competition with the United States? Why would it? Manufacturing consumer goods for export to the West drives China's booming economy and provides employment for tens of millions in a nation in which systemic unemployment is at dangerously high levels. A Cold War–style confrontation would sap China's economic vitality by diverting huge amounts of capital from manufacturing consumer goods for the international market to China's arms industries, thus threatening China's main business, the Wal-Marting of America.

That Red China and capitalist America are now bedmates in the economic sphere is a fact that few American politicians, Democrat or Republican, care to fully acknowledge. China needs U.S. consumers, the biggest single market for Made in China products, and American consumers seem comfortable with that. "The China Price," which denotes the lowest possible cost for manufactured goods, is now part of the American business lexicon.[9]

The downward competition among American manufacturers to meet the China Price means that American consumers buy many classes of imported manufactured goods more cheaply at discount stores than they could buy comparable American-made goods, even if those goods still existed. (One of the tragic side effects of the China Price system is that "comparable" American goods seldom exist. The export of manufacturing jobs to China's coastal cities—or to any "off-shore" location anywhere in the world that promises to meet or beat the China Price—has profoundly changed the character of American life.)

A quid pro quo relationship has developed between Washington and Beijing. Washington is generally OK with the idea that China will continue to supply inexpensive products to U.S. consumers; in turn, China continues to help finance the growing U.S. national debt by buying hundreds of billions of dollars of low-interest U.S. Treasury bonds that investors in the United States and elsewhere no longer covet. China is the Great Enabler that supplies the opium for America's budget-deficit addiction. The curious relationship between Beijing and Washington—that they have come to share a common economic bed—is a strange tale. Stranger still is the real possibility that a major downturn in either economy could lead to economic chaos in the other. If one nation drowns in an economic maelstrom, the other could be pulled down with it.

Nonetheless, old habits of thought persist. China is forever suspicious of the United States; U.S. "hegemonism" remains a powerful concern, even though Chinese rhetoric has been ratcheted down over the years. Likewise, the United States remains chronically wary of possible Chinese adventurism in East Asia, particularly in regard to Taiwan, where nationalist tensions are high on both sides of the Formosa Strait.

THE BIG SHOW

Is China the Next Great Threat? The official U.S. stance, under Presidents George H. W. Bush, Bill Clinton, and George W. Bush, has been agnosticism tempered by suspicion. There have been differences in emphasis, to be sure. The elder Bush, and especially Clinton, pursued policies of engagement with China; George W. Bush, influenced by neoconservatives, triumphalists, and certain Christian activists to whom the Chinese government was—and is—a continuing moral affront, tilted more toward Taiwan.

Nonetheless, a recent Quadrennial Defense Review Report, issued in February 2006, blandly asserts:

> Of the major and emerging powers, China has the greatest potential to compete militarily with the United States and field disruptive military technologies that could over time offset traditional U.S. military advantages absent U.S. counter strategies. U.S. policy remains focused on encouraging China to play a constructive, peaceful role in the Asia-Pacific region and to serve as a partner in addressing common security challenges, including terrorism, proliferation, narcotics and piracy.
>
> U.S. policy seeks to encourage China to choose a path of peaceful economic growth and political liberalization, rather than military threat and intimidation. The United States' goal is for China to continue as an economic partner and emerge as a responsible stakeholder and force for good in the world.[10]

Meanwhile, despite the force-for-good language, the Defense Department prepares for the worst. That's the way the game is played in Washington. A nation that lacks an existential threat is a nation with a modest military budget, and there is nothing modest about America's defense budget. The common comparison is that America spends more on defense than the next fifteen nations combined.[11] The Soviet Union was an existential threat; terrorism is not. Fighting terrorism has already cost the United States many hundreds of billions of dollars, most of it poorly spent on the war-of-choice in Iraq. But the Defense Department does not find year-after-year funding for big-ticket items—F-35 stealth fighters, common aerospace vehicles, and (perhaps) a new generation of specialized nuclear weapons—by pointing to Osama Bin Laden and his jihadist brothers. China is the Pentagon's best ally in the department's budget wars.

The United States has included China in its nuclear war plans since the 1950s. China's first nuclear test occurred in October 1964; by then, the United States had roughly twenty-four hundred nuclear weapons in Guam, South Korea, Okinawa, the Philippines, and Taiwan, all within striking distance of Chinese cities and military installations. If there has been a Sino-American nuclear arms race since 1964, the race has been distinctly lopsided. China's total nuclear stockpile is thought to be around two hundred warheads, only about twenty of which could credibly threaten the

U.S. mainland. The United States has about ten thousand nuclear weapons, hundreds of which could be quickly and precisely targeted on China, if necessary.

The "gap" may close a bit over the years; current estimates suggest that China will have about two hundred and twenty warheads by 2015. The United States, which is downscaling its nuclear stockpile along with Russia, will have about five thousand. Nonetheless, once the Cold War ended and Russia no longer proved to be much of a nuclear threat, China was moved squarely into Strategic Command's crosshairs.[12]

Sun City Extended: A USSTRATCOM Study of Future Force Structures, dated February 1, 1994 is especially intriguing. A declassified version of *Sun City's* briefing slides was obtained, with the help of the Freedom of Information Act, by Hans A. Kristensen, one of the nation's most diligent and reliable researchers into the arcana of America's nuclear war plans.[13]

The opening slide is curious: it contains the title and a stylized image of Chicago's downtown skyline. (Should Chicagoans be worried?) From then on, the slides get stranger and stranger. Of the sixty-one slides with (presumably) substantive information, all but one have the details blanked out. That's not too surprising; *Sun City Extended*, after all, is a sensitive document. But the truly odd bit is that the slide left intact concerns China. It reads:

CHINA SCENARIOS

2 POTENTIAL US/CHINA ADVERSARIAL SCENARIOS IDENTIFIED

1ST SCENARIO DEPICTS A US/NK/CHINA EXCURSION

— REGIONAL AS OPPOSED TO GLOBAL CONCERN

— CALLS FOR AN ADAPTIVELY PLANNED RESPONSE AGAINST NK NOT A FULL SCALE ATTACK AGAINST CHINA

— DPF, NSNF, OR CONVENTIONAL (CALCM/TLAM-) RESPONSE MORE APPROPRIATE SOLUTION

2ND SCENARIO FOCUSES ON A CHINA/CONUS CONFRONTATION

— IMPLIES A NEED FOR A MAJOR-ATTACK RESPONSE PLAN

The Defense Department's glorious affection for acronyms may not be shared by all. "NK" is North Korea; "DPF" is directed planning force; "NSNF" is non-strategic nuclear forces; "CALCM" is conventional air-launched cruise missile; "TLAM-C" is a version of the Tomahawk land attack missile; "CONUS" is the continental United States. Acronyms aside, *Sun City Extended* clearly suggests that China had finally made it to the Big Show. When StratCom says there is a need for "a major-attack response plan," it is likely speaking of the possible use of many dozens of nuclear warheads, at a minimum. But *why* was that particular slide, one in a pack of sixty-one, left untouched? An error, perhaps. But it is tempting to believe that the Defense Department's redactors wanted to get the message out to the powers in Beijing.

In the unlikely event that a military conflict between China and the United States ever erupts, it will probably be over Taiwan. China insists that Taiwan is a province of China, a position the United States has gone along with for more than three decades, mostly as a matter of diplomatic and balance-of-power expediency. For a host of geopolitical reasons, the Nixon administration in 1972 ended the charade that the Nationalist Chinese government, exiled on Taiwan for a generation, represented China and that the Beijing government, which actually ruled the world's most populous nation, was illegitimate.[14] Nonetheless, presidential administrations, from Nixon's onward, have retained close political, economic, and military ties to Taiwan.[15]

Today's Taiwan is a de facto independent state that edges ever closer to de jure status, at least rhetorically. And its economy, to understate the case, is famously vigorous. To further complicate matters, the United States regularly sells high-tech military gear to Taiwan, and it has arguably made a commitment to come to Taiwan's aid if China ever attacks Taiwan, although the exact nature of the U.S. commitment, embodied in the Taiwan Relations Act of 1979, is open to contradictory interpretations.[16]

Meanwhile, China remains truculent toward Taiwan's leadership and its drift toward formal independence. China's otherwise moderate 2004 *White Paper on National Defense* noted, for instance, that it is "the sacred responsibility of the Chinese armed forces to stop the 'Taiwan independence' forces from splitting the country." (To Beijing, "splitism" is the ultimate sin.) "Should the Taiwan authorities go so far as to make a reckless attempt that constitutes a major incident of 'Taiwan independence,'" says the White Paper, "the Chinese people and armed forces will resolutely and thoroughly crush it at any cost."[17]

THE WAR OF 2031

As noted in Chapter Two, U.S. Space Command's *Long Range Plan*, issued in April 1998, said the United States does not "expect to face a global military peer competitor within the next two decades." That was pretty good news, insofar as Space Command was concerned. "Now is the time," it added, "to begin developing space capabilities, innovative concepts of operations for warfighting, and organizations that can meet the challenges of the twenty-first century."[18]

Global military peer competitor. Those four words are behind the drive for space dominance. Space warriors generally acknowledge (off the record) that the Iraqs and Irans and North Koreas of the world are not—and never could be—existential threats to the United States. Under certain circumstances, of course, such states could cause America a lot of grief.[19] But the Big Show, the reason the United States must achieve a space-dominance capability, will not be a showdown with nations such as Iran or North Korea, no matter how retrograde their regimes may be. The Big Show is that presumptive "global military peer competitor"—China.

If presidential administrations tend toward pragmatic agnosticism regarding the "Chinese threat," America's space warriors seem to have little difficulty expressing their opinion. The Chinese are coming, they say, and we're not prepared. Space warriors regularly spin out imaginative America-wake-up scenarios in which the United States is bested in space by a combination of Chinese technical sophistication and audaciously clever Sun-tzu-style deception. One early scenario was published in the Spring 1994 issue of *Aerospace Power Journal*, predecessor of today's *Air and Space Power Journal.*

Author Michael E. Baum looked ahead to 2011 when the ever-deceptive Chinese launch a Pearl Harbor-style attack on U.S. space forces on the seventieth anniversary of the original Japanese Pearl Harbor attack. In Baum's fantasy, Chinese missiles strike terrestrial satellite uplink and downlink facilities and the United States suffers three to five thousand casualties. Despite that fearful toll, U.S. forces can't risk retaliation because the Chinese have also attacked American satellites in space with ground-launched and space-based weapons, rendering American forces blind and deaf.

If U.S. retaliation provoked the Chinese to strike the United States with nuclear-tipped missiles, the scenario went, the United States would have no warning. And too, in this imaginative scenario, the Chinese had a limited objective—they simply sought to take the Spratly Islands in the South China Sea, minute parcels of land they had long coveted and claimed, as had Vietnam and Taiwan. (The islands, Baum said in his scenario, were under the protection of the United States and the United Nations.)

Early in the 2011 conflict, Gen. William Smith, chairman of the Joint Chiefs of Staff, tells an aide, "It seems the Chinese have taken a page right out of our space doctrine. They have attacked us in space and from space. They have prevented us from getting the usual support our satellites give us, and they control the area not only above the battlefield but potentially the battlefield itself. The question is, how are we going to recover?"

The United States does not quite recover. The treacherous Chinese take the Spratlys. Four months after the conflict ends, General Smith berates Congress for worshipping too long at the space-for-peaceful-purposes altar. Lawmakers failed to proceed with the weaponization of space in the 1990s, when all manner of military strategists were recommending it. Meanwhile, he said, the Chinese surged ahead.

> Much as Billy Mitchell predicted and developed the initial vision-ary doctrine for how our aircraft forces would look in his future, so we should have heeded what the doctrinists wrote in the 1990s. The control of space—just like control of the air—is the most critical aspect of war. Our preconceived notions, assumptions, and biases that the next war would be just like the last allowed us to be surprised and cost us the battle for the Spratly Islands.[20]

Baum's scenario is a bit of a stretch. For one thing, why would the Chinese risk war with the United States over the Spratlys? The South China Sea is a strategic shipping crossroads, to be sure, but is it *that* strategic? A far more intriguing China-oriented scenario was offered in 2002 by Simon P. Worden, then director of development and transformation at Air Force Space Command's Space and Missile Systems Center, and Major John E. Shaw, a historian of space power. Worden has long been a major player in the space-warrior world.

The scenario, in a monograph titled *Whither Space Power? Forging a Strategy for the New Century,* begins in May 2003 and ends in 2075, a time span that hints at its intricacy.[21] A central episode is (once again) a Pearl Harbor-style strike on U.S. space assets. The attack comes, as you might guess, on

December 7, 2031. Many years later, according to the scenario, Tu Yu, the chief space marshal of the Asian Hegemony (China along with Vietnam, Korea, and Japan), recalls that wondrous day in 2031. It had been preceded by years of canny misdirection designed "to encourage the uniquely Western idea that the absence of war is peace." When the Chinese-led attack came (aided by China's Islamic allies), it was a classic bolt from the blue.

> Our D-Day strike was phenomenally successful. We used both ground- and space-based weapons to destroy over nineteen hundred satellites, nearly seventy percent of the adversary's space infrastructure, in that first day....
>
> After a mere twenty-four hours, Western economies and armed forces were in disarray. It was now our task to use our space superiority to wipe the Western devils from the seas, which they had dominated for five centuries.
>
> With unhindered space reconnaissance, we had quickly fixed all of their surface ships and most of their underwater assets. In the second twenty-four hours of the conflict, we had sunk eighty-nine of the enemy's vessels, including four aircraft carriers and fifteen submarines. Although we were saddened by the great loss of life this entailed, it was a small repayment for centuries of Asian blood extracted to satisfy Western greed.

The United States and its "imperialist" allies, blinded and confused by the loss of their eyes and ears in space (not to mention having been thoroughly buffaloed by the demise of many of their space-based weapons), quickly capitulated. The peace treaty, negotiated under the auspices of the United Nations, stipulated that the United States would assume "full responsibility for the war of 2031 and admits to having served as the primary instrument of imperialist expansion in the twenty-first century." The United States also agreed to pay reparations of $5 trillion for "past imperialist damages to oppressed peoples."

A grim scenario, at least for those of us who live in the West. But be of good cheer. Determined not to leave their readers too depressed, Worden and Shaw then spin out a Superwoman scenario (subtitled "Seizing the Solar System") in which retired U.S. space force officers, led by former Aerospace Force Chief of Staff Maria Barbicane, eventually win back space for the United States and its allies.[22]

THE FIVE IRONIES

In closed-door meetings, space warriors continue to wring their hands about the potential military-space capabilities of China. The penultimate paragraph of an article, "The Chinese Threat to U.S. Space Superiority," published in the Winter 2005 issue of *High Frontier*, a quarterly published by Air Force Space Command, distilled the conventional space-warrior wisdom regarding the Middle Kingdom: "China possesses both the intent and a growing capability to threaten U.S. space systems in the event of a future clash between the two countries."[23]

It is a schizophrenic and ironic future, isn't it? China persists in underwriting America's instant-gratification lifestyle by exporting cheap consumer goods to the United States while financing a substantial part of the U.S. national debt by buying hundreds of billions of dollars of U.S. Treasury notes; in the spring of 2007, China's central bank held about $1.2 trillion dollars in foreign reserves, most of it U.S. dollars.[24] And yet, China is portrayed by America's hardliners as the Next Great Threat.

Another irony: In its continuing enthusiasm for buying Treasury notes, China is underwriting the further development of America's new high-tech way of war. That is distinctly odd behavior for a nation presumed to be prepping for a *High Noon* showdown with the United States.

A third irony: China is intent on integrating itself into the global economic system—strange behavior indeed for a nation that is regularly depicted by American hardliners as a profound military threat to the United States and, by extension, to the Western world and Japan.

A fourth irony: China has long been the lead player in the global effort to negotiate a ban on *all* space-oriented weapons, not just weapons of mass destruction. That inconvenient fact is seldom mentioned in the United States by Air Force Space Command, by the Pentagon, by the White House, by hardline think tanks, by cable-news pundits, by America-first newspaper triumphalists, or by the assortment of neoconservatives determined to eliminate evil empires everywhere.

A final irony. Because of its ill-advised, ham-fisted, debris-producing antisatellite test in January 2007, China—the champion of a new and more comprehensive space-weapons treaty—shot itself in its collectivized foot.[25]

DO NO HARM

A comprehensive and demonstrated space-control capability ("defensive" and "offensive" counterspace) requires the development, testing, and deployment of antisatellite weapons. In the late 1970s and early 1980s, U.S.-Soviet relations had taken such a poisonous turn that many analysts, East and West, feared that ASATs might soon be deployed by both nations. On May 18, 1983, physicist Richard L. Garwin, one of the world's brightest lights in arms control, testified before a subcommittee of the Senate Foreign Relations Committee in support of a proposed ASAT ban, which he helped draft. Garwin concluded his testimony by suggesting that the United States was at a crossroads:

> [W]e can urgently negotiate a treaty along the lines of the draft presented here, or we can see the wealth and security of our nation imperiled by a needless conflict in space, brought about by a greater desire for advantage than for mutual benefit, and fostered by emerging doctrine and organizations which regard space as an opportunity for conflict rather than the marvelous tool and environment which it is. We can try to make space safe for all non-weapon activities, or we can risk our own continued military and civil use of space. Negotiation, without further ASAT tests, is an opportunity we will not have much longer.[26]

Garwin, who helped design America's first thermonuclear device, is no fuzzy let's-throw-all-the-swords-into-the-sea sort of guy.[27] However, throughout the Cold War he played a major role in developing the theory and implementing the practice of nuclear arms control. With the blessing of both Republican and Democratic administrations, Garwin and other Western scientists and policymakers met regularly with Soviet scientists and policymakers to work out the technical foundations for verifiable arms control measures.[28]

One of the core ideas of arms control, nuclear or conventional, is that adversarial nations might find a measure of armed peace by negotiating formal agreements designed to maintain a roughly equal balance of military power between them. If neither side has a clear-cut military advantage over the other—and if both sides know it—war is less likely. Why start a brawl if you are not sure you will win? More to the point, why begin a fight even if you think you *can* "win," but at an unacceptably high cost? King Pyrrhus gave us a way to understand such "victories" more than two thousand years ago.

Another basic principle in the arms control world, insofar as nations are concerned, is to avoid making bad situations worse by ill-conceived unilateral actions. Unilateral deployment of a comprehensive antisatellite capability in the twenty-first century—and certainly the deployment of weapons in space—would, in Garwin's opinion, do great harm. The United States is the world's greatest military power, a fact that no one disputes. But deployment of a full-blown space-dominance capability might well be the proverbial bridge too far.

During the Cold War, the United States and the Soviet Union experimented fitfully with antisatellite weapons, but in the end common sense prevailed, thanks largely to arms control analysts like Garwin. The United States and the Soviet Union knew that if one nation deployed a significant number of antisatellite weapons—or any kind of space weapon—the other nation would do likewise. During the Cold War, a space-related arms race would have been a destabilizing no-win bucket of vipers for each side. In the post–Cold War world, the situation is not as clear; there is no longer a head-to-head arms race. But in the twenty-first century, if space weapons come to be understood as conferring upon the United States hegemony, Garwin says, "nations or consortia of nations would oppose them."[29]

Years ago, Garwin suggested that national policymakers be guided by something he called the "Extended Golden Rule."[30] The Golden Rule is an ethical statement that stands near the center of a host of religions around the world, as well as many secular schools of thought. One formulation, a traditional Christian version found inscribed on the walls of many churches, goes like this: "Do unto others that which you would like them to do unto you."

That's a tough adjuration. In its positive formulation, the Golden Rule insists that you actively treat others as you wish them to treat you. In the real world of clashing national interests, conflicting values, and nationalistic, ethnic, and religious passions, it sets an impossibly high standard. The men and women who run the major powers tend to be a suspicious lot who routinely engage in worst-case analyses. They may host and toast rivals and potential rivals at state functions, but they seldom trust them and they are forever attempting to gain military advantage over them.

While the positive formulation of the Golden Rule sets a near impossible standard, Garwin's version, like the traditional Hebrew formulation, is different: "Do *not* do unto others what you would *not* like them to do unto you." In the military context, the suggestion is to refrain from doing something to others that—if done to you—would so alarm you that you would almost surely react.[31]

Once again, suppose another nation said that it intends to develop and deploy a comprehensive space-dominance capability. How would the United States react? With vigor, surely. The other nation would be defined by the president, the Congress, and the American people as a clear and present danger to America's freedom of action on the world stage as well as to its economic survival.

If the United States should definitively choose to unilaterally pursue and deploy a comprehensive space-control capability—even if "only" an on-demand pop-up capability—would other nations be similarly angered? To pose the question is to answer it.

Although no other nation is capable of taking on the United States in a symmetrical arms race in space, China would surely choose to have a partial go at it by deploying a variety of relatively high-tech antisatellite weapons, such as land-based lasers or co-orbital "space mines." Indeed, China experimentally "illuminated" at least one American spy satellite in 2006 with a ground-based laser. Why wouldn't China conduct such experiments? As Loren Thompson of the Lexington Institute, a highly respected defense-oriented think tank, said of the laser event:

> If you keep looking over the fence at your neighbor's back yard, you're going to get poked in the eye, so it's not surprising that China might be worried about U.S. forces stationed on their doorstep.... They don't like it and are figuring out how to poke us in the eye. Now I'm no great admirer of the Chinese leadership, but how would we feel if the Chinese had their aircraft carriers off Long Island?[32]

China's kinetic-kill ASAT test in January 2007 was an even more definitive statement. Off-the-record sources suggest that China has conducted low-key ASAT weapons research for many years, possibly since the 1980s, when the Reagan administration's Strategic Defense Initiative was at full throttle. States less capable than China of high-tech responses might someday choose to combat U.S. space dominance with simpler means—injecting satellite-damaging pellets into certain orbital planes, for instance, or detonating cunningly arranged nuclear weapons in space.

In the end, it is probably better, as Garwin suggests, for the United States to refrain from doing to others that which it would not want done to it. Anthony Lake, President Clinton's national security adviser, put it this way in 1996:

> Today, Asia faces a choice between two global visions for the twenty-first century. The first is a return to the zero-sum politics of the nineteenth century—a world where great powers are permanent rivals, acting as though what was good for one power was, by definition, detrimental to another. The second is a world where great powers act to increase cooperation, avert chaos, and strengthen economic growth, while preserving the balances of power that preserve the peace.

A "key element of regional stability," he added, "is our engagement with China. With its emergence as a great power, China will play a central role in deciding whether the next century is one of cooperation or zero-sum rivalry and conflict. As President Clinton has said, a secure, stable, open and prosperous China—in other words, a strong China—is in our interest. We welcome China to the great-power table. But great powers also have great responsibilities."[33]

Tony Lake was on point. A policy of engagement with China is likely to lead to an ever more capitalistic China, and perhaps—someday—to a marginally less repressive and more democratic China.[34] In its economic life and, to a far more limited degree, in its cultural life, China is already trending toward Western ways. Its future wealth is tied to economic integration with the West, not in burying the West.

Soviet and Western ambitious and worldviews were so greatly opposed to one another that the Cold War was probably inevitable; in contrast, a cold war with China is not inevitable. But if the United States talks of friendship with China while building a space-dominance capability, it may short-circuit China's evolutionary process, and the world will have a new, expensive, and potentially dangerous cold war.

16

The Irony of American History

A keen observer of American life, a man born in the state of Missouri, once recounted a conversation he had with a European statesman in the late 1940s, after it had become clear that the United States was preventing the Stalinist hordes from sweeping through Western Europe: "We are grateful to America for saving us from communism, the European said. "but our gratitude does not prevent us from fearing that we might become an American colony. That danger lies in the situation of America's power and Europe's weakness."

The Missourian reminded the European of the idealism that had helped shape American foreign policy, but the European was not soothed. "The idealism does indeed prevent America from a gross abuse of its power," the European said. "But it might well accentuate the danger Europeans confront. For American power in the service of American idealism could create a situation in which we would be too impotent to correct you when you are wrong and you would be too idealistic to correct yourself."[1]

The Missourian was Reinhold Niebuhr, philosopher, theologian, author, and a staunchly anti-communist "Christian realist." He recalled the anecdote in *The Irony of American History*, published in 1952. Niebuhr wrote in the context of the early Cold War, when the Soviet Union was thought to be the Western world's nemesis. But Niebuhr's understandings of the unfathomable mysteries of human nature, as well as the role American "idealism" played in shaping American foreign policy, speak directly to us today. America's power and idealism (its "exceptionalism") had become, in Niebuhr's view, an ironic and "vivid symbol of the spiritual complexities of modern man."

American power tends to generate illusions to which a techno-cratic culture is already too prone. This technocratic approach to the problems of history, which erroneously equates the mastery of nature with the mastery of historical destiny, in turn accentuates a very old failing in human nature: the inclination of the wise, or the powerful, or the virtuous, to obscure and deny the human limitations in all hu-man achievements and pretensions.[2]

American foreign policy should be bold and resolute in the face of evil, Niebuhr believed. But it must also be tempered by a measure of humility; America should not think of itself as being prescient about an "unknown future." Further, it must, to echo the Declaration of Independence, always preserve a "decent respect for the opinions of mankind."[3]

The fears expressed by Niebuhr's European friend so many decades ago presumably faded as the United States took the lead in containing the Evil Empire, underwriting decades of relative peace and prosperity in Western Europe. But in the years after the Soviet collapse, many Europeans once again began to fear that, over the long run, American idealism combined with its military power would prove dangerous to world peace.

That assumption pains Americans, who see the United States as the stead-fast nation that saved the world from multiple horrors in the last century and which is now engaged in defending virtually everyone from the global caliphate Islamic extremists claim is their objective. Why, then, don't we hear more pro-American cheers from the freedom-loving peoples of the world? Why are we assailed ever more loudly with accusations of "imperialism"?

The proximate cause of these accusations may have been the annoy-ingly provocative assertions of triumphalists and neoconservatives in the post–Cold War world, statements such as those made by William Kristol and Robert Kagan in 1996 (described in Chapter Fourteen) that the goal of U.S. foreign policy should be to preserve American hegemony as far into the future as possible.

That sort of thing is not designed to win friends abroad. But trium-phalists and neoconservatives are not concerned with winning friends; they believe America's mission is not to charm the world but to *fix* it. Friends are fine, but in the end what they want is a kind of Vito Corleone version of foreign policy—one that produces a mixture of ring-kissing respect and fear in other nations.

While triumphalists and neocons may be reasonably content with a foreign policy a *capo* would admire, it unsettles many Americans. We wonder how a nation long admired for its dedication to liberty, democracy, openness, and the rule of law—a nation that for decades provided refuge and opportunity to tens of millions of immigrants—could now be so widely accused of overweening arrogance. We are baffled that a nation whose contribution in blood and treasure helped rescue Europe and Asia from fascism and militarism and communism could now be indicted for seeking to run the world. And we are mystified that a nation whose popular culture, technology, and ways of doing business are ascendant throughout much of the developed world finds itself mistrusted and even feared.

The testimony of Serge Schmemann, editorial page editor of the *International Herald Tribune*, is especially poignant. Schmemann, who lived abroad for years, had become hardened to occasional expressions of anti-Americanism. But in January 2004 he wrote with regret and sadness that he was now hearing his nation regularly assailed as a "dangerous empire in its last throes, as a failure of democracy, as militaristic, violent, hegemonic, evil, callous, arrogant, imperial and cruel."[4]

For this reader at least, Schmemann's essay brought to mind the words of Senator J. William Fulbright, published in 1966: "Power tends to confuse itself with virtue and a great nation is peculiarly susceptible to the idea that its power is a sign of God's favor, conferring upon it a special responsibility for other nations—to make them richer and happier and wiser, to remake them, that is, in its own shining image."[5]

More than two thousand years ago, one of America's prime exemplars, Athens in its Golden Age, confused power with virtue, and ultimately brought ruin to itself and others in the world in which it dwelt.

A TALE OF HUBRIS

Ancient Athens was not sizable by modern standards. Although it was the most populous city-state in ancient Greece, it probably had no more than a quarter of a million people in the city and in the surrounding area called Attica. In contrast, the Roman Empire eventually embraced millions. Yet Athens in its Golden Age was in many respects more closely akin to modern America than Imperial Rome.

There were hundreds of Hellenic city-states, colonies, and settlements radiating outward from the Hellenic Peninsula and reaching Sicily and Italy and the southern coast of Spain, the northern coast of Africa, and the shores of the Black Sea. The heart of the Hellenic world was the Aegean Sea, bounded on the west and north by today's Greece and on the east by today's Turkey, where Hellenic culture dominated the coasts. The Aegean itself, Homer's lovely wine-dark sea, was liberally seasoned with islands, large and small.

But it was in Athens that Hellenic civilization, including respect for rational thought, flowered most vigorously. A substantial number of Athenians came to embrace systematic skeptical inquiry into the human condition. Debate on the mysteries of existence was encouraged and honored. Athenian poetry, drama, philosophy, sculpture, and architecture are still admired and studied in the West—and Americans generally venerate the concept of democracy that Athenians practiced.[6]

"Our constitution," said Pericles, for two decades the unofficial first citizen of Athens, "does not copy the laws of neighboring states; we are rather a pattern to others than imitators ourselves. Its administration favors the many instead of the few; this is why it is called a 'democracy.'" Indeed, said Pericles, Athens was the "school of Hellas."

The occasion for these comments was a traditional funeral rite in 431 B.C. at the end of the first year of the Peloponnesian War.[7] The speech itself (which was likely embellished by Thucydides, author of *The Peloponnesian War*) was so eloquent that Western historians generally accord it proper noun status—The Funeral Oration—and compare it to Lincoln's Gettysburg Address, a reasonable conceit. In each, the speaker honors the men who had died in battle by describing the transcendent worth of the state that sent them forth.[8]

"Far from needing a Homer for our eulogist, or other of his craft whose verses might charm for the moment only for the impression which they gave to melt at the touch of fact," Pericles said at one point, "we have forced every sea and land to be the highway of our daring, and everywhere, whether for evil or for good, have left imperishable monuments behind us." Translated: Athens was the acme of human civilization.

Thucydides, an Athenian of high rank, was a participant in some of the events he wrote about and he knew many of the key players on both sides. That makes his testimony regarding the origins of the war especially compelling. There were many reasons for the conflict, Thucydides says, but the most important was the inconvenient fact that Athens, the state in which democracy was born, brought the war upon itself by its excessive arrogance.

For decades, Athens had promoted its vision of democracy throughout the Hellenic world, often peacefully but sometimes by force. Athens, the city-state that insisted that every male citizen participate in governing the home *polis*, had become an empire in the years preceding the war, causing it to become increasingly envied and mistrusted.

The "real cause" of the war, the one that was "most kept out of sight," says Thucydides, was the "growth and power of Athens, and the alarm which this inspired in Sparta." That made war "inevitable."[9] In another remarkable passage, Thucydides observed that as war grew imminent, "Men's feelings [among the Hellenes] inclined much more to the Spartans, especially as they proclaimed themselves the liberators of Hellas....So general was the indignation felt against Athens, whether by those who wished to escape from her empire, or were apprehensive of being absorbed by it."[10]

Thucydides' account was a tale of honor and deceit, wisdom and stupidity, bravery and treachery. But above all, it was a tale of hubris. No analogy should be pushed too far, of course. The differences in scale between Athens and the United States are staggering. Athens was a tiny city-state important only in the Mediterranean context; the United States bestrides the world. But at least a few parallels are striking, especially the exceptionalist vision common to both.

Athens fostered public and private virtue to a degree unequaled for its time and built a reasonably democratic edifice at home. While doing so, its citizens came to believe that theirs was the most righteous civilization in the history of the world. That overweening exceptionalism, that unrelenting we're-Number-One-hubris, ultimately led to war and defeat. As the prolific, idiosyncratic, and still-controversial twentieth-century historian, Arnold Toynbee said years ago, "Great empires...do not die by murder, but suicide. And the moment of greatest danger is their moment of greatest strength, for it is then that complacency and hubris infect the body politic, squander its strength, and mock its virtues."[11]

WHO WE ARE

As you have discovered by now, *Twilight War* is more about values than technology. Values, however, is an exceedingly vague word, isn't it? Whose values—yours or mine? Ask any ten people what America's core values are and you'll get ten different and probably contradictory answers. And yet, one word is likely to pop up every time—"freedom."

"Freedom" is a lovely word, although I am partial to the more old-fashioned term, "liberty," as used in the Preamble to the Constitution: "We the People of the United States, in Order to form a more perfect Union, establish Justice, insure domestic Tranquility, provide for the common defense, promote the general Welfare, and secure the Blessings of Liberty to ourselves and our Posterity, do ordain and establish this Constitution of the United States of America." Fifty-two words that still stir the blood.

Liberty? Freedom? Either works. Both words play honorable roles in the American civic catechism; that was true even before there was a United States. John Adams wrote in 1765 "that liberty must at all hazards be supported. We have a right to it, derived from our Maker. But if we had not, our fathers have earned and bought it for us, at the expense of their ease, their estates, their pleasure, and their blood."[12] The "Liberty Song," an immensely popular ditty written in 1768 by John Dickinson, a citizen of Pennsylvania, expressed similar thoughts:

> *Come join hand in hand, brave Americans all,*
> *And rouse your bold hearts at fair Liberty's call;*
> *No tyrannous acts shall suppress your just claim,*
> *Or stain with dishonor America's name.*
> *In Freedom we're born, and in Freedom we'll live.*[13]

America's historical devotion to liberty as well as the rule of law, the foundation that supports the whole edifice, was created by the minds of men and women who willed these national values into being, values that have been nourished over the years by the blood of men and women who have honored them with their lives. In that respect, the United States *is* an exceptional nation. The idea that sovereignty somehow could be rooted in the liberty of ordinary individuals, and the notion that the rule of law could put limits on the behavior of a nation's leaders—even its highest official— were novel concepts in eighteenth-century Europe. The monarchs of Europe were certain this odd American experiment would fail and they were astonished when it didn't.

To be sure, liberty for all represents an ideal that has not yet been fully realized in the United States; much the same can be said for the rule of law, which has been battered, bruised and butchered here and there by federal, state, and local governments as well as by corporations, special interest groups, and individuals. And yet, the *aspirational* ideals of liberty, the rule of law, and the vesting of sovereignty in the people, still drive the American experiment.

The fact that the United States over the past sixty-plus years has not used its extraordinary economic and military might to build a classic do-as-we-say-or-face-the-consequences global imperium makes America an exceptional nation when judged by the miserable standards of world history. To be sure, the United States works diligently, either overtly or covertly, to make things go its way. That has been true of all great powers in the history of the world. But America does not attempt to run the world like a modern-day Rome.

And yet...now and then we produce threatening words and phrases such as those in "The Way Ahead," the final section of Air Force Space Command's *Strategic Master Plan FY06 and Beyond*. "Our vision calls for prompt global strike space systems with the capability to *directly apply force from or through space against terrestrial targets*."[14] (Italics added.)

Some years ago, Air Force Lt. Col. Bruce M. DeBlois wrote a brilliant essay exploring the many reasons why unilateral American space dominance was a bad idea. "Space Sanctuary: A Viable National Strategy" appeared in the Winter 1998–1999 issue of the Air Force publication *Airpower Journal* (now, *Air & Space Power Journal*), a must-read for space warriors. For a time, DeBlois was a professor at the School of Advanced Airpower Studies, where he edited *Beyond the Paths of Heaven: The Emergence of Space Power Thought*.[15] After retiring in 2001, DeBlois helped his friend Everett C. Dolman get *Astropolitics: The International Journal of Space Power and Policy* off the ground.[16]

DeBlois and Dolman seem mismatched. Dolman, whom you met in chapters one and two, is an ardent champion of U.S space dominance. The United States, he says, "should seize control of outer space and become the shepherd (or perhaps watchdog) for all who would venture there." Meanwhile, DeBlois promotes international cooperation on military-space issues.

Although Dolman and DeBlois have differing attitudes toward national security space, both believe the United States must take the lead in shaping the use of space for the twenty-first century, at least in the military sphere. Dolman says the United States must move smartly to develop space-control capabilities because it would be dangerous for the United States not to. Further, he and his space-warrior colleagues say, the United States would use its space power to benefit humankind.

U.S. control of space would place "as guardian of space the most benign state that has ever attempted hegemony over the greater part of the world," writes Dolman. "It is bold, decisive, guiding, and, at least from the hegemon's point of view, morally just." In contrast, DeBlois believes that America's role in space is to take the lead in keeping space free of weapons and conflict. In "Space Sanctuary," he offered this observation, which has ricocheted throughout the space-warrior community.

> The United States exports its national values of individual freedoms and democracy and maintains a pattern of not bullying other nations into accepting these ideals. The expectation is that the inherent worth of the ideals is self-evident. Maintaining the moral high ground in order to support this pattern is essential, even if it requires some risks.... The idea of putting weapons in space to dominate the globe is simply not compatible with who we are and what we represent as Americans.[17]

THE CONQUEST OF SPACE

Proponents of space control are surely right when they say that America's vital interests must be vigorously defended. They are correct when they say that the United States, more than any other nation, relies on its space assets, military and commercial, to help fight wars and to keep its economy vibrant; therefore, these space assets must be protected. But space warriors are mistaken when they say that the United States must achieve the capability to control space in order to protect its assets and ensure its security.

In a world based on the principle that nation-states are sovereign entities, a U.S. space-control capability and the deployment of weapons in space would surely raise vexing questions regarding the sovereignty of other nations. If one state becomes so overwhelmingly powerful on a global scale, in what sense do other states retain their full measure of sovereignty?

Most likely, a vigorous space-control capability and weapons in space would be regarded by many states as an expression of contempt for the global norms of the international nation-state system and a challenge to their sovereign rights.

In March 1775, with revolutionary fever rising in the Colonies, Patrick Henry is reported to have said to his fellow Virginians, "Is life so dear, or peace so sweet, as to be purchased at the price of chains and slavery? Forbid it, Almighty God. I know not what course others may take, but as for me: Give me liberty or give me death!"

The phrasing may not be exact; Henry's speech was later committed to paper by someone else. But surely the gist was right. A passion for liberty lay at the heart of the American Revolution. Liberty, most Americans believed, was something worth fighting for and even dying for. It was, and I hope it still is, the core American value.

The exact legalistic meaning and scope of "liberty" is endlessly disputed and debated, which is why the good Lord gave us the American Civil Liberties Union, God bless its contentious heart. But in a very rough sense, personal liberty seems to mean that individuals are free to do pretty much as they please as long as doing so does not dramatically curtail the rights of others to do as they please or endanger public safety.

In much of today's world, various forms of statism, sectarian or secular, still reign, and individual liberty is suppressed. The notion of individual liberty is not even a cultural concept in vast areas of the globe. But freedom of choice for nation-states has long been the worldwide norm; it is the essential element in any definition of national sovereignty. National sovereignty can be thought of as individual liberty applied to states.

Realists insist that nation-states exist in an anarchic world. They do not mean that the globe is in a constant state of chaos, although it often seems that way. They mean that nations, in theory, are subject to no higher coercive authority. There is no world government, no U.N. Secretariat that has the authority to tell them how to conduct their affairs. Far from being a black-helicoptered-global-government-in-waiting, as some of today's Know-Nothings insist, the United Nations is the principal guarantor of national sovereignty. Nonintervention in the internal affairs of nation-states is an iconic belief at the organization's East River headquarters.

The East-West nuclear standoff during the Cold War was more dangerous than most people realize and it was profoundly immoral insofar as the United States and the Soviet Union were prepared to destroy much of the world in the name of deterrence. Nonetheless, the Cold War was a prime example of another pivotal point made by realists: Throughout history, major military powers tend to "balance" one another, whether as individual states or as parties to an alliance.

In the years before the Cuban missile crisis in October 1962, the Soviet Union and the United States attempted to get the jump on one another in nuclear weaponry. After the crisis ended, the United States and the Soviet Union slowly but inexorably became committed to balancing their nuclear forces as they sought rough parity. Parity, went the conventional wisdom, would promote a degree of stability in times of high tension, as long as each side had a relatively secure second-strike retaliatory force.

The Cold War is now a chapter or two in history texts. Not since imperial Rome has a nation possessed such unbalanced power as the United States. The United States intends to keep a couple of thousand nuclear weapons deployed for quick use and thousands more in reserve. It has an ever-growing array of "conventional" weapons capable of attacking targets with unprecedented stealth, precision, and (in military-speak) "lethality." It has the best-trained and best-equipped military personnel in the history of the world and the air and sealift capacity to get sizable battle-ready units to any point on the globe within days or weeks. Its high-tech lead over other nations in all things military widens every year. And now it speaks of taking the high ground of space, controlling it, and possibly placing weapons in it.

Is it really conceivable that a nation that cherishes liberty and the rule of law as its core values would unilaterally deploy a global space-control capability and place weapons in space? National sovereignty is liberty writ large and that applies to all nations, not just to the United States. Would not unilateral space dominance be a flagrant violation of the rule "Do not do unto others what you would not like them to do unto you"?

National security space issues are not clear-cut. They do not lend themselves to sloganeering. There are compelling arguments on both sides of the space-control issue. But in the end, the choice is clear. An attempt by the United States to deploy a unilateral space-control capability—to appoint itself as the global space cop—would mean that the United States had truly declared war on its own core values of liberty and the rule of law. A nation that values liberty as a universal principle must not and should not pursue a policy that could potentially compromise the liberty of all nations.

The next few years are critical. The United States can drift along without decisively choosing how it will proceed regarding national security space. (Not choosing, goes the truism, is also a choice.) It can choose to begin working with other nations to craft a treaty to prevent an arms race in outer space. Or it can choose to unilaterally pursue a policy of space dominance. How the United States approaches and eventually decides these issues will tell the world just how deeply rooted America's democratic values really are.

My focus has been on the notion of space dominance, an idea with deep roots. As superficially prudent as space dominance may sound to many of us, the unintended consequences of such a policy could be extraordinarily damaging to U.S. security. You know that in your gut, don't you? An assertion by any other nation that it intended to develop and deploy a comprehensive space-dominance capability would be vigorously condemned by the United States as a potential instrument of international tyranny, and it would not be tolerated.

Imagine America's reaction if the folks in Beijing had said that "China's vision calls for prompt global strike space systems with the capability to directly apply force from or through space against terrestrial targets." One can almost hear a president telling the nation in a televised speech, "This *outrage*, this *violation* of international law and custom, this *insult* to the peoples of the world, this *tyranny* of the heavens, *shall not stand*."

Why would we expect the leaders of other great and powerful nations to feel differently about an American capability to control space? Space dominance, whether by the United States or by any other nation, would violate the democratic ideal of the rule of law as expressed in the Outer Space Treaty of 1967, which the United States championed and pushed to fruition. The treaty embodied the view that space was "the province of all mankind" and should be used for "peaceful purposes."

Is the push for space control and weapons in space evidence of a new kind of imperialism, as many critics suggest? Probably not. Space warriors, military and civilian, seek full spectrum dominance in space as a way of protecting the United States and its interests, not because they want to run the world. But the push for unilateral space dominance *is* consistent with American exceptionalism, the belief that the United States is entitled by its civic and moral virtue to do virtually anything it wants to do.

In the end, America's motives for seeking space dominance may not make much difference to the leaders of other great nations. Full spectrum dominance in space may not be part of any systematic imperial plan, but the men and women who guide other nations know that it could be employed for imperial purposes at some future time.

And yet, the United States still has moral authority in much of the world. Hundreds of millions of people in other lands still believe that the United States, despite its flaws, strives to be a fair, just, and reasonably democratic society, a live-and-let-live society. An accepting society. Millions of people seek to educate themselves in America, work in America, perhaps migrate to America, not because they hate it but because they believe they can build a better life in the United States. The Statue of Liberty still has a potent symbolic meaning, not just in the United States but in many nations.

Building and deploying the capability to unilaterally control space and placing weapons in space would not square with America's historic reverence for liberty and the rule of law. No nation should unilaterally declare itself as the policeman of space; if we permit our government to go that route, our great and grand nation will have squandered much of its moral authority.

Nonetheless, the Eisenhower vision of reserving space for peaceful purposes is fading. An increasingly likely scenario is that the United States will eventually attempt to deploy a space-dominance capability, thus alienating nations and peoples who might otherwise be allies and friends. The words we Americans would use to justify space dominance would be benign— competent spinmeisters would see to that. But other states would regard them as little more than phrases lifted from a Newspeak lexicon. They would call it by its right name: the conquest of space.

WORTHY GOALS...

We Americans ought to keep in mind the wisdom of a prominent political leader who spoke at West Point on January 5, 1993. His topic was not space; it was the broader issue of America's role in the twenty-first century. What he had to say in 1993, however, is relevant to America's attitude toward space in this century.

Global leadership, the speaker said, "can be political or diplomatic. It can be economic or military. It can be moral or spiritual leadership. Leadership can take any one of these forms, or it can be a combination of them." But whatever leadership is, it "should not be confused with either unilateralism or universalism.... No, the United States should not seek to be the world's policeman. There is no support abroad or at home for us to play this role, nor should there be. We would exhaust ourselves, in the process wasting precious resources needed to address those problems at home and abroad that we cannot afford to ignore."

The United States emerged from the Cold War, the speaker added, as the sole remaining superpower. It was right that America marshal its moral and material resources to promote a democratic peace. "It is our responsibility, our opportunity to lead. There is no one else." But leadership could not be simply asserted or demanded. "It must be demonstrated. Leadership requires formulating worthy goals, persuading others of their virtue, and contributing one's share of the common effort and then some. Leadership takes time. It takes patience. It takes work."

George H. W. Bush, then a lame-duck president in his final days, made sense in that address.[18] The United States should take the lead in global affairs but it should also eschew the unilateral and messianic mission of *fixing* the world or even policing it, whether from land, sea, air, or space. Nonetheless, a lot of influential Americans—particularly a wide array of neoconservatives and triumphalists—believe the United States should be the global policeman, with the assistance, now and then, of *ad hoc* "coalitions of the willing."

INSPIRING IDEALS

In August 1945, shortly after atomic bombs were used against the densely populated cities of Hiroshima and Nagasaki, the Manhattan Engineer District published an amazing little book, *Atomic Energy for Military Purposes*, usually called the Smyth Report after its author, Henry DeWolf Smyth, a Princeton physicist. Smyth outlined the history of the top-secret enterprise, including which scientific and industrial processes had been chosen to produce the "active material" needed to make the bombs work.[19]

The report startled many Manhattan Project scientists. During the war they had been so constrained by the demands of secrecy that they were often barred from talking to one another about certain aspects of the "the gadget" they were all working on, even though they might be in the next room or in a building a few yards across a leafy quadrangle. But now the entire project had been laid out in book form, although not in enough detail to show other countries how to build their own bombs straightaway.

Publication of the Smyth Report incited controversy. Leo Szilard, a Hungarian émigré who had been the catalytic figure in getting the bomb project under way, was horrified. In July 1945 Szilard was asked to read Smyth's draft in the presence of a military courier and approve it for release. After going over it, he scratched out the word "approved"; he simply acknowledged that he had read it.[20] David Lilienthal, shortly to become the first chairman of the Atomic Energy Commission, called the Smyth Report the worst breach of atomic security that had yet occurred.[21] Soviet leaders, as surprised as anyone by the appearance of the Smyth Report, translated it, printed thirty thousand copies, and gave it to their own bomb scientists and engineers.[22]

In August 1945, the United States had an atomic monopoly, which made it the world's sole superpower. Why did the U.S. government feel compelled to publish the report and risk giving the Soviet Union insights into how to put together a bomb program? The answer is that publication of the report, an act so unprecedented that President Harry S Truman had to sign off on it, served two purposes, one practical and one motivated by only-in-America idealism.

Ordinary men and women throughout the world would want to know what the atom bomb was and how it had come about. Hundreds of key scientists who had been part of the Manhattan Project and who were now returning to normal civilian life would be pumped for information. Publication of the report sent a message to those scientists; it defined the boundaries. Based on the report, scientists knew what they were free to talk about and, by its omissions, what they must *not* reveal. Publication was a prudent, practical, preemptive measure.

But the Smyth Report had a nobler purpose, stated in the final two paragraphs of the main text. During the war, public discussion of the bomb project had been off limits. And yet, the central issues regarding the bomb were not technical, the scientists said. They were, as Smyth put it, "political and social questions." How these questions were answered would "affect all mankind."

"We find ourselves," Smyth wrote, "with an explosive which is far from completely perfected. Yet the future possibilities of such explosives are appalling, and their effects on future wars and international affairs are of fundamental importance." These issues had been discussed during the war by some of the upper-tier bomb scientists, he noted, but not by the American people or by Congress. "In a free country like ours, such questions should be debated by the people and decisions must be made by the people through their representatives. This is one reason for the release of this report.... The people of the country must be informed if they are to discharge their responsibilities wisely."[23]

You will find no better definition of democracy than Smyth's free-country remarks. Unhappily, as the Cold War unfolded, it became clear that he and his colleagues had been too optimistic. There was too much paranoia, too much secrecy, too much misinformation and disinformation on both sides of the Iron Curtain to ensure a fully informed public discussion of nuclear issues in the West, much less in the police state that was the Soviet Union.

Nonetheless, the throw-the-issues-open-to-everyone sentiment behind the Smyth Report was magnificent. It spoke of a profound faith in the wisdom of the American people and the workings of the democratic process— of how ordinary people, whose rights of free speech and a free press were guaranteed by the Constitution, would be able to come to grips with the most profound life-or-death matters imaginable.

WE, THE PEOPLE

Twilight War is no Smyth Report. It reveals no previously classified information and it does not explore scientific matters that are only vaguely comprehensible to those of us who lack a degree in physics. And yet, the morally complex and culturally divisive issues examined in these pages are akin to those introduced by the Smyth Report. Whether or not the United States might deploy a unilateral space-dominance capability is an issue too important to be left solely to the president, any president, or to the Congress. The Constitution does not vest ultimate sovereignty in the national legislature or the president. It vests it in "We, the people."

The need for intense and active involvement in a major foreign policy issue has seldom been as important as it is now. We do not need to start a cold war with China or anyone else, in which the drive for space dominance would be the focus. There is a better way to build the future in space, and working toward a new space treaty is it. *Twilight War* is not rocket science. It is not about exotic hardware or black programs or Strangeloves stalking the halls of the Pentagon. It is not about secret plans and doctrines. In the end, it touches upon the meaning of America.

The moon belongs to everyone/The best things in life are free,/The stars belong to everyone,/They gleam there for you and me. Doggerel, certainly. Nonetheless, it is a pleasant rhyme that hints at a near-universal notion. The heavens *are* somehow different from land, sea, and sky, venues for conflict since the dawn of man. While our planet is a darkly troubled place, the stars and the sun, the moon and the planets still have the capacity to inspire poets and lovers. They cheer the soul and cause us to reflect on the meaning of existence. "The heavens proclaim the glory of God," begins the hymn of praise in Psalms 19. "The work of God's hands is revealed in the heavenly vault."

One need not believe in God to feel the wonder. Any clear night will do. The heavenly vault embodies the infinite and the eternal, concepts that can be named although not fully understood. Unfathomable mystery resides in the universe and the stars are just a visible manifestation of it. The proper role of the United States is to use its power, influence, and moral authority to ensure that space remains free of conflict, a weapons-free sanctuary. To fail in that task would be a truly tragic irony of American history.

Nonetheless, the space-dominance train left the station decades ago and it click-clacks steadily toward its destination. It is no stealth train, but it has managed to travel in hazy twilight. Few of us have noticed it. It is time for a close, hard look. A democratic society can do no less. Like the report of Donald Rumsfeld's Space Commission, *Twilight War* is a warning. Not of a "space Pearl Harbor" but of the perils of American hubris regarding space, and of our coming war with our own values.

Appendix A
Into Space, Anonymously

Humans have long dreamed of breaking the bonds of gravity and soaring toward the heavens. When Daedalus and his son Icarus decided to escape from Crete, where they had been imprisoned by King Minos, they fashioned wings of feathers, thread, and wax. "My son," Daedalus warned, "neither soar too high, lest the sun melt the wax; nor swoop too low, lest the feathers be wetted by the sea." As father and son flapped toward safety, Icarus disobeyed, as young men are wont to do. He flew too close to the sun, with a tragic outcome.

Centuries later, Icaro-Menippus, who adapted the wing of a vulture and the wing of an eagle to his body and took off from Mount Olympus, met a happier fate. According to Lucian of Samosata, a second-century satirist, Icaro reached the Moon but was not yet content. He then journeyed to the stars and finally to heaven itself. Mercury escorted the audacious young man back to Earth and relieved him of his wings.[1]

In 1638, Domingo Gonsales of Spain—the charming figment of a fertile British mind—told of his trip to the "Moone," to which he was carried by wild swans trained to pull a contraption that looked something like a giant box kite with a trapeze bar hanging from it. Gonsales, serenely puffing his pipe while sitting on the bar, noted that Nicolaus Copernicus, the iconoclastic Polish astronomer, had been right all along. The heavens did not revolve around the Earth, as the clergy had long said. Rather, the Earth "turneth round upon her own Axe every twenty-four howers from the *West* unto the *East*."[2]

And thanks to Jules Verne, we are familiar with the journey to the Moon by Messrs. Barbicane, Nicholl, and Ardan. Shortly after the end of the American Civil War, according to Verne's tale, the Baltimore Gun Club, composed of expert artillerymen with a lot of time on their hands, raised $6 million to build a nine-hundred-foot-long cannon. Too long and too heavy to sit on the surface, it was fabricated perpendicularly, like a very deep well, into the Florida soil and rock, somewhere between present-day Fort Myers and Sarasota.

The trio's aluminum man-carrying "cylindro-conical" shell weighed about twenty thousand pounds; some four hundred thousand pounds of guncotton propelled it into space with an initial velocity of about thirty-six thousand feet a second. (As Verne describes it, the "aerial coach was lined with strong springs and [hydraulic] partitions to lessen the shock of departure.") After whipping around the Moon, the men in the lunar coach splashed down in the Pacific. When picked up days later by a search vessel, Barbicane, Nicholl, and Ardan were engaged in a game of dominoes.

In 1898, five years before the Wright brothers got a powered glider off the ground at Kitty Hawk, a shy Russian mathematics teacher, Konstantin Eduardovitch Tsiolkovsky, born in 1857, calculated how a liquid-fueled "re-action-machine" might help humankind break the bonds of gravity. "The scientifically... verified mathematical conclusions," Tsiolkovsky wrote, "indicate the feasibility of an ascent into space with the aid of such machines and, perhaps, the establishment of settlements beyond the confines of Earth's atmosphere."[3]

Tsiolkovsky published his first article on rocketry, "Exploration of Space With Rocket Devices," in 1903 in a Russian scientific journal. He later churned out dozens of space- and rocket-related works before dying in 1935. He described how a rocket could be powered by a combination of liquid oxygen and liquid hydrogen, much as in today's space programs, and he imagined multi-stage rockets—a "passenger rocket train" some three-hundred-feet long and employing twenty rocket stages.

"Working under great difficulties, with pitifully meager resources," wrote Arthur C. Clarke in 1968, "Tsiolkovsky calculated, made models in his little workshop, and wrote numerous popular and technical articles advocating his ideas. Not only were most of these soundly based, they were also so astonishingly ahead of their time that even now we are still catching up with him."[4]

Nothing practical came of Tsiolkovsky's theories. The Czarist government was too busy building opulent palaces to rival those of France to pay attention to someone like Tsiolkovsky. Then came the Great War, the Revolution, and the transformation of Russia into the principal state of the Soviet Union. Lenin and Stalin were too deeply engaged in modernizing industry and agriculture—and in starving to death millions of Kulaks and murdering rivals, real or imagined—to think of building rocket ships. Years later, a giant crater on the far side of the Moon was named for Tsiolkovsky.[5]

In the early 1920s, many men in Europe and America were thinking along similar lines, including Hermann Oberth, a Transylvanian who taught mathematics in Romania. Oberth's *The Rocket into Interplanetary Space* was published in 1923. He believed that an early step toward space travel would have to be the construction of a space station—a large orbiting rocket with a mass of "at least" four hundred thousand kilograms.

Oberth's space station would be a marvelous astronomical observatory because "in space, telescopes of any size could be used." The station also would be a sensational platform for observing the Earth. Men with telescopes "could recognize every detail on the Earth" and the information gained could be transmitted by light signals "through the use of appropriate mirrors." Such observations would have prevented the *Titanic* from hitting an iceberg, said Oberth. He also imagined that huge orbiting mirrors might be constructed and used to focus the sun's energy on selected portions of the Earth.

> For example, routes to Spitzbergen or to the northern Siberian ports could be kept free of ice. If the mirror had a diameter of only one hundred kilometers [*only!*], it could make broad areas in the northern regions of the Earth inhabitable through diffused light, and in our latitude it could prevent the fearful spring freezes and protect fruit crops from damage by night frosts in both spring and winter.[6]

Herman Potocnik, an Austrian, was also enchanted with the notion of space travel. His *The Problem of Space Travel,* an obscure but marvelous work, was published in 1929. Potocnik, who adopted the pen name Herman Noordung, wrote of how rockets might be made to work and how trajectories eventually could be designed to land men on the Moon and to take them on "fly-bys" to the nearer planets, Mars and Venus—"an ancient dream of mankind!"[7]

Potocnik was especially intrigued by Mars. "Even water is probably found on Mars," he wrote. "However, a fairly large part of it is probably frozen, because the average temperature on Mars appears to be substantially below that of the Earth."[8] However, before we humans could go to the Moon and Mars, Potocnik said, we must first build a space station. His "space base" would be a three-part affair with a central structure—the "habitat wheel"—as its main component. (The wheel resembled the space station von Braun later "designed" for his 1952 *Collier's* article.) In Potocnik's scheme, thermal energy from the sun, focused by a concave mirror, would drive a steam generator, thus supplying electrical power.[9]

Unhappily, an even larger concave mirror could be fashioned into a "most dreadful weapon" capable of sweeping the Earth with "death rays." An enemy's munitions dumps could be ignited, cannons and tank turrets and iron bridges melted, and troops charred "when the beams of this concentrated solar light were passed over them." Important war factories, industrial areas, even cities could be set ablaze. Ships at sea would be vulnerable; they could be burned out "like bugs are exterminated in their hiding place with a torch."[10]

In the United States, Robert H. Goddard, like Tsiolkovsky, Oberth, Potocnik, Verne, and others, had visions of space travel. As World War I raged in Europe, Goddard made notes on "The Ultimate Migration." Humans, faced with a sun about to expire, would build "arks" (powered by "intra-atomic energy") and send them toward many different star systems where habitable worlds might be found. The voyages would be long and the crew and passengers would travel in suspended animation. Every ten thousand years or so—or perhaps every million years—the pilots would be temporarily reanimated to see if the arks were still on course. Goddard never developed his notes into a story; fearful of ridicule, he hid them in his files under the heading, "Special Formulae for Silvering Mirrors."[11]

Goddard was more than a space fabulist; he was a supremely competent engineer and experimentalist.[12] He won his first patent for a liquid-fueled "rocket apparatus" on July 7, 1914, on the eve of the Great War. On March 16, 1926, he launched the world's first such rocket, near Worcester, Massachusetts. It rose one hundred and eighty-four feet. Nine years later, one of his gyroscope-stabilized rockets soared to an altitude of seven thousand feet near Roswell, New Mexico. Goddard might have been *the* global pacesetter in rocketry if he had not been a little paranoid about other rocketeers stealing his ideas. Suspicion made him enormously secretive; he guarded his advances in rocketry zealously—registering two hundred and fourteen patents in all.[13] As a result, he played a less noted role in the development of rocket science than might otherwise have been the case. In the end, work done at von Braun's huge Peenemünde research and test operation in Nazi Germany led the way, at least insofar as a death missile that transited the lower reaches of space was concerned.

———————>●●<———————

When Soviet troops reached Germany's V-2 research and production centers in the latter stages of the Second World War, they found that the facilities had been largely stripped of parts and documents by Americans troops and special teams. The Americans had also persuaded many German rocket scientists, engineers, and technicians to move west of the line that would soon separate the Soviet zone of occupation from the remainder of Germany.

"This is absolutely intolerable," Josef Stalin told Col. G. A. Tokaty-Tokaev. "We defeated Nazi armies; we occupied Berlin and Peenemünde, but the Americans got the rocket engineers. What could be more revolting and more inexcusable?"[14]

Stalin was needlessly overwrought. Although the Soviets failed to get von Braun and the key members of his team (see Chapter Eight), they nonetheless harvested a respectable crop of men who had worked on the V-2s and who were now willing to work for the Soviet Union.[15]

A Soviet Army officer, Boris Chertok, was sent to Germany in the spring of 1945 to acquire as many V-2 parts, blueprints, engineers, and technicians as possible. When he and a colleague, Alexei Isaev, arrived in Bleicherode, near Mittelwerk—the V-2 factory where thousands of slave laborers had worked and died—they were "dirty and dusty." Chertok and Isaev were directed to von Braun's former home, where they could rest. The home had "four toilets and three great bathrooms," Chertok recalled. Isaev threw aside a white feather blanket and plopped down on a bed in a second-floor bedroom. There was a mirror on the ceiling. Isaev lit a cigarette and said, "You know, it's not bad at all, this Fascistic beast's pit."[16]

Chertok helped establish a rocket research institute in Bleicherode that soon had about a thousand people working for it, including fifty to sixty Peenemünde veterans. The Germans were well paid and got good rations. In October 1946, a delegation from the Soviet Union, headed by a general, visited the institute. After a briefing, the general praised the Germans, who had been "very industrious." As a reward, he invited them to dinner. A huge table had been set up, recalled one of the engineers, and the men were served a meal "the like of which we'd never seen before. Fruit in absolute abundance, which was unheard of at the time, and, of course, vodka, vodka, vodka, nothing else to drink."

After the party, the Germans were summarily shipped to the Soviet Union. Their homes were surrounded by armed Soviet soldiers and the Germans were told they could bring their families and "any woman" they wished, "even if she is not a wife." They could also bring their personal possessions.

Irmgaard Grottrup, wife of the most important German scientist in the group, Helmut Grottrup, put the latter promise to a severe test. When Helmut had gone to work for the Soviets, he had been given an elegant farm near Bleicherode. Irmgaard, who knew that famine was sweeping the Soviet Union, told Soviet officials she would not move without her cows and hay. The Soviets agreed. The cows and hay were transported, too.[17]

Some of the Germans feared the worst in the Soviet Union. To their relief, they were well treated. They were paid more than their Soviet counterparts and they got better housing and food. Like the Soviet scientists working elsewhere on the atom bomb project, they were expected to produce results.

Most of the German rocket men settled at institutes in Podlipki, about forty minutes by car northeast of Moscow. The Germans, working with Soviet engineers and technicians, cobbled together new V-2s from bits and pieces of the old Peenemünde program, and they worked on a variety of other rocket-related projects. But it was soon clear that their principal unstated mission was to teach young Soviet engineers and scientists rocketry. German brains were being picked by their Soviet handlers. We often asked ourselves, one of the Germans later said, why we were working with inexperienced people, some of whom were still students. Why were we not working with experienced specialists?

> Only much later did we realize what tricky means the Soviets applied so that we would not learn what they were really doing: the Russian top experts, organized in work teams like us, worked in the same factory, but carefully separated from us. They worked on the same subjects as we did, and they studied our reports with greatest care. The contact between them and us was maintained by young en-

gineers.... There was a group of experts parallel to ours, but anonymous to us! Its members were first-class specialists, they followed and controlled our work but remained invisible to us.[18]

Although the lines of authority were vague, the Germans soon came to believe that the man in charge of the Soviet operation was Sergei Pavlovich Korolev, whom they had previously met now and then in Bleicherode. The Germans were right. Korolev oversaw the "invisible" Soviet team and his knowledge and skills continually impressed the Germans.

Korolev was a superb and innovative engineer and an organizational genius. Before the war, he had been among the Soviet Union's most ardent rocket enthusiasts. Like von Braun and his friends, who conducted amateur experiments in rocketry long before the war began, Korolev and his friends also experimented with rockets.

On August 17, 1933, Korolev and colleagues launched the first reasonably successful liquid-fuel rocket in the Soviet Union. It weighed forty pounds and rose about four hundred meters before veering off and crashing into trees. The flight lasted eighteen seconds. Afterward, Korolev summarized the event on a poster, concluding with the admonition that "Soviet rockets must conquer space."[19]

Beginning in 1952, the German scientists, engineers, and technicians were shipped home to Germany. It is likely that Korolev was happy to see them go. He had been annoyed by the decision, made by Stalin, to devote so much time and energy to getting V-2s assembled and off the ground. Korolev believed the V-2s were already obsolete and that he could have advanced Soviet rocketry farther in the same amount of time by following his own path. Korolev's ego was not in need of German rocket Viagra.

In the 1950s and 1960s, Korolev—chief designer of the Soviet space program and the man behind the early sputniks—conquered space, as he had dreamed of doing in 1933. Korolev biographer James Harford, an expert on the U.S. and Soviet space programs, sums up Korolev's contribution:

> Korolev not only developed the first Soviet ICBM and launched the Space Age with Sputnik, he put into space the first dog, first man, first two men, first woman, first three men; he directed the first "walk in space"; he created the Soviet Union's first spy satellite and first communications satellite; he built the launch vehicles and the spacecraft that first reached the moon and Venus and passed by Mars.

He was frustrated, though, from achieving his biggest goal: sending a man to the moon before the United States did.[20]

Korolev died in 1966 at fifty-nine. In some measure, he *had* changed the world although his name would not be linked to rockets and spaceflight until after his death. Stalin had decreed years earlier that no one outside the space program's inner circle should know the identity of the chief designer, the man who first took humankind into space. Korolev was twice honored as a "Hero of Socialist Labor" but was not allowed to wear his medals in public. He wrote occasional articles on space for *Pravda*, but signed them "Professor K. Sergeev."[21]

Appendix B
Newton's Cannon

Physicists (not to mention the folks on TV's *Starship Enterprise*) like to say that we live in an Einsteinian universe featuring the "space-time continuum" and other extraordinary and cool phenomena that only people well versed in high-level mathematics can understand. They are right. Einstein and the folks who followed him have redefined what we know, or think we know, about the universe. But not about our own solar system. Insofar as exploring the solar system is concerned, a set of ideas promulgated more than three hundred years ago tells all we need to know.

As a young man in Britain, Isaac Newton helped invent the modern world with the publication of the *Principia—Mathematical Principles of Natural Philosophy*.[1] In it, he described the three "Laws of Motion" along with hundreds of pages of propositions and corollaries and mathematical proofs.[2] The first law says: "Every body continues in its state of rest, or of uniform motion in a right line, unless it is compelled to change that state by forces impressed upon it." (By "right line," Newton meant a straight line.)

The first law—sometimes called the "law of inertia"—does not fit our everyday observations. We know, of course, that objects "at rest" remain that way unless we propel them with our foot, hand, club, engine, or whatever. But the second part about a body keeping on in a "right line" at the same velocity forever is profoundly counterintuitive. Cars run out of gas and stop. Soccer balls go dead, too, if no one kicks them. Airplanes fall out of the sky if their engines fail. And yet satellites don't fall back to Earth, even though they lack a rocket engine to steadily propel them.

Newton presented an amazing and provocative "thought experiment" early in *Principia*.[3] Suppose that a "leaden ball" is "projected from the top of a mountain by the force of gunpowder." Newton, like his twentieth-century peer, Albert Einstein, was a man of almost unfathomably powerful insight. However, he was not always a graceful writer. In effect, he said in that passage, "Imagine hauling a cannon to the top of a very high mountain and firing cannonballs."[4] As a pivotally important part of his thought experiment, Newton also asked us to assume that there was *no air to retard the motion of the cannonball.*

The first cannonball, Newton suggested, might be fired toward the horizon with enough force that it would follow a downward curving arc until it fell to Earth in two miles. We could then progressively increase the charge of gunpowder so the cannonball would go farther each time we fired the cannon. Eventually, the cannonball "might go quite round the whole Earth before it falls; or lastly, so that it might never fall to the Earth, but go forwards into the celestial spaces, and proceed in its motion *in infinitum*." Don't forget that, according to Newton's first law of motion, the cannonball would *forever travel at the same velocity it had when it left the muzzle of the cannon.*

A few years later, Newton published a wonderful diagram illustrating his point. Newton traces the paths of four cannonballs shot from a mountain at the North Pole. One falls to Earth at the base of the mountain. The next one falls about a thousand miles away. The third one curves halfway around the Earth before it falls. The fourth cannonball *never* falls; it traces a circular path around the Earth.[5] (It must be said that Newton's mountain was peculiar in that it must have been several hundred miles high and a thousand miles wide at its base. The top of the mountain protruded well into the airless vacuum of space.)

Vacuum or no vacuum, why didn't the fourth cannonball fall—or sail off into deep space? This was where Newton's most magnificent insight, the law of universal gravitation, came into play. Today, we seldom think of gravity—it's a given, much like the sun will rise tomorrow. But in Newton's day, it was a world-changing idea. Everyone "knew" that it was simply the natural order of things that all terrestrial things were somehow rooted to the Earth—even tree leaves and birds. When they died, down they came. Some sort of mysterious attractive force was clearly at work. Otherwise, humans would simply fall off the face of the Earth as it turned on its axis. (Didn't you wonder about that when you were very young? If the Earth turned, as teachers said, didn't that mean you were upside down some of the time?)

Newton named the attractive or centripetal force "gravity" and asserted that every material object attracts every other material object. Mass attracts mass. Further, the force of that attraction is proportional to the mass of the objects and *inversely* proportional to the square of the distance between the objects. Newton did not explain what gravity was; he simply described its properties with uncanny precision. But that description—when linked to his laws of motion—explains virtually everything we need to know about how our solar system works.

In Newton's thought experiment, the law of inertia said the fourth cannonball should go in a straight line forever. In contrast, the law of gravity said the cannonball was attracted toward the center of the Earth. That's a conundrum. Newton solved it by saying that if the cannonball were accelerated to a sufficiently high velocity by the cannon's gunpowder, its straight-line inertial motion would be speedy enough that it would forever circle the Earth. That's because its onward motion and its falling motion would be synchronized with Earth. The cannonball would fall toward the center of the Earth at the same rate that the curvature of the Earth "fell" away from the cannonball.

In proposing his thought experiment, Newton had no interest in mountaintop cannons. He was explaining why the Moon stayed in orbit. His first law of motion said that the Moon should travel in a straight line at the same velocity until the end of time. But his law of universal gravitation said the Moon and the Earth were mightily attracted to one another. However, because the Earth was many times more massive than the Moon, the Moon was continuously falling toward the center of the Earth—or as a physicist would put it, "accelerating" toward the center of the Earth. Happily for us, the onward velocity of the Moon is precisely enough to balance the attractive force of gravity.

Gunpowder, as Newton knew, lacked the energy to propel a cannonball into orbit. Sir Isaac was conducting a thought experiment, not proposing a course of action. Today, satellites are launched by rocket "boosters" instead of gunpowder. Rockets loft satellites above the Earth and set them free at velocities sufficient to achieve orbit.[6]

—————⇒➤◄⇐—————

Space is mostly a whole lot of nothing.[7] It is an airless vacuum, which makes for some interesting phenomena. For one thing, it is soundless. Science fiction movies usually get that wrong—in the *Star Wars* movies you hear the low throaty sound of battle cruisers as they slide through space. In contrast, Stanley Kubrick's *2001: A Space Odyssey* got it right. In Kubrick's film, the spaceship *Discovery* makes no sound as it heads toward Jupiter. Sound, as we generally understand it, requires a medium such as air or water to carry sound waves to our ears. Similarly, there are no shock waves from explosions in space. Like sound, shock waves require a medium to propagate. The next time you see a spaceship buffeted about by shock waves, hiss at the screen (quietly, of course).

Because space is airless it is also frictionless. Objects launched into space will go forever, just as Newton said, unless they happen to run into something. By the time this book is published in 2008, *Voyager* I, a NASA probe launched September 5, 1977, will have traveled nearly nine and half *billion* miles.[8] One of *Voyager*'s (fictional) deep-space cousins even starred in the first *Star Trek* movie as the heart and soul of the hugely powerful and profoundly mysterious *V'ger*.

We have all seen film clips of "weightless" astronauts in orbit. They aren't really weightless; they simply seem to be because they float around, sometimes gracefully, sometimes awkwardly, in their spacecraft. But weight is a relative thing, a way of describing the interaction between mass and gravity. The Moon has about one-sixth of the mass of the Earth, which means astronauts "weigh" one-sixth as much on the Moon as they do on Earth. (Weight also can be a function of the interaction of mass and centrifugal force, as with a carnival ride in which your enhanced weight pins you and your screaming friends against the inside wall of a revolving cylinder as the floor drops away.)

Astronauts float around in orbit because they, along with their spaceships, are in continuous free fall toward the center of the Earth. The weight-giving effects of gravity are canceled for objects that are in free fall in the gravitational field of *any* large body—whether it is the Earth, the Moon, or Mars, Jupiter, or a star. Indeed, the Earth is in continuous free fall toward the center of the sun. Fortunately for us, Earth also has enough inertial motion to overcome that in-pulling solar force.[9]

So there you have it: satellites stay up because orbital space is airless and frictionless; moving objects in such an environment will continue to move at a constant velocity in a straight line unless acted upon by a force.[10] Gravity is a force and it continuously bends the course of satellites toward the center of the Earth; the downward motion is matched, yard for yard, you could say, by the downward curve of our spherical Earth. The whole thing also can be explained as the interaction of centripetal and centrifugal forces. That wasn't Newton's method, but the math works out just as well.[11]

———⟫●⟪———

Newton's cannonballs are just a start. *Twilight War* is not a technical book and orbital mechanics are frightfully complex. One need not understand orbital mechanics to know that America's unilateral military dominance of space is probably a bad idea. But if you do want to get a handle on it, *The Physics of Space Security* is a good place to start. The book, published by the American Academy of Arts & Sciences, is accurate, dispassionate, and immensely informative. It will not make you a Newton—Newtons do not come along often in the history of humankind. But at a minimum, it will give you a keen understanding of something that puzzles a lot of people—why things that go up don't necessarily come down.[12]

The *Physics of Space Security* can be downloaded—section by section—from the American Academy's website.[13] Section 6 is especially compelling. It outlines, in reasonably plain language, why dogfights in space—the sort of thing depicted in *Star Wars* movies—are just not going to happen. Maneuvering in space is a slow and complex thing, anything but instantaneous.

The *physics* of the *Star Wars* saga is just plain wrong. George Lucas, a very bright guy and the creator of *Star Wars*, knew that. He wanted action, adventure, and emotional punch, not accuracy. Accuracy would have been irredeemably boring. Lucas made a wide-screen comic book filled with heroes and villains, good and evil, mythology and swordplay. I'm not knocking the *Star Wars* saga, a multi-billion-dollar juggernaut. I enjoyed them, or at least the first three films, and so did my kids. But, dogfights in space are not in our future. Nor is orbital space likely to be an arena where the forces of good and evil will play out. Whatever nations may do regarding orbital space is likely to be justified on the basis of "national interest."

Appendix C

Space Control—A Very Old Idea

In the Defense Department's Dictionary of Military Terms, the definition of "space control" includes the following: "the surveillance of space; protection of U.S. and friendly space systems; *prevention of an adversary's ability to use space systems and services for purposes hostile to U.S. national security interests; negation of space systems and services used for purposes hostile to U.S. national security interests*; and directly supporting battle management, command, control, communications, and intelligence."[1] (Italics added.) That definition has long and deep roots.

—————————

In 1909, less than six years after the Wright brothers got their first kite-like *Flyer* into the air, an Italian Army officer, Giulio Douhet (see Chapter Six) wrote in an Italian newspaper that, strange as it might seem to men who had been "inexorably bound to the surface of the Earth," the sky was "about to become another battlefield no less important than the battlefields on land and sea.... We are fully conscious today of the importance of having command of the seas, but soon the command of the air will be no less important."[2]

The image of airpower in the Great War many of us carry in our heads was largely constructed by movies, with the 1927 William Wellman classic *Wings* the archetypal tale of gallantry, courage, and brotherhood among the knights of the air. But there's more to it than that. When the war began in August 1914, Germany had 232 airplanes serviceable for front-line duties; Russia, 190; France, 162; and Britain, Italy, and Austria-Hungary each had about 50 to 100 each. Belgium had 16 and the United States, which would not enter the war until 1917, possessed 8.[3]

These were not combat planes; their role was observation and reconnaissance. In the first weeks of the war, enemy pilots waved to one another as they passed by. That didn't last long. Soon, the airmen began to use pistols, rifles, bricks, *flechettes*, bombs, grenades, and even grappling hooks to bring down the other fellow. But it was not until 1915, with the invention of lightweight machine guns with synchronizers that enabled airmen to shoot through the arc of a spinning propeller, that matters turned truly ugly. Pilots could now aim their plane at the enemy and fire. Through the remainder of the war, they shot one another down by the thousands. Germany alone lost 3,128 planes.[4]

Compared to the slaughter on the ground, in which tens of thousands of men might die in a day, the war in the air seemed daring, even romantic. "If those who come back alive," said the *New York Times*, "feel henceforth that they are a little apart and resplendent, touched with the radiance of that thinner upper air, who will care to deny them?"[5] After the war, an American pilot wrote an epic 163-page poem, *Riders of the Sky*. At one point, Manfred von Richtofen, the "Red Baron," is said by the poet to have taken pity on a discombobulated enemy flyer:

> *Yet once, they say, he let an enemy*
> *Escape: some dashing boy tricked into battle*
> *With the Kaiser's kingly ace; who found himself*
> *With hopelessly jambed gun, helpless before*
> *That nerveless hand and that unerring eye.*
> *Perhaps in admiration for a spirit*
> *Whose skill matched not his quality of courage,*
> *Perhaps magnanimity of soul*
> *Remindful of the Nibelungenlied;*
> *But he withheld the sting of his Spandaus,*
> *And let him go.*[6]

In his first "victory," German pilot Max Immelmann, later called the "Blue Max," wounded a British pilot who then crash-landed. Immelmann, the story goes, landed nearby, pulled the Brit from the wreckage, dressed his wounds, treated him to fine food and French wines for two days, and then sent him to a comfortable prison camp reserved for airmen. In June 1916, Immelmann was killed. The British claimed that a pilot from the Royal Flying Corps had vanquished him. In Germany, Immelmann was said by some to have been downed by British ground fire rather than by a British air rival. In any event, British airmen dropped a wreath over the spot where Immelmann died, saluting him as a "brave and knightly opponent."[7]

It is no wonder that the press and the public often confused the war in the air with medieval jousts. Airmen were often chivalrous, although not as systematically so as the press on both sides suggested. After all, the best way to eliminate the other fellow was not to engage in propeller-to-propeller combat but to swoop down from the rear, like a falcon upon a pigeon. The victim learned of the attacker's presence when bullets ripped into him or his machine. "In any form of attack," said German ace Oswald Boelcke in his "rules" of aerial combat (*Dikta Boelcke*), "it is always essential to assail your opponent from behind." Also, it was preferable to attack in groups of four or six, he said, and always with the sun behind you. However, if caught by surprise by another plane coming from the rear, one must wheel around and face the foe head-to-head rather than flee.[8]

One American airman recalled the day when he saw a German plane coming toward him, "climbing in such a way as to head me off if I kept straight on." But there was a convenient cloud nearby. "I turned and dodged around the cloud, climbing all the time, evidently giving the German the impression I was running away, for when I completed the circuit, I found the enemy machine going in the direction he had last seen me take. I was now above and behind him." The rest was easy. "I came down on him, opening with both guns at a distance of 75 yards."[9]

Despite the knightly overtones, most aerial battles were more hunt than joust, with packs of pursuit planes prowling the skies hoping to catch the enemy unaware. The Red Baron became the war's most famous ace with eighty victories. For each, he ordered a silver cup engraved with the date and type of plane he had downed.[10] The hunters' prey, however, was seldom their opposite number, fellow hunters. The hunters mainly sought reconnaissance planes—scouts—or observation planes engaged in directing artillery fire. During the Great War, air battles became battles for control of the air as each side sought to blind the other side's ground troops by shooting down its aerial scouts and spotters as well as its ground-attack planes and bombers.

———⟫●⟪———

Battles for control of the air were seldom definitive. One side might claim it for a few hours or a few days in a given area and then the other side might regain it. Most often, though, neither side had a clear advantage. World War II was different. In the early days, Nazi Germany owned the skies over Europe. *Blitzkrieg* warfare required it. Later in the European war, the Allies asserted themselves ever more decisively. The Allies did not achieve total control of the air (often called "air supremacy" or "command of the air") at all times and in all places. But they achieved command of the air when it counted most.

The D-Day invasion in June 1944 would not have been possible without Allied control of the air. One hundred and two squadrons of Allied fighters patrolled the skies on D-Day. Supreme Allied Commander Dwight D. Eisenhower later told Congress that the "Normandy invasion was based on a deep-seated faith in the power of the Air Forces, in overwhelming numbers, to intervene in the land battle." Without the Army Air Forces and their "ability to sweep the enemy air force out of the sky," the invasion "would have been more than fantastic, it would have been criminal."[11]

German officers echoed Eisenhower. After the war, Adolph Galland, chief of German fighter forces, recalled "that whenever a fighter plane rolled out of its camouflaged lair, an enemy immediately pounced on it. The danger of being detected and destroyed by the enemy was ever present. At last we retired into the forests. Before and after each sortie the planes were rolled in and out of their leafy protection with great difficulties and much damage." Two weeks after the D-Day invasion, said Galland, his fighters were no longer an effective fighting force.[12]

Field Marshal Erwin Rommel, whose duty it was to repel the Allied invasion force, said "the enemy's air superiority is having a grave effect on our movements. There's simply no answer to it." A little later, a Canadian reconnaissance pilot spotted Rommel's staff car on a road. Although he didn't know who the occupant was, he assumed it must be someone important and he called in a strike by Spitfires. Rommel was seriously wounded, removing him from the war.[13]

On December 16, 1944, 17 German divisions attacked thinly defended American positions in the Ardennes offensive—the Battle of the Bulge—Hitler's last big push to disrupt the invasion. Fog and clouds kept Allied planes virtually grounded for seven days. America's Ninth Air Force flew only 1,800 sorties that week as the Germans advanced. But when the sun returned on December 23, U.S. planes began to sweep the skies; the Ninth flew 1,920 sorties on Christmas Day alone. The official U.S. Army history of the war resorted to purple prose to describe the event.

> The morning of 23 December broke clear and cold. "Visibility unlimited," the air-control posts happily reported all the way from the United Kingdom to the foxholes of the Ardennes front. To most of American soldiery this would be a red-letter day—long remembered—because the bomber and fighter-bombers were once more streaming overhead like shoals of silver minnows in the bright winter sun, their sharply etched contrails making a wake behind them in the cold air.[14]

By the spring of 1945, following Germany's failed Ardennes offensive, allied control of the air over Germany was so complete that U.S. and British bombers and fighters could have operated with near-complete freedom if ground-based antiaircraft fire—flak—had not been so deadly, and if not for the appearance of a new German weapon, the jet-powered Messerschmitt-262. But even the twin-jet Me-262s, the most potent bomber interceptors of the war, were too few and too late to make a significant difference in the war's outcome.

Chuck Yeager, a supremely gifted pilot (who would become in October 1947 the first man to break the sound barrier and live to tell about it) recalls that the Me-262 had a hundred and fifty mile-per-hour speed advantage over his P-51 Mustang. Me-262 pilots were supposed to go after bombers, Yeager said; they were not supposed to engage in dogfights and thus risk getting shot down. "Some [Me-262] pilots were damned arrogant and didn't bother about dropping their wing tanks in a chase," said Yeager. "They just teased around, let a Mustang get close, then cobbed the throttle and thumbed their nose."

Yeager's only confirmed Me-262 "kill" was of a plane coming in for a landing at two hundred miles per hour. "He never saw me, but the damned control tower did. Ground gunners began blasting at the lunatic American swooping right at them, who was trying to line up a quick burst and pull out there. I came in full-throttle at five hundred feet and fired.... I'd rather have brought down the son of a bitch in a dogfight, but it wasn't an easy kill—one quick accurate burst, with flak banging all around me."[15]

Karl Baur, a German civilian who had been the chief test pilot for Messerschmitt, later told of testing a new version of the Me-262 at a time when the Allies had control of the air throughout Germany. In the spring of 1945, Baur was stationed at a base near Lechfeld in southern Germany, where he was wringing out two new versions of the Me-262.

"One morning I started with the Me-262 to test the 50mm cannon when I saw [an American] bomber squadron already approaching. A few seconds after I was airborne, they dropped their bombs in the middle of the runway." After completing the program, Baur decided to land at the Memmingen air base. "Just as I approached to land, the Americans bombed the runway approximately one hundred meters in front of me."

Baur next tried to set down at Landsberg. "From a ten kilometers distance, I saw smoke and flames on the runway there." By then Baur's fuel warning light was on and he decided to return to Lechfeld, his only alternative. Although the bombers that morning had cratered the runway, there was a short stretch that looked promising. "If I could manage to touch down within the first meter of [the runway]—and if my brakes worked properly—then the stretch should be long enough to roll out."[16]

Exceptional skill pulled Baur through; he stopped just short of the first crater, his fuel gone. *Luftwaffe* pilots were seldom as able or as lucky as Baur. "Between late 1944 and early 1945," said Lt. Gen. Johannes Steinhoff, a fighter pilot who became inspector general of the *Luftwaffe*, "the average young pilot flew only two missions before he was killed."[17]

"Warfare is not like an athletic contest," observes military historian Richard P. Hallion, "where one desires the excitement of the close match; rather, since the days of Sun-tzu, it has been recognized that a nation should use military force swiftly, decisively, and overwhelmingly." The art and science of war, ancient and modern, is to gain "asymmetric advantage" over the enemy, and control of the air is fundamental to that. Hallion adds:

> Broadly speaking, control of the air enables a nation to prosecute the fullest range of offensive operations by all its forces against a foe while at the same time, insulating those forces defensively from meaningful enemy counterattacks. Coming from this are obvious advantages, particularly what might be termed the "three freedoms": the freedom of initiative, the freedom to operate, and the freedom to maneuver.[18]

By the end of the Great War, the development of a recognizably modern U.S. airpower doctrine, which featured control of the air as its starting point, was well under way. A few years later, and certainly by the end of the war, their thoughts had become conventional wisdom among airpower partisans. "The first battles of any future war," Gen. Billy Mitchell, America's most ardent champion of airpower, said in 1921, "will be air battles. The nation winning them is practically certain to win the whole war, because the victorious air service will be able to operate and increase without hindrance."[19]

Air doctrine has been refined over the years to the point that achieving control of the air during war is, metaphorically speaking, Commandment No. 1 in America's military lexicon. Today, that paradigm embraces space. The first paragraph of the first chapter in the Air Force's key space document says:

> Military forces have always viewed the "high ground" as one of dominance and advantage in warfare. With rare exceptions, whoever owned the high ground owned the fight. Space assets offer an expansive view of the Earth operating high above the planet's surface; satellites can see deep into an adversary's territory, with little risk to humans or machines. Today, control of the ultimate high ground is critical for space superiority and assures the force-multiplying capabilities of space power. Tomorrow, space superiority may enable instant engagement anywhere in the world.[20]

Insofar as space warriors are concerned, Douhet was prescient. Take another look at his 1909 comment, cited a few pages back, and simply substitute "space" for "sky" and "air."

Appendix D
From Silverbird to FALCON

In 1948, Col. Grigori A. Tokaev, former chief of the Aerodynamics Laboratory of the Moscow Military Air Academy, defected to the British.[1] Tokaev had worked closely with high-ranking Soviet officials after the war, including Vasili Stalin, Josef Stalin's son. Given that background, Tokaev could offer his debriefers considerable insight into the Soviet regime—but perhaps his most startling revelation was about Stalin's interest in building a space bomber that could someday strike the United States.

In 1946, Tokaev had been posted to Berlin, where he was charged with recruiting German scientists to work for Moscow. He had little success. Before going to Berlin, he had "heard of the outrages perpetrated by Red Army troops against the inhabitants—particularly the women—of every German village or town they had entered. But I never could have credited the bitter loathing the Germans had for everything Russian if I had not directly encountered it in Berlin."[2] That antipathy toward the Soviet Union did not help Tokaev in his recruiting.

Tokaev soon came across details of the "Saenger project," a rocket plane scheme put together by Eugen Saenger and his associate (and later, wife), Irene Bredt. Both were extraordinarily talented jet and rocket scientists. From time to time, Tokaev sent reports on the Saenger project back to his handlers in Moscow.

It seems that Saenger, as a young man in pre-war Germany, had imagined he would someday play a major role in designing an orbital space station that could be used as a "factory" to construct the machines necessary for visiting the planets.[3] But first, he would have to develop the science of rocketry.

In the early 1930s, Saenger and Bredt came up with a concept they called *Silbervogel–Silverbird*—a sleek rocket plane that could transport people anywhere in the world in a couple of hours or so. It would do that by flying into the lower reaches of space under rocket power. Then its engines would cut off and *Silverbird* would employ *Rikoschettier*—or "skipping flight"—to glide to its destination.[4]

From its highest point above the Earth—perhaps ninety miles or more, depending on the destination—*Silverbird* would nose downward and skip off the top of the atmosphere like a flat stone skips off water when properly thrown. The bounce would send *Silverbird* upward; then it would head obliquely down for another skip. Each skip would sap some of the rocket plane's kinetic energy, like cars on a roller coaster whose ups and downs become less steep after the first big plunge. No matter. The skipping technique, Saenger believed, would get the job done.

In the mid- and late-1930s, Germany was interested in war machines, not in rocket planes that might ferry wealthy passengers to New York or Rio de Janeiro. In 1936, Saenger and Bredt began work at the Hermann Göring Institute, the research arm of the *Luftwaffe*. They were charged with converting *Silverbird*, which existed only on paper, into an *Amerika* bomber that could skip/glide through the lower regions of space and drop payloads on American cities—perhaps bombs packed with radioactive sand, according to historian David Myhra.[5]

How would the bomber be launched? From a track nearly two miles long, something like the rocket-launch track in the 1951 end-of-the-world movie, *When Worlds Collide*. A rocket-propelled sled would give *Amerika* a boost to more than a thousand miles per hour; once in the air, the bomber's own rocket engines would take over and carry it into the lower reaches of space. The *Amerika* bomber would become an unpowered glider when it reentered the atmosphere.

New York was a priority target. According to one ambitious Saenger scenario, the bomber, with a crew of one, would be launched eastward over the Soviet Union. After reaching its maximum height, it would head downward for its first skip. Nine skips, each smaller than the last, would presumably bring it back to Germany.[6] On the backstretch the bomber would release its payload over Indianapolis and the radioactive bomb would glide on to New York, striking without warning and contaminating a wide area.

Nothing came of Saenger's ideas during the war for a variety of reasons, the most compelling being the staggering disconnect between concept and that which might be technologically feasible in the real world. A competing rocket project, Wernher Von Braun's short-range ballistic missile—the V-2 —was one of the most complex and challenging undertakings of the war. Nevertheless, it was easy stuff compared to Saenger's brainchild.

It is likely that much of what Tokaev, the Soviet aeronautics expert, had to say in his debriefing sessions was reflected in his book *Stalin Means War*, published in 1951. Tokaev wrote that Stalin became interested in the Saenger project in 1946 because Tokaev's reports had worked their way up the bureaucratic chain to the top. The book's dramatic highlight describes how the author was hustled back from Berlin to Moscow to give his opinion of Saenger's work directly to Stalin.

Tokaev's face-to-face midnight meeting with Stalin was surreal, at least in his description of it. Stalin was surrounded by seven key henchmen, including Vyacheslav Molotov ("minister for assassination," according to Tokaev) and Georgi Malenkov (a man who looked like "an overfed scullion" who "spent his worthless life roaring, 'Glory to Stalin!'"). Stalin grilled Tokaev about the Saenger plane. Tokaev explained that Saenger's ideas were interesting—"they could teach us a good deal"—but the bomber itself was technologically out of reach.

"Do you mean, then, that there is no point in our pursuing the plan," Tokaev reports Stalin as asking. No, said Tokaev; much could be learned from research. "Certainly," said Stalin, "research is necessary. But we still need Saenger planes, and their construction should be our immediate objective." Their possession, Stalin added, "would make it easier for us to talk to the gentleman-shopkeeper, Harry Truman, and keep him pinned down where we want him."[7]

Tokaev was ordered to find Saenger and put him on the Soviet payroll. Saenger, it seems, had gone to ground at the end of war and Tokaev never found him. Perhaps Tokaev did not want to find him; he loved Russia but loathed Stalin and his inner circle. In any event, Tokaev came to fear that his failure to produce Saenger would shortly lead to his own early demise. Stalin was not a forgive-and-forget boss, a fact that gave Tokaev and his wife ample reason to defect.[8]

Without Saenger to guide them, Moscow's interest in skip-glide bombers faded. Conventional intercontinental ballistic missiles would eventually become Moscow's weapon of choice to keep the United States "pinned down." The story of Saenger would be little more than an intriguing Cold War anecdote if not for the fact that Saenger still inspires, however indirectly, many twenty-first century space warriors. His *Silverbird* seed produced an American tree with many branches.

⟶⟶≫●≪⟵⟵

After the war, the United States Air Force picked up the Saenger idea, which has been reincarnated with seemingly endless permutations and digressions and variations for more than six decades.[9] The latest reincarnation—or at least a kissin' cousin three generations removed—is the Common Aero Vehicle, discussed in Chapter Five. For that, credit or blame can be largely assigned to Walter R. Dornberger, Wernher Von Braun's Army boss during most of World War II and a Saenger-plane enthusiast.

Dornberger was held by the British as a prisoner for a couple of years after the war, but once the Brits determined he was not a war criminal, he was allowed to migrate to the United States. He soon became an adviser to the Air Force on guided missiles and a consultant to Bell Aircraft, the company that built the X-1 rocket plane in which Air Force test pilot Chuck Yeager cracked the sound barrier on October 27, 1947.

Bell Aircraft was an ardent promoter of advanced aerospace concepts and Dornberger was the keenest of champions of the Saenger space bomber. By April 1952, Dornberger had persuaded Bell to submit a proposal to the Air Force for a manned Saenger-like bomber-missile known as Bomi (bomber-missile).[10]

Dornberger was also high on the possible commercial use of the Saenger plane. In a fanciful (or downright fantastical) essay published in 1956, he went into considerable detail about how rocket-propelled "airliners" would someday fly anywhere in the world in a matter of hours. They would blast off from "rocket ports" and soar into the very thin atmosphere of suborbital space—like *Silverbird*—before returning to the denser atmosphere and gliding to a landing. At one point, he described the emotions passengers would experience during their brief sojourns in space.

In the darkness of space above and beside us, the Moon and the stars are shining with a brightness unknown to the dust-bound human of the past. The outside air pressure is but one five-hundredth of what it is on the ground. The tremendous speed of our rocket plane still gives it a substantial lift. But otherwise we do not feel the speed. The Earth seems to rotate only very slowly underneath us. We feel like being in space, and this is the most unforgettable experience of our trip.[11]

By 1957, several Saenger-like ideas for a space bomber—or, in some schemes, reconnaissance craft that would glide back into the atmosphere from space to investigate suspicious activities by adversaries—were consolidated into Project Dyna-Soar, short for "Dynamic Soaring."

Dyna-Soar was one of the most interesting space-related projects the Air Force has ever mounted, mainly because so much truly visionary work was done without ever reaching a consensus as to its mission. In part because of the incoherence regarding mission objectives, the Dyna-Soar—officially known as the X-20—never flew, although its partisans often spoke breathlessly of its potential, whatever that might be. Moments before the public unveiling of the space plane in September 1962, the undersecretary of the Air Force referred to it as "the vehicle you are about to see." The thing unveiled that day was not, however, a "vehicle." It was a mockup of what Dyna-Soar *might* look like, if it were ever built.

In fairness, a huge amount of pioneering research had been conducted over the years on Saenger-like boost/glide concepts, including Dyna-Soar—research that later would become helpful in developing NASA's Space Shuttle orbiters. But in September 1962, no one had any clear idea as to how to make Dyna-Soar work or what its purpose might be. By then, the United States was well along with developing and deploying intercontinental missiles, spy satellites, and it had the Gemini manned satellite program, which was believed to have military applications. Why *would* the United States need Dyna-Soar, in many respects a duplicative program?

The program was officially killed on December 10, 1963 by Defense Secretary Robert McNamara because it was both expensive and pointless, although he didn't put it quite that way. Herbert York, director of the Advanced Research Projects Agency during the Dyna-Soar years, was more direct. He later observed that Dyna-Soar—as well as an even more fantastic contemporary project, the Aerospace Plane—"involved getting Air Force pilots into space," a "basic goal" that the Air Force pursued with "great zeal and emotion." And yet, "What became of all the new [military-space] ideas born out of the reactions to Sputnik? Where did they lead us? What did they contribute to our security in general and to closing the missile gap in particular? The surprising, perhaps unbelievable, yet most significant answers to these three questions are: Nothing, nowhere, nothing."[12]

———❖———

Despite the skepticism expressed by McNamara, York, and others, the dream of Saenger-like projects did not die with Dyna-Soar. Sporadic research continued and it was given a major boost in the 1980s, when President Reagan said in his 1986 State of the Union speech that the United States was moving ahead on several exciting scientific and technological projects, including a space plane. "We're going forward with our shuttle flights. We're going forward to build our space station. And we are going forward with research on a new Orient Express that could, by the end of the next decade, take off from Dulles Airport, accelerate up to twenty-five times the speed of sound, attaining low Earth orbit or flying to Tokyo within two hours."[13]

The president was referring to research then underway on a National Aero-Space Plane, not to be confused with the Air Force's ill-fated Aerospace Plane of the late 1950s and 1960s. (Hyphenating "aerospace" was supposed to be enough to separate the two projects in people's minds.) As the president suggested, the National Aero-Space Plane might become a civilian transport as well as a military plane. The key word was "might." The program was exclusively a military project. Among the Air Force missions it might perform were strategic bombing, reconnaissance, in-orbit inspection of satellites launched by other nations, and even the "interdiction" of these satellites, should that prove necessary.[14]

Once again, little came of the idea. The people running the program—officially called the "X-30"—counted on the maturing of technologies not yet invented. The National Aero-Space Plane, said Richard P. Hallion, one of the nation's most respected historians of the Air Force, "engendered extraordinary controversy over its lifetime (which coincided with an era of declining military budgets, a decline in aerospace research investment, and new demands for what investment monies did exist)." One 1992 review of the program, quoted by Hallion, noted: "The NASP program's seven-year history has been characterized by turmoil, changes in focus, and unmet expectations." The program died in 1995, Hallion added, "amid a welter of problems, including declining support, rising costs, questionable performance, and serious and persistent technical challenges."[15]

⟩⟩⦿⟨⟨

The space bomber idea, whether manned or unmanned, has more lives than any feline, domestic or feral. Early in the research game, American aficionados of Saenger understood that he and Bredt had been far too optimistic or just plain wrong about many things in their technical analyses, especially his beloved *Rikoschettier* skip-glide-skip concept. Repeated dips into the atmosphere and bounce-backs would stress the ship beyond its breaking point. But space bomber partisans believed that Saenger and Bredt had been on target about one big thing: If it were possible to launch a certain kind of machine into space, it could then reenter the atmosphere and glide to any point on Earth. The Space Shuttle's orbiters hinted at the many possibilities.

The orbiters in the Space Shuttle program, however, were not and are not highly maneuverable once they reenter the atmosphere. They have to hit their reentry "window" precisely in order to glide to a safe landing on the target runway. But what if one could design a reentry vehicle that would be highly maneuverable once it reentered the atmosphere? Would that not be the near-perfect, stealthy, unstoppable, strike-at-a-distance weapon?

That is what the Project FALCON/Common Aero Vehicle program, in its 2003 incarnation, was all about. But, as noted in Chapter Five, Congress balked at the weapons implications of FALCON—after all, the acronym, *F*orce *A*pplication and *L*aunch from *CON*us left little to the imagination. The name of the project was soon changed to the Falcon Hypersonic Technology Vehicle program.

With that change, "Falcon" was no longer an acronym. That not-so-subtle change may have been designed to assuage members of Congress who fretted over the baldly described weapons mission of FALCON, circa 2003. DARPA's new description of Falcon, publicly issued in January 2006, no longer referred to a weapon system. It did, however, assert that the program was designed to "enable prompt global reach missions and demonstrate affordable and responsive space lift." The old "global strike" language was gone. But what, precisely, was meant by the reference—*wink-wink*—to "global reach"? In the Falcon Fact sheet, the first paragraph under the heading, "Program Vision," said:

The Government's vision of an ultimate prompt global reach capability (circa 2025 and beyond) is engendered in a reusable hypersonic cruise vehicle. This autonomous aircraft would be capable of taking off from a conventional military runway, carrying a 12,000-pound payload, and reaching distances of 9,000 nautical miles in less than two hours. This hypersonic cruise vehicle will provide the country with a significant capability to conduct responsive missions with quick turn-around sortie rates while providing aircraft-like operability and mission-recall capability.[16]

Twelve-thousand-pound payload? Responsive missions with quick turn-around sortie rates? Falcon still quacked like a duck and walked like a duck. Any system with such capabilities would be able to launch Common Aero Vehicles—potential do-anything global-strike weapons.

If he were alive today, Eugen Saenger would be amused. He would immediately understand the FALCON/Falcon concept. To be sure, whatever the United States comes up with over the next several years as work continues will be far removed from his cherished *Silverbird*. Yet, in a fundamental way, it would be the same old thing. In the military, some old ideas die; others are simply restructured, renamed, and reborn.

Appendix E
Useful Websites

The Air Force Association, the premier lobbying organization for the Air Force. Plug "space" into search box and proceed.
http://www.afa.org/aef/

Air Force Space Command
http://www.afspc.af.mil/

Air & Space Power Journal, a must-read Air Force publication. Current and back issues are easily accessed.
http://www.airpower.maxwell.af.mil/airchronicles/apje.html

Air War College Gateway to the Internet, an extraordinary site that can be used for deep explorations of many military-related topics, including space.
http://www.au.af.mil/au/awc/awcgate/awcgate.htm

Center for Defense Information, a global leader in the space arms control movement. Click on "Space Security."
http://www.cdi.org/

Center for Nonproliferation Studies at the Monterey Institute for International Studies. Click on "Current and Future Space Security" for first-rate analyses.
http://cns.miis.edu/

Disarmament Diplomacy, an online journal that provides factual information and analyses relevant to all aspects of arms control, including space.
http://www.acronym.org.uk/

Eisenhower Institute, a think tank with expansive and in-depth analyses and studies. Plug "space" into search box.
http://www.eisenhowerinstitute.org/

Global Network Against Weapons and Nuclear Power in Space, an online meeting place for the activist community.
http://www.space4peace.org/

GlobalSecurity.org, a site maintained by John Pike, who has been deeply engaged in military space issues for many years. Click on "space."
http://www.globalsecurity.org/

George C. Marshall Institute, a comprehensive space-warrior site.
http://www.marshall.org/

Missile Defense Advocacy Alliance.
http://www.missiledefenseadvocacy.org/

Missile Defense Agency.
http://www.mda.mil/mdalink/html/mdalink.html

NASA gateway to military-space sites.
http://www.hq.nasa.gov/office/hqlibrary/pathfinders/milspace.htm

NASA's list of key documents in the history of space policy.
http://history.nasa.gov/spdocs.html

James Oberg, the personal website of one of the country's most astute space commentators.
http://www.jamesoberg.com/

OnPower.org, a project of the Center on Peace & Liberty at the Independent Institute.
http://www.onpower.org/

Reaching Critical Will, a complete source of statements made at the Conference on Disarmament, including space-related issues.
http://www.reachingcriticalwill.org/

Secure World Foundation, a site with a growing focus on space issues.
http://www.secureworldfoundation.org

Russian Space Web, a fascinating window into the history of the old Soviet space program, as well as up-to-date information on the Russian program.
http://www.russianspaceweb.com/

Space Review, an easy-to-read online magazine on all manner of space-related topics, commercial, scientific, military, historical, and futuristic.
http://www.thespacereview.com/

Space.com, an invaluable resource.
http://www.space.com/

SpaceDebate.org, a relatively new blog-like site that grows more useful every week.
http://www.spacedebate.org/

Spacewar.com, another good resource.
http://www.spacewar.com/

Henry L. Stimson Center, a think tank that has refined the "rules of the road" concept to a high degree. Plug "space" into the search box.
http://www.stimson.org

Union of Concerned Scientists, a major site for factual data and rigorous analysis. Plug "outer space" into the search box.
http://www.ucsusa.org/

Notes

PREFACE

1. Herman Melville, *White-Jacket* (New York: 1892), chapter 36.

CHAPTER I

1. Bill Gunston and Sharon Lucas, eds., *Aviation Year by Year* (London: Dorling Kindersley, Ltd., 2001), 17.

2. F. Stansbury Haydon, *Aeronautics in the Union and Confederate Armies* (New York: Arno, reprinted 1980), 2.

3. Peter Mead, *The Eye in the Air: History of Air Observation and Reconnaissance for the Army 1785–1945* (London: Her Majesty's Stationery Office, 1983), 14.

4. Paul Dickson's *Sputnik: The Shock of the Century* (New York: Walker Publishing Co., 2001) is lively reading. James R. Killian's *Sputnik, Scientists, and Eisenhower: A Memoir of the First Special Assistant to the President for Science and Technology* (Cambridge, MA: MIT Press, 1977), is less lively but offers a fascinating inside-the-Oval-Office perspective. For another insider look, see Chapter Six of Herbert York's *Race to Oblivion: A Participant's View of the Arms Race* (New York: Simon and Schuster, 1970).

5. Howard E. McCurdy, *Space and the American Imagination* (Washington, DC: Smithsonian Institution Press, 1997), 75.

6. Ibid., 74. Senator Johnson was echoing an already-old idea. Producer George Pal's *Destination Moon*, released in 1950, was a minor Cold War classic. At a pivotal point in the movie, industrialist Jim Barnes tells a gathering of fellow tycoons that they must help the Air Force build a rocket to get to the Moon. "We're not the only ones planning to go there," he says ominously. "The race is on, and we better win it, because there is absolutely no way to stop an attack from outer space. The first country that can use the Moon for the launching of missiles will control the Earth. That, gentleman, is the most important military fact of our century."

7. The speech, "Space Control and National Security," was reprinted in *Space Weapons: A Handbook of Military Astronautics*, James H. Straubel et al., eds. (New York: Frederick A. Praeger, Publishers, 1959). The book was a collection of articles from *Air Force Magazine*.

8. Diplomat Paul H. Nitze, a national security adviser to presidents from Truman to Reagan and a quintessential hardliner, regarded massive retaliation as "merely a declaratory policy,

while our action policy was graduated deterrence." He defined graduated deterrence "as a policy of limiting wars—in weapons, targets, area, and time—to the minimum force necessary to deter and, if necessary, to repel aggression." (Paul Nitze (*From Hiroshima to Glasnost*, (New York: Grove Weidenfeld), 152.) See also Robert R. Bowie and Richard H. Immerman, *Waging Peace: How Eisenhower Shaped an Enduring Cold War Strategy* (Oxford and New York: Oxford University Press, 2000); Harold Stassen and Marshall Houts, *Eisenhower: Turning the World Toward Peace* (St. Paul: Merrill/Magnus Publishing Corp, 1990; Campbell Craig, *Destroying the Village* (New York: Columbia University Press, 1998).

9. U.S. Department of State, *Foreign Relations of the United States, 1955–1957*, Vol. XI, "United Nations and General International Matters," 1988, 725, points 7 and 8.

10. *Department of State Bulletin*, October 30, 1967, 565.

11. For a close look at the development of the treaty, with an emphasis on U.S.-Soviet Cold War posturing, see "The Emergence of Cooperative Restraint: 1962–1975," Chapter Four of James Clay Moltz's *The Politics of Space Security, 1957–2007: Strategic Restraint and the Pursuit of National Interests* (Palo Alto, CA: Stanford University Press, forthcoming).

12. Glenn H. Reynolds and Robert P. Merges, *Outer Space Problems of Law and Policy* (Boulder, CO: Westview Press, 1997), 48.

13. The treaty can be found at http://www.state.gov/t/ac/trt/5181.htm.

14. Sen. Bob Smith, "The Challenge of Space Power," *Airpower Journal* (now *Air & Space Power Journal*), Spring 1999, http://www.airpower.maxwell.af.mil/airchronicles/apj/apj99/spr99/smith.html.

15. In spring 2006, the name of the Space Warfare Center was changed to the less provocative "Space Innovation and Development Center." "One of the things I want people to understand is that there's no change in our mission," said the unit's commander. Air Force Space Command news release dated March 10, 2006, http://www.afspc.af.mil/news/story.asp?storyID=123017237.

16. The majority of the other twelve members of the Rumsfeld-chaired Space Commission were retired military men. Retired Generals Howell M. Estes, Ronald R. Fogleman, Charles A. Horner, and Thomas S. Moorman, Jr., had served in the Air Force, as had Duane P. Andrews, who had also served as a House staffer and assistant secretary of defense. Lt. Gen. Jay M. Garner and Gen. Glenn K. Otis were retired from the Army, as was Douglas H. Necessary, who had also served as a House staffer. Admiral David E. Jeremiah was retired from the U.S. Navy. Robert V. Davis had served as House Staffer and an under secretary of defense, and William R. Graham had served as science adviser to President Ronald Reagan. Malcolm Wallop was a retired senator from Wyoming.

17. For a succinct and prescient resume of Rumsfeld's career before becoming George W. Bush's secretary of defense, see "Darth Rumsfeld" *American Prospect*, February 26, 2001, http://www.prospect.org/print/V12/4/vest-j.html. For a more adoring view, see an interview by neoconservative doyen Midge Decter, *National Review Online*, http://www.nationalreview.com/interrogatory/decter200310300716.asp.

18. One wonders, for instance, if Donald Rumsfeld ever framed the grip-and-grin photo of him shaking hands with Saddam Hussein on December 20, 1983. The photo-op occurred in Baghdad nearly four years into the Iraq-Iran war, which Iraq had begun by attacking Iran. By then, U.S. intelligence agencies had established that Saddam had used chemical weapons (a.k.a. "weapons of mass destruction") against Iranian soldiers. That fact discomfited the U.S. government, but only to a modest degree. Iraqi oil was important to America. Rumsfeld, then head of G.D. Searle, was dispatched to the Middle East as a

special presidential envoy. Although the United States remained officially neutral during the war, part of Rumsfeld's mission was to reassure Saddam that the United States still favored Iraq. According to an official State Department summary, Rumsfeld failed to bring up the unpleasant topic of chemical weapons. But the future defense secretary did say that "independent and sovereign nations had a right to undertake activities with which we or others did not agree." The State Department summary of the meeting said that Saddam Hussein showed "obvious pleasure" with "Rumsfeld's visit and remarks." The meeting is documented in *National Security Archive Electronic Briefing No. 82* titled "Shaking Hands with Saddam Hussein: The U.S. Tilts Toward Iraq, 1980–1984," http://www.gwu.edu/~nsarchiv/NSAEBB/NSAEBB82/index.htm.

19. Go to http://www.fas.org/irp/threat/missile/rumsfeld/.

20. The Report of the Commission to Assess United States National Security, Space Management and Organization, 2001 (hereinafter, "Space Commission"). It can be downloaded, section by section, from http://www.fas.org/spp/military/commission/report.htm.

21. Space Commission, 25.

22. Ibid., 17; Steven Lambakis, *On the Edge of Earth: The Future of American Space Power* (Lexington, KY: University Press of Kentucky, 2001) is an excellent summary of the evolution of national space policy from Eisenhower to Clinton.

23. Space Commission, 28–32.

24. Ibid., 33.

25. Go to http://www.defenselink.mil/Transcripts/Transcript.aspx?TranscriptID=1087.

26. *Vision 2020* may be difficult to find. For a pdf version, see http://www.middlepowers.org/gsi/docs/vision_2020.pdf (as of May 2007). For an htm version, see http://www.fas.org/spp/military/docops/usspac/lrp/ch02.htm.

27. The *Long Range Plan* can be accessed chapter-by-chapter at http://www.fas.org/spp/military/docops/usspac/lrp/toc.htm. See Chapter Six, the section titled "Force Application."

28. Ibid., Chapter One, section titled "Foreign Threat," "Future Strategic Environment."

29. For a comprehensive look at mutual U.S.-Soviet restraint in space during the Cold War, see Moltz, *The Politics of Space Security.*

30. Air Force Space Command, *Strategic Master Plan 06,* can be found at http://www.cdi.org/news/space-security/afspc-strategic-master-plan-06-beyond.pdf.

31. Everett C. Dolman, *Astropolitik: Classical Geopolitics in the Space Age* (London: Frank Cass, 2002), 158.

CHAPTER 2

1. Robert Coram, *Boyd: The Fighter Pilot Who Changed the Art of War* (New York: Little Brown, Back Bay Books, 2004) is immensely readable. There are thousands of references to Boyd on the Internet—use the search terms "John Boyd" and "Strategy."

2. Sun-tzu, *The Art of Warfare*, trans. R. T. Ames, ed. R. G. Henricks (New York: Ballantine Books, 1998), 95.

3. Boyd may have been a military genius, but he was sorely lacking in traditional communications skills. His briefing slides were complex, often arcane, and always repetitive. See Boyd's "Patterns of Conflict" at http://www.d-n-i.net/boyd/patterns.ppt, particularly slide 131. See also Coram, 334–39.

4. Coram, 335.

5. Ibid., 226.

6. "Network-Centric" or "netcentric" defines the way America's armed forces fight. For an overview, see Defense Department, Office of Force Transformation, *The Implementation of Network-Centric Warfare*, 2004, http://www.oft.osd.mil/library/library_files/document_387_NCW_Book_LowRes.pdf.

7. "U.S. Mulls Air Strategies in Iraq," *Christian Science Monitor,* http://www.csmonitor.com/2003/0130/p06s01-woiq.htm. Whether the early air attacks against Iraq in March 2003 actually constituted "true" shock and awe is controversial. The prevailing view among military analysts seems to be that the actual bomb and missile attacks were a limited shock-and-awe effort. For an excellent summary of the controversy, sees "What Happened to Shock and Awe," *Air Force,* November 2003, http://www.afa.org/magazine/Nov2003/1103shock.asp.

8. Directorate of Advanced Concepts, Technologies, and Information Strategies, *Shock & Awe: Achieving Rapid Dominance* (National Defense University, 1996), http://www.ndu.edu/inss/books/books%20-%201996/Shock%20and%20Awe%20-%20Dec%2096/.

9. Ibid., "Introduction to Rapid Dominance."

10. "What Happened to Shock and Awe," *Air Force*, endnote 5.

11. Bob Woodward, *Plan of Attack* (New York; Simon & Schuster, 2004), 102.

12. Defense Department, *Joint Vision 2020*, http://www.dtic.mil/jointvision/jvpub2.htm. See "Full Spectrum Dominance."

13. The 2002 *National Security Strategy* can be found at http://www.whitehouse.gov/nsc/nssintro.html. The 2006 *Security Strategy* can be found at http://www.whitehouse.gov/nsc/nss/2006/.

14. *Army Space Journal*, Fall 2004, 12, http://www.smdc-armyforces.army.mil/SpaceJournal/ASJ_fall_2004_VOL_3_NO_2_Final.pdf. The entire issue is devoted to future concepts of space-aided warfare.

15. Arthur K. Cebrowski , Statement before the Senate Subcommittee on Strategic Forces, March 25, 2004, http://www.fas.org/irp/congress/2004_hr/032504cebrowski.pdf.

16. Alfred Thayer Mahan, *The Influence of Sea Power Upon History 1660–1783* (New York: Dover Publications, 1987), 138.

17. Department of Defense Directive No. 3100.10, dated July 9, 1999, paragraph 4.2.1, http://www.fas.org/spp/military/docops/defense/d310010p.htm.

18. Air Force Space Command, *Strategic Master Plan FY04 and Beyond*, Foreword. The plan, superseded by a FYO6 plan (http://www.cdi.org/news/space-security/afspc-strategic-master-plan-06-beyond.pdf), is no longer easily found on the Worldwide Web. As of May 2007, it could be found at http://www.thememoryhole.org/mil/space-command-plan-fy2004.pdf.

19. Dolman, *Astropolitik*, 156.

20. John J. Mearsheimer, *The Tragedy of Great Power Politics* (New York: W. W. Norton & Co., 2001), 2. See especially Chapter Two, "Anarchy and the Struggle for Power," and Chapter Ten, "Great Power Politics in the Twenty-first Century."

21. Richard Rhodes, *The Making of the Atomic Bomb* (New York: Simon & Schuster, A Touchstone Book), 1988, 388.

22. Fred Kaplan, *The Wizards of Armageddon* (Stanford, CA: Stanford University Press, 1991), 347.

23. *National Security Strategy 2002.*

24. A transcript of Rumsfeld's press briefing on September 26, 2002, is at http://www.defenselink.mil/Transcripts/Transcript.aspx?TranscriptID=3669. Here is the section of the briefing in which Rumsfeld's word confusion reigned:

Question: I want to return to the question of preemption, if I could. In the new national security strategy, and also in your testimony last week up on the Hill, the word preemption and prevention was used almost interchangeably. But as a matter of military doctrine, and of international practice, there is a distinction. I was curious if in this current threat environment you see that distinction blurring? And when we talk about Iraq, although no decision's been made, do you see it as a preemptive war against an imminent threat or a preventive war to keep them from becoming a greater threat?

Rumsfeld: I would have to go get my dictionary and talk to some experts on international law. You're right, there are differences in those words and their meanings and their historical use. And I may be a bit sloppy in using them somewhat interchangeably. I often use more than one, and the reason I do is for—is to try to add dimension to what people are hearing.

I mean, if you think about it, defense is one word, and you can do that in a variety of different ways. Everyone agrees that self-defense is legitimate, legal, domestically, internationally, and it's accepted. The concept of anticipatory self-defense is also something that goes back historically a long time. People have always preferred to have battles take place not on their real estate, but on somebody else's real estate. And as they see things developing, they have attempted to stop them before they actually adversely affected their population and their real estate.

Prevention is also—has a connotation that's somewhat more acceptable than preemption. It sounds a little fairer—if there is such a word; that you're trying to prevent something from happening at the last minute is the implication—the connotation of that word to me.

Preemption is slightly different in the sense that it suggests that you have reason to believe something's going to happen, could happen, that is notably unpleasant, and you make a conscious decision to go out and stop that from happening.

25. See http://www.dtic.mil/doctrine/jel/doddict/.
26. Selig S. Harrison, "The United States and South Asia: Trapped by the Past?" *Current History*, December 1997, http://www.currenthistory.com/archivedec97/harrison.html.
27. *U.S. Coercion in a World of Proliferating and Varied WMD Capabilities: Final Report for the Project on Deterrence and Cooperation in a Multi-Tiered Nuclear World*, February 2001, page 8, http://globalsecurity.org/wmd/library/report/2001/deterrence.doc. Study conducted under contract for DARPA's Advanced Systems and Concepts Office by DFI International, Anthony Fainberg, Supervising Project Officer.

CHAPTER 3

1. Stockholm International Peace Research Institute (SIPRI), http://www.sipri.org. For the most up-to-date information, see "Recent Trends in Military Expenditure."
2. Perhaps the best inside look at the war is Wesley K. Clark's, *Waging Modern War: Bosnia, Kosovo, and the Future of Combat* (New York: Perseus Books Group, Public Affairs, 2001). Clark was supreme allied commander, Europe, at the time of the conflict over Kosovo and his book examines the conflict in its full political and diplomatic context.
3. See, for instance, Peter Grier, "The Sensational Signal" *Air Force,* February 2005, http://www.afa.org/magazine/Feb2003/02signal03.asp.
4. For a time, the Pentagon attempted to keep precise details about the accuracy of JDAMs a secret. That was hopeless. During the conflicts in Afghanistan and Iraq, journalists caught

on to the fact that JDAMs were unbelievably accurate. Top Air Force brass now speak freely about it. Maj. General Thomas Taverny, mobilization assistant to the commander of Air Force Space Command, described JDAM accuracy at a Space Warfare Symposium in Keystone, Colorado in June 2006. A Space Command news release contained this paragraph: "The general said JDAMs allow B-52s to attack targets from twelve to twenty miles away without risking harm to aircrews. The weapon's accuracy is honed from three-hundred-meters using conventional bombs, to three meters using the Global Positioning System satellite constellation." The news release can be found at http://www.afspc.af.mil/news/story.asp?storyID=123022940.

5. Human Rights Watch, "The Crisis in Kosovo," http://www.hrw.org/reports/2000/nato/Natbm200-01.htm.

6. There has been a long and sometimes contentious debate in recent years on the meaning and the reality of the "Revolution in Military Affairs," now often called "transformation." The Project for Defense Alternatives has compiled an online guide to the debate, http://www.comw.org/rma/fulltext/overview.html.

7. Richard B. Myers, "Space Superiority is Fleeting," *Aviation Week & Space Technology*, January 1, 2000.

8. Go to http://www.aef.org/pub/teets1102.asp.

9. Space Commission, 19.

10. A background paper, "Threats to United States Space Capabilities" by Tom Wilson, a member of the Space Commission's staff, is especially useful, See http://www.globalsecurity.org/space/library/report/2001/nssmo/article05.html.

11. The director of the super-secret National Security Agency also heads the equally super-secret Joint Functional Component Command Network Warfare, which works closely with the Defense Information Systems Agency and the Joint Task Force for Global Network Operations. The other principal mission of the Joint Functional Component Command Network Warfare is to figure our how best to paralyze potential enemies with American cyber attacks.

12. Frank Tiboni, "DoD's 'Manhattan Project'," *Federal Computer World*, August 29, 2005, http://www.fcw.com/article90416-08-29-05-Print.

13. Bruce M. Deblois, Richard L. Garwin, R. Scott Kemp, and Jeremy C. Maxwell, "Space Weapons: Crossing the U.S. Rubicon," *International Security* 29, no. 2 (Fall 2004).

14. David A. Fulghum and Douglas Barrie, "Cracks in the Net," *Aviation Week & Space Technology*, June 30, 2003.

15. "Ensuring America's Space Security: Report of the FAS Panel on Weapons in Space," September 2004, Appendix B, 81, http://www.fas.org/main/content.jsp?formAction=297+contentid=311. See also Michael E. O'Hanlon, *Neither Star Wars nor Sanctuary: Constraining the Military Uses of Space* (Washington, DC: Brookings Institution Press, 2004), 125–26.

16. Government Accountability Office, *Space Acquisitions: DoD Needs Additional Knowledge as it Embarks on a New Approach for Transformational Satellite Communications System*, "Background" (Washington, DC: Government Accountability Office, May 2006), http://www.gao.gov/new.items/d06537.pdf.

17. Ibid.

18. Deblois et al., "Space Weapons," 61.

19. A description of the Mid-Infrared Advanced Chemical Laser (MIRACL) test can be found at http://www.fas.org/spp/military/program/asat/miracl.htm. News of the Chinese laser test or tests was leaked in September 2006. See Vago Muradian, "China Attempted

to Blind U.S. Satellites with Laser," DefenseNews.com, http://www.defensenews.com/story.php?:F=2121111&C=america.

20. Deblois et al., "Space Weapons," 59.

21. Space Commission, 29.

22. Ibid., 21.

23. For a description of the 1962 nuclear test series that included Starfish Prime, see the Nuclear Weapons Archive, http//nuclearweaponarchive.org/Usa/Tests/Dominic.html. A nighttime detonation of a 1.4 megaton weapon 248 miles above tiny Johnston Island on July 9, 1962 "appeared quite spectacular from Hawaii (800 miles away) and at Kwajalein (1600 miles away), with impressive light displays from an artificial aurora lasting up to seven minutes. The electromagnetic pulse (EMP) from this test sent power line surges throughout Oahu, knocking out street lighting, blowing fuses and circuit breakers, and triggering burglar alarms." The archive includes color photos.

24. Although the 2006 update is difficult to find, the 2001 version, "Twenty-first Century Threat Reduction: Nuclear Study Results from DTRA/ASCO" can be found at http://www.globalsecurity.org/wmd/library/report/2001/nuclearstudies.doc. The quotation is on page eight under the heading, "Assessing Nuclear Threats to Low-Earth Satellites."

25. Ibid., 9. Military satellites in low-Earth orbit are only lightly hardened against radiation. (Higher-orbit satellites are more fully hardened because they must contend with greater levels of natural radiation.) Further hardening of low-Earth-orbit satellites would make a big difference. With additional hardening, low-yield nuclear detonations in space "would still pose a prompt radiation threat to the 5–10 percent of low-Earth-orbit satellites within line of sight but would no longer substantially threaten 85–90 percent of satellites in low-Earth orbit. Such hardening has been estimated to add three percent to the cost of a low-Earth-orbit constellation."

26. "Report of the Commission to Assess the Threat to the United States from Electromagnetic Pulse (EMP) Attack," Volume 1, Executive Report, 2004, page 1, http://globalsecurity.org/wmd/library/congress/2004_r/04-07-22emp.pdf. Many knowledgeable people believe the threat to terrestrial systems was overblown by the commission. Philip Coyle, for example, the Pentagon's director of operational test and evaluation during the Clinton administration, questions the conclusion that small, kiloton-scale nuclear weapons would produce catastrophic consequences. "The U.S. military does not know how to do this today, and has no way of demonstrating the capability in the future without returning to nuclear testing," he says. "The fact is that a rogue nation or terrorists that tried this would be very unsure of the results, and would risk massive retaliation from the United States for having achieved nothing," http://www.nti.org/d_newswire/issues/2004/9/24/71161847-7641-4D8D-AF3A-D1819B145C42.html.

27. O'Hanlon, *Neither Star Wars*, 67. "Some argue that adversaries would desist from using nuclear weapons in space out of fear of retaliation. It is true, certainly, that this would be a provocative action with considerable potential for inciting some type of escalation from the United States. But the assumption that an enemy would be deterred for that reason is unconvincing and too optimistic. What better way to use nuclear weapons than to destroy a key military capability of an enemy country without killing any of its population? The United States could threaten nuclear retaliation after such an attack, but it is far from clear that such a threat would be credible—or even appropriate."

28. Limiting factors are the weight and size of the warhead. The ability to make a nuclear device of some sort is not the same as making a nuclear weapon compact and light

enough to be carried aloft by a low-performance missile. North Korea conducted its long anticipated first nuclear test in October 2006. It was a very low-yield device, a "fizzle" according to some American analysts. Currently, no one outside of North Korea's military program seems to know whether that backward state possesses the technological savvy to miniaturize a nuclear explosive device, a necessary step in the making of a weapon deliverable by a missile.

29. See, for instance, David Albright, "North Korea Drops Out," *Bulletin of the Atomic Scientists*, May 1993, 9–11.

30. See, for instance, David Albright and Mark Hibbs, "Iraq's Bomb: Blueprints and Artifacts," *Bulletin of the Atomic Scientists*, January/February 1992, 30–40.

31. James E. Oberg, *Space Power Theory* (U.S. Air Force Academy, 1999), 67. Available at http://space.au.af.mil/books/oberg/.

32. See especially David Wright, Laura Grego, and Lisbeth Gronlund, *The Physics of Space Security* (Cambridge, MA: American Academy of Sciences, 2005).

33. Philip J. Baines, "Prospects for Non-Offensive Defenses in Space," http://cms2000.isn.ch/pubs/ph/details.cfm?id=14393.

CHAPTER 4

1. Paul B. Stares, *The Militarization of Space: U.S. Policy 1945–1984* (Ithaca, N.Y.: Cornell University, 1985), 49.

2. The statement, drafted by the President's Science Advisory Committee, can be found at http://history.nasa.gov/sputnik/16.html.

3. Ibid.

4. James B. Gavin, *War and Peace in the Space Age* (London: Hutchinson & Co., 1959), 200.

5. Ibid., 213.

6. Ibid., 215.

7. Philip J. Klass, *Secret Sentries in Space,* (New York: Random House, 1971), 62. In February 1963, the chief of the Soviet Union's Strategic Rocket Forces asserted that "it has now become possible at a command from Earth to launch missiles from satellites at any desired time and at any point in the satellite trajectory." Robert Salkeld, *War and Space* (Englewood Cliffs, NJ: Prentice-Hall, 1970).

8. George B. Kistiakowsky, *A Scientist at the White House: The Private Diary of President Eisenhower's Special Assistant for Science and Technology* (Cambridge, MA: Harvard University Press, 1976), 229. See also Major General Oris B. Johnson, *Air University Review*, November/December 1968, http://www.airpower.maxwell.af.mil/airchronicles/1968/nov-dec/johnson.html. Johnson, commander of the Ninth Aerospace Defense Division, wrote: "Recognition of space as today's front line of defense demands commensurate emphasis on studies of defenses for every space weapon we can foresee, designs to counter every space weapon we find the enemy testing, and deployment of defense weapons against the existing space threat just as rapidly as cost-effective systems become available. We must be prepared, since the price of technological and operational surprise in the space age can be disaster. We can, and must, expend the effort to deter or win."

9. Laura Grego's "A History of ASAT Programs," http://www.ucsusa.org/global_security/space_weapons/a-history-of-asat-programs.html, is a concise introduction to the topic.

10. Clayton K.S. Chun, *Shooting Down a Star,* 21. This short but illuminating study of

the history of ASATs can be found at http://www.fas.org/spp/military/program/asat/ADA377346.htm.

11. The history of the Soviet co-orbital ASAT program, from a Russian perspective, is at http://www.russianspaceweb.com/is.html. RussianSpaceWeb.com is a rich source.

12. T. A. Heppenheimer, *Countdown: A History of Space Flight* (New York: John Wiley & Sons, 1997), 261. A somewhat different insight was offered by Herbert York in *Making Weapons, Talking Peace: A Physicist's Odyssey from Hiroshima to Geneva* (New York: Basic Books, 1987), 274–75. York, one of the nation's principal Cold War-era scientists and arms control negotiators was preparing for negotiations (the Strategic Arms Limitation Talks II) in 1978. He met privately with a top Soviet negotiator, a man who understood how things really worked in the Soviet Union. York asked about the Soviet ASAT system, which had greatly complicated the talks. "His reply was classic. In essence, he said, 'You know how it is. You have the same thing in your country. Some young, ambitious technicians get hold of an idea they believe is both practical and important, and they promote it and push it until finally the authorities let them go ahead with it.' I believed him. The Soviet ASAT was less the result of an action-reaction mechanism, or a calculation of military need, than a case of an interesting technology sold to a gullible and poorly informed leadership by aggressive salesmen. It happens often enough in the United States; how could it fail to happen in the Soviet Union?"

13. Stares, *Militarization of Space*, 197.

14. Roger C. Hunter, *A United States Antisatellite Policy for a Multipolar World*, University Press monograph, 18, at http://www.au.af.mil/au/aul/aupress////saas_Theses/SAASS_Out/Hunter/hunter.pdf.

15. Ibid., 202.

16. Ibid., 18.

17. See Stares, *Militarization of Space*, 192–200, for a succinct description.

18. See "The Death of the Solwind Satellite," Henry L. Stimson Center, http://www.stimson.org/?SN=WS20050714867.

19. David N. Spires, *Beyond Horizons: A Half Century of Air Force Space Leadership* (Maxwell Air Force Base, AL: Air University Press, 1998), 261.

20. Edgar Snow, *Journey to the Beginning* (New York: Random House, 1958), 360.

21. J. Robert Oppenheimer, "Atomic Weapons and American Foreign Policy," *Foreign Affairs*, July 1953, 529. See John Newhouse, *War and Peace in the Nuclear Age* (New York: Alfred A. Knopf, 1989), 92, for Eisenhower's role in encouraging Oppenheimer to write the article.

22. U.S. Department of State, *Foreign Relations of the United States*, 1952-54, Vol. XV, part 2, 1839.

23. See, for instance, Fred Inglis, *The Cruel Peace: Everyday Life and the Cold War* (New York: Basic Books, 1991); Spencer R. Weart, *Nuclear Fear: A History of Images* (Cambridge: Harvard University Press, 1988); Allan M. Winkler, *Life Under a Cloud: American Anxiety About the Atom* (New York and Oxford: Oxford University Press, 1993).

24. See "Launch on Warning: The Development of U.S. Capabilities, 1959–1979," a comprehensive online briefing book compiled by the non-profit National Security Archive, issued in April 2001, http://www.gwu.edu/~nsarchiv/NSAEBB/NSAEBB-43.

25. Albert Wohlstetter's classic, "The Delicate Balance of Terror," published in 1958, at http://www.rand.org/publications/classics/wohlstetter/P1472/P1472.html, was a product of the bomber age. For insight into presumed Soviet perfidy during the missile age, see Charles

Tyroler II, ed., *Alerting America* (Washington, DC: Pergamon-Brassey's, 1984), a compendium of papers produced by the Committee on the Present Danger, which included Ronald Reagan on its rolls.

26. Gregg Herken, *Counsels of War* (New York: Alfred A. Knopf, 1985), 116.

27. Nitze, *From Hiroshima*, 166. Nitze's chilling observation: "In a situation in which two countries or blocs are more or less even in nuclear military capabilities, and those capabilities are vulnerable to destruction if struck before they are used, the value of an initial strike would be immense. This could result in serious instability in a crisis.

"The United States, for example, would look with grave suspicion on any action on the part of the Russians that would indicate they were preparing a first strike. This could well lead the United States to consider a preemptive strike.

"The Soviet Union, in an effort to keep one or two moves ahead of us, might well feel that it should strike even sooner than planned to head off our preemptive blow. I could foresee the possibility of a situation arising in which there would be such an interaction of fear that it would be almost impossible to conceive how statesmen could prevent the situation from deteriorating into war."

MAD was supposed to enhance "crisis stability," thus promoting a climate in which the United States and the Soviet Union could engage in nuclear arms control talks. Nitze offers a detailed insider's account of such talks in his book.

28. Hundreds of books deal with the nuclear arms race. One cannot go wrong by starting with *Counsels of War* by Gregg Herken, *The Wizards of Armageddon* by Fred Kaplan, and *War and Peace in the Nuclear Age* by John Newhouse.

29. "Nuclear Notebook," *Bulletin of the Atomic Scientists*, November/December 1997, 67.

30. I had an uneasy conversation some years back with a man familiar with the arcana of U.S. nuclear targeting. He said that Americans commonly believed that major American cities would be struck by "only" one or two nuclear weapons in the event of all-out war, meaning that people living several miles from ground zero would have a decent chance of survival. I noted that I lived in Chicago, about twelve miles from the city's center. Don't sleep easy, he said. "If the Soviets target the United States the way we target the Soviet Union, the Chicago area probably would be hit by something like thirty or forty weapons."

31. A cyber-mountain of material on the ABM treaty can be found on the Web. But Matthew Evangelista's *Unarmed Forces: The Transnational Movement to End the Cold War* (Ithaca, NY: Cornell University Press, 1999) does a terrific job of putting the treaty into historical context.

32. An added benefit: If both sides believed they had sufficiently "robust" survivable retaliatory forces, they would presumably have the confidence to engage in the kind of diplomacy that would—over time—further stabilize East-West relations. These diplomatic efforts would eventually end the arms race and even scale back the numbers of nuclear weapons and missiles. Over the past two decades, a series of bilateral arms control talks, treaties, and agreements have reduced the combined nuclear stockpiles to the point that weapons are now counted in the thousands instead of *tens* of thousands. That looks like progress to some; to others, it is small comfort.

33. Reagan's "ash heap" speech can be found at http://www.reagan.utexas.edu/archives/speeches/1982/60882a.htm.

34. Paul Lettow, *Ronald Reagan and His Quest to Abolish Nuclear Weapons* (New York: Random House, 2005), 132. Reagan sought to achieve clear military dominance of the Soviet

Union as a way of forcing an end to the Cold War. Only then could the two nations aggressively pursue nuclear disarmament. Most of Reagan's advisers supported military dominance, full stop. The pursuit of nuclear abolition was, in their view, irrational.

35. Reagan's "Star Wars" speech can be found at http://www.reagan.utexas.edu/archives/speeches/1983/32383d.htm.

36. Lettow, *Ronald Reagan and His Quest*, 23.

37. Ibid., 19.

38. See, for instance, Frances Fitzgerald, *Way Out There in the Blue: Reagan, Star Wars and the End of the Cold War* (New York: Touchstone/Simon & Schuster, 2000), and William J. Broad, *Teller's War: the Top-Secret Story Behind the Star Wars Deception* (New York: Simon & Schuster, 1992). Both paint a picture of a man who was in over his head regarding the scientific end of Star Wars.

39. Go to the Missile Defense Agency website at www.mda.mil/mdalink/html/mdalink.html. It describes a sharply limited system compared to President Reagan's Strategic Defense Initiative.

40. See, for instance, Nitze, *From Hiroshima*, 405.

41. Fitzgerald, *Way Out There*, 248–255.

42. Go to "Star Wars and Geneva" at http://www.fas.org/rlg/850909-sdi.htm.

43. For background on North Korea's missile program see "North Korean Ballistic Missile Capabilities, http://cns.miis.edu/research/korea/index.htm.

44. *Countermeasures*, http://www.ucsusa.org/assets/documents/global_security/CM_all.pdf, is extraordinarily eye-opening.

45. See, for instance, Jeremy Singer, "Test Ease Overheating Concerns With MKV Technology," at Space.com, http://www.space.com/spacenews/archive05/MKV_101705.html.

46. Press Release, "Economists Predict Missile Defense to Cost $1 Trillion," January 2, 2003, http://www.armscontrolcenter.org/archives/000255.php.

47. "Reinventing Multilateralism," study by the Program in Arms Control, Disarmament, and International Security, University of Illinois, http://www.acdis.uiuc.edu/Reinventing/ch_P.shtml.

48. David Wright and Laura Grego, "Anti-Satellite Capabilities of Planned US Missile Defence Systems," *Disarmament Diplomacy*, December 2002/January 2003, offers a succinct description of how antiballistic missile systems can be adapted for use against satellites, http://www.acronym.org.uk/dd/dd68/68op02.htm.

49. Charles Aldinger, "General Warns: High-Tech Warfare Could Litter Space with Debris," Space.Com, March 28, 2001, http://www.space.com/news/spaceagencies/space_war_debris_010328_wg.html.

CHAPTER 5

1. Eugene M. Emme, ed., *The Impact of Air Power: National Security and World Politics* (Princeton, NJ: D. Van Nostrand, 1959), 671–72.

2. Paul Lashmar, *Spy Flights of the Cold War* (Thrupp, England: Sutton Publishing, 1996), 84–88. One of the most provocative of the early spy flights occurred on May 8, 1954. The plane, a B-47 equipped for reconnaissance, was piloted by Harold "Hal" Austin, who took off from an airbase near Oxford, England and headed northeast over Norway, Sweden, and Finland to Murmansk, on the northern edge of the Kola Peninsula, far above the

Arctic Circle. Then Austin turned southeast over the White Sea toward Arkhangel.

The region, studded with military installations, was one of the most sensitive areas of the Soviet Union. Soviet interceptors attempted to down Austin's plane. Although the plane was hit, it made it to safe territory, Finland. As the plane left the Soviet Union, said Austin's co-pilot, Carl Holt, "One of the remaining fighter pilots flew up to our right wing and gave us a salute and then turned back."

Austin and his two-man crew later met with LeMay, who presented each man with a Distinguished Flying Cross, as he often did when his men completed a deep reconnaissance mission. He apologized for the fact that it was not a Silver Star. But Silver Stars would have to be approved in Washington, LeMay said, and "I'd have to explain this mission to too damn many people who don't need to know."

Later, Austin recalled a puzzling conversation with LeMay at the pre-mission briefing, "Well, maybe if we do this overflight right, we can get World War III started." Austin thought that was probably a "loose comment, for his staff guys." General Thomas S. Power, LeMay's second in command, chuckled. "General Power never laughed very much, so I always figured that was kind of a joke between them in some way or another."

Some thirty years later, Austin was marketing director for Air Force Village West retirement community and LeMay was chairman of the board. The two often talked. One day Austin brought up the May 8, 1954 mission. LeMay remembered it "as if it were yesterday," said Austin. They chatted about it for a while and then LeMay said, "Well, we'd have been a hell of a lot better off if we'd got World War III started in those days." See "A Cold War Overflight of the USSR" by Hal Austin, http://www.b-47.com/Stories/austin/austin.html.

3. Curtis E. LeMay, with MacKinlay Kantor, *Mission with LeMay: My Story* (Garden City, NY: Doubleday, 1965), 481–82.

4. Strategic Command mission statement, http://www.stratcom.mil. It reads: "Provide the nation with global deterrence capabilities and *synchronized DoD* [Defense Department] *effects to combat adversary weapons of mass destruction worldwide.* Enable decisive global kinetic and non-kinetic combat effects through the application and advocacy of integrated intelligence, surveillance and reconnaissance (ISR); space and global strike operations; information operations; integrated missile defense and robust command and control." (Italics added.) The phrase, "synchronized DoD effects to combat adversary weapons of mass destruction worldwide" opens the door for preemptive attack.

5. Quoted in William H. Kauffman and John D. Steinbruner, *Decisions for Defense: Prospects for a New Order* (Washington, DC: Brookings Institution Press, 1991), 45.

6. See, for instance, Thomas Schelling, "The Legacy of Hiroshima: a Half-Century Without Nuclear War," http://www.publicpolicy.umd.edu/IPPP/Summer00/legacy_of_hiroshima.htm.

7. William M. Arkin and Robert S. Norris, "Tiny Nukes for Mini-minds," *Bulletin of the Atomic Scientists*, April 1992.

8. *Nuclear Posture Review* [Excerpts], 2001. Despite its December 2001 date, the document was not a response to the attacks of September 11, 2001. It had been in the works for several years. Go to http://www.globalsecurity.org/wmd/library/policy/dod/npr.htm.

9. Ibid., "Defeating Hard and Deeply Buried Targets."

10. *National Strategy to Combat Weapons of Mass Destruction*, 2002, http://www.fas.org/irp/offdocs/nspd/nspd-17.html.

11. Linton F. Brooks, speech to the Heritage Foundation, May 12, 2004. The speech is no

longer on the foundation's website or the website of Los Alamos National Laboratory, although in February 2007 there was an inoperative link at the lab site. (Brooks oversaw America's nuclear-weapons complex, including Los Alamos.) A copy may be found at http://partnershipforglobalsecurity.org/documents/speech_heritage_nuclear_policy_ (5-04).pdf.

12. James E. Cartwright, StratCom commander, Testimony, Senate Armed Services Committee, April 18, 2005, http://www.fas.org/ssp/docs/GlobalStrikeReport.pdf, p. 33. This exchange took place with Jeff Sessions, a Republican from Alabama:

Sessions: How do you share—how would you explain to us a global strike concept? How do you utilize that, what the president and secretary of defense would like to see? And how are you getting along toward achieving it?

Cartwright: Global strike is one of our mission areas. It provides to the nation the ability to rapidly plan and rapidly deliver effect to any place on the globe. It allows us to provide effect for a regional combatant commander, if that's appropriate. Say, in the case of Central Command, [Lt.] General [John P.] Abizaid allows us to provide a strategic capability which, again, is not necessarily nuclear, for that regional combatant commander, to tailor it for his target and deliver it very quickly with very short timelines on the planning and delivery, any place on the face of the earth.

Sessions: Is that possible? Can we—do we have the technology that's available today that—if you had the money, that you could, within a short period of time, deliver a conventional weapon anywhere in the world?

Cartwright: Even with the money right now, we have technical challenges that we have to overcome in order to get this capability. If we're talking about non-kinetic [information warfare], we can move pretty much anyplace on the Earth at the speed of light in cyber-type capabilities. But the conventional-type capabilities and the nuclear type capabilities, nuclear right now is delivered in our missiles at very high speeds, at very long ranges. Our bombers have very long ranges, not quite the speeds. But trying to pull those attributes together with both conventional and nuclear kinetic effects is a little bit of what we're trying to work at in the global strike arena....

Sessions: That's the joint strike capability you're working on?

Cartwright: The global strike? Yes, sir....

Sessions: But in terms of explosive power, a nuclear weapon on a missile, for example, would have far more explosive power than a conventional munition would?

Cartwright: Yes, sir. But, again, if it—

Sessions: I would say it does, but the point is that a conventional munition might not be sufficient under certain circumstances.

Cartwright: Under certain circumstances. And there are circumstances in which that is the case.

Sessions: With regard to the hard and deeply buried targets, I know a number of our adversaries are proud of their tunneling ability and have worked hard to place deep in the ground and in mountains and other areas their strategic capability. Would you explain, General Cartwright, what your concerns are in that regard? What you feel like is—we need to be capable of neutralizing that capability that our adversaries have.... So are we there? Is a study of the capabilities of [the proposed] Deep Earth Penetrator, in your opinion, justified to see if something like that is feasible? And do you support it and why?

Cartwright: Yes, sir. First, I would say that this target set of buried and deeply buried and hardened targets is a very real target set and that it is growing. And...if an enemy has a capability that they want to protect, they generally move towards some way to disguise, deceive us about its capability and its location to thwart our targeting and our weapons capabilities. Oftentimes they go to mobility, sometimes they go to cover, sometimes they bury deeply.… The Robust Nuclear Earth Penetrator is one of several capabilities that I think will be necessary. Whether it is a nuclear capability or whether we have other capabilities is the work that's being done in the study.

13. William Arkin, "Not Just a Last Resort?" *Washington Post*, May 15, 2005, B01, http://www.washingtonpost.com/wp-dyn/content/article/2005/05/14/AR2005051400071_pf.html.

14. StratCom press release, December 1, 2005, http://www.stratcom.mil/News/SGS_IOC.html.

15. William Arkin, "Nuclear War in… Alabama," *Washington Post* online, http://blog.washingtonpost.com/earlywarning/2005/10/nuclear_war_in_alabama.html.

16. Arkin, "Not Just a Last Resort?"

17. General James E. Cartwright, Strategic Command, Statement before the Senate Armed Services Committee, Emerging Threats and Capabilities subcommittee, http://armed-services.senate.gov/testimony.cfm?wit_id=3638&id=1813.

18. George Richie, "The Common Aero Vehicle: Space Delivery System of the Future," (Analytic Services Inc. (ANSER), 1999), endnote 27. ANSER, an independent research organization based partly on the RAND model, is heavily involved in national security work. The paper is available, for a fee, at http://www.aiaa.org/content.cfm?pageid=406&gTable=mtgpaper&gID=3140.

19. For a popularized but still accurate article on global strike, see Noah Shachtman, "Bullet from the Blue," *Popular Mechanics*, January 2007, http://popularmechanics.prelive.smartmoney.com/technology/military_law/4203874.html.

20. Air Force Space Command, *Strategic Master Plan 06 and Beyond*, Section 5.3.4.

21. Ibid., Section 6.1.5.2.

22. Go to http://www.aiaa.org/content.cfm?pageid=406&gTable=mtgpaper&gID=3140.

23. Ibid.

24. Go to http://stinet.dtic.mil/oai/oai?&verb=getRecord&metadataPrefix=html&identifier=ADA333343. In 1997, RAND, the defense-oriented think tank, offered this definition: "Transatmospheric vehicles (TAVs) are envisioned as a new type of reusable launch vehicle that could insert payloads into low Earth orbit or deliver them to distant targets within minutes. Such a vehicle may be able to carry out several types of military, civil, and commercial missions. In past decades, a number of military TAV concepts have been proposed, but a complete operational vehicle has never been built. The promise of TAVs is that because of their reusability they could launch payloads at much lower cost than existing rockets. In addition, if they were operated more like aircraft and less like rockets, they could enable responsive and flexible space operations, features that would be useful for a number of military missions."

25. U.S. Air Force Air University, *SpaceCast*. 1994. Black Horse-specific material can be found at http://www.fas.org/spp/military/docops/usaf/2020/app-h.htm.

26. U.S. Air Force Air University, *Air Force 2025*, Executive Summary, "Space Strike Systems," August 1996, http://www.fas.org/spp/military/docops/usaf/2025/index.html.

27. See "Falcon: Force Application and Launch from Conus Technology Demonstration," a draft solicitation from DARPA dated June 17, 2003, http://www.globalsecurity.org/space/library/report/2003/falconsolicitationdraftrev1.pdf.

28. Lance Lord, Testimony to the Senate Armed Services Committee, Strategic Forces sub-committee, March 16, 2005, http://www.spaceref.com/news/viewsr.html?pid=15798.

29. Go to http://thomas.loc.gov/cgi-bin/cpquery/?&sid=cp108wxoo8&refer=&r_n=hr622.108&db_id=108&item=&sel=TOC_292378&.

30. Walter Pincus, "Pentagon Has Far-Reaching Defense Spacecraft in Works," *Washington Post,* March 16, 2005, http://www.washingtonpost.com/wp-dyn/articles/A38272-2005Mar15.html; Tim Weiner, "Air Force Seeks Bush's Approval for Space Weapons Programs," *New York Times,* May 18, 2005, http://www.nytimes.com/2005/05/18/business/18space.html?ex=1274068800&en=e2a17a59b511f204&ei=5088.

31. Robert E. Levin, Director, Acquisition and Resource Manager, Government Accountability Office, testimony to the House Armed Services Committee, Strategic Forces subcommittee, "Space Acquisitions: Stronger Development Practices and Investment Planning Needed to Address Continuing Problems," http://www.gao.gov/new.items/d05891t.pdf.

32. Loren Thompson, "Can the Space Sector Meet Military Goals for Space," 2005, http://lexingtoninstitute.org/docs/662.pdf. Problems abound in the national security space sector and should not be minimized. Thompson, a respected military analyst and chief operating officer of the Lexington Institute, a first-rank military-oriented think tank, stressed technological difficulties:

"The armed forces are changing the way they prepare for and wage war, in a complex process called 'military transformation.' Military transformation has many facets and features, but virtually all of them are linked in some manner to the promise of new technology. Proponents of change argue that by assimilating emerging technologies and linking them to appropriate revisions of doctrine and organization, the military can achieve revolutionary progress in warfighting performance.

"Although the concept of military transformation predates Donald Rumsfeld's tenure as defense secretary, he has given the movement for change momentum and focus. One area of particularly heavy emphasis is space. Rumsfeld and his key advisors believe that orbital systems offer unique advantages in providing military forces with timely intelligence, precise targeting, and robust communications.

"Few experts would disagree. However, even as ambitious plans to leverage space technology have gained the support of policymakers, a troubling pattern has appeared in the execution of national security space programs. Every one of the next-generation [space satellite] constellations being developed has encountered unanticipated cost growth, schedule slippage and technical difficulties. The problems are so pervasive that they raise doubts about whether government and industry can successfully execute military plans for space.

"Doubts that they can reached a climax in the Spring of 2005, when congressional committees reviewing defense budget requests for the next fiscal year threatened to terminate or drastically scale back several of the Pentagon's most important space initiatives. Among the endangered programs were the nation's next generation of missile-warning satellites, its next generation of photo-reconnaissance satellites, its next generation of secure communications satellites, and its first-ever constellation of space-based radars.

"It isn't surprising that such programs face developmental challenges. Not only are they the most technologically complex military systems ever built, but many were burdened with demanding new performance requirements in the aftermath of 9–11 terrorist attacks. Nonetheless, problems have become so widespread and chronic that they threaten to undermine the viability of the entire transformation agenda."

33. For a quick overview of future-years spending by the Defense Department, see "Long-Term Implications of Current Defense Plans: Summary Update for Fiscal Year 2007," http://www.cbo.gov/showdoc.cfm?index=7671&sequence=0.

34. Steven M. Kosiak of the Center for Strategic and Budgetary Assessments estimates that "black" programs account for about $30 billion in the Fiscal Year 2007 Defense Department Budget. See "Classified Funding in the FY 2007 Defense Budget Request," in the Publications section of the Center for Strategic and Budgetary Assessments web site, http://www.csbaonline.org.

35. Robert S. Dudney, "Back to Demolition Derby?" *Air Force Magazine,* August 2006, http://www.afa.org/magazine/aug2006/0806edit.html.

36. Andy Pasztor, "Pentagon Lowers Space Horizons: Satellite Effort Is Likely to Face Budget Pressures," *Wall Street Journal,* February 5, 2007, 3.

37. For a fine (but short) dissection of a high-priority military space program, space radar, see Dwayne A. Day's "Radar Love: The Tortured History of Space Radar Programs," *The Space Review,* an online magazine, http://www.thespacereview.com/article/790/1.

38. Kaplan, *Wizards,* 246. General Thomas S. Power was a passionate advocate of hitting the Russkies with an American bolt from the blue. In December 1960, he was briefed by a high-level Defense Department analyst on the virtues of restraint in the nuclear age. "Why do you want us to restrain ourselves," Power bellowed. "Restraint! Why are you so concerned with saving *their* lives? The whole idea is to kill the bastards.... Look. At the end of the war, if there are two Americans and one Russian, we win!"

39. Dwayne A. Day, "General Power vs. Chicken Little," *The Space Review,* www.thespacereview.com. Emme (*Impact of Air Power,* 871) describes an early example of the sort of thing Dwayne Day was writing about. On January 28, 1958, Air Force Brigadier General Homer A. Boushey, director of advanced technology for the Air Force, spoke to the Aero Club of the National Press Club. Among many things, he promoted the idea that U.S. Moon bases would be the ultimate deterrent to war. Perhaps nuclear-tipped missiles, he said, could be "catapulted from shafts sunk deep into the Moon's surface." The missiles would not require much energy to launch because the Moon's gravity was about one-fifth that of Earth.

    Further, a Soviet missile attack launched from Earth against U.S. Moon bases would be observed from the Moon. America's Moon troops would then have forty-eight hours or so to determine where the missiles would hit, giving them time to seek safety in bunkers.

    More important, the Moon would provide "a retaliation base of unequalled advantage.... If we had a base on the Moon, either the Soviets must launch an overwhelming nuclear attack towards the Moon from Russia two and a half days prior to attacking the continental United States (and such launchings could not escape detection), or Russia could attack the continental U.S. first, only and inevitably to receive from the Moon some forty-eight hours later, sure and massive destruction." It has been said, added Boushey, that "he who controls the Moon, controls the Earth."

40. The Soviet Union under Mikhail Gorbachev did eventually ignore the potential threat posed by Ronald Reagan's Strategic Defense Initiative, but only because Gorbachev's scientific advisers persuaded him that the Americans would ultimately fail; the technologies envisioned by the many proposed Star Wars systems were too advanced to be realized, even by the United States. See Fitzgerald, *Way Out There,* 407–11.

41. George Lee Butler, Speech to National Press Club, February 2, 1998, http://www.brook.edu/fp/projects/nucwcost/deter.htm.

42. Air Force, *Counterspace Operations*, August 2004, http://dtic.mil/doctrine/jel/service_pubs/afdd2_2_1.pdf.

43. A description of MIRACL can be found at http://www.fas.org/spp/military/program/asat/miracl.htm.

44. "Service More Tight-lipped About MIRACL's ASAT Mission: Army Continuing to Refine Laser's Ability to Track, Defeat Satellites," *Inside the Army*, November 30, 1998, http://jya.com/miracl-asat.htm.

45. William Broad, "Administration Conducting Research into Laser Weapons, *New York Times*, May 3, 2006, http://select.nytimes.com/gst/abstract.html?res=F3091 7F73A5B0C708CDDAC0894DE404482&n=Top%2fReference%2fTimes%20 Topics%2fSubjects%2fM%2fMissiles%20and%20Missile%20Defense%20Systems. See also Jeff Hecht, "US Plans Anti-satellite Lasers," *NewScientistTech.com*, May 3, 2006, http://www.newscientisttech.com/article/dn9104-us-plans-antisatellite-lasers.html.

46. Tom Wilson, "Threats to United States Space Capabilities," background paper prepared for the Space Commission, http://www.fas.org/spp/eprint/article05.html, 29–30.

47. See http://www.ph.surrey.ac.uk/ugrad/courses/microsatellite.

48. The XSS-11 is the latest in one line of research; fact sheet published by the Air Force Research Laboratory, http://www.wpafb.af.mil/AFRL. For DART, see NASA fact sheet at http://www.nasa.gov/centers/marshall/pdf/100402main_dart.pdf; for MiTEx, see Jeremy Singer, "Critics Worry There May Be More to MiTEx than Meets the Eye," *Space News*, July 5, 2006, http://www.space.com/spacenews/archive06/Mitex_070306. html. For Angels, see Rita Roland, "Heavenly Hosts to Improve Satellites," *SIGNAL* Magazine (journal of the Armed Forces Communications and Electronics Association), January 2007, http://www.afcea.org/signal/articles/templates/Signal_Article_Template. asp?articleid=1242&zoneid=196. Finally, see "Orbital Express Space Operations Architecture," a DARPA fact sheet, http://www.darpa.mil/tto/programs/oe.htm.

49. See Brian Berger, "Fender Bender: NASA's DART Spacecraft Bumped into Target Satellite," Space.Com, http://www.space.com/missionlaunches/050422_dart_update.html.

50. Today's smallsat programs are at least vaguely reminiscent of America's first theoretical and largely untested antisatellite program, Project SAINT ("SAtellite INTerceptor). SAINT was conceived in the late 1950s as an unmanned satellite that could closely rendezvous with a target satellite, inspect it by television, and—if the target satellite seemed threatening—destroy or disable it. The technology that would be required for SAINT was too sophisticated for the day, and it seemed to violate America's space-for-peaceful-purposes policy. The project was canceled in December 1962, http://www.astronautix.com/craft/saint.htm. See also Stares, *Militarization of Space*, 112–17.

CHAPTER 6

1. Marc Ash, "Massive Human Slaughter," March 16, 2003, http://www.truthout.org/cgi-bin/artman/exec/view.cgi/11/179/printer.

2. Woodward, *Plan of Attack*, 278.

3. Ibid., 325.

4. Human Rights Watch, *Off Target: The Conduct of the War and Civilian Casualties in Iraq*, Part II, http://www.hrw.org/reports/2003/usa1203/.

5. Ibid., Part I.

6. "President Bush Announces Major Combat Operations in Iraq Have Ended," http://www.whitehouse.gov/news/releases/2003/05/20030501-15.html.

7. See http://www.Iraqbodycount.net. Given the nature of the violence in Iraq, it is not possible to obtain an accurate number of deaths directly attributable to the invasion and its aftermath. The most conservative (but reasonably reliable numbers) are produced by a non-governmental organization called Iraq Body Count, from which the seventy thousand figure was taken. The organization records deaths that are clearly documented. Although it concedes that there surely have been many more deaths, they are not included for lack of clear-cut documentation.

8. Carefully targeted JDAMs and other precision weapons are appropriate when fighting a conventional war against conventional military targets; that is, when the other side wears uniforms, operates within a readily identifiable chain of command, and generally tries to follow the "rules of war." Conversely, precision weapons can be indiscriminate killers when used in guerrilla-style wars in which the targets are elusive, the intelligence is faulty, and the enemy hides among civilians.

9. Friedrich Nietzche, *Thus Spake Zarathustra,* (Ware, Hertfordshire: Wordsworth Editions Limited, 1997), "Old and New Tables," Verse 22.

10. Lee Kennett, *The First Air War: 1914–1918* (New York, Simon & Schuster, 1991), 48.

11. See Tom Morgan, "The Great Zeppelin Raid," http://www.hellfire-corner.demon.co.uk/zeppelin.htm.

12. Raymond H. Fredette, *The Sky on Fire: The First Battle of Britain 1917–1918 and the Birth of the Royal Air Force* (New York: Holt, Rinehart and Winston, 1966), 30.

13. Ibid., 262.

14. Ibid., 29.

15. Ibid., 72.

16. Ibid., 262.

17. Ibid., 241.

18. Ernest Hemingway, *A Farewell to Arms* (New York: Charles Scribners Sons, 1929; reprinted 1957), 310.

19. Giulio Douhet, *The Command of the Air,* trans. by Dino Ferrari (Washington, DC: Office of Air Force History, 1942; reprinted 1983), 5–10.

20. Ibid., 14.

21. Ibid., 58.

22. Ibid., 61.

23. Phillip. S. Meilinger, "Molding Airpower Convictions: Development and Legacy of William Mitchell's Strategic Thought," in Phillip S. Meilinger, ed., *The Paths of Heaven: The Evolution of Airpower Theory.* (Maxwell Air Force Base, AL: Air University Press, 1997), 98.

24. William Mitchell, *Winged Defense: The Development and Possibilities of Modern Air Power—Economic and Military* (New York: G. P. Putnam's Sons, 1925), 19.

25. Ibid., 16.

26. Michael S. Sherry, *The Rise of American Air Power: The Creation of Armageddon* (New Haven: Yale University Press, 1987), 58.

27. Meilinger, *Paths of Heaven,* 80.

28. Burke Davis, *The Billy Mitchell Affair* (New York: Random House, 1967), 218. The book is a must-read for anyone interested in Mitchell's career.

29. Beginning in January 1907, H. G. Wells, the British novelist, historian, and futurist, published a novel in serial form called *The War in the Air.* It described a global conflict in

the 1920s initiated by one Prince Karl Albert of Germany, the man chiefly responsible for building a fleet of massive dirigibles, each capable of carrying many tons of bombs, mostly incendiaries.

New York City—"the largest, richest, in many respects the most splendid, and in some, the wickedest city the world had ever seen"—was the first city to be attacked by the prince's aerial armada. New York, said Wells, was chosen because it was the de facto capital of the United States, which was Germany's "leading trade rival" and the chief barrier to Germany's imperial expansion.

Prince Albert directed the attack from his airship, the *Vaterland*. Although an unpleasant fellow, he was not overly barbaric when judged by historical standards. He was simply a nineteenth-century militarist with twentieth-century weapons that included ocean-hopping dirigibles (ranging from eight hundred to two thousand feet in length!) as well as tiny fighter planes, *drachenfliegers* (dragon-fliers) suspended from the airships.

The prince was reluctant to destroy so great a city as New York; he "sought to be moderate even in massacre." It was sufficient for his purposes do away with only a small portion of the city by using incendiaries. The prince transformed lower Manhattan into a "furnace of crimson flames, from which there was no escape."

Unhappily for the prince and for humanity, the German attack triggered a global air war. According to Wells, all major nations had been secretly preparing for aerial combat, with Japan and China, working together, having developed the most formidable air fleets. Within weeks, war in the air had set all of the world's great cities ablaze. Global civilization, as it was wont to do in Wells's stories, collapsed into anarchy, famine, and pestilence.

In Wells's later novel, *The World Set Free*, published in 1914, the great cities of the world also perished in "unquenchable crimson conflagrations," this time triggered by atomic bombs dropped from the air. *The War in the Air* is available at http://www.online-literature.com/wellshg/warinair/; *The World Set Free* at http://www.online-literature.com/wellshg/worldsetfree/.

30. Maxwell Air Force Base, Ala: Air University Press, 1999.
31. Peter R. Faber, "Interwar U.S. Army Aviation and the Air Corps Tactical School: Incubators of American Air Power," in Meilinger, *Paths of Heaven*, 212.
32. Charles Griffith, *The Quest: Haywood Hansell and American Strategic Bombing in World War II* (Maxwell Air Force Base, AL: Air University Press, 1999), 49.
33. The B-17 "co-starred" with Gregory Peck in the 1949 classic air-war film, *Twelve O'Clock High*, a fictional story based on actual events.
34. Michael E. Brown, *Flying Blind: The Politics of the U.S. Strategic Bomber Program* (Ithaca, NY and London: Cornell University Press, 1992), 59.
35. ACTS did not invent the American version of strategic bombing; it refined ideas that began to develop during World War I. As early as August 1917, a mission headed by Major Raynal C. Bolling recommended building an American Air Force so large that it would be "in excess of the tactical requirements of the Army in France." Some 37.5 percent of that "excess" force would be night bombers, which would be useful against industrial targets in Germany. Later that year, Col. Edgar S. Gorrell was asked to formulate ideas for a war-winning bombing campaign, pending the arrival of American bombers in Europe. Assisted by three other men (and borrowing freely from British theorists), Gorrell quickly came up with a plan—and a plea: It was "of paramount importance that we adopt at once a bombing project… at the quickest possible moment, in order that we may not only wreck Germany's manufacturing centers but wreck them more completely than she will wreck ours next year." Up to a hundred squadrons of bombers should be directed

against industrial plants around Dusseldorf, Cologne, Mannheim, and in the Saar Valley, the Gorrell Plan said. The plants would be destroyed and the morale of the workmen shattered. The Great War ended before the United States had the bombers in place. See, for instance, T. D. Biddle, *Rhetoric and Reality in Air Warfare*, (Princeton, NJ: Princeton University Press, 2002), 53–57; and R. F. Futrell, *Ideas, Concepts, Doctrine: Basic Thinking in the United States Air Force, 1907–1960* (Maxwell Air Force Base, AL, Air University Press, 1989), 24–26.

36. Kennett, *The First Air War*, 119.
37. Meilinger, *Paths of Heaven*, 51–68.
38. Haywood S. Hansell, Jr., *The Air Plan That Defeated Hitler* (Atlanta, GA: Haywood S. Hansell, Jr., 1972), 304.
39. Stephen A. Garrett, *Ethics and Airpower in World War II: The British Bombing of German Cities* (New York: St. Martin's Press, 1993), 12.
40. Ibid., 11.
41. Ibid., 13.
42. Arthur Harris, *Bomber Offensive* (London: Greenhill Books; Novato, CA: Presidio Press, 1990), 77.
43. Ibid., 83.
44. Ibid., 105.
45. Ibid., 173–76.
46. Ibid., 261.
47. Frederick Taylor, *Dresden: Tuesday, February 13, 1945* (New York: HarperCollins, Washington, DC: Air Force History and Museums Programs, 2004), 429–48. See also Earl R. Beck, *Under the Bombs: The German Home Front, 1942–1945* (Lexington, KY: The University Press of Kentucky, 1986), 177–80; Conrad C. Crane, *Bombs, Cities, and Civilians: American Airpower Strategy in World War II* (Lawrence, KS: University Press of Kansas, 1993), 114–19; Sherry, *The Rise of American Air Power*, 260–64; and Garrett, *Ethics and Airpower*, index entries under Dresden, 247.
48. Taylor, *Dresden*, 375.
49. Harris, *Bomber Offensive*. 242.
50. Ibid., 177.
51. Hansell, *The Air Plan*, 153.
52. For an excellent behind-the-scenes account of the meeting, see Herman S. Wolk, "Decision at Casablanca," *Air Force Magazine*, January 2003, http://www.afa.org/magazine/jan2003/0103casa.asp.
53. Crane, *Bombs, Cities*, 82.
54. Ibid., 111.
55. Ibid., 72.
56. Field Marshall Erhard Milch's comments can be found at http://www.au.af.mil/au/awc/awcgate/cbo-afa/cbo05.htm.
57. Crane, *Bombs, Cities*, 126.
58. Ibid., 127. Arnold had long championed incendiary bombs, and before the war, he believed that American incendiaries were not up to snuff. In the spring of 1941, Arnold called a conference with representatives from the Ordnance Department and the Chemical Warfare Service. Vannevar Bush, chairman of the newly created National Defense Research Committee, was present. "It was during those discussions," Arnold later wrote, "that Dr. Bush first told me about an incendiary jelly. When the container broke after

one of these bombs hit its objective, the jelly was thrown in gobs in all directions. The gobs stuck to the wall and ignited.... These new bombs, which we later called 'Napalm,' burned with such intensity and with such explosive force that if dropped near the entrance to a cave or building, they caused all the air to rush out; and anyone inside died from lack of oxygen. Henry "Hap" Arnold, *Global Mission* (New York: Harper & Brothers, 1949), 243.

59.   Arnold, *Global Mission*, 564.

60.   Martin Caidan, *A Torch to the Enemy: The Fire Raid on Tokyo* (New York: Ballantine Books, 1960). See also Sherry, *Rise of American Air Power*, 271–82.

61.   Curtis E. LeMay, with MacKinlay Kantor, *Mission with LeMay: My Story* (Garden City, NY: Doubleday & Co., 1965), 352.

62.   Ibid., 384.

63.   Ibid., 387. See Sherry, *Rise of American Air Power*, endnote 76, page 406, for a discussion of Tokyo casualty figures. For a brief but illuminating look at the evolution of the fire-bombing strategy, see also William W. Ralph, "Improvised Destruction: Arnold, LeMay, and the Firebombing of Japan" *War in History* 13, no. 4, http://wih.sagepub.com/cgi/content/abstract/13/4/495.

64.   See Sherry, *Rise of American Air Power*, endnote 43, page 413, for a thoughtful discussion of the difficulty of arriving at reasonably accurate casualty figures.

65.   Robert S. McNamara, "We Need Rules for War," *Los Angeles Times*, August 3, 2003, http://www.wagingpeace.org/articles/2003/08/03_mcnamara_rules-for-war.htm.

66.   Stephen L. McFarland, *America's Pursuit of Precision Bombing, 1910–1945* (Washington, DC: Smithsonian Institution Press, 1995), 100.

67.   Buster C. Glosson, "Impact of Precision Weapons on Air Combat Operations in Airpower" *Airpower Journal*, Summer 1993, http://www.airpower.au.af.mil/airchronicales/apj/glosson.html#glosson

CHAPTER 7

1.   H. H. Arnold and Ira C. Eaker, *This Flying Game* (New York: Funk & Wagnalls, 1926), 47.

2.   H. H. Arnold, *Global Mission* (New York: Harper & Brothers, 1949), 1–29.

3.   Ibid., 48.

4.   Ibid., 50–54.

5.   Ibid., 61–64.

6.   Arnold and Eaker, *This Flying Game*, 149.

7.   The saga of the "Flying Bug" can be found in Arnold, *Global Mission*, 74–76. Arnold may have come up with the first cruise missile but Nazi Germany produced the second, in massive numbers. In 1944 and 1945, the Luftwaffe launched some twenty thousand pilotless V-1 "buzz bombs" against targets in England, Belgium, and France. V-1s had a pulsejet engine, which gave them greater speed than the Bug. Like the Bug, buzz bombs had a propeller; unlike the Bug, the propeller was not used for propulsion. The slipstream whirled the prop, providing a rough measure of distance traveled. At the proper number of revolutions, the fuel was cut off and the bomb nosed downward.

8.   Ibid., 260–61.

9.   Ibid., 490.

10. Crane, *Bombs, Cities,* 78–85. Crane offers far more detail on the "Weary Willies" scheme than does Arnold.

11. Dik A. Daso, *Architects of American Air Supremacy: Gen. Hap Arnold and Dr. Theodore von Karman* (Maxwell Air Force Base, AL: Air University Press, 1997), 3.

12. Ibid., 109.

13. Michael H. Gorn, *The Universal Man: Theodore von Karman's Life in Aeronautics* (Washington, DC: Smithsonian Institution Press, 1992), 5.

14. For a fine profile of von Karman, see Walter J. Boyne, "Von Karman's Way," *Air Force Magazine,* January 2004, http://www.afa.org/magazine/jan2004/0104vonkarman.asp.

15. Daso, *Architects of American Air,* 48.

16. Arnold, *Global Mission,* 165.

17. Daso, *Architects of American Air,* 57.

18. Arnold, *Global Mission,* 173.

19. Daso, *Architects of American Air,* 70–72.

20. Bryce Walker, *Fighting Jets* (Alexandria, VA: Time-Life Books, 1983), 28–29.

21. Arnold, *Global Mission,* 532–33; Theodore von Karman and Lee Edson, *The Wind and Beyond: Theodore von Karman, Pioneer in Aviation and Pathfinder in Space* (Boston: Little, Brown and Co., 1967), 267.

22. Daso, *Architects of American Air,* 217–20.

23. Ibid. *Where We Stand* is at 211–307.

24. Frederick I. Ordway III and Mitchell Sharp, *The Rocket Team: From the V-2 to the Saturn Moon Rocket—The Inside Story of How a Small Group of Engineers Changed World History* (New York: Thomas Y. Crowell, 1979), 284.

25. Daso, *Architects of American Air,* 239–43.

26. Von Karman and Edson, *The Wind and Beyond,* 306.

27. Daso, *Architects of American Air,* Appendix C, "Science: the Key to Air Supremacy," 410–14. *Toward New Horizons,* a huge work, is not widely available.

28. Spires, *Beyond Horizons,* 11. Von Karman was not universally admired. In December 1945, Vannevar Bush, who had served as director of the Office of Scientific Research and Development during the war, told the special Senate Committee on Atomic Energy: "We have plenty enough to think about that [is] very definite and very realistic—enough so that we don't need to step out into some of these borderlines, which seem to me more or less fantastic. Let me say this: There has been a great deal said about a three thousand-mile high-angle rocket. In my opinion such a thing is impossible and will be impossible for many years. The people who have been writing these things that annoy me have been talking about a three thousand-mile high-angle rocket shot from one continent to another carrying an atomic bomb, and so directed as to be a precise weapon which would land on a certain target such as this city. I say technically I don't think anybody in the world knows how to do such a thing, and I feel confident it will not be done for a very long period of time to come. I think we can leave that out of our thinking. I wish the American public would leave that out of their thinking."

29. Sherry, *Rise of American Air Power,* 187.

30. Emme, *Impact of Air Power,* 305.

31. General Henry Arnold, "Air Power for Peace," *National Geographic,* February 1946, 139.

32. *New World Vistas* can be downloaded, section by section, at http://www.au.af.mil/au/awc/awcgate/vistas/index.htm.

33. "Space Technology Volume," http://www.au.af.mil/au/awc/awcgate/vistas/sabmnst.htm, paragraph 4.17.

34. America's modern military/industrial/scientific complex was hardly the product of Hap Arnold or of any one man. It was the product of World War II and the insistence by many men—especially Vannevar Bush who, as director of the Office of Scientific Research and Development during the war, was the closest thing America has ever had to a science czar. Bush believed that the United States must become—and forever remain— the global leader in *all* phases of scientific research after the war. That meant substantial government investment in all phases of science.

Bush's report to the president in July 1945, *Science—the Endless Frontier,* suggested that the government, in the form of a National Research Foundation, take near-total control of basic and applied research for everything from medicine to submarines.

The Bush proposal didn't fly. It was too extreme, too centralized, and it incited too much opposition from men and women who feared that it would lead to excessive governmental control. But over the years, *Frontier* has been cited, time and again, as one of the intellectual pillars of the military/industrial/scientific complex that began growing rapidly during the Korean War.

Bush, a brilliant scientist and engineer and an adept organizer of scientific talent during the war, was disappointed that his National Research Foundation was never established. (The National Science Foundation, established in 1950, was a paler shadow of Bush's original proposal.) Bush never tired of pushing the idea that civilian scientists must carry the heaviest load for military research, even in times of peace. Bush put it plainly, if arrogantly, in *Modern Arms and Free Men* (New York: Simon and Shuster, 1949), 252–53:

"We have arrived at the point where military planning of adequate comprehensiveness is beyond the capacity of military men alone. Either they will learn to cope with the new situation or they will lose their franchise. So far, the course of events has come close to the latter alternative. The days are gone when military men could sit on a pedestal, receive the advice of professional groups in neighboring fields who were maintained in a subordinate or tributary position, accept or reject such advice at will, discount its importance as they saw fit, and speak with omniscience on the overall conduct of war.

"For one thing, professional men in neighboring fields have no present intention of kowtowing to any military hierarchy, in a world where they know that other professional subjects are just as important in determining the course of future events in the nation's defense as are narrowly limited military considerations."

Military leaders must "avail themselves of the collaboration of the best minds that the country produces… in physics, chemistry, biology, mathematics, engineering, medicine, psychology, statistics, law, organizational theory and practice, and other fields that now enter intimately into the whole."

CHAPTER 8

1. *Collier's* reprinted von Braun's March 22, 1952 article, as well as other space-related articles that appeared in the magazine, in a coffee-table book, *Across the Space Frontier* (New York: The Viking Press, in cooperation with *Collier's* magazine, 1952).

2. Von Braun was not the first entrant in the satellite race. Unitarian clergyman and journalist Edward Everett Hale (grandnephew of Revolutionary War hero Nathan Hale) beat him by many decades. Hale, a prolific writer, is best known today for his short story, "The Man Without a Country." "The Brick Moon," his story about a navigation satellite made of brick to withstand fire, was published in 1869 in *The Atlantic Monthly.* An engaging

piece, it can be accessed at http://www.gutenberg.org/etext/1633.

3. Von Braun's inclusion of the United Nations in the scenario was pro forma. By 1952, the U.N. Security Council, which included the Soviet Union, was paralyzed by Cold War tensions. Cornelius Ryan, von Braun's editor at *Collier's*, was more direct in his introduction to *Across the Space Frontier*. The United States alone had the wherewithal to become guardian of the peace, Ryan said, and it should immediately embark on a long-range program to secure "space superiority" for the West. Otherwise, a "ruthless power" might build a space station and "subjugate the peoples of the world."

    "We have the scientists and the engineers. We have the inventive genius. We have vast industrial superiority. We should begin a space program immediately, for in the hands of peace-loving nations the space station could be man's guardian in the skies.... No nation could undertake preparations for war without the certain knowledge that its massing troops were being observed by the ever-watching eyes aboard the 'sentinel in space.' It would be the end of Iron Curtains wherever they might be."

4. John Norton Leonard, *Flight into Space* (New York: Random House, 1953), 105.

5. Ibid., 105. Leonard added, somewhat archly, "They [the critics] say that von Braun's great shuttle rockets—to say nothing of his space station—would surely fail, probably in a gigantic fiasco that would sour the world on space flight for the next hundred years."

6. Von Braun's early years are described in Ernst Struhlinger and Frederick I. Ordway III, *Wernher von Braun: Crusader for Space* (Malabar, FL: Krieger Publishing Co., 1994), 9–20. When the war began, Stuhlinger worked with physicist Werner Heisenberg on Germany's stillborn atomic bomb project. In 1943, he joined von Braun's V-2 program. Ordway, a rocket expert, worked for a time on von Braun's U.S. Army missile team and later became von Braun's principal biographer.

7. Michael J. Neufeld, *The Rocket and the Reich: Peenemünde and the Coming of the Ballistic Missile Era* (New York: The Free Press, 1995).

8. Ibid., 264.

9. Stuhlinger and Ordway, *Wernher von Braun*, 44.

10. Daso, *Architects of American Air*, 136.

11. Neufeld, *The Rocket and the Reich*, 258.

12. Ordway and Sharpe, *The Rocket Team*, 1–2.

13. Stuhlinger, *Wernher von Braun*, 62.

14. Ibid., 62–63.

15. That reasoning was more about bureaucratic infighting than reality. Or perhaps it had more to do with Buck Rogers and Flash Gordon than with logic. By definition, space is utterly different from the atmosphere. The two mediums are so unlike that nothing about flight carries over into space. Indeed, space is not even a "medium," although the Air Force routinely uses that term. When the Air Force speaks of the "medium" of air, it means that air is a substance that provides aerodynamic lift to aircraft. In contrast, space has no substance; it is a vacuum or near vacuum and it is also a maelstrom of gravitational forces that must be handled very precisely to get anywhere.

16. See Spires, *Beyond Horizons*, 14–15: Stares, *Militarization of Space*, 25–26.

17. RAND, *Preliminary Design of an Experimental World-Circling Spaceship*, 1946. RAND sells facsimile reprints. The report also can be found at http://www.rand.org/pubs/special_memoranda/SM11827/.

18. Arthur C. Clarke's seminal article can be found at http://lakdiva.org/clarke/1945ww/1945ww_oct_305-308.html.

19. RAND, *Preliminary Design,* Introduction.

CHAPTER 9

1. David Holloway, *Stalin and the Bomb: The Soviet Union and Atomic Energy, 1939–1956* (New Haven: Yale University Press, 1994), 132.

2. It is a persistent Cold War myth that Soviet spies "stole the secret of the bomb" from the Americans. There were Soviet spies in Los Alamos and elsewhere and they provided useful information to Soviet scientists, especially for the first Soviet bomb. But Soviet physicists were already among the best in the world.

    In early 1943, Igor Kurchatov was named scientific director of the Soviet Union's atom bomb project. Kurchatov, who had been exploring nuclear physics for more than ten years, assembled a first-rate team. During the war, little progress was made; the Soviet Union was fighting for its survival and resources were scarce. After the surrender of Japan, Stalin told Kurchatov to produce a bomb within five years.

    The members of the A-bomb team were eager to comply; it was their patriotic duty. One member of the team spoke for all when he said in 1990 that he had an "inner feeling that our confrontation with a very powerful opponent had not ended with the defeat of Fascist Germany." After Hiroshima and Nagasaki, historian David Holloway, writes, "the feeling of defenselessness increased.... For all who realized the realities of the new atomic era, the creation of our atomic weapons, the restoration of equilibrium became a categorical imperative." (*Stalin and the Bomb*, 204)

    In early September 1949, air samples gathered by American reconnaissance planes over the Pacific suggested unusual amounts of radioactivity. After isotopic analyses, experts from Los Alamos National Laboratory and the Naval Research Laboratory said the samples were "consistent with the view that the origin of the fission products was the explosion of an atomic bomb whose nuclear composition was similar to the Alamogordo [test] and the explosion occurred between the 26th and 29th of August." John T. Farquhar, *A Need to Know: The Role of Air Force Reconnaissance in War Planning, 1945–1953* (Maxwell Air Force Base, AL: Air University Press, 2004), 116.

    America's leading bomb scientists were not greatly surprised. Many had predicted that it might take the Soviet Union about five years or so to produce a bomb. The Air Force brass was not greatly surprised, either. Accustomed to the rigors of worst-case analyses, they had generally assumed the Soviet Union would acquire atomic weapons by the mid-1950s or earlier.

    Others were startled. According to author Robert S. Norris, Gen. Leslie R. Groves, who headed the wartime Manhattan Project, had been famously contemptuous of Soviet technology; it might take the Soviet Union "ten, twenty, or even sixty years" to produce a bomb. "Those people can't even make a jeep," he told one audience (*Racing for the Bomb: General Leslie R. Groves, the Manhattan Project's Indispensable Man* (South Royalton, VT: Steerforth Press, 2002), 475). President Truman had been even more skeptical. He believed the proper answer to the "when" question was "never," according to John Newhouse. *War and Peace in the Nuclear Age* (New York: Alfred A. Knopf, 1989), 73.

3. Holloway, *Stalin and the Bomb*, 217.

4. Allan M. Winkler, *Life Under a Cloud: American Anxiety About the Atom* (New York: Oxford University Press), 115.

5. Ray Bradbury, *The Martian Chronicles* (New York: Random House, Bantam Books, 1978).

6. Robert R. Bowie and Richard H. Immerman, *Waging Peace: How Eisenhower Shaped an Enduring Cold War Strategy* (Oxford and New York: Oxford University Press, 2000),

247. Robert H. Ferrell, ed., *The Diary of James C. Hagerty: Eisenhower in Mid-Course, 1954–1955* (Bloomington, IN: Indiana University Press, 1983), 99–102.

7. Carl Spaatz, "Atomic Warfare," *Life*, August 16, 1948. Spaatz took an oddly optimistic stance about an actual atomic war. The Russians might well "send against us a striking force of some hundreds of long-range bombers," he said. "Who can doubt the destruction and chaos that an enemy could bring us through the air?"

Nonetheless, Spaatz added, "I agree with those who maintain that such an attack would not be decisive. The U.S. industrial capacity is too big to be permanently destroyed by a single attack." The Russians, he believed, would understand that. "The flash attack upon the U.S. must be understood as essentially a preventive measure aimed at impeding the development of an American counteroffensive" as the Soviet Union took over Western Europe with ground troops.

One way to ensure that such an attack would never happen, wrote Spaatz, was to build an American Air Force so powerful that it would "overawe" the Russians. But if an attack did come, the United States must be prepared to retaliate with an equally "stunning blow" followed by even more attacks against the Soviet heartland.

Spaatz's articles are intriguing today not only because of what he says about the Russians, but also because of what he says about the Navy. The article was part of an intense multifaceted Air Force campaign to persuade the American people that the Air Force was now America's first line of defense; therefore it should receive the lion's share of the defense budget.

8. Killian, *Sputnik, Scientists, and Eisenhower*, 68. Eisenhower was unlikely to forget the events of 1944 when, as Christmas approached, things were looking good for the Allies. They had reclaimed huge swaths of German-held territory in France and Belgium since D-Day. But the good news was deceptive. In the weeks preceding the massive German counter-offensive in the Ardennes—the "Battle of the Bulge"—that began December 16, the Germans made a show of moving men and materiel in daylight into an area north of Cologne, the gateway to Germany's industrial heartland. They were attempting to persuade the Allies that the German army was preparing for a last-stand defense at the Rhine. Meanwhile, the buildup for the Ardennes offensive into Belgium took place farther south under cover of darkness. Despite reconnaissance flights, the Allies failed to catch on to the buildup. The Battle of the Bulge, said General Andrew Goodpaster, General Eisenhower's closest aide, "deeply impressed upon (Eisenhower) the value as well as the limitations of intelligence, together with the dangers of being caught off guard." Dwayne A Day, John M. Logsdon, Brian Latell, *Eye in the Sky: The Story of the Corona Spy Satellites* (Washington, DC: Smithsonian Institution Press, 1998), 173.

9. Norris, *Racing for the Bomb*, 471.

10. Major Gian E. Gentile, "Planning for Preventive War, 1945–1950," *JFQ (Joint Forces Quarterly)*, Spring 2000, http://dtic.mil/doctrine/jel/jfq_pubs/1424.pdf.

11. Ibid.; see also Lashmar, *Spy Flights*, 97.

12. Harry S Truman, *Memoirs by Harry S Truman: Volume Two, Years of Trial and Hope* (Garden City, NY: Doubleday & Company, 1956), 383.

13. Kaplan, *Wizards*, 134. LeMay and the Strategic Air Command were wedded to preemption. According to an official history prepared by SAC for the period of 1954–1956, the command's "ultimate objective was the ability to launch a multiple wing strike over EWP [Emergency War Plan] targets in a minimum amount of time.... The only way to protect the nation was to be able to destroy the enemy's offensive power before it could

be completely unleashed," (Kaplan, *Wizards*, 402, note 108.) LeMay's successor, Thomas "Tommy" Power, shared LeMay's vision, although he called preemptive or preventive nuclear war "assumption of the initiative." Thomas S. Power, *Design for Survival* (New York: Coward-McCann, 1965), 79.

14. Michael I. Handel, *Master of War: Classical Strategic Thought* (London: Frank Cass, 2001), 244.

15. Philip Taubman, *Secret Empire: Eisenhower, the CIA, and the Hidden Story of America's Space Espionage* (New York: Simon & Schuster, 2003), 14.

16. Strobe Talbott, ed. and trans., *Khrushchev Remembers* (Boston: Little, Brown and Company, 1970, 393.

17. Taubman, *Secret Empire*, 171.

18. Ernest R. May, "Strategic Intelligence and U.S. Security: The Contributions of CORONA," in Day et al., *Eye in the Sky*, 22.

19. Newhouse, *War and Peace*, 122.

20. For an especially good discussion of the missile gap, the hottest issue in the 1960 Kennedy-Nixon presidential campaign, see Kaplan's *Wizards*, 155–73.

21. George W. Goddard, *Overview: A Lifelong Adventure in Aerial Photography* (Garden City, NY: Doubleday & Company, 1969), 381.

CHAPTER 10

1. Emmet John Hughes, *The Ordeal of Power: A Political Memoir of the Eisenhower Years* (New York: Athenaeum, 1963), 103. The speech, known as "A Chance for Peace" or "The Cross of Iron" can be found at http://millercenter.virginia.edu/scripps/diglibrary/prezspeeches/eisenhower/dde_1953_0416.html. Hughes, speechwriter for Eisenhower (and, ultimately, a critic of the president's administration) recalls how Eisenhower and his staff pondered for days how to react to Stalin's death. At one point, Hughes went to the president's office on another matter, but the conversation soon turned to Stalin's death. Eisenhower grew excited and intense, writes Hughes, and began pacing the Oval Office in a wide arc. Then the president began to speak "slowly and forcefully": "Look, I am tired—and I think everyone is tired—of just plain indictments of the Soviet regime. I think it would be wrong —in fact, asinine— for me to get up before the world now to make another one of those indictments. Instead, just one thing matters: what have *we* got to offer the world? What are *we* ready to do, to improve the chances of peace." Then, writes Hughes, the president proceeded to outline, point by point, what he wanted to say in his speech.

2. Ibid., 251. Secretary of State John Foster Dulles opposed the summit. Eisenhower, who admired Dulles, often followed Dulles's lead. But not always. At one point in his second term, the president told Hughes that he knew Dulles did not command great confidence either at home or abroad. But he also said: "People just don't like that personality of Foster's, while they do like me. The fact remains that he just knows more about foreign affairs than anybody I know. In fact, I'll be immodest and say that there's only one man I know who has seen *more* of the world and talked with more people and *knows* more than he does—and that's *me*."

Nonetheless, Eisenhower believed that when it came to the Soviet Union, his secretary of state was too rigid, too confrontational. Throughout both terms, the president was intent on pursuing tension-easing negotiations with Moscow; he believed that if he could find the right key, he could work creatively with Soviet leaders on disarmament issues. Dulles never warmed to the idea.

3. The text of the Open Skies proposal can be found at http://tucnak.fsv.cuni.cz/~calda/Documents/1950s/Ike_OpenSkies_55.html. Harold Stassen and Marshall Houts, *Eisenhower: Turning the World Toward Peace* (St. Paul, MN: Merrill/Magnus Publishing, 1990), 295–96, 350–51. Historians often credit Nelson Rockefeller, a special assistant to the president, with originating Open Skies. Not so, said Harold Stassen, Eisenhower's chief disarmament adviser. The source was World War II hero Gen. James H. Doolittle, chairman of the National Advisory Committee for Aeronautics.

4. Robert J. Donovan, *Eisenhower: The Inside Story* (New York: Harper & Brothers, 1956), 345.

5. Michael R. Beschloss, *Mayday: Eisenhower, Khrushchev, and the U-2 Affair* (New York: Harper & Row, 1986), 103.

6. Stassen and Houts, *Eisenhower: Turning the World*, 340. Stassen, Eisenhower's "secretary for peace," was standing next to Eisenhower. He later wrote that nearly everyone in the room, including Eden, Faure, and Dulles formed a ring around Eisenhower and Khrushchev, straining to hear. Meanwhile, the Russian delegation hung back, "silent, expressionless, listening to Khrushchev talk, but choosing not to interrupt. I think that everyone in that circle made the same discovery at about the same moment. They saw and heard the real Russian ruler, Joe Stalin's stubborn successor… the dumpy, feisty, flamboyant man who confronted Eisenhower." According to his memoirs, Khrushchev returned to Moscow well pleased. The Soviet delegation, he said, now realized that "our enemies probably feared us as much as we feared them."

7. Beschloss, *Mayday*, 104; Stassen and Houts, *Eisenhower: Turning the World*, 117. General Andrew Goodpaster, the aide closest to Eisenhower throughout his presidency, later said the president thought at the time there was "at least a chance" that Open Skies might be accepted. In any event, the Soviets didn't buy it. In April 1956, Khrushchev confronted Harold Stassen in London and confirmed that Open Skies had flamed out: "You treat the Soviet Union like a rich uncle treats a pauper nephew!" The Soviet Union didn't want pictures of anyone else's land, Khrushchev said. Why were the Americans always so eager to peek into other people's bedrooms? Soviet leaders had not turned down Open Skies outright at Geneva, he added, only because of their respect for Eisenhower.

8. Lashmar, *Spy Flights*, 117.

9. Ibid., 119.

10. Talbott, *Khrushchev Remembers*, 356.

11. V. D. Sokolovskiy, *Soviet Military Strategy, Third Edition*. Edited, with analysis and commentary by Harriet Fast Scott (New York: Crane, Russak & Co., 1975), 62.

12. Lashmar, *Spy Flights*, 42–45. Marquis Childs, one of the nation's most reliable reporters, said in the *Washington Post* that the "Russians believed that the American plane was carrying a recently developed type of reconnaissance equipment" that made "it possible to conduct reconnaissance at much greater distances than has ever before been possible." Columnist Drew Pearson said the Russians "knew the plane was equipped with high-powered radar and electronic equipment that could watch amphibious maneuvers and the flight of rockets over the Russian's most secret testing ground—the Baltic."

13. Farquhar, *Need to Know*, 37.

14. Ibid., 70.

15. Lashmar, *Spy Flights*, 70.

16. Ibid., 75.

17. Taubman, *Secret Empire*, 47. The secret spy flights were dangerous undertakings at best, and the U.S. government was seldom helpful in providing casualty statistics (or any information at all) to anyone, including the families of airmen. *New York Times* journalist Philip Taubman believes that "at least" two hundred and fifty-two crewmen were shot out of the sky between 1950 and 1970 in the reconnaissance war. Most of these flights were directed at the Soviet Union; others at China or Soviet satellites. Ninety of the men are known to have survived, rescued either by American forces or confirmed to have been captured by communist forces. "But the fate of one hundred and thirty-eight men is unknown. It is possible, even likely, that some of them survived for years in captivity, while Washington made little effort to determine if they were alive and to make arrangements for their repatriation."

18. See R. Cargill Hall, "Postwar Strategic Reconnaissance and the Genesis of Corona" in Dwayne Day, John M. Logsdon, and Brian Latell, eds., *Eye in the Sky: The Story of the CORONA Spy Satellites* (Washington, DC: Smithsonian Institute Press, 1998), 86–101.

19. Taubman, *Secret Empire*, 51.

20. Gregory W. Pedlow, Donald E. Welzenbach, and J. Kenneth McDonald, *The CIA and the U-2 Program, 1954–1974* (Springfield, VA: Center for the Study of Intelligence, Central Intelligence Agency, 1998), 19. The study was named after a secretarial school in Boston's Beacon Hill neighborhood where the top-secret meetings were held.

21. Ibid., 5.

22. Ibid., 11.

23. See especially *Mayday* by Michael R. Beschloss and *Secret Empire* by Philip Taubman.

24. Killian, *Sputnik, Scientists, and Eisenhower*, 228.

25. Ibid., 227. Killian recalled a breakfast meeting that he and Herbert York, the thirty-five-year-old director of Lawrence Livermore National Laboratory (a nuclear weapons facility), had with Eisenhower. The president remarked that some of his political advisers had noted that a large number of Democrats served on the President's Science Advisory Committee. Eisenhower told his political advisers that he had never raised the question of politics with his scientists, nor did he intend to. York responded, "Well, don't you know, Mr. President, that all scientists are Democrats?" Eisenhower laughed.

26. Ibid., 218.

27. Ibid., 82.

28. Taubman, *Secret Empire*, 107–08.

29. Killian, *Sputnik, Scientists, and Eisenhower*, 84.

30. Pedlow et al., *The CIA and the U-2*, 175.

31. Taubman, *Secret Empire*, 185.

32. Pedlow et al., *The CIA and the U-2*, 10.

33. Taubman, *Secret Empire*, 305.

34. Ibid., 309.

35. Pedlow et al., *The CIA and the U-2*, 84.

36. Symbolism played no role in the timing of U-2 flights. Near-perfect weather—low turbulence at takeoff and landing sites as well as clear air along the flight path—were the chief determinants.

37. Beschloss, *Mayday*, 44.

38. Ibid., 178.

39. Beschloss's *Mayday*, 243–272, provides a particularly good blow-by-blow account of the U-2 affair. The Federation of American Scientists maintains an online file of government

documents relating to the U-2 shoot-down at http://www.fas.org/irp/imint/doc_u2/in-dex.html.

40. Strobe Talbott: *Khrushchev Remembers: The Last Testament* (Boston and Toronto: Little, Brown and Company, 1974. 449). In this second installment of his memoirs, Nikita Khrushchev said he was certain that he had handled the matter in the "best way." U.S. spy flights were an outrage. By shooting down Francis Gary Powers, he had told the Americans "that we were both willing and able to fire on any plane that flew over our territory. We had no use for the policy of the Gospels: if someone slaps you, just turn the other cheek. We had shown that anyone who slapped us on our cheek would get his head kicked off" (p. 449). In his book's epilogue, Khrushchev unwittingly gave startling testimony to the mutual madness, miscommunications, misunderstandings, and misjudgments that drove the Cold War. The Soviet Union had been receptive to some arms control measures that would require on-site inspections and aerial reconnaissance, Khrushchev suggested—"up to a certain distance inside our borders." The Soviet Union simply could not allow "the U.S. and its allies to send their inspectors crisscrossing around the Soviet Union. They would have discovered that we were in a relatively weak position, and that realization might have encouraged them to attack us" (p. 536).

41. Kistiakowsky, *Scientist at the White House*, 375.

42. Day et al., *Eye in the Sky*, 174.

43. Ibid., 1.

CHAPTER II

1. Beschloss, *Mayday*, 150.

2. Kaplan, *Wizards*, 248.

3. U.S. Department of State, *Foreign Relations of the United States*, 1958–60, Vol. X, Part I: E. Europe Region; Soviet Union; Cyprus, Section 9, Editorial Note 74, http://dosfan.lib.uic.edu/ERC/frus/frus58-60x1/09soviet3.html.

4. Bowie and Immerman, *Waging Peace*, 47.

5. See Walter J. Boyne, "The Man Who Built the Missiles," *Air Force Magazine,* October 2000, http://www.afa.org/magazine/oct2000/1000bennie.asp.

6. Emme, *Impact of Air Power*, 844.

7. See Lance Lord, "We Walked With a Legend," a commentary on Bernard A. Schriever, http://www.schriever.af.mil/news/story.asp?id=123023129.

8. Bernard A. Schriever, "Military Space Activities: Recollections and Observations," in R. Cargill Hall and Jacob Neufeld, eds., *The U.S. Air Force in Space, 1945 to the Twenty-first Century* (Washington, DC: United States Air Force History and Museums Program, 1998).

9. Emme, *Impact of Air Power*, 858–59.

10. Killian, *Sputnik, Scientists, and Eisenhower*, 128. Killian rounded out his comment by suggesting that military officers "were convinced that their service, be it Army or Air Force, was best qualified to develop the exotic technology that would be needed for space warfare—and for civilian use, too. In recalling these (interservice) conflicts and fantasies, I also recognize that most of these star-struck officers were also motivated by a laudable concern for the defense of the nation. I cannot say the same for some parts of the aerospace press which outrageously conjured up even wilder fantasies and scare talk, usually in the interest of circulation and advertising from the aerospace industry."

11. Spires, *Beyond Horizons*, 27–28.

12. Walter A. McDougall, *The Heavens and the Earth: A Political History of the Space Age* (Baltimore and London: Basic Books, 1985), 108.

13. U.S. Department of State, *Foreign Relations of the United States, 1955–1957*, Vol. XI, "United Nations and General International Matters," 725.

14. Kurt R. Stehling, *Project Vanguard: The Story of Project Vanguard by its Head of Propulsion* (Garden City, NY: Doubleday & Co., 1961), describes the project from the perspective of a man deeply involved from day one; it is a wonderfully lively account. Stuhlinger and Ordway's *Wernher von Braun*, tackles the topic from the perspective of the von Braun team, 121–40.

15. Stehling, *Project Vanguard*, 23.

16. Paul Dickson, *Sputnik: The Shock of the Century* (New York: Walker Publishing, 2001), 158.

17. Nikita S. Khrushchev, *For Victory in Peaceful Competition with Capitalism* (New York: E.P. Dutton & Co., 1960), 32. On January 22, 1958, for instance, Khrushchev told a gathering of "front-rank agricultural workers" In Byelorussia that "the favorite idea of the imperialists" was that "the socialist system was not conducive to the development of science and culture." The imperialists had even come to believe their own "lies." But Sputnik proved the Americans wrong. Nonetheless, Khrushchev said, the Soviet feat was ridiculed. "One American general even said that the launching of a satellite did not require much brain and that anyone could take a piece of metal and throw it into the sky. Well, why don't *you* do it if *you* are so clever and strong?" (The official Soviet account of the speech said Khrushchev was interrupted here and there by "stormy applause.")

18. McDougall, *The Heavens and the Earth*, 129–31. Insiders in the Eisenhower administration and many scientists considered Vanguard a gamble from the start.

19. Day et al., *Eye in the Sky*.

20. James Harford, *Korolev: How One Man Masterminded the Soviet Drive to Beat America to the Moon* (New York: John Wiley & Sons, 1997), 161. While conducting medical research for manned space shots, Soviet scientists had been sending dogs on their final journeys since 1951, when Dezik and Tsygan were first rocketed to the edge of space. Some dogs, however, were luckier and came back—Albina and Tsyganka wore doggy space suits; they were ejected at about fifty miles in altitude and safely recovered.

21. U.S. Department of State, *Foreign Relations of the United States, 1955–1957*, Vol XI, "United Nations and General International Matters," 759.

22. John Lewis Gaddis, "The Evolution of a Reconnaissance Satellite Regime," in Alexander L. George, Philip J. Farley, and Alexander Dallin, eds., *U.S.-Soviet Security Cooperation: Achievements, Failures, Lessons* (New York and Oxford: Oxford University Press, 1988), 355.

23. Spires, *Beyond Horizons*, 312, endnote 8.

24. Ibid., 101.

25. Another outspoken proponent of military space supremacy was General Curtis LeMay, by then Air Force chief of staff. In March 1962, he spoke at Assumption College in Worcester, Massachusetts. The title of his speech was "Military Implications of Space." At one point, he touched on a possible space weapon that has been a space-warrior favorite for more than four decades: "Beam-directed energy weapons may be used in space. And the energy directed by these weapons could travel across space essentially with the speed of light. This would be an invaluable characteristic for the interception of ICBM warheads and their decoys." *Vital Speeches of the Day,* XXVIII, no. 15, May 15, 1962, 452.

26. Schriever, "Military Space Activities," 17.
27. Talbott, *Khrushchev Remembers: The Last Testament*, 47.
28. Kennedy's speech can be found at http://www.rice.edu/fondren/woodson/speech.html.

CHAPTER 12

1. James Oberg, *Space Power Theory*, 146–49. The book can be downloaded at http://space. au.af.mil/books/oberg/.
2. Space Commission, 100.
3. Lee Kennett, *A History of Strategic Bombing* (New York: Charles Scribner's Sons,1982), 5–6. Austria besieged Venice during the summer, but cholera and other diseases forced the Austrian troops to abandon the swampy ground near the city, where artillery batteries had been emplaced. Meanwhile, Austria's warships could not get close enough to shell the city; the water was too shallow. No problem, said artillery officer Franz Uchatius. He would construct unmanned hot-air balloons that would drop bombs. The balloons were small and the bombs didn't amount to much—a few pounds of gunpowder packed into cast-iron casings.

   By observing the wind conditions, Uchatius estimated how long it would take his little war machines to drift over the city. Then he cut fuses to a suitable length, lit them, and released the balloons from a ship, the aptly named *Vulkan*. When the fuses burned down, the links between bombs and balloons were severed and the bombs fell. The exact number of balloons launched is uncertain, but it may have been as many as two hundred.

   The Austrian press spoke of the "frightful effects" of the bombardment. In fact, most of the bombs fell harmlessly into the Gulf of Venice or into Venetian lagoons. Those that landed in the city seemed to have caused no great consternation. But a precedent had been established.
4. See, for example H. G. Wells, *The War in the Air*, described in Chapter 6, endnote 29.
5. Kennett, *History of Strategic Bombing*, 10.
6. Mead, *The Eye in the Air*, 35. In 1909, Lord Montague of Beaulieu said Britain could be paralyzed by air attacks on government buildings including the Houses of Parliament, railway stations, telephone and telegraph offices, and the stock exchange (Kennett, *The First Air War*, 44.) Attacks on cities, however, would not go unpunished. In 1913, a French aviator published a book with the remarkable title, *How We Are Going to Torpedo Berlin with Our Squadron of Airplanes as Soon as the War Begins*. In it, he describes twenty German Zeppelins striking Paris, causing "indescribable horrors." French aircraft then retaliate by raining 1,360 "torpedoes" on Berlin, forcing Germany to surrender (Kennett, *A History of Strategic Bombing*, 17.)
7. The U.S. Army was a little slow to realize the potential military value of the flying machine. Not long after their first powered flights in 1903, the Wright brothers realized that they had something that might be useful in war. In 1905, a myopic Army Board of Ordnance and Fortification turned down an offer by the Wrights to sell the Army their latest machine. The Wrights were not dismayed. France and Germany seemed to be on the brink of war and the brothers offered their machine to the French. The asking price: two hundred thousand dollars, a tidy sum when two thousand could build a splendid mansion. The French did not go for the deal; they believed they would soon develop their own airplanes, which could be used in the coming war.

8. Lambakis, On the Edge of Earth, 274–76.

9. Perhaps out of diplomatic courtesy, the United States, along with Israel, had traditionally abstained from voting on the annual PAROS resolution in the U.N. General Assembly. In December 2005, both voted "no" for the first time.

10. Another barrier to negotiations has been a long-running dispute between China and the United States over beginning negotiations for a Fissile Material Cut-Off Treaty (a "fissban"). The United States, which has stockpiled enough fissile material for tens of thousands of new nuclear weapons, seeks to negotiate a treaty that would prevent other nations from producing bomb-grade plutonium and highly enriched uranium. A fissile material cutoff treaty is America's highest priority at the Conference on Disarmament; in contrast, a new space treaty is China's highest priority. Since 1999, when President Bill Clinton green-lighted further development of a national antiballistic missile system, China has insisted that both treaties be worked on at the same time. The administrations of Presidents Clinton and Bush described that as "linkage" and thus unacceptable. The dispute, which is exceedingly arcane, has been notable for the high degree of political posturing and cynicism practiced by both sides. For background, see "Time for a Fissban—or Farewell" by Jenni Rissanen, Disarmament Diplomacy, no. 83, Winter 2006. Go to http://www.acronym.org.uk/dd/dd83/83fissban.htm.

11. Go to http://www.reachingcriticalwill.org/political/cd/speeches06/index2.html#second; statements made on June 13, 2006.

12. Satellites in very high orbits will remain in orbit even after they have "died." Satellites in low-Earth orbit, where there are enough air molecules to eventually slow them, will eventually reenter the atmosphere, in weeks, months, years, or decades, depending on how distant their orbits are from Earth.

    When a satellite's time has come, ground controllers remotely fire small retro-rockets embedded in the satellite, which slow it until it enters a lower "decay" orbit in which atmospheric drag slows it to a predictable rate. Eventually, ground controllers send it on its final plunge into the atmosphere.

    All of this is an immensely complicated and time-consuming business. (Another method used to dispose of satellites that no longer serve a useful purpose is to fire them into higher and thus permanent orbits.) See Appendix B, "Newton's Cannon," for a brief introduction into orbital mechanics.

13. Bob Preston et al., Space Weapons; Earth Wars (Santa Monica, CA: RAND and Project Air Force, 2002), 174.

14. Go to http://www.lanl.gov/quarterly/q_spring03/asteroid_text.shtml.

15. Go to http://www.space.com/scienceastronomy/050309_meteor_crater.html.

16. Objects in orbit still have mass but they no longer "weigh" anything. "Weight" describes the interaction of gravity and mass; in orbit, the force of gravity has been, in effect, cancelled out. See Appendix B, "Newton's Cannon."

17. In 1970, Gen. Bernard A. Schriever, as noted in the previous chapter, was America's most influential space warrior. That year he wrote this in a forward to an early space-warrior book: "The deterioration of the U.S. strategic posture has led many to conclude that our only recourse is strategic arms limitations agreements with the Soviet Union. It is, of course, the sincere hope of every logical person that an agreement can be reached with the Soviet Union for strategic arms control. However, an honest interpretation of Communist doctrine and of Soviet history does not suggest that we should place high hopes that an accord can be reached which will guarantee our security. Therefore, it is essential that we

vigorously search for other strategic capabilities to provide additional options. Is there an alternative to disarmament negotiations if they should fail?... That answer lies in the most advanced field of technology, namely space technology. It lies in the development of strategic space weapons." See Salkeld, War and Space, iv.

18. Space Commission, 37–38.

19. The American notion that "peaceful" could be equated with "non-aggressive" dates back to 1958. See "The Legal Aspects of Peaceful and Non-Peaceful Uses of Outer Space" by Ivan A. Vlasic in Peaceful and Non-Peaceful Uses of Space, Bhupendra Jasani, ed. (New York and London: Taylor & Francis, 1991), 37.

20. An excellent source of information on space treaty issues is a website maintained by a non-governmental organization called Reaching Critical Will. Hundreds of original documents can be found at http://www.reachingcriticalwill.org/legal/paros/parosindex. html#Negotiations.

21. A good summary of the Sino-Russian position can be found at http://www.reachingcriti-calwill.org/political/cd/speeches04/topic.html#PAROS.

22. Go to http://www.marshall.org/category.php?id=8. Scroll down to "Saving Space: Securing Our Space Assets," July 2005.

23. Zhang Hui, "Space Weaponization and Space Security: a Chinese Perspective," China Security (World Security Institute), No. 2, 2006.

24. See http://www.stimson.org/space/programhome.cfm. Theresa Hitchens's Future Security in Space: Charting a Cooperative Course (Washington, DC: Center for Defense Information, 2004) is also a useful primer on the rules-of-the-road concept.

25. See, for instance, a list of treaty precedents compiled by the Henry L. Stimson Center at http://www.stimson.org/?SN=WS20040408639.

26. International Security Advisory Board, "Report on U.S. Space Policy, 7–8, http://www.state.gov/documents/organization/85263pdf.

27. Ibid., 10.

28. When political scientists speak of an "anarchic world," they do not mean the globe is in utter chaos, although at times that seems to be the case. Rather they mean there is no global government that can enforce some measure of law and order. In contrast, functioning nation-states have hierarchical governments that, in theory, can maintain order within the boundaries of the states. No moral judgment is implied; the order can be relatively benign, such as found in most modern democracies, or it can be a cruel and inhumane order such as under Stalin, Mao, Hitler, and Saddam Hussein. Many idealists used to hope that the United Nations might someday evolve into a quasi world government capable of maintaining global law and order. At best, that was a misinterpretation of the purposes of the United Nations. Despite the grand rhetoric of the U.N. Charter, the central role of the United Nations has been the protection and preservation of national sovereignty.

29. Michael E. O'Hanlon, Neither Star Wars Nor Sanctuary: Constraining the Military Uses of Space (Washington, DC: Brookings Institution Press, 2004), 121.

30. One of the earliest and keenest proponents of U.S. control of space was Air Force General Homer A. Boushey. In the late 1950s, he was director of advanced projects for the Air Force and a prototypical right-stuff guy. In August 1941, for instance, he became the first American to get an airplane off the ground using rocket motors, an extraordinarily gutsy act. Previous tests of the rockets (JATOs for "Jet Assisted Take-Off") had often ended in explosions. (Daso, Architects of American Air, 66.)

Boushey was especially enamored of controlling space from the Moon. On January 28, 1958, he spoke to the Aero Club of the National Press Club. Among many things, he promoted the idea that U.S. bases on the Moon would be the ultimate deterrent to war. Nuclear-tipped missiles, he said, could be "catapulted from shafts sunk deep into the Moon's surface." That would not require much energy because escape velocity would be "only one-fifth or one-sixth" that of Earth.

The heart of his speech, however, was this assertion: "It has been said that 'He who controls the Moon, controls the Earth.' Our planners must carefully evaluate this statement, for, if true (and I for one think it is), then the United States must control the Moon." (Emme, The Impact of Air Power, 871.)

31. What is meant by "relatively decent"? Consider the kind of world we would live in if the Soviet Union had "won" the Cold War.

32. See, for instance, Randy Rydell, "Looking Back: Going for Baruch—The Nuclear Plan That Refused to Go Away," Arms Control Today, June 2006, http://www.armscontrol. org/act/2006_06/LookingbackBaruch.asp.

33. Eugene Rabinowitch, ed., Minutes to Midnight: The International Control of Atomic Energy (Chicago: The Bulletin of the Atomic Scientists, 1950), 68.

34. Robert Jay Lifton and Richard Falk, Indefensible Weapons: The Political and Psychological Case Against Nuclearism (New York, Basic Books, 1982), 199–200.

35. Dean Acheson, Present at the Creation: My Years in the State Department (New York: Norton, 1969), 155.

36. A definitive account of the tests is in Jonathan Weisgall, Operation Crossroads: The Atomic Tests at Bikini Atoll (Annapolis, MD: Naval Institute Press, 1994).

37. Gar Alperovitz is a leading "revisionist." See his classic, Atomic Diplomacy: Hiroshima and Potsdam—The Use of the Atomic Bomb and the American Confrontation With Soviet Power (New York: Simon & Shuster, 1965).

38. For an early and tentative analysis of the alleged Iranian nuclear weapons program, see David Albright and Mark Hibbs, "Spotlight Shifts to Iran," Bulletin of the Atomic Scientists, March 1992.

39. Space Commission, 29.

40. Richard L. Garwin and Frank N. von Hippel, "A Technical Analysis: Deconstructing North Korea's October 9 Nuclear Test," Arms Control Today, November 2006, http:// www.armscontrol.org/act/2006_11/tech.asp.

41. China's January 2007 ASAT test employed a "road-mobile" medium-range ballistic missile that did not require a spaceport. A sophisticated spacefaring nation, such as China, presumably could develop the capability to launch kill-vehicles to intercept satellites in low-Earth orbit from areas other than a formal spaceport. However, kill-vehicles capable of reaching satellites in higher orbits require much more powerful rockets that, in turn, would need the services provided at a true spaceport. In any event, America's surveillance satellites were so sophisticated that China's preparations for the test (and for at least two previous tests) were detected.

42. Go to http://www.reachingcriticalwill.org/political/cd/papers06/, May 22, 2006, for the People's Republic of China and the Russian Federation's working paper, "Verification of PAROS."

43. America's negotiators might even pick up on an intriguing idea conceived by Ronald Reagan during his Star Wars days. Reagan repeatedly said he wanted to share Strategic Defense Initiative technology with the Soviet Union, an idea that his top national security

advisers furiously opposed. See, for instance, the share-the-technology discussion in Lettow, Ronald Reagan and His Quest, 209. If the United States were willing to share its technical knowledge regarding land-, sea-, or air-based missile defense, it would be proof that the United States was serious about a new space treaty.

44. Go to http://www.fas.org/nuke/control/paros/news/treaty-paros-000915.htm.

45. Go to http://www.gsinstitute.org/bsg/docs/05_09_07_Grey_space.pdf.

CHAPTER 13

1. *Arsenal of Hypocrisy: The Space Program and the Military Industrial Complex*, produced by Randy Atkins (http://www.ArsenalofHypocrisy.com) and hosted by Bruce Gagnon, Global Network Against Weapons & Nuclear Power in Space. Go to http://www.space4-peace.org.

2. Hubert Vedrine with Dominique Moïsi, *France in an Age of Globalization* (Washington, DC: Brookings Institution Press, 2000), 2.

3. *World Policy Journal*, "America's Virtual Empire," XIX, no. 2. Also, http://www.world-policy.org/journal/sum02-2.html.

4. Go to http://www.mtholyoke.edu/acad/intrel/winthrop.htm.

5. Thomas Jefferson, "Comments to the Citizens of Washington," 1809. Go to http://etext.virginia.edu/jefferson/biog/lj33.htm.

6. Go to http://www.yale.edu/lawweb/avalon/washing.htm.

7. Go to http://www.mtholyoke.edu/acad/intrel/jqadams.htm.

8. In the late 1700s, for instance, Jonathan Mitchel Sewall, a New Hampshire lawyer and Revolutionary War poet, wrote in his "Epilogue to Addison's Cato" a couple of lines that came to be enormously popular: *No pent-up Utica contracts our powers! But the whole boundless continent is yours!* Albert K. Weinberg, *Manifest Destiny: A Study of Nationalist Expansion in American History* (Chicago: Quadrangle Paperbacks, 1963), 62.

9. Ibid., 31.

10. Go to http://www.newhumanist.com/md4.html.

11. For a brief overview, go to http://www.pbs.org/kera/usmexicanwar/prelude/md_expansionism.html.

12. McDougall, *Promised Land, Crusader State*, 1997, 118.

13. Joseph's Pulitzer's New York *World* and William Randolph Hearst's New York *Journal*, which were in a thuggishly brutal circulation war, featured generous helpings of bizarre and sensational stories as well as doses of imaginative or wholly fictional "news"— including lurid (if sometimes true) tales of Spanish oppression in Cuba. Both newspapers carried enormously popular color comic strips drawn by different artists but starring the same character, "The Yellow Kid." Hence the term, "yellow journalism."

14. Letter to Teddy Roosevelt, July 17, 1898. See the commentary by Joseph R. Stromberg, "The Spanish American War: the Leap into Overseas Empire," at http://www.independent.org/newsroom/article.asp?id=1344.

15. Joseph L. Stickney, *Life and Glorious Deeds of Admiral Dewey Including a Thrilling Account of Our Conflicts with the Spaniards and Filipinos in the Orient* (Philadelphia, PA: Bell Publishing Company, 1899), 273.

16. Ibid., 277.

17. Charles S. Olcott, *William McKinley, Vol. II* (Boston and New York: Riverside Press, 1916), 109.

18. Both comments as well as many more can be found at "Anti-Imperialism in the United States, 1898–1935," a website edited by Jim Zwick. Go to http://www.boondocksnet.com/ai/index.html.

19. Max Boot, *The Savage Wars of Peace: Small Wars and the Rise of American Power* (New York: Basic Books, 2002), 125.

20. C. B. Bowers, *Beveridge and the Progressive Era* (New York: The Literary Guild, 1932), 74.

21. The "March of the Flag" speech can be found at http://www.historytools.org/sources/beveridge.html.

22. For a shortened version of Beveridge's Senate speech, go to http://www.isop.ucla.edu/eas/documents/phlpqust.htm.

23. Alfred Thayer Mahan, *Retrospect & Prospect: Studies in International Relations—Naval and Political* (Port Washington, NY: Kennikat Press, 1902, reissued 1968), 16–17.

24. Josiah Strong, *Expansion Under New World Conditions* (New York and London: Garland Publishing, 1971), 213.

25. Brooks Adams, with a new evaluation by Marquis W. Childs, *America's Economic Supremacy* (New York and London: Harper & Brothers, 1947), 136.

26. Ibid., 169–70.

27. This amazing poem can be found at http://www.historymatters.gmu.edu/d/5478/.

28. William Thomas Stead, *The Americanisation of the World: The Trend of the Twentieth Century* (London: "Review of the Reviews" Office, 1902), 1.

29. See Edmund Morris, *Theodore Rex* (New York: Random House, 2001), 176–209.

30. Go to http://www.historicaldocuments.com/TheodoreRooseveltscorollarytotheMonroeDoctrine.htm.

CHAPTER 14

1. Thomas J. Knock, *To End All Wars: Woodrow Wilson and the Quest for a New World Order* (New York: Oxford University Press, 1992), 199.

2. Ibid., 194.

3. Herbert Hoover and H. Lawrence Hoffman, *The Ordeal of Woodrow Wilson* (New York: McGraw-Hill, 1958), 256.

4. Walter E. Weyl, "Prophet and Politician," reprinted in Robert B. Luce, ed., *The Faces of Five Decades: Selections from Fifty Years of the New Republic, 1914–1964* (New York: Simon and Schuster, 1964), 45.

5. Publisher Henry Luce (*Time, Life, Fortune*) was one of the most influential exceptionalists. As early as February 17, 1941, he said this in an editorial in *Life* called "The American Century": "In the field of national policy, the fundamental trouble with America has been, and is, that whereas their nation became in the twentieth century the most powerful and the most vital nation in the world, nevertheless Americans were unable to accommodate spiritually and practically to that fact. Hence they have failed to play their part as a world power—a failure that has had disastrous consequences for themselves and mankind.

   And the cure is this: to accept wholeheartedly our duty and our opportunity as the most powerful and vital nation in the world and in consequence to exert upon the world the full impact of our influence, for such purposes as we see fit and by such means as we see fit." Luce added, however, that he "emphatically" did not mean that the United States should "police the whole world" or to "impose democratic institutions on all mankind including the Dalai Lama and the good shepherds of Tibet."

6. Go to http://reagan2020.us/speeches/To_Restore_America.asp.

7. Eugene V. Rostow, *A Breakfast for Bonaparte: U.S. National Security Interests From the Heights of Abraham to the Nuclear Age* (Washington, DC: National Defense University Press, 1992), 22. His comment did not suggest approval. He believed that a proper foreign policy should be based on a grand strategy, a coherent and systematic definition of America's role in the world.

8. See *Sojourners* magazine, published by an evangelical organization that is distinctly liberal in its outlook, www.sojo.net.

9. Irving Kristol, *Neoconservatism: The Autobiography of an Idea* (New York: Free Press, 1995), 33.

10. Irving Kristol often expressed a degree of "wonderment" over the term, "neoconservatism." It was not a movement but a "persuasion," he said. Writing in the August 25, 2003 issue of *The Weekly Standard*, a glossy neoconservative magazine co-founded by his son, William Kristol, he wrote: "Neoconservatism is the first variant of American conservatism in the past century that is in the 'American grain.' It is hopeful, not lugubrious; forward-looking, not nostalgic; and its general tone is cheerful, not grim or dyspeptic. Its twentieth-century heroes tend to be TR, FDR, and Ronald Reagan. Such Republican and conservative worthies as Calvin Coolidge, Herbert Hoover, Dwight Eisenhower, and Barry Goldwater are politely overlooked."

11. *Commentary*, April 1976.

12. Go to http://www.opinionjournal.com/forms/printThis.html?id=110001926.

13. Ibid.

14. Ibid.

15. Ibid.

16. Charles Krauthammer, "The Unipolar Moment," *Foreign Affairs*, 70, no. 1 (special issue dated 1990–91).

17. *Foreign Affairs*, 75, no. 4, July/August 1996. (William Kristol is the son of Irving Kristol and Gertrude Himmelfarb, godparents of the neoconservative movement.)

18. Go to http://www.whitehouse.gov/news/releases/2005/02/20050202-11.html.

19. Go to http://www.newamericancentury.org/statementofprinciples.htm.

20. Go to http://www.yale.edu/lawweb/avalon/washing.htm.

CHAPTER 15

1. *Asia 2025* embraced all of the states of Asia, including Asiatic Russia, India and Pakistan. It was published in a plastic binder for a relatively small circle of Defense Department and government policymakers. It is not easily found, but references to it can be found on the web by using "net assessment" and "Asia 2025" as search terms.

2. Go to http://www.newamericancentury.org/chinanov0497.htm.

3. Mearsheimer, *Tragedy of Great Power Politics*, 401.

4. See, especially, Michael P. Pillsbury, "An Assessment of China's Anti-Satellite and Space Warfare Programs, Policies and Doctrines," U.S.-China Economic and Security Commission, January 19, 2007, http://www.uscc.gov/researchpapers/comm_research_archive.php.

5. The Chinese economy ranks second to that of the United States. See the *World Factbook* published by the Central Intelligence Agency, http://www.cia.gov/library/publications/the-world-factbook/geos/ch.html#Econ.

6. Frank J. Gaffney, Jr., "Chinese Penetration of the Global Capital Markets: Are American Investors Unwittingly Buying the Rope To Be Used for Their Hanging?" testimony before the U.S.-China Economic and Security Review Commission, August 11, 2005, http://www.uscc.gov/hearings/2005hearings/written_testimonies/05_08_11wrts/gaffney_frank_wrts.php.

7. See, for instance, Vaclav Smil, "China's Great Famine: 40 Years Later," http://www.bmj.com/cgi/content/full/319/7225/1619.

8. For a short biography of Deng Xiaoping, see http://www.asiaweek.com/asiaweek/features/aoc/aoc.deng.html.

9. "The China Price," *Business Week*, December 6, 2004, http://www.businessweek.com/magazine/content/04_49/b3911401.htm.

10. Quadrennial Defense Review, 2006, 29, http://www.defenselink.mil/pubs/pdfs/China%20Report%202006.pdf.

11. See Robert S. Dudney, "What It Means To Be No. 1," *Air Force Magazine*, February 2006, http://www.afa.org/magazine/Feb2006/default.asp. After noting that the United States far outspends everyone else, Dudney added:

    "The 15 countries in question—China, Russia, France, Britain, Japan, Germany, Italy, Saudi Arabia, India, South Korea, Spain, Australia, Canada, Turkey, and Israel—have small economies, compared to us. As a group, their GDP totals $17 trillion. The United States GDP, by itself, is nearly as great—approaching $13 trillion. One would expect comparable defense spending levels.

    "There are other, more significant factors that make the United States the No. 1 spender.

    "Start with the obvious strategic considerations. The United States, unlike any other nation, is a global power with worldwide interests, responsibilities, and allies. No other nation would be called on to extend its deterrent power around the world or would even want to. None have [sic] the power to fight and win two major regional wars at a time. Only Washington can do that.

    "Indeed, the scale of U.S. military might enables some other major nations—Germany, say, or Japan—to be relaxed about their own defenses. Another factor to consider: Americans have decided that, if war comes, it will be waged far from U.S. shores. That decision imposes certain military demands, all of them expensive.

    "Fighting far from home requires lots and lots of transport—especially airlift—to haul bullets, beans, parts, and troops. It also requires costly overseas bases. Because every war they fight is an 'away game' in an enemy's backyard, U.S. combat forces can't be just a little stronger; they must be much stronger—in the air, on land, or at sea—and that requires high-technology weapons.

    "It also requires a huge amount of combat support. At present, about 50 percent of U.S.A.F.'s budget goes to so-called "joint force enablers"—tankers, satellites, and surveillance aircraft.

    "Much of today's defense cost flows from the kind of force to which we Americans have committed ourselves psychologically. It is an all-volunteer force, not conscripted. Attracting and keeping high-quality personnel costs a fortune—$111 billion a year just for pay—and grows more expensive each year. Health care costs and other benefits have been soaring.

    "Such a professional combat force, in turn, requires extensive, realistic training, which pushes up outlays on fuel, spare parts, repairs, and depot labor. The U.S. military spends $150 billion a year on these accounts, twice as much as it spends on weapons....

"A bigger point to make is this: Even today's relatively high level of defense spending imposes no undue burden on Americans or their economy. The best measure of 'afford-ability' is not the amount of dollars spent, but rather the percent of GDP that a nation devotes to its military equipment and operations, and that figure is near a historic low.

"In a Nov. 21 memo, Adm. Edmund P. Giambastiani, Jr., vice chairman of the JCS [Joint Chiefs], raised that issue with Rumsfeld. 'A common comparison of defense spending cited in the press is that, in absolute terms, the U.S. spends more than the next "X" countries combined,' he wrote. He pointed out that, at 3.8 percent of GDP, the U.S. ranked no better than 29th.

"In other words, we stand just behind Belarus (3.9), just ahead of Morocco (3.7), and dead even with Tanzania. As Rumsfeld himself might say, it is useful to keep this in mind."

12. Hans Kristensen, Robert S. Norris, and Matthew G. McKinzie, *Report: Chinese Nuclear Forces and U.S. Nuclear War Planning*, http://www.nukestrat.com/china/chinareport.htm.

13. Go to http://www.nukestrat.com/us/stratcom/suncityex.htm.

14. President Richard Nixon, whose anti-communist credentials were impeccable, began to establish relations with communist China in 1972, in part because he wanted to enlist China as a de facto ally in America's continuing Cold War confrontation with the Soviet Union. China would "balance" Soviet ambitions in East Asia. See, for instance, James Mann, *About Face: A History of America's Curious Relationship with China, From Nixon to Clinton* (New York: Alfred A. Knopf, 1999).

15. For Beijing's view, see "The One-China Principle and the Taiwan Issue," February 21, 2000, at http://taiwansecurity.org/IS/White-Paper-022100.htm.

16. The Taiwan Relations Act can be found at http://www.taiwansecurity.org/IS/TRA.htm. For a thoughtful overview of U.S.-China relations, see *Foreign Affairs*, September/October 2005, an issue devoted to China.

17. From the introduction to chapter two of China's 2004 *White Paper*, go to http://www.fas. org/nuke/guide/china/doctrine/natdef2004.html#2. That document was written at a time when a presidential campaign in Taiwan had focused on the issue of independence and tensions between the Mainland and Taiwan were high. In contrast, the waters had calmed a bit by 2006. The 2006 paper simply said:

"The struggle to oppose and contain the separatist forces for 'Taiwan independence' and their activities remains a hard one. By pursuing a radical policy for 'Taiwan inde-pendence,' the Taiwan authorities aim at creating 'de jure Taiwan independence' through 'constitutional reform,' thus still posing a grave threat to China's sovereignty and territorial integrity, as well as to peace and stability across the Taiwan Straits and in the Asia-Pacific region as a whole. The United States has reiterated many times that it will adhere to the 'one China' policy and honor the three joint communiqués between China and the United States. But, it continues to sell advanced weapons to Taiwan, and has strength-ened its military ties with Taiwan." Section One: The Security Environment, http://news. xinhuanet.com/english/2006-12/29/content_5547029.htm.) The three joint communiqués as well as the text of the Taiwan Relations Act can be found at http://www.taiwansecurity. org/TSR-US.htm.

18. *Long Range Plan*, Introduction, paragraph four.

19. A couple of scenarios commonly bruited about behind closed doors in national security circles go something like this: If Iran seems to be on the edge of going nuclear, Israel might launch preemptive strikes against its nuclear infrastructure. In that event, the entire

Gulf region would be in play. Similarly, if North Korea develops a true nuclear capability, Japan might build a nuclear arsenal virtually overnight; it has the expertise and the plutonium to do so. If that happens, the ancient tensions between China and Japan would greatly increase. Despite considerable Japanese investment on the Chinese mainland, the reservoir of Chinese mistrust of Japan is extraordinarily wide and deep. China suffered horribly during the 1930s at the hands of a brutally racist and imperial Japan. The United States would be entangled in either the Gulf or a North Korean–Japanese–Chinese scenario, with unpredictable but almost surely unfortunate consequences.

20. The "space Pearl Harbor" scenario can be found at http://www.airpower.maxwell.af.mil/airchronicles/apj/apj94/baum.html.

21. Simon P. Worden and John E. Shaw, *Whither Space Power? Forging A Strategy for the New Century* (Maxwell Air Force Base, AL: Air University Press, 2002), http://aupress.au.af.mil/fairchild_papers/worden_shaw/worden_shaw.pdf.

22. Maria Barbicane? You may recall that Jules Barbicane was the hero of Jules Verne's *From the Earth to the Moon.*

23. Richard J. Adams and Martin F. France, "The Chinese Threat to U.S. Space Superiority," *High Frontier*, Winter 2005, http://permanent.access.gpo.gov/lps67359/2005/Journal-Winter05.pdf.

24. See, for instance, Clay Chandler, "China's $1.2 Trillion Cash Hoard," *Fortune*, May 14, 2007, http://money.cnn.com/magazines/fortune/fortune_archive/2007/05/14/100024842/index.htm.

25. Bret Stephens, "China's Gift," *Wall Street Journal*, January 23, 2007, 18.

26. Quoted in Richard L. Garwin's "Toward International Security: the Role of Space Weapons, Antisatellite Weapon Tests, and National Missile Defense," a presentation to the United Nations, October 21, 1999, http://www.fas.org/RLG/102599-lakhdhir.htm.

27. Although Garwin is one of the world's most accomplished physicists, he has almost always worked, as do most scientists, far off the public stage. In the late 1940s and early 1950s, he was Enrico Fermi's star student at the University of Chicago. (Fermi was then arguably the world's premier experimental physicist, a Nobel laureate who, on December 2, 1942, initiated the first manmade, self-sustaining nuclear chain reaction, a milestone in the Manhattan Project.)

Garwin went on to become one of IBM's key research scientists, doing path-breaking work in low-temperature physics and superconductors, communications systems, gravitational radiation, and the like. He has published more than five hundred scientific papers and has been granted forty-four patents. He was director of the IBM Watson Laboratory and director of the IBM Applied Research Center during IBM's glory years.

In another life, Garwin focused on the intersection of science and public policy, especially national security policy. Beginning in the mid-1950s, he evolved into one of world's leading advocates of nuclear arms control. Over the decades, he served on the President's Science Advisory Committee and the Defense Science Board, and he has counseled a host of government bodies and non-governmental organizations on national security matters. He taught public policy at Harvard's Kennedy School of Government for three decades and he has been a principal participant in many dozens of international arms control meetings, conferences, seminars, and working groups.

In yet another life, Garwin helped design nuclear weapons for a time. In the early 1950s, for instance, while a faculty member at the University of Chicago, he spent his summer breaks at Los Alamos National Laboratory in New Mexico, where the first atomic bombs were designed and built. Some of the scientists at Los Alamos, especially Edward Teller, had been working on the theory of a hydrogen bomb (which they called the "Super") for several years. But exactly how the Super might be made to work eluded everyone until early 1951, when Teller and Stanislaw Ulam came up with the idea of "radiation implosion." Teller asked Garwin in May 1951 to design an experimental device that would test the theory. Garwin, then twenty-three years old, did so. Teller later recalled that Garwin came up with a workable blueprint in "a week or two."

The experimental device, built with additional input from other Los Alamos scientists, was tested November 1, 1952 on an island in the Pacific. It had a yield of about ten million tons of TNT, making it some seven hundred times more powerful than the bomb dropped on Hiroshima. Its fireball was three miles wide and the test site, a mile-wide island, Elugelab, disappeared. See also "An Evening with Richard L. Garwin: Conversation with David Kestenbaum of National Public Radio," a transcript of an American Association for the Advancement of Science meeting, January 10, 2006, http://www.fas.org/rlg/060110-aaas.pdf.

28. Organizations such as the Pugwash Conferences on Science and World Affairs (http://www.pugwash.org/); the Federation of American Scientists (http://www.fas.org); International Physicians for the Prevention of Nuclear War (http://www.ippnw.org/); the Natural Resources Defense Council (http://www.nrdc.org); and *The Bulletin of the Atomic Scientists* (http://www.thebulletin.org) have been deeply involved for decades in promoting an international exchange of ideas and data to buttress arms control efforts. See, especially, Matthew Evangelista's *Unarmed Forces: the Transnational Movement to End the Cold War* (Ithaca, NY and London: Cornell University Press, 1999).

29. See Richard L. Garwin, "Space Weapons or Space Arms Control?" presentation to the American Philosophical Society, April 29, 2000, http://www.aps-pub.com/proceedings/1453/0600toc.htm.

30. See, for instance, "Scientist, Citizen, and Government—Ethics in Action (or Ethics Inaction,)" presented to the Illinois Mathematics and Science Academy, May 4, 1993. Go to http://www.fas.org/rlg/930504-imsa.htm.

31. Some years ago during a lively debate at the University of Chicago, John J. Mearsheimer, the world-class political scientist mentioned earlier, observed that it is not wise "to poke a sleeping dog in the eye with a stick." The topic of the hour had nothing to do with military space. Mearsheimer was expressing his view that a great nation should have enough economic, diplomatic, and military power to protect its vital interests, but it should not go out of its way to needlessly provoke a fight.

32. See "China Attempted to Blind U.S. Satellites with Laser," http://www.defensenews.com/story.php?F=2121111&C=america. For a later wrap-up of the test evidence, see Yousaf Butt, "Satellite Laser Ranging in China," http://www.ucsusa.org/global_security/space_weapons/chinese-lasers-and-us-satellites.html.

33. Anthony Lake, remarks to the Japan-America Society, October 23, 1996, http://www.mtholyoke.edu/acad/intrel/lakeapec.htm.

34. For a contrary view, see James Mann, *The China Fantasy: How Our Leaders Explain Away Chinese Repression* (New York: Viking, 2007).

CHAPTER 16

1. Reinhold Niebuhr, *The Irony of American History* (Charles Scribner's Sons, 1952), 132.
2. Ibid., 147.

3. Ibid., 148.

4. Serge Schmemann, "The Coalition of the Unbelieving," *New York Times Book Review*, January 25, 2004, 12, http://query.nytimes.com/gst/fullpage.html?res=9D06E5D61E30F 936A15752C0A9629C8B63.

5. J. William Fulbright, *The Arrogance of Power* (New York: Random House, Vintage Books, 1996), 2.

6. Life in Athens was not as democratic as we like to suppose. Like the American South be fore the Civil War, the standard of living for Athenian citizens was almost wholly depen- dent on slave labor, as was true in many parts of the ancient world. The Athenian variety of slavery is commonly thought to have been relatively "humane," except for the tens of thousands of men condemned to labor in the yard-high tunnels of the silver mines, where life was hard, brutish, and short. Athenian slaves could even testify in law cases, although they were first tortured to ensure truthfulness.

7. The Funeral Oration can be found in Thucydides, *The Peloponnesian War* (any edition), Book II: 35-47.

8. Did Thucydides get the history of the conflict between Athens and Sparta right? There is no way to know. His book laid the foundations of historiography and is chockablock with facts and figures, speeches and events—but it is also a morality tale, a dispiriting story of how a long and probably preventable war brought financial, material, and moral exhaus- tion to Athens, the most enlightened state in Hellas.

    Thucydides tried to set down events as objectively as possible, in part by consult- ing multiple sources in researching facts and events. Unlike Herodotus, a contemporary whose history of the Persian wars is filled with gossip and supernatural explanations, Thucydides described the fate of Hellas as determined by men, not gods.

    Like today's historians, Thucydides recognized that total objectivity was not always possible. Sources were often confusing, ambiguous, or contradictory. In one passage, for instance, he explains how he handled speeches. "Some I heard myself, others I got from various quarters." But "in all cases" it was "difficult to carry them word for word in one's memory, so my habit has been to make the speakers say what was in my opinion demanded of them by the various occasions, of course adhering as closely as possible to the general sense of what they really said." (I: 22)

    That raises an intriguing question. Was Pericles really as wise and eloquent as he is presented? Or was Thucydides practicing the art of making "speakers say what was in my opinion demanded of them"?

9. Thucydides, *History of the Peloponnesian War*, I: 23.

10. Ibid., II: 8.

11. Quoted in Walter A. McDougall, "America and the World at the Dawn of a New Century," keynote address, Foreign Policy Research Institute annual dinner, November 10, 1999, http:// www.fpri.org/fpriwire/0712.199912.mcdougall.americaworldnewcentury.html.

12. John Adams, "A Dissertation on the Canon and Feudal Law," 1765, http://www.found- ing.com/library/lbody.cfm?id=140&parent=54.

13. John Dickinson, "The Liberty Song." A copy can be found at http://sniff.numachi.com/ pages/tiHARTOAK2;ttHEARTOAK.html.

14. *The Master Plan* can be found at http://www.cdi.org/news/space-security/afspc-strategic- master-plan-06-beyond.pdf.

15. Bruce M. DeBlois, "Space Sanctuary: A Viable National Strategy," *Airpower Journal*, Winter 1998, http://www.airpower.maxwell.af.mil/airchronicles/apj/apj98/win98/deblois. html.

16. *Astropolitics* is published by Routledge, Taylor & Francis Group.

17. DeBlois, "Space Sanctuary."

18. George H.W. Bush, speech at West Point, January 5, 1993, http://dosfan.lib.uic.edu/ ERC/briefing/dispatch/1993/html/Dispatchv4no02.html.

19. Henry DeWolf Smyth, *Atomic Energy for Military Purposes* (The "Smyth Report"), August 1945, http://www.atomicarchive.com/Docs/SmythReport/index.shtml.

20. William Lanouette, *Genius in the Shadows: A Biography of Leo Szilard—the Man Behind the Bomb* (New York, Charles Scribner's Sons, 1992), 272.

21. Alice Kimball Smith, *A Peril and a Hope: The Scientists' Movement in America, 1945–47* (Chicago: University of Chicago Press, 1965), 84.

22. Holloway, *Stalin and the Bomb,* 173.

23. Smyth, *Atomic Energy,* Chapter Thirteen, paragraphs seven and eight.

APPENDIX A

1. Lucian's "Trips to the Moon" is marvelous satire. Go to http://www.gutenberg.org/ files/10430/10430-h/10430-h.htm.

2. Francis Godwin's "The Man in the Moone, or, a Discourse of a Voyage Thither" is a minor classic in space lore. Go to http://onlinebooks.library.upenn.edu/webbin/book/ lookupid?key=olbp17985.

3. William J. Walter, *The Space Age* (New York: Random House, 1992), 6.

4. Arthur C. Clarke, *The Promise of Space* (New York: Harper & Row, 1968), 14.

5. Ibid., 15.

6. See Chapter One of "The Space Shuttle Decision," an online document published by the NASA History Office, http://history.nasa.gov/SP-4221/contents.htm.

7. Herman Potocnik, a.k.a. Herman Noordung's *The Problem of Space Travel: The Rocket Motor* is online at the NASA History Office, http://www.hq.nasa.gov/office/pao/History/ SP-4026/contents.html.

8. Ibid., "Distant Worlds."

9. Ibid., "The Habitat Wheel."

10. Ibid., "The Most Dreadful Weapon."

11. Walter, *The Space Age,* 20.

12. A short sketch of Goddard can be found at http://www-istp.gsfc.nasa.gov/stargaze/Sgoddard.htm.

13. Spires, *Beyond Horizons,* 6.

14. Loyd. S. Swenson, Jr., James M. Grimwood, and Charles C. Alexander, *This New Ocean: A History of Project Mercury* (Washington, DC: National Aeronautics and Space Administration, 1966), 18.

15. Moltz, *The Politics of Space Security.* Chapter Three, "Roots of the U.S.-Soviet Space Race: 1920s to 1962" is a useful summary of the years described in this appendix.

16. James Harford, *Korolev: How One Man Masterminded the Soviet Drive to Beat America to the Moon* (New York: John Wiley & Sons, 1997), 67.

17. Ibid., 75–77.

18. Ibid., 80.

19. Ibid., 41.

20. Ibid., 2–3.

21. Ibid., 3.

APPENDIX B

1. Isaac Newton's *Principia* is available in well-stocked libraries, either as a standalone or in Volume 34 of *Encyclopaedia Britannica's Great Books of the Western World*, first published in 1952. *Principia*, however, is somewhat unreadable for those of us not well up on calculus, a mathematical system Newton invented (according to some accounts) or "discovered," as if it were an artifact of nature. (Newton called the calculus "fluxions.") *Principia* can be found online at http://members.tripod.com/~gravitee/principia.htm.

2. The first several pages of *Principia* are taken up with "Definitions." The section titled "Axioms, or Laws of Motions" immediately follows.

3. See *Principia*, "Definition V."

4. In contrast to Newton, Arthur C. Clarke was always a graceful writer. His 1968 book, *The Promise of Space*, is "dated" in that it does not recount anything more current than the summer of 1967. Nevertheless, it is a space-lore classic. It can be found in many libraries as well as on the used-book market. Its first seven chapters explain Newtonian concepts with admirable clarity. See also "Newton's Life" by Michael Fowler at http://galileoandeinstein.physics.virginia.edu/lectures/newton.html.

5. See "Newton's Life" by Michael Fowler at http://galileoandeinstein.physics.virginia.edu/lectures/newton.html.

6. A velocity of just over 17,000 miles an hour is sufficient to achieve a minimal orbit. However, a velocity of 25,000 miles an hour is required to escape Earth's "gravity well," the first step toward the exploration of the solar system. The Soviet Union and the United States began sending scientific probes beyond Earth's gravity well in the late 1950s. The first human-made spacecraft to reach the Moon was Luna One, a Soviet spacecraft dubbed *Mechta* (dream) by its designer, Sergei Pavlovich Korolev. Launched January 2, 1959, the unmanned craft was supposed to hit the Moon and leave behind Soviet memorabilia. Instead, it missed by a few thousand miles and eventually went into orbit around the sun.

7. Space may be a whole lot of nothing in that it lacks air, but otherwise it is exciting and challenging territory. In the words of one expert, orbital space—the region we are concerned with here—is a domain in which the "gravity wells" of the Earth, Moon, and sun intersect in complex ways. "What appears at first as a featureless void is in fact a rich vista of gravitational mountains and valleys, oceans and rivers of resources and energy alternately dispersed and concentrated, broadly strewn danger zones of deadly radiation, and precisely placed peculiarities of astrodynamics." Dolman, *Astropolitik*, 61.

8. For background on *Voyager*, see A. J. S. Rayl's article at http://www.planetary.org/news/2006/0815_Voyager_1_Sailing_Past_100_AU_en_route.html.

9. Because future interplanetary travelers always will be in free fall toward one heavenly body or another—whether the Moon, or Mars, or Jupiter—they will be weightless. Weightlessness, however, can be partially counteracted by having some portion of the ship rotate, as in Kubrick's *2001*. Centrifugal force from the rotation substitutes for gravity.

10. Remember, we're talking Newtonian physics here, not Einsteinian and post-Einsteinian physics. In twenty-first-century physics, everything is far more weirdly complicated than Newton's physics. But at the velocities that humans will presumably deal with, Newtonian physics is all we need to explore the solar system.

11. Wright et al., *Physics of Space Security*, 20.

12. Satellites *do* fall out of orbit from time to time. That's because of "atmospheric drag." Air thins at a rapid rate with altitude. Nonetheless, widely scattered air molecules can

be found as high as a thousand miles or so above the Earth. Below that altitude, there are enough air molecules to create friction, albeit minuscule. The friction gradually saps the inertial energy of the satellite, causing its orbit to decay until it falls back into the atmosphere. Depending on how high the satellites are, serious orbital decay can take a matter of weeks, months, years, decades, or even centuries. A satellite's fiery reentry can be forestalled, as with the International Space Station, with occasional rocket boosts. Newton, however, spoke in the pristine language of mathematics. In his *Principia*, there was no atmospheric drag.

13. Go to http://www.amacad.org/publications/rulesSpace.aspx.

APPENDIX C

1. Go to http://www.dtic.mil/doctrine/jel/doddict/.
2. Douhet, *Command of the Air*, 27.
3. Kennett, *The First Air War,* 21.
4. Ibid., 175.
5. Ibid., 156.
6. Leighton Brewer, *Riders of the Sky* (Boston and New York: Houghton Mifflin, 1934), 26.
7. Jack Wren, *The Great Battles of World War I* (New York: Madison Square Press, 1971).
8. See "Dicta Boelcke," an online commentary by Micheal Shackelford, http:www.lib.byu.edu/estu/wwi/comment/dicta-b.html.
9. James J. Hudson, *Hostile Skies: A Combat History of the American Air Service in World War I* (Syracuse, NY: Syracuse University Press, 1968), 163.
10. Wren, *The Great Battles,* 234.
11. See Jeffery R. Barnett, "Great Soldiers on Airpower." *Airpower Journal*, Winter 1998, http://www.airpower.au.af.mil/airchronicles/apj/apj98/win98/barnett.html.
12. Richard P. Hallion, "Control of the Air: the Enduring Requirement," a 1999 online-only document published by the Air Force Historical Studies Office, https://www.airforce-history.hq.af.mil/Publications/Annotations/hallioncontrol.htm. See Part III, subhead: "Normandy and Afterwards."
13. Ibid.
14. Barnett, "Great Soldiers on Airpower."
15. Chuck Yeager, with Leo Janos, *Yeager* (Toronto, New York, London: Bantam Books, 1985), 61.
16. Isolde Baur, *Karl Baur, a Pilot's Pilot: Chief Test Pilot for Messerschmitt* (Winnipeg, Canada: J. J. Fedorowicz Publishing, 2000), 168.
17. Lieutenant General Johannes Steinhoff, "The German Fighter Battle Against the American Bombers," Office of Air Force History, 1968, http://www.au.af.mil/au/awc/awcgate/cbo-afa/cbo10.htm.
18. Hallion, *Control of the Air*.
19. William Mitchell, *Our Air Force: The Keystone of National Defense* (New York: E. P. Dutton & Co., 1921), xix.
20. See "Space Operations: Air Force Doctrine Document 2-2," issued November 27, 2006. Go to www.fas.org/irp/doddir/usaf/afdd2_2.pdf.

APPENDIX D

1. Tokaev is also known at Tokaty-Tokaev or Tokady-Tokaev.
2. Grigori A. Tokaev, *Stalin Means War* (London: George Weidenfeld & Nicolson, 1951), 80–81.
3. David Myhra, *Saenger: Germany's Orbital Rocket Bomber in World War II* (Atglen, PA: Schiffer Publishing, 2002), 120–29.
4. Ibid., 79.
5. Ibid., see "radiation-spreading device," Index, 171.
6. Ibid., 99.
7. Tokaev, *Stalin Means War*, 111–18.
8. Ibid., 194–207.
9. "The Need for Speed: Hypersonic Aircraft and the Transformation of Long Range Air-power," a June 2005 thesis written by Kenneth F. Johnson at the School of Advanced Air and Space Power Studies, is an excellent introduction to the topic. Go to https://research.maxwell.af.mil/papers/ay2005/saas/Johnson.pdf.
10. Swenson et al., *This New Ocean*, 531, note 43.
11. Walter R. Dornberger's lengthy fantasy, "The Rocket Propelled Commercial Airliner," was written in 1956 for limited distribution. It can be found in Robert Godwin, compiler and editor, *Dyna-Soar: Hypersonic Strategic Weapons System* (Burlington, Canada: Collector's Guide Publishing, 2003), 35–36.
12. York, *Race to Oblivion*, 129–33.
13. Go to http://www.presidency.ucsb.edu/ws/index.php?pid=36646.
14. See Stares, *Militarization of Space*, 43. For a thumbnail look at the military side of the "Orient Express" program prepared by the Federation of American Scientists, see "X-30: the National Space Plane," http://www.fas.org/irp/mystery/nasp.htm.
15. Richard P. Hallion, "The History of Hypersonics: or, 'Back to the Future – Again and Again,'" January 2005. (This short history of space plane projects can be obtained, for a fee, from the American Institute of Aeronautics and Astronautics. http://www.aiaa.org/content.cfm?pageid=406&gTable=Paper&gID=23008.
16. Go to http:www.darpa.mil/body/news/2004/falcon_fs_jan06_final.pdf.

Index

About the Author

Mike Moore is Research Fellow at the Independent Institute and the former editor of *The Bulletin of the Atomic Scientists,* a science-oriented, peace-and-security magazine founded by key members of the Manhattan Project.

He has been a reporter and editor for the *Kansas City Star, Chicago Daily News, Chicago Tribune,* and *Milwaukee Journal,* as well as the editor for *Quill,* the magazine of the Society of Professional Journalists.

He has contributed articles on national security, conflict resolution, nuclear proliferation, and space weaponry to journals such as the *Brown Journal of World Affairs, Foreign Service Journal, Yes! A Journal of Positive Futures,* and *SAIS Review of International Affairs;* and to the books *The Domestic Sources of American Foreign Policy* (St. Martin's Press), *Cyberwar, Netwar and the Revolution in Military Affairs* (Palgrave Macmillan), and *Asia-Pacific Cooperative Security in the 21st Century* (Taipai). Moore is also the editor of the anthology, *Health Risks and the Press,* published jointly by the American Medical Association and the Media Institute.

In addition to his work in journalism, he has participated in several professional conferences sponsored by organizations such as the Council on Foreign Relations, the Stanley Foundation, the International School on Disarmament and Research on Conflicts, the Eisenhower Institute, the Nuclear Policy Research Institute, the Pugwash Conferences on Science and World Affairs, Business Leaders for Sensible Priorities, Shanghai's Fudan University, the National Atomic Museum, the Lawyers Alliance for World Security, and the Nuclear-Free Future Foundation

He lives in Missouri with his wife, Sandy.

INDEPENDENT STUDIES IN POLITICAL ECONOMY

For further information and a catalog of publications, please contact:
THE INDEPENDENT INSTITUTE
100 Swan Way, Oakland, California 94621-1428, U.S.A.
510-632-1366 · Fax 510-568-6040 · info@independent.org · www.independent.org